The Power of the Mind

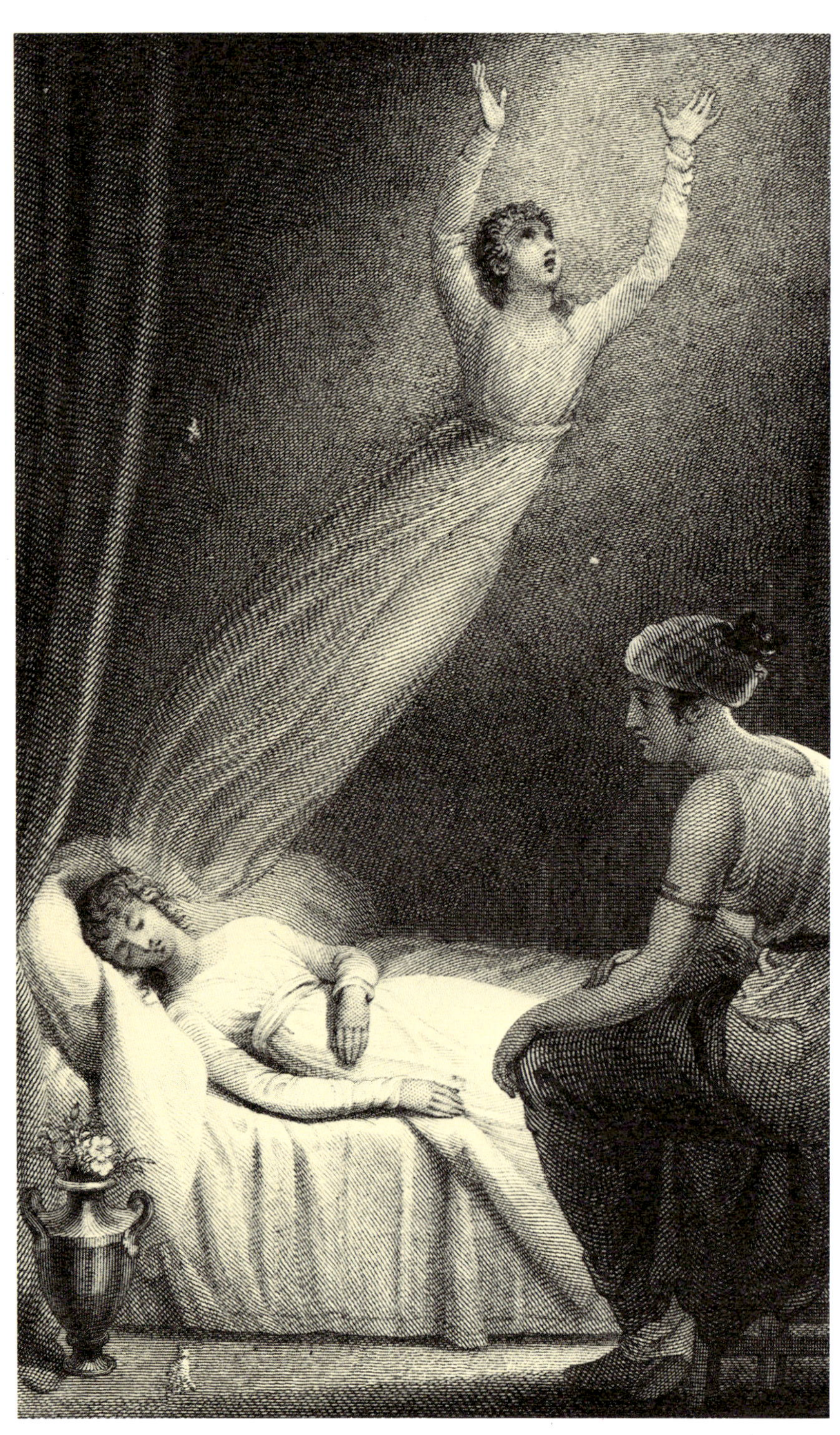

The Power of the Mind

Edited by Peter Brookesmith

Orbis · London

Acknowledgements
Photographs were supplied by Chas Addams/The New Yorker Magazine, Aerofilms, Robert Aird Photography, Aldus Archive, All-Sport, Ardea, Associated Newspapers, Associated Press, BBC Hulton Picture Library, BBC TV, Bildarchiv Preussischer Kulturbesitz, British Museum Department of Prints and Drawings, Richard Burgess, Eldon Byrd, Cambridge Evening News, Camera Press, Jean-Loup Charmet, Bruce Coleman, Colorific!, William E Cox, John Cutten, Daily Star, Arnold Desser, Edimedia, Mary Evans Picture Library, Evening Echo, Explorer, Fate Magazine, Field Museum of Natural History, Vivien Fifield, Joel Finler, Foundation for Research on the Nature of Man, J Friedman, Leif Geiges, Gemeentelijk Archiefdienst Amsterdam, General Motors, John Glanvill, Alison Goodall, Elmer Gruber, Sonia Halliday, Robert Harding, John Hasted, Keith M T Hearne, John Hillelson Picture Agency, Toby Hogarth, Holiday Inns, Michael Holford, John Hughes, Robert Hunt Library, Illustrated London News, Imperial War Museum, Brian Inglis, Julian Isaacs, Alix Jeffry, Kadima Productions Inc, Kobal Collection, Neil Lancashire Photography, Frank Lane, Beverley Lebarrow, Lawrence LeShan, London Scientific Fotos, MARS, Macmillan Publishers, William MacQuitty, Mansell Collection, Medical Illustration Support Service, National Enquirer, National Film Archive, National Gallery of Art Washington, National Maritime Museum, National Portrait Gallery London, Natural Science Photos, Peter Newark's Western Americana, Bob Okon, S Ostrander, Kit Pedlar, Philosophical Research Society Los Angeles, The Photo Source, Photri, Guy Lyon Playfair, Popperfoto, Press Association, Psi Search, Psi Search/David Eisendrath, Psychic Magazine, Psychic News, Psychic Press, The Psycho-Physical Research Foundation, Lucy Quill, Rank Xerox, J J Ratcliffe, Rex Features, J B Rhine, David Rumbelow, SORRAT, Carl Sargent, Dr Morton Schatzman, Science Photo Library, Ronald Sheridan, Spectrum Colour Library, Sport and General Press Agency, Stanford University News and Publications Service, Roy Stemman, St Louis Democrat, The Sun, Syndication International, Targ and Puthoff/*Mind-reach*, Thames TV, John Topham Library, David Towersey, UPI, Montague Ullman, Victoria and Albert Museum, John Watney, Wellcome Institute for Medical History, World Government of the Age of Enlightenment, Yorkshire Post, ZEFA.

The publishers would like to thank the following authors for contributing to this book:
Paul Begg 108–114; David Christie-Murray 59–67; Jenny Dawson 125–130; Joe Friedman 210–213; A.J. Ellison 131–138, 156–164; Melvin Harris 104–111; David Harvey 219–228; Piet Hein Hoebens 98–101; Brian Inglis 198–209; Julian Isaacs 42–57, 178–184; Francis King 72–75; Lynn Picknett 116–123; Guy Lyon Playfair 39–41, 229–232; Archie Roy 76–79, 93–96, 144–147, 165–177, 186–197; Carl Sargent 214–217, 233–236; Roy Stemman 10–25, 68–71, 81–92, 102–103, 140–143, 148–154; Colin Wilson 27–38.

First published in Great Britain 1986 by
Orbis Book Publishing Corporation Ltd
A BPCC plc company

Printed in Italy.
ISBN 1-85155-033-x hardback
1-85613-037-2 paperback

Contents

Introduction

Do psychic (or 'psi') phenomena exist, and if they do, how can we relate them to what we know of the normal workings of the human mind? And can we reconcile them at all with what we know of the physics of matter? These questions just might dominate scientific thinking in the 21st century, and perhaps some answers can be found in this book.

Scientists who study psi – parapsychologists – usually divide psi into two types of phenomena, extra-sensory perception (ESP) and psychokinesis (PK) or mind-over-matter and, these terms are explained fully in this volume. Scientific study of psi has been under way for well over 50 years and has developed some sophisticated methods of enquiry – but there is still particular antagonism on the part of scientists toward the two types of psi that seem to dominate the headlines. These involve *people* who seem to have some special psi gifts, and *happenings* of what I will call the 'Gee whizz' variety – spectacular phenomena like teleportation (the disappearance of an object at one location and its subsequent reappearance, 'out of the blue', at another) and levitation.

There are good reasons for distrust of apparently gifted individuals – the 'Psi Stars' – by scientists. Sometimes, when these personalities have been happy to work with scientists, spectacular results have been forthcoming. Good examples would be the researches of the brilliant Victorian scientist Sir William Crookes with the gifted medium D.D. Home, and the more contemporary scientific study of the Czech Pavel Stepanek – you'll find him listed in the *Guinness book of records* as the world's most psychic person. But often the Psi Stars have been reluctant to co-operate with researchers, and just as often it has been claimed that their feats are just sleight-of-hand and trickery. The most obvious recent case would be the bewildering Israeli Uri Geller. Does Geller really bend metal (and a lot more besides) by PK, or is he just a brilliant magician who deceives people by trickery and personal charisma? Or (and lots of people overlook *this* possibility) might he be both? Geller is perhaps the most controversial Psi Star of the 20th century and this book examines his personality, his background, and the remarkable (and sometimes almost incredible) powers it's claimed he possesses. It looks too at the people who are sceptical about his claims and have attempted to debunk him. It's got to be said that there is something of the music hall about all this, and scientists usually steer well clear of media circuses. But fortunately some adventurous ones – notably Hal Puthoff and Russ Targ in America and John Hasted in London – have taken the plunge with Geller and tried to make some documentation of his abilities.

Whatever you think of Geller – and there are as many shades of opinion about him as there are varieties of psi effects reported in association with him – he's not the only contemporary Psi Star; controversy rages about the others too, and this is particularly true of the 'psychic detectives' – people with apparent ESP gifts that enable them to solve crimes and to find lost or stolen property or even corpses. Stories about such people – Peter Hurkos and Gerard Croiset are the most famous examples – delight the popular press. Unfortunately the popular press often has a gullible attitude to such things and the truth in cases of psychic detection is often quite different from the reports in newspapers and magazines. Piet Hein Hoebens, one of a dwindling band of rational sceptics (often sceptics are as irrational as the more extreme believers they try to debunk) shows how many stories about Hurkos, for example, have been exaggerated in the re-telling (page 98). And although many psychics and mediums claimed to have given the police helpful psychic impressions of criminals like the Yorkshire Ripper, the police usually have other views on the matter, and the success rates of these individuals is often greater in the matter of getting publicity for themselves than in providing accurate information.

If Psi Stars make fastidious scientists uneasy then the Gee Whizz effects almost give them apoplexy. As some early essays in this book explain, scientists have traditionally studied psi by simplifying – using laboratory tests of a controlled, precise, but ultimately mechanical and boring nature. When confronted by the possibility of people levitating before their eyes, most parapsychologists would run back to the laboratory muttering about hallucinations. And this is where they would definitely be wrong: there is some fine evidence for the reality of levitation (see page 116) and not everyone who has observed it can be demented, hallucinating or lying. Just because the evidence doesn't come from controlled scientific studies does *not* mean that it can be ignored. In the end, every type of evidence is in fact human testimony of one kind or another.

This brings us to some important changes in parapsychology that have taken place in the last 25 years. Rather than seeking out Psi Stars for study, or developing ever more sophisticated and even more boring variants of card-guessing tests for ESP, scientists – following the pioneering lead of the Maimonides team in Brooklyn, New York (see page 89) – have gone back to a careful study of the 'ordinary', unsensational, everyday psi experiences of common people. And one finding from almost every survey ever conducted of spontaneous psi experiences is that a disproportionate number of them occur when people are asleep, deeply relaxed, or daydreaming – in other words not in their 'normal', alert state of consciousness. The Maimonides team tested for telepathy (mind-to-mind ESP) in just such a state (dreaming) and with exciting new test techniques (using richly-detailed, realistic pictures instead of numbers or simple, abstract symbols), and they reaped a rich harvest of strong ESP effects. Following their lead others have used hypnosis, relaxation exercises, or the sensory-deprivation-like *Ganzfeld* procedure (see page 229) to cultivate 'altered states of consciousness' (or ASCs) and have also been able to obtain startling evidence for the reality of ESP. And this research may spin off into two areas that are vastly important scientifically – and not just for psi research.

Firstly, these ASC studies may tell us something about how psi works within the mind. It seems as if our rational, 'normal' minds are not amenable to psi influences, but if the cause-and-effect, logical workings of the mind are suspended in dreaming or daydreaming, then psi gets to work. And this conclusion is strengthened if we look at the twilight world of the psychiatrist. Hallucinations, multiple personality and madness are often linked with psi, and there may be good reasons for this (see pages 186 and 198). These 'abnormal' states of mind are also non-rational, and the 'normal' inhibitions that get in the way of psi may not operate here. Those pioneers of the study of the mind, Freud and Jung, were both deeply interested in psi and sympathetic towards parapsychology; they had good reason to be, from their experiences. And it may not be simply that 'abnormal' states of mind somehow favour the expression of psi. As we discover in this book (page 198), there may be a psi element that partly *causes* such abnormal phenomena as mass hysteria.

The other intriguing thing about ASCs is that they may open up possibilities other than merely stronger psi. Genius, inspiration, creativity – these aspects of human achievement may be crucially dependent on ASCs. There is only so much that can be done by logical, black-and-white analysis of a problem – the rest needs something extra. That 'extra' factor lies within the unconscious mind, and out of the labyrinthine workings of that part of our personalities arise creativity, dreams, seeing into the future, 'hunches' that may actually be psychic (see page 152), hallucinations and madness. Quite some mixture, and we're not going to find out about *this* with card-guessing tests.

Fascinating as the varieties of ESP – telepathy and the others – may be, it might be the case that the final secrets of the workings of psi will be unravelled through study of its sister phenomenon, PK. If possible, PK has an even murkier history than ESP; the number of fraudulent physical mediums' (those who claim to use PK to levitate objects and suchlike, rather than claiming communications from the spirits of the dead as 'mental' mediums do) is enormous. And just as Uri Geller is controversial, so scientific PK research has expanded into some pretty mind-boggling areas. Research into metal-bending, the craze Geller started, has almost become orthodox now – and some brilliant and ingenious approaches to PK metal-bending have been developed (see page 39). But these seem almost mundane compared to the 'minilab' system for studying PK which is described in this volume. The minilab grew out of the work of an American group who were able, they claimed, to produce the full gamut of PK effects, including the levitation of heavy tables and other objects. The minilab is a sealed system, an allegedly tamper-proof locked glass tank where researchers can attempt to localise and capture PK effects on film. The minilab is extremely controversial among parapsychologists and it has never proved possible to replicate the original American findings. But in principle this kind of experiment could bridge the gap between scientific rigour and spontaneous PK happenings. This has already happened with ESP – witness the dream telepathy research – but it is a bright new development in PK research.

The real reason, though, why PK research may ultimately hold all the answers lies as much in modern physics as it does in parapsychology. Quantum physics does not explain psi, but what it does do is twofold. First, quantum physics is itself so bizarre, and the ideas that are played around with in that science are so counter-intuitive and alien to our experience, that it makes such things as telepathy seem almost mundane by comparison. But more importantly, quantum physics provides a framework of theory in which psi effects are at the very least *possible* and even, according to some theorists (a minority, but not a tiny one), predictable. Modern physics could end the banishment of parapsychology by science over decades, during which time it was shunned by all but the most intrepid soils. Archie Roy (page 170) describes how parapsychology and modern physics might link one with the other.

But the truth might go even deeper than this. It may be that rather than seeing existing science as able to 'handle' psi after all, we may have to admit that the very structure of science could be changed by psi. This is because it's possible that the people conducting the experiments – the scientists themselves – use PK to influence their work. This concept opens up a veritable Pandora's box of possibilities in science and while this volume (page 161) considers many of the implications of the 'experimenter effect', it's so important that we can consider it here too.

Basically, psychologists have known for many years that the personality and behaviour of experimenters in psychology experiments can affect what their subjects (the people being studied) do. This set of findings – which comes from well over 300 experiments, since that number were surveyed together as far back as 1977 – is usually carefully ignored in psychology courses in universities and colleges because it's rather embarrassing. Psychologists badly want to play at being Real Scientists like physicists and chemists, and one of the basic tenets of Real Science is that the scientist and the object of his study are quite separate things. The observer and the observed are intrinsically different, and ne'er the twain shall meet. Unfortunately the experimenter effect that psychologist Robert Rosenthal and others unearthed knocks this idea squarely on the head. And really, psychologists have always *known* about the experimenter effect because it's part of their experience. It's just that playing at being Real Scientists made them turn their back on the world of experience – a fatal mistake. Parapsychologists can at least claim that they were aware of (and did research on) the experimenter effect while psychologists were still avoiding it.

But now the experimenter effect threatens to invade the citadel of Real Science itself. If experimenter effects can be not just psychological but actually psi-based then the implications for science are stunning. It means that the basic scientific philosophy we have accepted for the last 300 years at least is built on a massive self-deception. This, in turn, explains why scientists are often so hostile to the very possibility of psi. Something within them senses this threat and wishes to dismiss the spectre. But it isn't going to be that easy; the evidence for psi-based experimenter effects is growing, and radical philosophers of science like the maverick Paul Feyerabend have already begun the task of dismantling the cherished illusions of scientific philosophy.

So, from the world of out-of-the-body experiences, telepathy, reincarnation, metal-bending and a hundred other extraordinary happenings – most of which are reported in the pages you're about to read – comes something which really *can* transform the nature of scientific thinking in the view of a small but not insignificant group of thinkers. The earliest pioneer thinkers and researchers in parapsychology always thought that what they were studying had enormous implications, although their primary interest was in the possibility of establishing that the human mind survived in some form after death (and that's a problem very much still alive, if you'll excuse the pun, and one I can't go into here for space reasons). Yet behind that was the belief that psi was a maverick factor in nature that could change the inhuman, secular face of a science that seemed to have little room in its philosophy for human values or the spiritual side of life. Resurrecting that inspiration could be rather important for us a century later, looking out on a science that has given us the ability to destroy our planet by irradiation, biological toxins and chemical warfare. This may seem like heavy business (and indeed it is) and the reader may wonder whether it really connects with parapsychology – the claim seems almost absurd. Yet I don't think it is; the baneful malevolence of science has everything to do with a philosophy that alienates the observing scientist from the object of his study and makes it merely a thing to be manipulated, controlled and observed in cold, clinical detachment. Understanding the place of psi in nature could be just one of the factors that undermine this dismal and ultimately destructive philosophy. If psi exists – and you can decide for yourself; much of the evidence is reviewed in this book – then the mystics who described the essential Oneness of all things were a lot closer to the truth than many scientists, and quantum physics may finally have understood the mystical insight. But the more inspired parapsychologists have never forgotten that the Power of the Mind as demonstrated by psi confirms that truth too!

Dr Carl Sargent

ESP: an introduction

Of all the mysteries that tax human understanding, the nature of the mind itself remains one of the most impenetrable. Are telepathy, precognition and clairvoyance really possible, and if they are, can they be subjected to scientific investigation?

In search of the sixth sense

The human mind has powers of understanding that are beyond the reach of the five senses. Extra-sensory perception is an undeniable fact – but one that is still shrouded in mystery

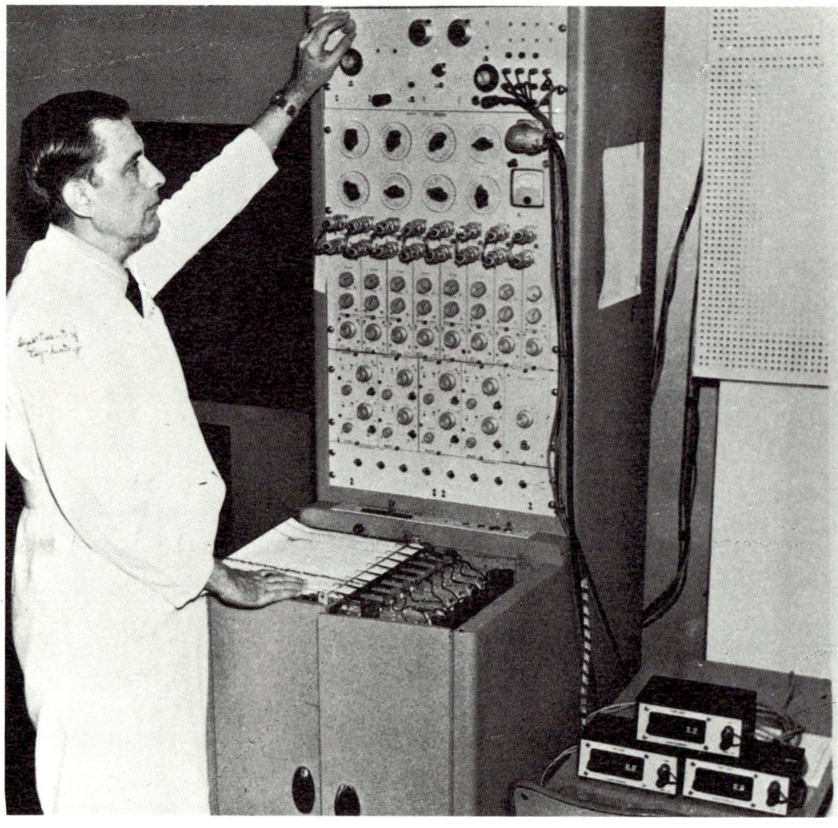

FOURTEEN-YEAR-OLD Stanley Krippner wanted an encyclopedia very badly. His parents had to refuse his request; they were apple farmers and a bad harvest had left them very short of money. Stanley went to his room and cried. After a while he began thinking of ways of raising the money himself and his thoughts turned to his rich Uncle Max. How could he best approach him for funds?

Suddenly the teenager sat bolt upright in bed as a horrible thought flooded his mind: 'Uncle Max can't help me because he's dead.' Many years later, Krippner – now one of America's leading psychic investigators – recalled: 'At that moment I heard the telephone ring. My mother answered the phone, then began sobbing as my cousin told her that Max had unexpectedly taken ill, was rushed to hospital, and had just died.'

Thousands of people have had similar experiences. Somehow information reaches them in a way that bypasses their 'normal' senses. During the past 50 years investigators have used the term *extra-sensory perception* (ESP) to describe the phenomenon and hundreds of experiments have been conducted around the world in an attempt to confirm its existence scientifically and understand how it works.

What is clear from this research, and from a study of spontaneous cases, is that ESP is not an isolated phenomenon. Take Krippner's experience, for example. There are three 'psychic' ways, all classified as types of ESP, in which he might have found out about his uncle's unexpected death:

Telepathy It is possible that the teenager's mind 'tuned in' to his cousin's mind and read his thoughts just as he was about to telephone with the bad news.

Clairvoyance It is just as likely that young Krippner had an awareness of his uncle's death – he sensed it had happened – without having any mind-to-mind communication.

Precognition Yet another possibility is that his knowledge came not from past or present events but from the future. Somehow he jumped fractionally ahead in time and knew what his mother was about to learn from the telephone call.

There is a fourth possibility: the dead uncle could have been communicating with his nephew. If that were the case, Krippner would have needed extra-sensory powers of *some* kind to be aware of the dead man's presence. Such communication is usually called mediumship and is outside the province of scientific research into ESP.

The strange case of Mrs Luther

People who investigate ESP – parapsychologists – are dealing with a very complex subject where many alternative explanations (including those in terms of conventional science) must be considered. At times it is difficult to determine where telepathy ends and clairvoyance begins.

The early investigators in the late 19th century began by collecting and collating an impressive range of cases. Books appeared, full of testimonies from reliable men and women – judges, doctors, lawyers – who had had unusual experiences. One example is Professor F. S. Luther, a mathematician of Trinity College, Cambridge, whose wife was asked by a friend if she had a book about the poet Ralph Waldo Emerson. She said she did not, but that night she dreamed she was giving such a book to her friend. The friend also had a dream in which she received the book from Mrs Luther. Next day the professor saw his wife suddenly turn to the bookshelves, prompted by an unexplained compulsion. She reached down a copy of *Century Magazine* and it opened immediately at an article entitled 'The homes and haunts of Emerson'.

Above: Dr Stanley Krippner conducting an ESP experiment with an electro-encephalograph – a device for measuring brain waves. ESP research now uses the latest micro-chip technology

Below: Cambridge scholar F. W. Myers, author of the pioneer work, *Human personality and its survival of bodily death*. First published in 1903, Myers' book documents hundreds of ESP cases

Top: a set of Zener cards (*top row*) used to test ESP in individual subjects. Each of the five symbols is designed to make a distinct impression on the memory. Below are some of the cards used by Dr Soal, who devised these after becoming bored with Zener cards.

Above: Dr Joseph Rhine, who with his wife Louisa, began the first major scientific investigation into ESP in 1927

Such spontaneous cases occur when people least expect them, so they cannot be studied objectively. Waiting for ESP to manifest itself in a laboratory is as futile as waiting for ball lightning to strike your house or for a meteorite to land in your garden. But early spontaneous cases were easily dismissed by sceptics as coincidence and something had to be done to put the study of ESP on a scientific basis.

Dr Rhine deals the cards

It became apparent that there were people to whom psychic experiences were relatively common, and psychical researchers began to conduct controlled tests with them, aiming principally to prove the existence of telepathy. The pioneer of this work was Dr Joseph Banks Rhine who, together with his wife Louisa, ran the first large-scale ESP research project at Duke University, North Carolina, USA, under the sponsorship of Professor William McDougall, head of the psychology department. The Rhines were originally biologists until, in the mid-1920s, their interest in the paranormal became their chief concern. Through Professor McDougall's initiative they were able to start a full-time investigation of ESP in 1927 and with their work the science of parapsychology was born. Dr Rhine coined the term 'ESP', and he devoted over 50 years to its study before his death early in 1980.

The Rhines' method of researching ESP was to give their subjects guessing tasks. They used a pack of 25 cards, which was divided into five sets of five cards, each set carrying a different symbol: star, circle, cross, wavy lines, rectangle. These cards, called Zener cards after one of the researchers at Duke University, were shuffled, then looked at one at a time by the sender, or agent. In another part of the university the receiver, or subject, would point to the symbol he thought the agent was looking at. According to the laws of chance, a subject would get 5 out of 25 right if only guesswork was involved. Occasionally, luck might enable him to guess more than five correctly, but on other occasions he would do less well so that, in an extended series of tests, the results would even out. If, on the other hand, the subject had ESP abilities, the results should be above average. And that is precisely what Rhine found.

One of Rhine's early 'star' subjects was a man named Linzmayer, who liked to be provided with some means of distraction while making his guesses. Rhine would sometimes arrange for him to do this by taking him on country drives and stopping the car to carry out impromptu tests. On one occasion, using this procedure, Linzmayer correctly named all 15 cards Rhine looked at. Under better controlled conditions in Rhine's laboratory Linzmayer continued to record above-average scores, but his ESP subsequently declined and then vanished.

In the card-guessing experiment in Rhine's car, Linzmayer appears to have read the researcher's mind. But he also took part in tests in which he was asked to name a card before it was turned over. Since no one knew what the card would be, Linzmayer had to use clairvoyance to make his guesses. Again, his scores were significantly above average, and there were other subjects who were just as good at 'seeing through' the cards. Rhine's work soon demonstrated that there was much more to ESP than pure telepathy. Within 10 years he was exploring the possibility of looking into the future, or precognition. Subjects were asked to guess *in advance* what the order of Zener cards would be when shuffled. The results were just as impressive as his other ESP laboratory work.

The struggle for the truth

There was, unexpectedly, tremendous public interest in Dr Rhine's work when it was first published in 1934. Not surprisingly, there were sceptics among his scientific colleagues who endeavoured to find fault with his laboratory techniques and conditions. Rhine provided satisfactory answers to all these criticisms. If these were not at fault, the sceptics continued, then Rhine's statistical analysis might be wrong. Perhaps the above-average results he was recording were not a manifestation of ESP but a statistical quirk. That argument was silenced in 1937 when the American Institute of Mathematical Statistics issued a statement, following its own investigation of the Duke University results, which said that the statistical methods used to evaluate ESP phenomena in Rhine's tests were completely valid.

If the subjects were not allowed to cheat, if the conditions made it impossible for the information to be transmitted to the subject by 'normal' means, and if the statistical methods used to analyse the results were correct, then surely the critics *had* to believe that ESP did exist? But there was still one other possibility that had to be taken seriously: experimenter fraud. Perhaps Rhine had 'cooked the books'. This suggestion was put forward in 1955 by a medical researcher, G. R. Price, in an article for *Science*, the prestigious official journal of the American Association for the Advancement of Science. He argued that experimenter fraud was 'the one explanation that is simplest and most in accord with everyday experiment'. Most of his criticisms were aimed at Rhine and Dr S. G. Soal, an eminent British parapsychologist.

Many people regarded Price's attack as an 'exposure' of parapsychology, but Rhine took it very calmly. He entered into correspondence with Price, answering his various allegations and discussing in depth the procedures used in his work. The result, many years later in 1972, was the publication by Price of another article in *Science*. The headline tells its own story: 'Apology to Rhine and Soal'.

Although the apology to Rhine was well deserved and long overdue, later discoveries indicated that Price's suspicions were right as far as Soal was concerned, Soal's is a strange case, and one that sounds a warning to those who are tempted to put their trust in a single set of ESP experiments. Many researchers regarded Soal's results as a cornerstone of ESP and the new evidence means that the history of parapsychology will have to be rewritten.

Soal, who was a mathematician, originally became interested in psychical research when he conducted a lengthy series of ESP tests, hoping to provide independent corroboration of Rhine's work. He tested 160 people over a five-year period and analysed the total of 128,350 guesses against the targets (symbols on the cards) they were attempting to 'see'. He found nothing but chance results and promptly stopped his ESP research, criticising Rhine for what he considered must be errors in the methods he used to produce positive results.

That might have been the end of the story, had it not been for the influence of another English researcher, Whately Carington. In his own ESP tests, using drawings as targets, Carington had discovered a strange displacement effect. Sometimes a subject would miss

Above: a practical demonstration of Dr Rhine's techniques. An agent outside the laboratory is given a set of Zener cards to look at. The subject inside the laboratory is asked to 'guess' which of the five symbols the agent is looking at and to indicate her choice on the display panel.

Below: Dr S. G. Soal, the mathematician whose research into ESP has been seriously questioned

Random numbers

Consider the sequence: 1 2 3 4 . . . If Dr Soal had used a sequence like this one in his ESP experiments, Basil Shackleton – or anyone else – could have scored a 100 per cent success rate simply by working out what the pattern was and calculating the next number. To ensure that Shackleton could not cheat – that he was really using ESP and not arithmetic to score his 'hits' – Soal should have made sure that, at any point in the sequence, the chance of any one of the card symbols being next in line was the same as that of any other symbol.

This is, in fact, the idea behind the mathematical definition of a random number: a string of digits in which each digit is selected according to a procedure in which all the numbers from 0 to 9 have an equal chance of being selected.

The strange thing about random numbers is that they are very difficult to come by: you cannot simply ask someone to think of a random number since, however randomly he thinks he is selecting the digits, you will always be able to find some kind of pattern in the sequence. The mathematical definition demands that you use a mechanical method, independent of human bias. The easiest way is to throw a die repeatedly and to record the number on the uppermost face each time.

But this is a slow and laborious method and, besides, a die has only six sides. In laboratory experiments standard lists of random numbers, generated on computers by a variety of methods, are often used. In the U.K., for example, a machine called ERNIE (electronic random number indicator equipment) selects the prize-winning number for a national lottery. In the days before it was possible to use computers to generate long sequences of random numbers, logarithmic tables were used to obtain 'pseudo-random' sequences.

Below: Dr R. G. Medhurst, a parapsychologist, who appeared in a dream to Betty Markwick. It was after her dream that Miss Markwick began analysing Dr Soal's research methods. She found that he may have manipulated the results and that his work was generally unreliable. Later, however, Miss Markwick came to recognise that had it not been for the appearance of Dr Medhurst in her dream she would never have begun work on Dr Soal

the target he was trying to guess and instead reproduce the previous day's target or even the one to be selected at random the next day. Carington urged Soal to re-examine his statistics and look for such a 'psychic displacement'. The mathematician did this, and sure enough the effect was found in the results produced by two subjects, Basil Shackleton and Gloria Stewart. Both showed positive and negative displacements at times, and Soal continued his ESP work using Shackleton and Stewart as his subjects.

Real evidence?

The results of experiments conducted with Shackleton between 1941 and 1943 were extremely impressive and were taken up by parapsychologists as evidence of the existence of ESP. But 20 years later Mrs Gretl Albert, who had been involved in the tests as an agent, claimed she had several times seen Soal altering the figures. A recent re-examination of the Soal statistics suggests that this is exactly what he did.

In order to ensure that the cards used in the experiments were picked at random, Soal used the standard laboratory technique of referring to Chambers' logarithmic tables and Tippett's random number tables (although he did not indicate exactly how he used them). What has been discovered is that the random lists Soal used in his experiments do not match the standard published ones. A study by Betty Markwick, published in 1978, has revealed that certain long sequences of numbers are repeated many times. This need only mean that Soal was using a small pool of random numbers and would not necessarily affect the validity of the experiment. However, Miss Markwick has discovered that the long repeated sequences are in fact not identical; they are sometimes interrupted by extra numbers, and that these, where they occur, show a remarkable correspondence with the ESP 'hits' recorded by Soal. Remove them and the scores fall to chance levels.

Summing up this evidence, Miss Markwick states that 'all the experimental series in card-guessing carried out by Dr Soal must, as the evidence stands, be discredited.'

The Soal case is a sad chapter in the chequered history of parapsychology. But the evidence for ESP does not depend on a single set of experiments. Over the last half century, as we will see in future chapters, the evidence for extra-sensory perception has grown stronger. Although researchers cannot yet produce telepathy, clairvoyance and precognition to order in their laboratories, their investigations show that ESP *is* a very real phenomenon. The latest research even holds out the hope that we may all, one day, be able to use our psychic powers at will.

Messages in the mind

Even though modern research has succeeded in actually recording the 'tuning in' of one mind to another, scientists still cannot tell us precisely how telepathy works

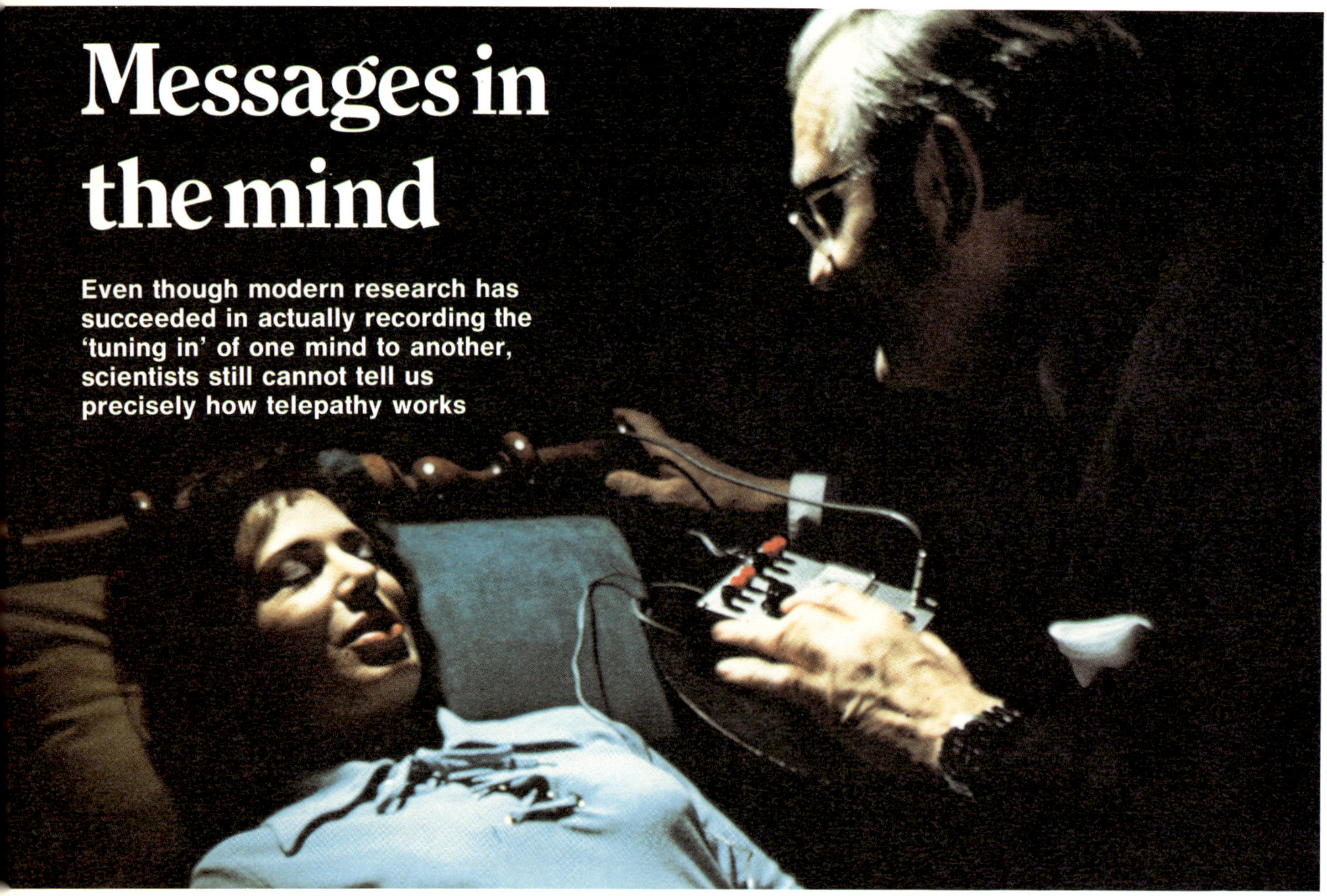

Above: Douglas Dean, one of America's leading psychical researchers, using a plethysmograph to monitor blood volume. The machine shows that telepathic activity can actually increase blood volume.

Below: Sir William Barrett (1845–1926), Professor of Physics at the Royal College of Science, Dublin, who was one of the first psychical investigators

EARLY ONE MORNING in 1980, a very frightened old lady walked feebly into a Barcelona police station. Señora Isabel Casas, an 81-year-old widow, had been so scared by a terrible dream that, despite her age and infirmity, she had managed to walk to the local police station to raise the alarm. Almost incoherent with fear, she told the officer on duty that she had seen the face of her friend and neighbour, Rafael Perez, 'twisted in terror' – and heard a voice say, 'They are going to kill us.'

The Spanish police were inclined to dismiss Señora Casas's experience as a mere nightmare. But they became curious when they learned that she had not seen Perez, the only other resident in the block of flats where she lived, for 10 days. Normally the 56-year-old chef called to see her every day, but he had written her a note saying he was going away for several weeks. It was odd, the police thought, that this note had not been delivered until three days after she had last seen her neighbour. And why had Perez not called to see her personally?

They decided to investigate and eventually found Perez tied up in a shed on the roof of the block of flats. He told them two men had broken into his apartment, made him sign 28 cheques so that they could draw his £15,000 life savings a little at a time, then forced him to write the note to Señora Casas so that her suspicions would not be aroused. Then they tied him up and said they would be back, once they had all the money, to kill him and his neighbour.

Astonishingly, the old woman seems to have picked up the thoughts of her friend as he waited in terror for his captors to return. His life was saved by her vivid telepathic dream – and the police ambushed and arrested the men when they returned to the scene of their crime.

This ability of one person to 'look into' the mind of another was one of the first subjects to be studied by the early psychical researchers a century ago.

The case of Canon Warburton

Typical of the spontaneous cases of telepathy investigated by early researchers was the experience of an English clergyman in 1883. Canon Warburton sat in an armchair in his brother's flat and began to doze. Suddenly, he woke up with a start exclaiming, 'By Jove! He's down!' The canon had just had a vivid dream in which he had seen his brother come out of a drawing-room on to a brightly illuminated landing, catch his foot on the edge of the top stair and fall headlong down the stairs, just managing to save himself from serious injury by using his hands and elbows. The house in the dream was not one he recognised. All the canon knew, having just

Above: Sir Oliver Lodge (1851–1940), who carried out psychical experiments with two girls who claimed to be able to read each other's minds. But later investigations have cast doubt on Lodge's results

arrived in London from Oxford, was that his brother had left him a note explaining that he had gone to a dance in the West End and would be back at about 1 a.m.

Recovering from the experience, Canon Warburton dozed off again for half an hour until his brother came in and woke him up. 'I have just had as narrow an escape of breaking my neck as I ever had in my life!' he exclaimed. 'Coming out of the ballroom, I caught my foot, and tumbled full length down the stairs.'

The canon's uncanny dream experience is one of many hundreds of equally impressive cases of spontaneous telepathy collected by the Society for Psychical Research in Britain and America.

The word 'telepathy' was coined in 1882 by a leading Cambridge scholar and investigator, F. W. H. Myers, and the first major study of such experiences – the *Census of hallucinations*, published in 1890 – examined replies to 20,000 questionnaires. But science needed to examine telepathy under more controlled conditions.

One of the pioneers of scientific research into telepathy was Sir William Barrett, professor of physics at the Royal College of Science, Dublin, who conducted experiments with hypnotised subjects that satisfied him that telepathy was real.

When Sir William submitted his paper, *Some phenomena associated with abnormal conditions of the mind*, to the British Association for the Advancement of Science, it was refused by the biological committee. He eventually presented it to the anthropological sub-section, where it was accepted only on the casting vote of its chairman, Dr Alfred Russell Walace, who was also a keen investigator of psychical phenomena.

By the early part of this century many groups of researchers were involved in imaginative telepathy tests. In the 1920s René Warcollier conducted group telepathy experiments between France and the United States, many of which produced very impressive results. But not all early research is acceptable by today's strict scientific standards. The famous physicist Professor Oliver Lodge (later Sir Oliver Lodge) carried out tests with two girls who claimed to be able to read each other's minds. He found their demonstrations convincing and published them in 1909 in his book *The survival of man*. But since the girls were allowed to hold hands while 'sending' their telepathic images of playing cards, the possibility that they were using a code cannot be eliminated. This suspicion is reinforced by Lodge's statistics, which show that when the girls were not touching, results fell nearly to chance levels.

'Sinclair goes spooky'

In the 1930s the work of the well-known writer Upton Sinclair caught the public imagination. Sinclair's wife had considerable psychic abilities and was able to 'receive' by telepathy pictures that were drawn by her husband or other senders. Sometimes these experiments were carried out in adjoining rooms, at other times over long distances. Sinclair published his results in his book *Mental radio*, revealing that in 290 experiments Mrs Sinclair scored 23 per cent successes, 53 per cent partial successes and 24 per cent failures.

The similarity between the original drawings and Mrs Sinclair's 'copies' was often striking, ruling out coincidence, but making a statistical analysis of the results difficult. In fact, partial successes were often as impressive as direct hits because they gave an interesting insight into how Mrs Sinclair perceived the images. On one occasion, Upton Sinclair drew a volcano with billowing black smoke. His wife drew a very good likeness, but was unable to identify it and guessed that the smoke was a beetle. Had this been a telepathy test which required a verbal response, her description of a beetle would have been judged a miss. In fact, her drawing showed that she had picked up the image very accurately.

Sinclair, a committed socialist, was well aware that most intelligent people still regarded the phenomenon of telepathy with scepticism. Some of his socialist friends felt that his interest in ESP conflicted with their rationalist outlook on the world, and one of them attacked him in a newspaper article headed 'Sinclair goes spooky'.

All in the mind's eye

Pictures drawn by American novelist Upton Sinclair and their images 'received' telepathically by his wife Craig reveal a startling degree of similarity. In the first pair (left) Sinclair's original was of a volcano erupting. His wife interpreted it as a beetle – which, as Sinclair put it, 'hardly sounds like a triumphant success.' But in fact the billowing smoke looks very like a beetle's body in Mrs Sinclair's drawing, while the sides of the mountain can easily be interpreted as its antennae.

The second and third pairs of pictures need no explanation. Mrs Sinclair had difficulty, however, with her husband's drawing of a cow. She failed to identify it, but noted that she saw 'something sending out long lines from it.'

In the last pair of pictures Mrs Sinclair again failed to identify the target picture – but the similarity between the two drawings is striking. Her comment reads, 'May be elephant's snout – but anyway it is some kind of a running animal. Long thing like a rope flung out in front of him.'

It was to give the subject respectability in the eyes of science that Dr J. B. Rhine began to research telepathy in the laboratory. Rhine used new methods and easily identifiable targets – Zener cards – to ensure that there was no doubt whether a subject was scoring a hit or a miss in his tests. The results were impressive and satisfied Rhine and many other scientists that mind-to-mind communication was real.

But there were still sceptics, one of whom was the psychologist Bernard Riess. When Dr Rhine was invited to lecture about his ESP work at Barnard College, Riess questioned him so fiercely and in such a manner that Rhine protested he was, in effect, accusing him of being a liar. Instead of defending his own experiments, however, Rhine suggested to Riess that he should carry out his own tests, using all the controls he believed necessary. Riess's students urged him to accept the challenge and they found a young lady with psychic abilities who agreed to act as subject. For several months, Riess conducted his own card-guessing experiments with the girl. Seventy-four runs of 25 cards were made (1850 trials) and they averaged a phenomenal 18 hits out of 25.

Riess, once a denigrator of ESP research, was called upon to defend his experiment in 1938 when the American Psychological Association organised an ESP symposium. He told the meeting:

> There can be no criticism of the method used. I had the deck of cards on my desk, shuffled them, and at the stated time turned them over one by one, making a record of each card. I kept the records locked up in my desk and sometimes it was a week before I totalled up the scores and found the number of high scores she was making. . . . The only error that may have crept in is a possibility of deception, and the only person who could have done the deceiving was myself since the subject at no time knew how well she was doing nor had any idea of cards which were being turned by myself. . . .

ESP in dreams

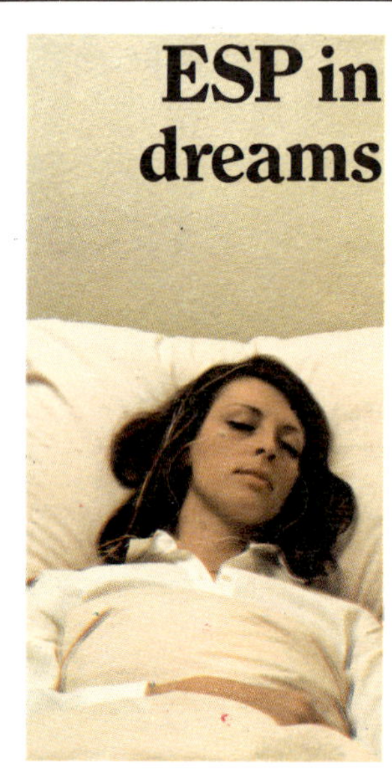

Recent research suggests that telepathy may occur much more often than is generally thought.

In a series of dream telepathy experiments carried out at the Dream Laboratory in Brooklyn, New York, an 'agent' studied a picture postcard and transmitted the image telepathically while the subject was asleep in another room. An electro – encephalograph monitored brain patterns: when a change in the patterns indicated the subject was dreaming, he or she was woken up and asked to describe the dream.

There was a high degree of similarity between the transmitted images and the dreams, although the target pictures were never received whole. The images were interwoven with the dream the subject was having at the time.

ESPionage!

Rhine's work continued to be a subject of public debate for many years, but with more and more researchers carrying out their own research programmes into various ESP subjects, telepathy was soon overshadowed by subjects such as clairvoyance and precognition, which brought startling experimental results. Then, in the late 1950s, telepathy was suddenly back in the news with the publication in the French press of reports that successful telepathy tests had been carried out between a subject in the submerged American submarine USS *Nautilus* and an agent on shore. The military implications of such methods of communication, if they proved to be reliable, were obvious; and they aroused great interest.

Despite the United States Navy's denial of the *Nautilus* story, the Soviets took it seriously – with the result that the work of Russian psychical investigators, which had been classed as top secret for 30 years, was made public. Among them was physiologist Dr Leonid Vasiliev. He claimed that Soviet parapsychologists had received encouragement for their research from high up in the party organisation – which suggests that Stalin himself may have been interested in the use of telepathy for military purposes.

Dr Vasiliev had been using hypnotised subjects to investigate 'mental radio', and when a book about his work was published in 1962 he revealed that he and other researchers had been able to make hypnotised

patients carry out actions by telepathic order, and even hypnotise people by telepathy. In one extraordinary case, a woman whose body was paralysed down the left side was the subject of the experiments. Her condition was psychosomatic, and under hypnotism she was able to move her left arm and leg with ease. Vasiliev discovered, however, that he had only to give *mental* commands and she would move her left hand, arm, or foot as requested – without the use of hypnotism.

He was able to demonstrate this mental communication before a group of observers. As an extra precaution the patient was blindfolded and not a word was spoken. Each instruction was written down and witnessed by the group before either Vasiliev or his co-worker, hypnotist Dr Finne, concentrated on it. The woman obeyed with remarkable accuracy, and she was even able to say whether it was Vasiliev or Finne who was giving the instruction.

More recently, the Russians have carried out even more startling demonstrations of telepathy using a biophysicist, Yuri Kamensky, and a Moscow actor and journalist, Karl Nikolaiev. Kamensky was in Novosibirsk in Siberia, Nikolaiev in Moscow, and a committee of scientists supervised the session. The results provided overwhelming evidence for mental communication between the two men.

In one test, Nikolaiev correctly described six objects that had been given to Kamensky; he was also able to identify 12 out of 20 ESP cards. What is particularly impressive about this Russian series is that the scientists succeeded in producing independent instrumental confirmation that something paranormal was going on.

They wired Nikolaiev to an electroencephalograph (EEG) machine, which monitors brain waves. They found that as soon as Kamensky began to transmit images, Nikolaiev's brain waves altered. Using this knowledge they devised a technique for sending messages in Morse code. Instead of asking Kamensky to think of an object, they asked him to imagine he was fighting Nikolaiev. As the scientists in Moscow watched the recording of Nikolaiev's brain waves on the EEG, they found that there was a distinct change in the pattern whenever Kamensky imagined he was fighting him. Kamensky was able to transmit Morse 'dots' and 'dashes' by imagining 'fighting bouts' of various lengths: a 45-second bout produced a burst of activity that was interpreted as a dash, while a 15-second bout was read as a dot. In this way, the scientists in Moscow were able to identify the Russian word *mig* – meaning 'instant' – which Kamensky had transmitted in Morse code from 2000 miles (3200 kilometres) away in Siberia.

Interestingly, a similar technique using different methods has been successfully demonstrated in the West. It followed the accidental discovery by a Czechoslovakian researcher, Dr Stepan Figar, that intense thought about a person produced an increase in that individual's blood volume – a change that could be accurately measured by a device called a plethysmograph.

Top: the nuclear submarine USS *Nautilus*. In the late 1950s it was rumoured that the US Navy had been carrying out telepathy experiments with an agent on shore and a sender aboard the submerged craft

Above: Karl Nikolaiev (left) and Dr Yuri Kamensky (second from right). They devised a method of sending Morse messages by telepathy

Left: Dr Leonid Vasiliev, the Soviet psychical researcher

Mental radio

Douglas Dean, a British-born electrochemist and professor of computing who is also a leading psychical researcher, saw the potential of this discovery for telepathy tests. His research revealed that, when a telepathic sender concentrates on the name of someone with whom a subject wired to a plethysmograph has an emotional tie, a change in the subject's blood volume is often recorded. Together with two engineers of the Newark College of Engineering in New Jersey, Dean designed a system using a plethysmograph for sending messages in Morse code.

If the sender concentrates on the name of a person who is emotionally significant to the subject, the plethysmograph produces a measurable response which is interpreted as a Morse dot. If no response is registered during a specified period of time, this is noted as a Morse dash. Using this technique, Dean has successfully communicated over short and long distances. In one remarkable instance he sent a Morse message over a distance of 1200 miles (2000 kilometres), between New York and Florida.

Despite these discoveries and the outstanding individual results that some experiments have produced, not all researchers are so successful when they attempt to duplicate telepathy tests. Mental radio remains an elusive phenomenon, although it is one that has occurred often enough – spontaneously and in the laboratory – to satisfy most investigators of its reality.

Clues from clairvoyance

The uncanny ability that we call clairvoyance takes many forms, from a vague awareness of a distant event to a vivid revelation. Though not always reliable, clairvoyance has provided startling and unexpected clues in crime cases, as many of those documented reveal

ONE DAY in late October 1978, seven-year-old Carl Carter disappeared from his Los Angeles home. The police were baffled; they did not know whether he had been kidnapped, or had simply wandered off and got lost.

It was then that a retired police officer suggested that a local psychic – who is known only by the name of Joan – might be able to help. Within hours of her involvement, the case had changed from a lost child investigation to one of triple murder.

The psychic told the police that the boy was dead and she described the man she thought was responsible for his murder. Joan tried drawing his portrait and a police artist was called in to make a more accurate sketch of the suspect, based on her description. When the drawing was shown to Carl's parents his father said at once, 'That looks like Butch.'

Within an hour, Harold Ray 'Butch' Memro was arrested and by the end of the day he had confessed to strangling Carl, and to murdering two other boys two years earlier.

Psychics often volunteer their services to the police and there are countless stories of people whose extra-sensory powers have given them glimpses of crimes. But all too often the accuracy of their statements cannot be verified until after the criminals have been caught by conventional means. In other words, ESP seldom leads the police to a culprit as it appears to have done in the Memro case.

It has to be remembered that, for every impressive case reported in the press, there are probably a hundred or more where volunteered 'psychic' help only leads the police on a wild goose chase. Following the mysterious disappearance of schoolgirl Genette Tate in August 1978, for example, the Devon police received calls from over 200 mediums and other people interested in psychic detection who believed their paranormal powers could produce useful clues.

The definition of clairvoyance is 'extra-sensory knowledge about material objects or events which is not obtained from another person's mind' – in other words, not simple telepathy. It can take many different forms, ranging from a vague awareness of a distant event to a vision in which scenes unfold

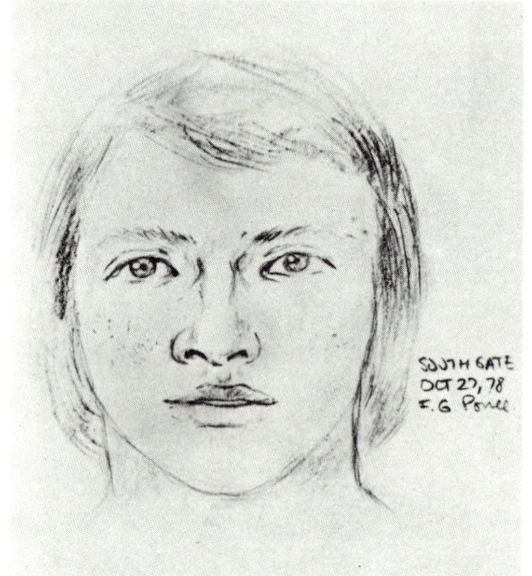

Left: late in 1978 Los Angeles police called in a local psychic, Joan (top), to help solve the case of a small boy's mysterious disappearance. The psychic told the police the boy was dead and, on the basis of her description, a police artist was able to make a sketch of the murderer (centre). The victim's parents immediately recognised the man in the picture as 'Butch' Memro (bottom), who was quickly arrested and confessed to the crime

Croesus tests the oracles

In ancient times clairvoyants were known as oracles and their visions were subject to as much scrutiny as they are today. Two and a half thousand years ago Croesus, the fabulously rich king of Lydia, conducted a fascinating psychic experiment to test the powers of seven oracles, six Greek and one Egyptian. According to the historian Herodotus, the king was becoming increasingly alarmed at the power of the Persians and decided to consult an oracle as to what course of action he should take. But which one could he trust? He decided to test them.

He sent out seven messengers, one to each oracle, instructing them that on the hundredth day each should ask his oracle, 'What is King Croesus, son of Alyattes, now doing?' Their answers were to be written down and brought back to the King. Only one of the answers – the most accurate – remains on record. The oracle at Delphi – the Pythoness, as she was called – induced her prophetic trances by sitting over a volcanic fault and inhaling the fumes while chewing mulberry leaves. The moment the Lydian messenger entered her sanctuary, she answered him, without even hearing his question, in verse:

I can count the sands, and I can measure the ocean;
I have ears for the silent and know what the dumb man meaneth;
Lo! on my sense there striketh the smell of a shell-covered tortoise,
Boiling now on a fire, with the flesh of a lamb in a cauldron –
Brass is the vessel below, and brass the cover above it.

After sending his messengers to the oracles, the king set about deciding on what would be the most improbable thing anyone could conceive of him doing. On the appointed day he took a lamb and a tortoise, cut them to pieces with his own hands, and boiled them together in a brass cauldron covered with a brass lid.

Not surprisingly, the clairvoyance of the oracle at Delphi got her the job as psychic adviser to the king.

vividly before the eyes of the clairvoyant.

For ordinary people, clairvoyance is most likely to occur in stressful situations or when people or places connected with them are in danger. A well authenticated instance concerns the 18th-century Swedish scientist and seer, Emanuel Swedenborg, investigated and recorded by the distinguished German philosopher Immanuel Kant. On one occasion Swedenborg arrived in Gothenburg from England at around 4 p.m. on a Saturday. Soon he became restless and disturbed and left his friends to go for a walk outside.

On his return, he described a vision he had had of a fire which, he said, had broken out just three doors away from his home, 300 miles (480 kilometres) away. A fierce blaze was raging, he said, and he continued to be disturbed until 8 p.m. when he announced that the fire had been extinguished. News of this clairvoyant vision spread rapidly through the city and Swedenborg was asked to give a first-hand account to the Governor of Gothenburg. It was not until a royal messenger arrived in Gothenburg on the following Monday that the events of Swedenborg's vision were confirmed.

The pioneer of ESP research, Dr J. Rhine, and his colleagues at Duke University, decided in the 1930s to investigate clairvoyance. They had earlier conducted successful telepathy tests in which one person concentrated on a symbol while someone else, in another room, tried to read his mind; the symbols of a pack of Zener cards were generally used. The Duke University investigators decided to see what would happen if, instead of looking at the cards, the agent simply shuffled them and then removed them one at a time from the pack, face

Below: Emanuel Swedenborg (1688–1772), the Swedish scientist, philosopher and theologian, who was well known during his lifetime as a clairvoyant

down. The subject of the experiment had to use clairvoyance, instead of telepathy, to guess their running order. (The agent could then note down the order of the cards by going through the pack after the experiment.)

In one series of experiments in which J. Pratt was the experimenter and Hubert Pearce the subject, Pearce scored 558 correct responses out of a total of 1850 guesses. If chance alone had been at work, he should have scored only 370 correct answers. On this basis, the odds against Pearce's score were calculated as 22,000 million to one.

Not everyone is impressed with laboratory results. One criticism that has been levelled at the Pearce-Pratt experiments is that Pearce was unsupervised while making his guesses. Professor C. E. M. Hansel, a non-believer in ESP, has argued that, under the circumstances, the results cannot be taken seriously. It was possible, after all, for Pearce to have sneaked out of the building after the experiment and peered through the window of the room Dr Pratt was in to see what cards

he was turning over. He could have noted them down or memorised them, then dashed back to his room to compile a running order with enough mistakes to make it look genuine.

Another psychical researcher, Professor Ian Stevenson, has subsequently investigated the theory and asserted that it would have been physically impossible for Pearce to have cheated in this way, since the cards would not have been visible through the window.

But even where the methodology of clairvoyant research is beyond criticism, the statistical nature of the results leaves many people unimpressed. For them, individual cases of spectacular clairvoyance are more impressive than repeated card-guessing tests that produce above-average results.

The clairvoyance of Polish engineer Stephan Ossowiecki attracted the attention of top psychical researchers in the early 1900s. Holding a sealed envelope or a folded piece of paper, he could often describe its contents or give the name of the signatory.

During an international conference on psychical research held in Warsaw in 1923, Ossowiecki's powers were put to the test. An English investigator, Dr Eric Dingwall, sketched a flag with a bottle etched in its upper left-hand corner. He then wrote the date, 22 August 1923, beneath his drawing and sealed it in a package consisting of three envelopes, one within the next. Dingwall sent the package from England to Baron Albert von Schrenck-Notzing in Warsaw.

Some important research into clairvoyance was carried out at Duke University, USA (top) during the 1930s. The experiments used Zener cards as targets: the agent, Dr Pratt (above left) sat in either room A or room B and withdrew cards one at a time, face down, from a pack while the subject, Hubert Pearce (above right) sat in room C and tried to name the cards as they were drawn from the pack. He was spectacularly successful: the odds against his results were 22,000 million to one

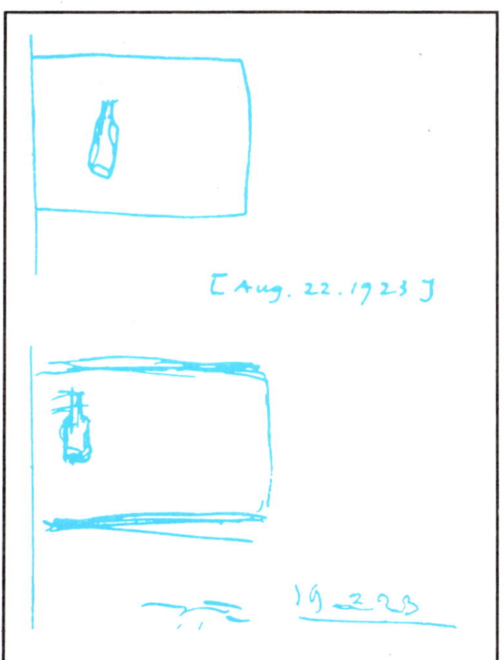

Polish engineer Stephan Ossowiecki (far left, pictured with his wife) had extraordinary clairvoyant powers. His abilities were tested in an experiment: an English investigator sketched a flag with a bottle on it, wrote the date beneath it and sent it in a sealed package to a noted Polish psychic researcher, Baron von Schrenck-Notzing (below), in Warsaw. The Baron handed the sealed envelope to Ossowiecki and asked him for his impressions.

Ossowiecki immediately realised that the Baron had not written the message. Then he suddely grabbed a pen and agitatedly began to draw what he 'saw' inside the envelope. His drawing (left) is startlingly similar to the original

Baron von Schrenck-Notzing was a well-known pathologist of the day, who was also a noted psychical investigator. Neither the Baron, nor the two other researchers involved in the experiment knew what was inside the envelope. They simply gave it to Ossowiecki without explanation and asked for his impressions.

The Polish clairvoyant told them that the Baron had not written the message; there were several envelopes, something greenish – cardboard – and a little bottle. Then he grabbed a pen and, in an agitated manner, drew an almost identical replica of the target. He also wrote '1923' and said something was written before it, but he was unable to say what it was. This test left Dingwall and the other researchers in no doubt that Ossowiecki had paranormal powers.

Measuring the soul

The ability to pick up impressions from objects was investigated as early as 1949 by J. Rhodes Buchanan, a physician in Ohio, USA. He found that some people he tested were able to identify medicines hidden in sealed envelopes or give accurate descriptions of the writers of letters. He coined the word *psychometry* – which means, in Greek, 'measure of the soul' – to describe the ability.

One of the most detailed studies of clairvoyance and psychometry was carried out, from 1919 onwards, by a German physician, Dr Gustav Pagenstecher, who practised medicine in Mexico for 40 years. One day Señora Maria Reyes Zierold consulted Dr Pagenstecher, complaining of insomnia. He decided to treat her by hypnosis. While in trance, she told him she could see his daughter listening at the door. To his surprise, when he opened the door the child was there just as the patient had claimed. With her permission he set about investigating Señora Zierold's paranormal vision and soon discovered that, if an object was put in her hand while she was in trance, she was able to give a vivid description of events connected with it.

Once, for example, she was handed a piece of string. She began describing a battlefield on a cold, foggy day, with groups of men and continuous rifle fire. 'Quite of a sudden,' she said, 'I see coming through the air and moving with great rapidity a big ball of fire . . . which drops just in the middle of the 15 men, tearing them to pieces.' The string had originally been attached to a German soldier's dog tag (identity disc). The psychic had reported with startling accuracy a scene that the man described as 'the first great impression I received of the war.'

In an attempt to discover whether some element of telepathy was involved, or whether Señora Zierold was a genuine clairvoyant the American Society for Psychical Research sent its research officer, Walter Prince, to conduct tests with her. One experiment he carried out involved two identical pieces of silk ribbon, enclosed in identical boxes. He mixed them up so that even he did not know which was which. Holding one box, Señora Zierold described a Mexican church and dancing Indians. The other gave her impressions of a French ribbon factory. She was absolutely right: one piece had come direct from the manufacturers, the other from a church altar.

With many outstanding cases of clairvoyance on record, it is not surprising to find possessors of these abilities being consulted in particularly baffling crime cases. The consolation for criminals is that few clairvoyants are as spectacularly successful or as reliable as Ossowiecki or Zierold!

Putting the power to work

Scientific research suggests ESP is a gift we all have – if only we could 'tune in' our minds to it. How could this elusive gift be put to use? The possibilities are limitless

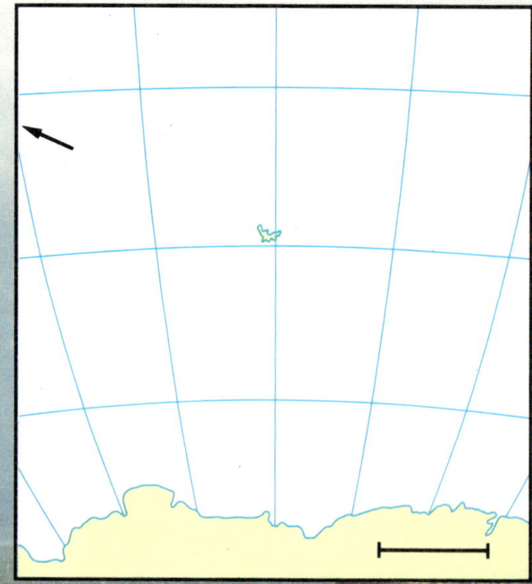

A TELEPHONE RANG in the office of Doctors Russell Targ and Harold Puthoff at Stanford Research Institute (SRI), California. A sceptical scientist who had heard about their research into extra-sensory perception was calling to issue a challenge. He had heard that Ingo Swann, one of the psychics they used in their tests, could apparently describe places given their geographical co-ordinates.

The man on the telephone asked Swann to describe what he could 'see' at 49° 20′S, 70° 14′E. Naturally, the psychic was not allowed to consult a map. But instantly he described a rocky island. The climate was cold and there were buildings, one of them orange, with a few trucks in front of them.

Swann described the coastline and continued with his description, drawing attention to specific points on the island, which he marked on a sketch map.

The psychic was absolutely right. The sceptic had come up with co-ordinates that marked the island of Kerguelen in the southern Indian Ocean. The island is administered as part of the French Southern and Antarctic lands and is a base for a joint French-Soviet research project that is studying the upper atmosphere. Many of the features described by Swann seemed to refer to Kerguelen, about which it was impossible for him to have had prior knowledge.

This case, quoted by Puthoff and Targ in their book *Mind-reach*, is one of many that the SRI scientists have investigated as part of their research into an aspect of ESP called 'remote viewing'. The geographical co-ordinate tests represent a variation of their normal procedure, which was to get Swann and other psychics to describe places being visited by one of the investigators.

For example, psychic Pat Price (an ex-police commissioner and vice-mayor of Burbank, California) sat talking to Targ while Puthoff left the SRI building carrying a sealed envelope that had been selected at random from a large number. Once outside the building, he opened the envelope and found instructions directing him to a particular destination. He stayed at this place for half an hour, just looking at it, while Price attempted telepathically to 'see' what Puthoff was seeing.

The psychic began describing a scene in terms that were general and rambling. But then, the scientists report, his account 'became tighter and more coherent, gradually zeroing in on a description of a tower-like structure until finally we heard "seems like it would be Hoover Tower".' Price's impressions were tape recorded and played back to Puthoff on his return to the SRI building. He then produced the envelope: the target site was, as Price had 'seen', the Hoover Tower, a well-known landmark of the Stanford University campus.

Not surprisingly, Puthoff and Targ's

In some remarkable ESP tests conducted at Stanhope Research Institute (SRI), California, psychic Ingo Swann (below) was given the co-ordinates of Kerguelen Island in the Indian Ocean (top). He immediately began to describe an island with a rocky terrain. The climate, he said, was cold, and there were buildings, one of them orange. The photograph (above) shows just how accurate his description was

In this SRI experiment, the subject attempted to 'see' what an agent in another part of the campus was looking at. Psychic Pat Price accurately identified the Hoover Tower of Stanford University (above)

Above right: these drawings indicate extrovert (top) and introvert (bottom) personalities. Dr Betty Humphrey of Duke University says such drawings can predict how a subject will score in ESP tests

Below: Dr Gertrude Schmeidler of City University, New York, who has shown that subjects who believe in ESP score higher in tests than those who do not

Below right: a subject in a state of sensory deprivation, or *Ganzfeld state*, which makes him receptive to ESP

work has excited great interest – particularly as they claim that remote viewing is an ability that most of us possess. Others have succeeded in producing similar results, but not all scientists have been able to do so. And critics claim that, for various technical reasons, the SRI scientists' results are not as impressive as they seem at first glance.

Executive ESP

If some people *can* learn to view remotely, there are all sorts of exciting possibilities. Could they eavesdrop on top secret political or commercial talks? Could they 'see' confidential plans or documents? Could they visit sensitive sites and give information about their layout and the people who work there? The very best cases of ESP suggest that such possibilities are not far-fetched; the problem is that psychic powers are notoriously unreliable. A fortune awaits the person who discovers a way of 'switching' ESP on and off at will.

Many people have searched for a key to psychic success in the hope of producing repeatable ESP experiments, but their results have been disappointing. Some of the most fascinating studies have examined personality in relation to psychic abilities: what kind of person is most likely to experience ESP? One of the first researchers to delve into the subject was Dr Gertrude Schmeidler.

In thousands of clairvoyance tests in the late 1940s and early 1950s, Dr Schmeidler, of the City University of New York, asked each person before he was tested whether he believed ESP was possible under the conditions of the experiment. The purpose was to see whether those who believed ESP was possible scored more highly than those who did not. And, indeed, Dr Schmeidler's score sheets showed such a difference: the believers scored consistently slightly above chance, whereas the scores of the non-believers were slightly below.

Another link between ESP and personality was discovered by Dr Betty Humphrey of the Duke Parapsychology Laboratory. Before testing individuals for ESP she gave them a blank sheet of paper and asked them to draw anything they liked. Bold pictures

that filled most of the sheet indicated the person was an 'expansive' type; small, timid or conventional drawings showed that the person was a 'compressive'. Analysis of their ESP results showed that the expansives scored more highly than the compressives.

This work has continued into the 1980s, with different researchers using slightly different methods to gauge their subjects' personalities. The current trend is to divide people into extroverts (expansives) and introverts (compressives) using a detailed questionnaire.

The reasons for this link between extrasensory abilities and personality are still the subject of considerable conjecture, but many researchers regard it as powerful evidence for ESP. But does it mean that people who are not believers, or who are not extrovert by nature, do not have ESP experiences? Not really. Research suggests that ESP can be induced by altering our state of consciousness. This may sound difficult, but, in fact, we do just that every time we fall asleep – and early researchers soon realised that dreams were a rich source of psychic experience. Numerous case histories were compiled of vivid dreams that either recorded events that were happening elsewhere at the time of dreaming, or gave the sleeper a glimpse of the future.

Modern parapsychologists use a technique that induces a state of altered consciousness easily at any time of day or night. The subject is asked to rest on a mattress. His eyes are then covered with half ping-pong balls onto which a soft coloured light is shone and his ears are covered with headphones into which 'white noise' (a gentle hissing sound) is fed. In this state of sensory deprivation the subject's mind has no visual or auditory distractions to occupy it and is, at least theoretically, more open to receiving telepathic signals from an agent some distance away, who is concentrating on a picture chosen at random. This technique induces a *Ganzfeld state* in the subject, and Dr Carl

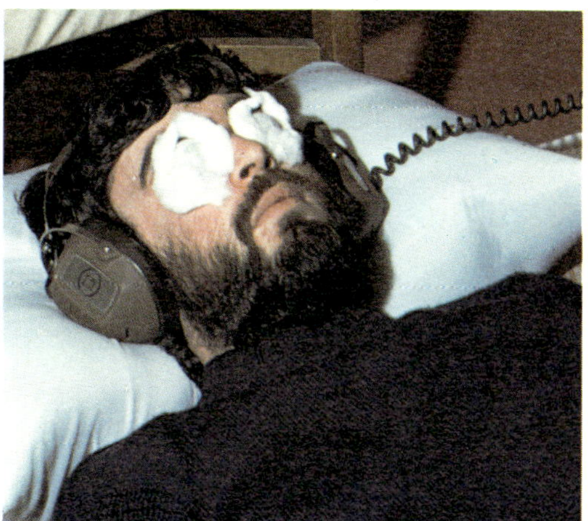

Sargent of Cambridge University is one of the researchers who has had outstanding results with it, with average scores of 17 per cent above chance expectancy. One of his top-scoring subjects is a young computer expert, Hugh Ashton. In one session he described seeing buildings in a corner, adding:

> 'Keep thinking of firemen and fire station . . . Firemen definitely seen, black and white. People but not faces. I think one man at bottom in foreground: facing . . . Young face, as if photographer says, 'Oi' and only he turned round'.

The description contained much more detail. At the end of the session the agent brought into the room four pictures. They were a duplicate set of the pictures contained in the target envelope, of which only one had been selected for the test. Hugh Ashton was asked to identify the one he thought had been used for the experiment, and he was able to do so instantly. The agent had been concentrating on a picture that showed firemen playing their hoses on their special training building. They all had their backs to the camera – with the exception of one, who was looking straight at the photographer.

In another session at Cambridge University a subject was even able to name the picture being 'sent' by telepathy: William Blake's *The ancient of days*.

Another technique that has been used successfully to induce telepathy is hypnosis. Mesmerism – the variant of hypnotism that was popular two centuries ago – was used by several practitioners to produce paranormal effects in their patients. The Marquis du Puységur found that a peasant, Victor Race, could at times repeat what was going through Puységur's mind when he was deep in a mesmeric trance.

Puységur was also the discoverer of medical clairvoyance. Subjects were mesmerised and then asked to diagnose the ailments of people brought into the room who were complete strangers. Though they had no medical knowledge, their diagnoses were often astonishingly accurate.

Russian psychical researchers have been particularly keen to use hypnosis to induce ESP, and their influence was responsible for similar work carried out by the Czechoslovak Dr Milan Ryzl, who now lives and works in the USA. While still in Czechoslovakia he experimented with precognitive clairvoyance. He would hypnotise a subject and ask him or her to visualise an unpleasant event that would happen to a friend in the future so that he or she could be warned about it.

As soon as one girl, Josefka, was hypnotised she became distressed, and began describing in vivid detail a scene in which a girlfriend, who lived 50 miles (80 kilometres) away, was approached by a stranger in a restaurant. They left and drove away together on a motorcycle at high speed. Suddenly they stopped. Josefka cried: 'Oh my God! He's torn her skirt.' She described the horrific scene as her friend was savagely raped.

Next day, thinking she had foreseen a future event, Josefka telephoned her friend to warn her not to accept a lift on a motorcycle from a stranger. 'You're too late,' came the response. 'It's already happened – last night.' Josefka's hypnotic vision matched the real event in every detail.

Josefka's ESP was just as impressive in the laboratory. Dr Ryzl enclosed standard Zener cards in opaque wrappings and asked her,

Dr Carl Sargent (above) of Cambridge University has gained outstanding results in ESP tests using the *Ganzfeld* state. One of his top-scoring subjects is Hugh Ashton, who described this photograph (left), which was sent telepathically by an agent, in accurate detail

Below: Jacques de Chastenet, Marquis du Puységur (1751-1825), an early exponent of mesmerism and the discoverer of medical clairvoyance, in which clairvoyants can diagnose illnesses by means of ESP

Left: in an experiment at Cambridge University, a subject was even able to name the picture being 'sent' – William Blake's *The ancient of days*

What causes ESP?

The first scientists to study one of the aspects of ESP – telepathy – thought its mechanics would be easy to understand once enough evidence had been collected. ESP seemed to be a simple matter of the mind being somehow 'tuned in' to receive messages, like a radio.

But the reality of ESP appears to be more complex. Successful telepathy experiments have been conducted with one of the participants shielded by a Faraday cage, which prevents the penetration of radio waves and other electromagnetic radiation. Whatever carries information from one mind to another is apparently not a straightforward physical process.

Finding an explanation for ESP is made even more difficult by the strange way in which it seems, at times, to ignore the natural limits of time and space; even if we could find a 'wavelength' on which minds make contact, we would still be left with the mystery of people who use ESP to see into the past or the future.

There is another complication that has to be taken into account in studying ESP. The latest research indicates that, in Zener card experiments that were originally carried out to test ESP, the results may actually have been due to psychokinesis (mind over matter), with the subject somehow influencing the order of the cards. An acceptable ESP theory, then, will have to take account of psychokinesis.

It is possible that research into particle physics may shed new light on ESP. Subatomic particles appear to be able to react instantaneously to the behaviour of other particles vast distances away – to 'communicate' by no known means, and faster than the speed of light. This is impossible according to the rules of quantum mechanics. But an attempt to explain the phenomenon has been made by Professor David Bohm of London University. The way in which particles 'communicate' may be similar to ESP contact, claim some parapsychologists. Professor Bohm's theory may provide the missing link between ESP research and science.

Above: Pavel Stepanek, the 'star' of ESP experiments conducted by Dr Milan Ryzl in the 1960s. In one experiment he attained a score against odds of a billion to one

while under hypnosis, to guess what they were. Out of 250 guesses she got 121 right – chance alone would have produced only 50 correct answers. When she tried the same experiment in a normal state her score was exactly at chance level.

Dr Ryzl went on to develop a method of ESP training, for which he claimed exceptional results. His six-stage method uses hypnosis and puts a heavy emphasis on inducing visual hallucinations. His claims created something of a controversy among other researchers, but the achievements of some of his subjects are beyond question. The star was Pavel Stepanek, a Czech library clerk. During the 1960s he was the most sought-after ESP subject and was tested by many researchers, usually with exceptional results. In his first series of 2000 guesses he scored hits with 1144; the odds against such a result are a billion to one.

Psychical researcher Rosalind Heywood found that ESP frequently impinged on her own life; she called her psychical impressions 'Orders'. In her book *The infinite hive* she tells of an experience that occurred in July 1949, when she was shutting up house for a month:

> Orders said that the water should be turned off at the main as a pipe in the attic bathroom was going to burst. I knew that this irrational prediction would stand little chance with my rational husband – it looked far more like fussing than ESP – and, as I expected, when I told him of it he kindly gave me the technical reasons why pipes did not burst in high summer.
>
> At this I decided on a fatuous compromise: I would leave the water turned on as he wished and take a key to our builder for use when the pipe did burst. Although he, too, explained that pipes never burst in the summer I just had the strength of mind to press the key into his reluctant hand, thank him and fly. When the pipe did burst, as Orders had warned me, his charge for repairing the damage was £20.

Francis Kinsman, an eminent British futurologist, has attempted in a unique way to put ESP to practical use. Between March and July 1979 he interviewed 15 leading clairvoyants and psychics, asking the same simple question: 'What do you think will be the role of Britain in the world context during the 1980s?' The questioning then branched off to include politics, economics, technology and sociological developments, and the results were published in a booklet, *Future tense*. The prophecies include the collapse of the current world economic system, major earthquakes and floods, a new Middle East war, and the abdication of the Queen.

But perhaps the most fascinating aspects of the predictions concern ESP. They claim that there will be an increase in the use of psychic techniques in the field of medicine. The Russians, they say, are leaders in the field of psychic research and are secretly carrying out experiments in psychic warfare. Fear for its own safety, they predict, will lead the West to concentrate its energies and develop the extra-sensory powers that are latent in everyone.

Above: Francis Kinsman, who has conducted a series of interviews with clairvoyants about the future of Britain and the world

Mind over matter

We assume that the laws of nature are immutable, but when we are faced with metal that bends with no apparent pressure, and solid objects that rise in the air by themselves or appear and disappear inexplicably, it is hard to avoid the conclusion that these laws can sometimes be suspended – at least by a few gifted individuals.

The world of Uri Geller

Uri Geller's metal-bending magic has made him famous throughout the world. But how does he perform such baffling feats? What is the source of his rare and remarkable power?

IN THE SUMMER of 1971, the teenagers of Israel were beginning to talk about a new pop idol – not a singer or a disc jockey, but a stage magician. His name was Uri Geller, and his popularity was undoubtedly influenced by the fact that he was tall, good-looking, and only 24 years old. But the act itself was startlingly original. Who had ever heard of a 'magician' repairing broken watches by merely looking at them? Or bending spoons by gently massaging them with his finger? Or breaking metal rings without even touching them? Yet these were just a few of the 'tricks' in Geller's dazzling repertoire.

Tales of this 'magic' reached the ears of a well-known psychical researcher named Andrija Puharich, who was so intrigued that he flew from New York to Israel to investigate. On 17 August 1971, Uri Geller was performing at a discotheque in Jaffa, and it was there that Puharich went to see him.

The first thing that struck him was that Geller was a born showman; he obviously loved performing in front of an audience. Yet Puharich found most of his act disappointing. Geller began with a demonstration of mindreading. He was blindfolded, then members of the audience were asked to write words on a blackboard. It was impossible for Geller to see the board; yet he guessed correctly every time. The enthusiasm of the teenage audience showed that they found it amazing; but Puharich knew that such feats are simple if the magician has a few confederates in the audience.

But the last 'trick' impressed him more. Geller announced that he would break a ring without touching it, and a woman in the audience offered her dress ring. She was told to show it to the audience, then hold it tightly in her hand. Geller placed his own hand above hers and held it there for a few seconds. When she opened her hand, the ring had snapped in two.

After the show, Puharich asked Geller if he would submit to a few scientific tests the next day. So far, Geller had consistently refused to be examined by 'experts'. But this time he readily agreed – to his own surprise, as he later admitted. It was a fateful decision: Geller's first step on the road to world fame.

Geller duly arrived at Puharich's apartment the next day. And his first demonstration convinced Puharich that this was genuine 'magic'. Geller placed a notepad on the table, then asked Puharich to think of three numbers. Puharich chose 4, 3 and 2:

Geller began giving demonstrations of his powers in 1968, first to groups of school children and at private parties, then to large audiences in theatres all over Israel. He said he was surprised at how well the experiments worked in front of so many people – having an audience even seemed to help

American psychical researcher Andrija Puharich who investigated Uri Geller in the early 1970s. His account of his experiences with Geller was published in 1974 and made the astonishing claim that Geller was the messenger of the Nine, a group of extra-terrestrial beings who were the 'controllers of the Universe'

'Now turn that notepad over,' said Geller. Puharich did, and found himself looking at the figures 4, 3 and 2 – written *before* he had thought of the numbers. Geller had somehow 'influenced' him into choosing those three figures.

The point is worth remembering, for it suggests that Geller could hypnotise people by means of 'telepathy'. Yet whether this helps to explain the weird and incredible events that followed is open to debate.

At further demonstrations, Geller went on to raise the temperature of a thermometer by staring at it, move a compass needle by concentrating on it, and bend a stream of water from a tap by moving his finger close to it. Puharich's conclusion was that Uri Geller was no mere conjuror: he was a genuine psychic, with a definite power of 'mind over matter' – a faculty known as psychokinesis.

Geller admitted that he had no idea of how he came to possess these curious powers. He had become aware of them when he was little more than a baby. At the age of six, he realised he could read his mother's mind. She came back one day from a party at which she had played cards for money. Geller took one look at her, and was able to tell her precisely how much she had lost.

When he started to go to school, his stepfather gave him a watch. But it always seemed to be going wrong. One day, as Geller stared at it, the hands began to go faster and faster, until they were whirling around. It was then that he began to suspect he might be causing it. Yet he seemed to have no control over this freakish ability. One day, when he was eating soup in a restaurant, the bowl fell off the spoon. Then spoons and forks on nearby tables began to bend. Geller's parents were so worried they even thought of taking him to see a psychiatrist.

By the age of 13, he was beginning to gain some kind of control over his powers. He broke a lock on a bicycle by concentrating on it, and learned to cheat at exams by reading the minds of more diligent pupils – he said he only had to stare at the backs of their heads to see the answers.

Puharich was intensely excited; it looked as if he had made the find of the century. Ever since the formation of the Society for Psychical Research in 1882, scientists have been studying psychics and mediums, trying to prove or disprove their claims. They have never succeeded in doing either. And the reason is mainly that most psychics claim they cannot switch their powers on and off at will. Yet Geller's powers seemed to work to order, whenever he wanted them to. If they would work in a laboratory as well as on stage, it would be one of the greatest triumphs in the history of psychical research.

At this point, events took a completely unexpected turn. On the morning of 1 December 1971 Geller was hypnotised by Puharich in the hope of uncovering clues about the origin of his powers. Puharich asked him where he was; Geller replied that he was in a cave in Cyprus – where his family had lived

Interest in Geller and his paranormal powers grew rapidly and a multitude of books about him appeared in the 1970s. Geller himself is an author – his autobiography, *My story*, was published in 1975, and many of his poems, which he says seem to 'come through' him rather than being composed by him, have been set to music and recorded

when he was 13 – and that he was 'learning about people who come from space.' He added that he was not yet allowed to talk about this. Puharich regressed him further, and Geller began to speak in Hebrew – the first language he had learned. At this point he described an episode that, he said, had taken place when he was three years old. He had walked into a garden in Tel Aviv, and suddenly become aware of a shining, bowl-like object floating in the air above his head. There was a high, ringing sound in the air. As the object came closer, Uri felt himself bathed in light, and fell down in a faint.

As Geller recounted these events, Puharich and his fellow investigators were startled to hear a voice speaking from the air above their heads. Puharich described it as 'unearthly and metallic'. 'It was we who found Uri in the garden when he was three,' said the disembodied voice. 'He is our helper, sent to help man. We programmed him in the garden.' The reason, it explained, was that mankind was on the point of a world war. Uri, it implied, had been 'programmed' to avert the catastrophe.

The voice stopped speaking. When Geller woke up, he seemed to have no memory of what had happened; so Puharich played the tape back. As he listened to his voice recounting the episode in the garden, Geller looked worried. 'I can't remember any of this.' And then, as the metallic voice began to speak, Geller snatched the cassette off the recorder. As he held it in his hand, it vanished. Then Geller rushed from the room. When they found him, some time later, he seemed to be confused, and there was no sign of the tape.

What had happened? The sceptical explanation is that Geller performed a little ventriloquism, then palmed the tape and made sure it 'disappeared', so that subsequent tests would not reveal the resemblance between his own voice and the 'space being' on the tape. But Puharich and the others said the voice came from above their heads, and that it sounded mechanical, as if manufactured by a computer. And even if Geller could have tricked a number of trained observers on this first occasion, it would certainly have been quite impossible on some later occasions described by Puharich. For the bodiless voice was only the first in a series of weird and inexplicable events – events that finally destroyed all Puharich's hopes of convincing the world that Geller's powers were genuine.

These events are described by Puharich in his book *Uri: a journal of the mystery of Uri Geller*. And they sound so confused and preposterous that the reader ends by doubting Puharich's common sense, then his sanity. He describes how, the following day, he recorded yet another hypnotic session with Geller, and how the 'voice' again interrupted and talked about war. Then Puharich and Geller went for a drive, taking the recorder with them, and the tape suddenly vanished into thin aír. From then on, hardly a day went past without the mysterious 'entities' performing some mind-boggling trick to convince Puharich of their reality. They made the car engine stop, and then start up again. They 'teleported' Puharich's briefcase from his house in New York to his apartment in Tel Aviv. When Geller and Puharich went to an army base to entertain the troops, they were followed by a red light in the sky that was invisible to their military escort. Geller actually photographed a 'space ship' on the orders of the metallic voice.

Was it a joke? Or some kind of trickery? Puharich, at least, was convinced that no

Geller's powers began to manifest themselves when he was a small child: he found that he could read his mother's mind, affect the workings of clocks and watches simply by looking at them, and cause spoons and forks to bend or break. At first his parents were merely embarrassed by the extraordinary events that occurred, but then they became concerned that something was wrong with him, and even considered consulting a psychiatrist

fraud was involved. A few years before, a psychic had given him messages from some mysterious beings who called themselves the 'Nine', and who said they came from outer space. And at one of the hypnotic sessions with Geller, Puharich asked whether the voice was one of the Nine, and it answered 'Yes'. He went on to ask if the Nine were behind the UFO sightings that had been taking place since Kenneth Arnold saw the first 'flying saucer' in 1947; again the answer was 'Yes'. The voice told Puharich that the Nine were beings from another dimension, and that they lived in a star ship called *Spectra*, which was '53,069 light ages away'. They had been watching Earth for thousands of years, and had landed in South America 3000 years ago. And they would soon prove their existence by landing on planet Earth. . . .

It is easy to jeer at all this, and to condemn Puharich for his gullibility. The simple explanation seems to be that Geller had been reading Erich von Däniken's *Chariots of the gods?* and decided to fool the naïve Puharich with this preposterous gobbledegook about space beings and star ships. Yet if Puharich's description of the various events is accurate, this is totally impossible. No doubt Geller could have palmed the cassettes, imitated the metallic voice, and faked the photograph of a UFO. But it is hard to see how he could have transported Puharich's briefcase from New York, caused the car engine to stop and start, and arranged for them to be followed by a red light that was invisible to the soldiers who were escorting them.

A photograph taken on 4 November 1972 by Geller when travelling by jet from London to Munich. According to Geller, his camera rose into the air of its own accord and stopped in front of him, as if signalling him to take a picture. Geller could see nothing in the sky but nevertheless took several shots. When the film was developed, five frames contained images of UFOs alongside the aeroplane

Could Puharich himself be telling lies? This hypothesis must also be ruled out. Puharich's aim was simply to prove that Geller possessed paranormal powers, and all he had to do was to arrange for scientific tests of these powers – as he later did in the United States. Far from making his case more convincing or interesting, all this talk about *Spectra* and the Nine only makes it sound absurd. By writing about it, he only destroyed his own credibility.

Does this mean, then, that the Nine were genuine, and that they have really chosen Geller to be their emissary on Earth? This is equally difficult to accept – and Geller says that he himself does not accept it. Then what *does* he believe? The answer is: nothing. He declares that the events described by Puharich leave him totally bewildered, and that he has no idea of their explanation.

Geller himself was becoming rather worried by all these strange events by the beginning of 1972. Unlike Puharich, he had no desire to convince the scientific establishment of the reality of his powers; he was more interested in becoming rich and famous. And the bewildering tricks performed by the Nine seemed unlikely to bring him closer to that goal. The same thing applied to Puharich, with all his talk about scientific proof and laboratory testing. Geller must have heaved a sigh of relief when, in April 1972, Puharich flew back to New York, promising to return in a few weeks. He proceeded to finalise plans to display his psychic talents in Germany, under the guidance of a professional impressario.

A sign from the Nine

Another curious event, described in *Uri*, guaranteed that Geller was able to make this trip to Germany alone. According to Puharich, Geller went into his apartment on 1 June 1972, and found a letter from Puharich on the mat. It stated simply that Puharich was unable to leave the United States for another three months, and would join Geller later. Accordingly, Geller flew on to Rome – en route for Munich – and telephoned Puharich to ask about the delay. Puharich was amazed, and denied writing any such letter. At which point, it struck them both that the letter must be yet another 'sign' from the Nine. The 'proof' was that it had vanished from Geller's shirt-pocket while he was on the aeroplane – obviously dematerialised by the owner of the metallic voice. A simpler explanation might be that Geller had invented the letter. But then, its appearance and disappearance are no more incredible than all the other baffling events described by Puharich.

Whatever the explanation, the letter incident convinced Puharich that the Nine wanted him to remain behind in the United States, trying to convince various eminent scientists that Geller was worth investigating. Meanwhile, his volatile and unpredictable protégé flew on to Munich, to keep his first appointment with fame and fortune – or at least, with notoriety and publicity.

Under the eyes of scientists

After a successful tour of Germany it seemed that Uri Geller had at last been accepted as a genuine psychic. But in the USA he was not so well received, and faced serious accusations of fraud

URI GELLER ARRIVED in Munich in June 1972, and immediately displayed that gift for publicity that would make him the most famous – and the richest – 'psychic' in the world. The tour had been arranged by an agent named Yasha Katz, who made sure that Geller was met by crowds of reporters. One of them asked him: 'What can you do that would be really astounding?' 'Suggest something,' said Geller. 'How about stopping a cable car in mid-air? After a moment's hesitation, Geller said: 'Sure, why not.' And the crowd of goggle-eyed reporters trailed behind him to the Hochfelln funicular line outside Munich.

The car left on its journey to the mountain top, and Geller concentrated hard. Nothing happened. It came down again, and still nothing happened. Then up and down again. By this time, Geller's confidence had drained away, and the reporters were losing interest. Then suddenly, to everyone's astonishment, the cable car stopped in mid-air. The mechanic called the control centre – and was told that the main switch had suddenly flipped off. Minutes later, the reporters were scrambling to get to the nearest telephones.

Inevitably, they wanted him to do something else. Someone suggested stopping an escalator in a department store. This time, Geller's luck seemed to have run out. Up and down, up and down they went. Then, at the twentieth attempt, the escalator stopped. . . .

Not surprisingly there were sceptics who felt that the amazing feat could be explained by a large bribe to a friendly electrician. Yet Geller also impressed a German scientist, Friedbert Karger, with his ring-breaking trick. Karger held the ring tightly in his hand; Geller held his own hand above it for a few moments – and when Karger opened his hand, the ring was broken. Karger was so excited that he rang Geller's mentor, Andrija Puharich, in New York, suggesting that Geller should stay on in Germany to be thoroughly investigated by scientists. Puharich squashed that one. Geller was already booked by some of America's most eminent scientific investigators.

Geller himself was not that enthusiastic

Geller and the cable car that halted halfway up the mountainside after he had been concentrating on stopping it. This was just one of the 'stunts' Geller performed in Germany in 1972

either. He was tasting fame, and enjoying the flavour. One impresario even wanted Geller to play in a musical about 'unknown powers', and Geller loved the idea. When told about all this over the telephone, Puharich gave a heartfelt sigh, and flew to Germany. And the young celebrity was persuaded to drop his plans to become the world's first singing mystic, and accompany his distraught Svengali back to the United States.

In fact, he was not too difficult to persuade. After weeks of non-stop exposure in the German media, Geller's feats were beginning to lose their impact on the public.

One of the oddest things about the Geller story is that he failed to achieve the same instant fame in the United States that he had found in Germany. There seem to be two explanations. One is that the Americans are hardened to publicity, and tend to become sceptical at the sight of 'miracle workers'. The other is that Geller's reputation had preceded him, and he found himself faced with considerable 'sales resistance'. Tales about Puharich's new protégé had already reached the world of paranormal research in the United States – a world in which Puharich was regarded as an eminent scientific investigator. According to the rumours, Puharich had been completely 'taken in' by this Israeli 'pop-magician', even to believing that he was an emissary from outer space. There were whispers that Geller was Puharich's 'evil genius'. So when Geller arrived in New York in the autumn of 1972, he found the atmosphere distinctly chilly.

From the beginning, he was surrounded by eminent scientists – men like Ed Mitchell, the Moon astronaut, Wernher von Braun, inventor of the V-2 rocket, and the physicist Gerald Feinberg. Geller was suspicious and unhappy; yet his powers seemed to be working excellently. In von Braun's office, he performed an interesting variant on his ring-breaking, flattening the gold wedding ring that von Braun held tightly in his own hand. Then von Braun found that his calculator battery was flat, although it had been put in that morning. Geller held the calculator between his hands. And when von Braun pushed the 'on' switch, the battery was no longer dead, but the display flashed random numbers. Geller had another try, and this time the calculator worked normally. There was no way in which it could have been faked – even a conjuror cannot get at the circuitry of a sealed calculator. Von Braun concluded that Geller could produce some strange electrical currents – a reasonable and probably correct assumption.

In the years since he began demonstrating his powers, Uri Geller has been seen to bend thousands of metal objects, either by stroking the metal lightly with his finger or simply by concentrating on it. In some cases the object has continued to bend after it has left his hand

Geller with John Lennon, talking about UFOs. Geller became interested in UFOs when he heard the voice of a 'space being' talking about the starship *Spectra*. After that, he claimed to have seen a 'red, disc-shaped light' that seemed to be following him, and managed to capture UFOs on film – even though he had not seen them in the sky at the time he took the photographs

Return of the 'space spooks'

In spite of these successes, Geller was tense and miserable. Apart from anything else, the 'space spooks' were at it again. In a room in a Washington hotel, an ashtray floated off the table, as if moved by invisible hands. Then the tape recorder began to work of its own accord. When Puharich – who was present – played the tape back, the weird metallic voice they had first heard in 1971 spoke again, explaining that the starship *Spectra* would soon be making a landing on Earth – but only for refuelling. The 'mass landing' promised in earlier interviews was evidently to come later. They also – to Puharich's surprise and irritation – told him not to start experiments with Geller for the time being, and not to tell anyone about these strange messages. When all this was over, the tape – according to Puharich – simply dissolved into thin air. Later messages that arrived through the tape recorder again insisted that Puharich should

Left: American astronaut Ed Mitchell, who met Geller on his first trip to the United States in 1972. Mitchell himself experimented with telepathy, and was intrigued by the so-called 'Geller phenomenon' – so much so that he offered to pay for scientific investigation of Geller's powers at the Stanford Research Institute (SRI) in California

scrap his plans for scientific tests. Understandably, Puharich was distraught. These beings from outer space – if that is where they came from – were wrecking his plans. Even Geller was unexpectedly sceptical; in one indignant outburst he said that he thought the 'space beings' were clowns playing practical jokes.

All this culminated in one highly significant event that Puharich dismisses in a single paragraph in his book on Geller, yet that could well provide the key to the mystery.

A psychic storm

When Puharich told Geller that he intended to ignore the 'space beings', and go ahead with the plans for scientific testing, Geller lost his temper and hurled a sugar bowl at his head. Puharich exploded in violent indignation. At that moment, an immense wind blew up outside, shaking the trees, and a grandfather clock shot across the hall and shattered into a thousand pieces. Overawed but still determined, Geller begged Puharich to forget the scientists. Puharich dug in his heels, and eventually won his point.

These incredible events – assuming that Puharich is reporting them accurately – may seem to confirm that some 'superhuman' powers were involved. Yet every paranormal researcher is aware that poltergeists can often produce equally amazing effects. And there is general agreement that poltergeists are closely connected with the unconscious minds of some human being or beings.

If the 'space beings' really existed, why should they suddenly order Puharich to drop the scientific investigations that they had earlier approved? On the other hand, if the strange manifestations originated in Uri Geller's unconscious mind, it would be perfectly understandable. He wanted to be famous and (if possible) rich, and the idea of being tested by sceptical scientists worried him. Significantly, the one project to which the 'space beings' gave the go-ahead was a film about the life of Geller.

Puharich tells how, the morning after the 'storm', his friendly black Labrador dog suddenly bit Geller on the wrist. The day before this same dog had suddenly vanished from the kitchen before their eyes, and a few moments later, was seen walking towards the house from 70 yards (65 metres) away – mysteriously 'teleported' by the space men, according to Puharich, to demonstrate their power. But perhaps the dog knew better. Perhaps it knew intuitively that the real culprit was Geller himself – or rather a stranger living in Geller's unconscious mind.

A few days later, the scientific tests began. They were held at the Stanford Research Institute in California, and conducted by Dr Hal Puthoff and Russell Targ. And as soon as the tests began, Geller knew he had nothing to worry about. Most psychics find it hard to perform under laboratory conditions; Geller

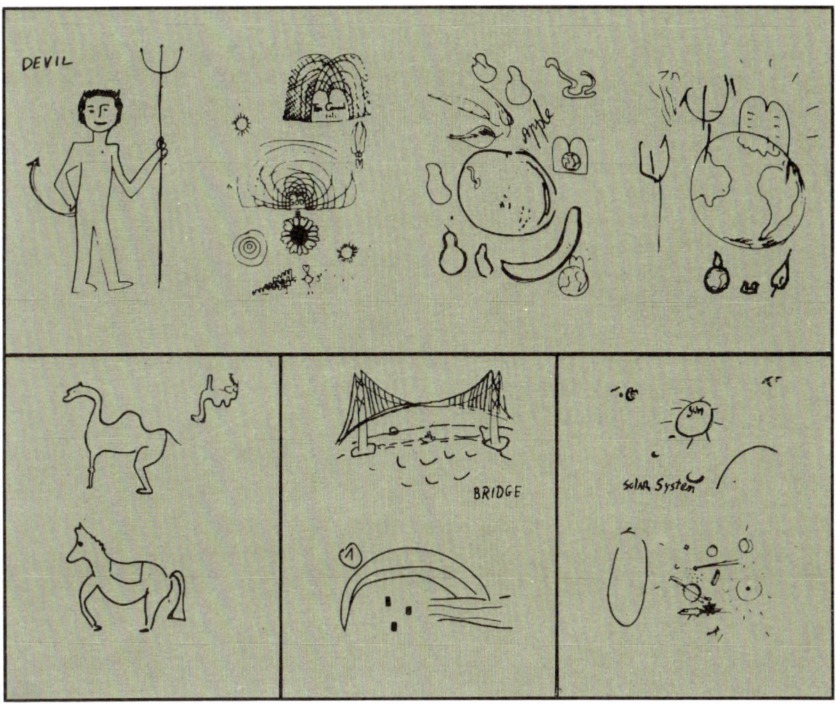

Target pictures and responses drawn by Geller during the SRI series of tests. Before each experiment Geller was isolated from the researchers in a shielded room – only then was the target chosen and a picture drawn

had no such problems. As soon as he began to concentrate on trying to bend a brass ring out of shape, the television monitor through which he was being watched began to distort, and its distortions occurred every time Geller's face distorted with concentration. Obviously, he was producing some kind of mysterious electrical effect. At the same moment, a computer on the floor below began to go wrong.

Next, Geller was tested for extra-sensory perception (ESP). Here his success was spectacular. A die was placed in a closed box and shaken; then Geller was asked to guess which side was uppermost. His guesses were right every time. Ten empty cans were placed upside down on a table, with a small object hidden under one of them; then Geller was brought into the room and asked to guess which can concealed the object. Again, his score was incredible – 12 out of 14 correct guesses. He was then asked to try to duplicate drawings sealed inside double envelopes; again and again, his response was breathtakingly accurate. Yet when 'target drawings' were selected at random from a huge pile made by many people in the building – so that the experimenters themselves had no idea of what was in the sealed envelope – Geller's score fell dramatically. This suggests that his success in the drawing experiments depends heavily upon telepathy or 'mindreading'. Yet this failed to explain the experiments with the dice, which prove genuine ESP *without* telepathy.

Challenged by the sceptics

Just as it seemed that Geller had passed his most difficult tests, and proved the genuineness of his powers, his American visit began to go badly wrong. He was asked to present himself at the offices of *Time* magazine; but the 'photographer' who made the appointment was, in fact, a professional 'magician' named Charles Reynolds. Puharich guessed that the magicians of America were plotting to 'lynch' Geller – and he was right. James Randi – one of the most celebrated illusionists since Houdini – was convinced that Geller was a fake, and was determined to expose him. Puharich was inclined to refuse to allow Geller to be tried by this kangaroo court of stage magicians; but Geller realised that his refusal would only be interpreted as guilt. So on 6 February 1973, he and Puharich presented themselves at the *Time* offices.

Geller was understandably nervous, faced with the obvious hostility of two 'magicians' and two *Time* editors. But he succeeded in demonstrating his telepathic powers by duplicating a drawing in a sealed envelope. After this, he bent a fork by stroking it lightly with his finger; the fork went on bending after he put it down. Charles Reynolds offered Geller his own apartment key – to make sure there could be no 'switching' – and Geller bent it by concentrating; again, the key continued to bend after it had left his hand. On the whole, Geller performed very creditably, and might have been justified in expecting a favourable report. In fact, the article that appeared in *Time* a few weeks later was damning. The two magicians claimed that they could easily duplicate every one of Geller's 'tricks', and that Randi actually did so after Geller had left the office. It ended by stating – quite untruthfully – that Geller had been forced to leave Israel in disgrace after a computer expert and some psychologists had duplicated his feats and accused him of fraud.

Above: Russell Targ who, with Harold Puthoff, conducted the experiments on Geller at Stanford in 1972

Right: stage magician James Randi is convinced that Uri Geller is a fraud, and claims that he can duplicate every one of Geller's 'paranormal' effects. Here Randi demonstrates his own apparent control over metal: he was handcuffed and locked into a high security bank safe – and escaped in less than four minutes

Randi and Charles Reynolds even asserted later that they themselves had caught Geller cheating – or at least, had seen him bending the fork by pressing it against the desk. Oddly enough, this extremely important accusation is not mentioned in the *Time* article – which seems strange in view of its determination to prove Geller a fake.

As far as the great American public was concerned, the Geller myth had now been exploded; he had been 'proved' to be a mere trickster. And since *Time* had such an immense worldwide circulation, there was little that either Geller or Puharich could do about it. By the end of March 1973, it looked as if the amazing career of Uri Geller had come to an end – a mere 18 months or so after it had begun. Yet as Puharich sat down at his desk, and wrote the opening lines of his book *Uri: a journal of the mystery of Uri Geller*, he experienced a quiet conviction that there was more to come.

What Geller experienced was more than quiet conviction; it was an outraged determination to make the sceptics eat their words.

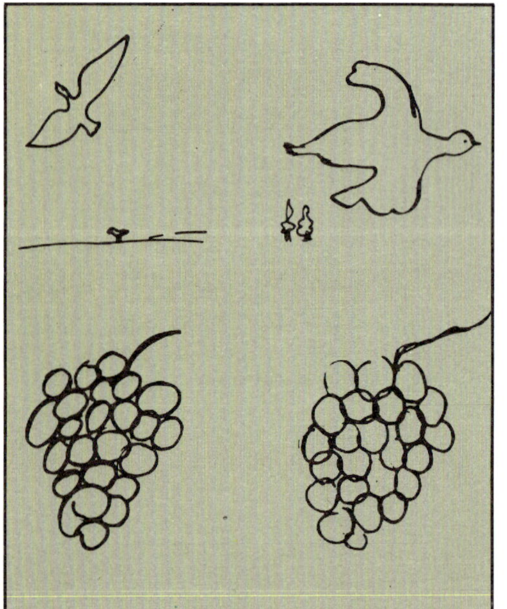

More target pictures and Geller's responses during the SRI tests. Geller's success with the 'grape' target is astonishing: he drew exactly the same number of circles as in the original drawing

The psychic superstar

Scientific investigation largely redeemed Uri Geller from accusations of fraud, but the controversy still raged. Many independent researchers have attempted to assess the 'Geller phenomenon'

Uri Geller at the first World Congress of Sorcery in Bogotá, Colombia, in 1975. Geller was billed as the main attraction of the show, the intention of which was 'to discuss and analyse the New Dimensions of Man and Life'. Besides demonstrating his power to bend metal, Geller started 50 broken watches, including one that, its owner claimed, had not worked for 40 years

FAME ARRIVED FOR URI GELLER on the evening of 23 November 1973 when he appeared on BBC-TV's *David Dimbleby Talk-in*. Overnight, that television programme turned Geller into the most controversial man in the British Isles.

By his own standards, the feats Geller performed that evening were not spectacular. With his eyes closed, he duplicated a drawing that had been made just before the programme and sealed in an envelope. Then he bent a fork – which Dimbleby held in his own hand – by gently stroking it. He started two broken watches by rubbing them, and caused the hands of one of them to bend upwards inside the glass. A fork on the table began to bend of its own accord. At the end of the programme, the producer came on to announce that they had received dozens of telephone calls from viewers saying that their own forks and spoons had begun to bend.

The next morning, there was probably not a single office or factory in England where Geller was not the main topic of conversation. Possibly the British are more gullible than the Americans. Or possibly, as J. B. Priestley once suggested, they are simply less accustomed to high-pressure advertising, and therefore less cynical. Not that there was any absence of cynicism after the programme. One journalist stated authoritatively that Geller had invented a powder that could cause metal to crumble instantaneously – then had to admit this was pure speculation. The science editor of the *Sunday Times*, Brian Silcock, was also a sceptic, until he rode with Geller in a taxi to the airport, and offered his own front door key for experiment. The moment Geller began to stroke it with one finger, the key bent like melting wax.

Metal bending nationwide

The excitement in England was reported all round the world. After two false starts – in Germany and the United States – Geller had achieved what he always wanted: the instantaneous fame of a pop star. Even the Americans, who had declined to take him seriously, suddenly had second thoughts: when Geller went back there later, they made up for their former indifference and treated him like a returning hero. Meanwhile, in England, a Sunday newspaper – the *People* – organised an experiment at short notice. They announced that at noon on the Sunday following the broadcast, Geller would concentrate his powers, and try to make spoons and forks bend all over England. They asked readers to report any such phenomena. The following Sunday, they described the flood of mail and telephone calls that began soon after the appointed time; 300 spoons and forks had curled up, and over 1000 broken clocks and watches had started up again.

The British seem to have broken the 'scepticism barrier'. Only two days after his triumph on the Dimbleby programme, Geller was demonstrating his powers in

Paris; then he moved on to Scandinavia, Spain, Italy and Japan. Luck – or perhaps his guardians from outer space – continued to favour him with amazing coincidences. In Oslo, he told a reporter jokingly that his psychic powers could fuse lights – and all the street lights in Oslo fused. On a ship in the Mediterranean, Geller said he would try stopping the ship – and a few minutes later, it slowed down and stopped. (A crimped fuel line was found to be the cause.)

Back in the United States, he received the kind of attention and adulation he had hoped for the first time – and also discovered that old enemies like Charles Reynolds and James Randi had lost none of their hostility. *Time* magazine once again denounced him, and took the opportunity to pour scorn on the whole 'psychic' scene, from Kirlian photography and psychic surgery to the 'secret life of plants'. Reynolds and Randi took this belated opportunity to assert that they had seen Geller bending a fork manually against the desk in the previous *Time* interview, although they failed to explain why they had withheld this important piece of information for so long. On the other hand, the publication of the report from the Stanford Research Institute – in the influential magazine *Nature* – convinced many scientists that Geller's powers were basically genuine. And the affirmative reports of various British scientists – like John Taylor and Ted Bastin – supported this view. (John Taylor, however, has since concluded that there is nothing paranormal about Geller's powers.) So instead of being merely the helpless victim of a campaign of defamation, Geller was now a figure of controversy.

Right: housewife Dora Portman of Harrow, England, was listening to a radio programme featuring Uri Geller in November 1973. Geller invited listeners to hold a piece of cutlery and try to bend it by concentration. To Mrs Portman's surprise the ladle she was using suddenly began to bend and the enamel to crack

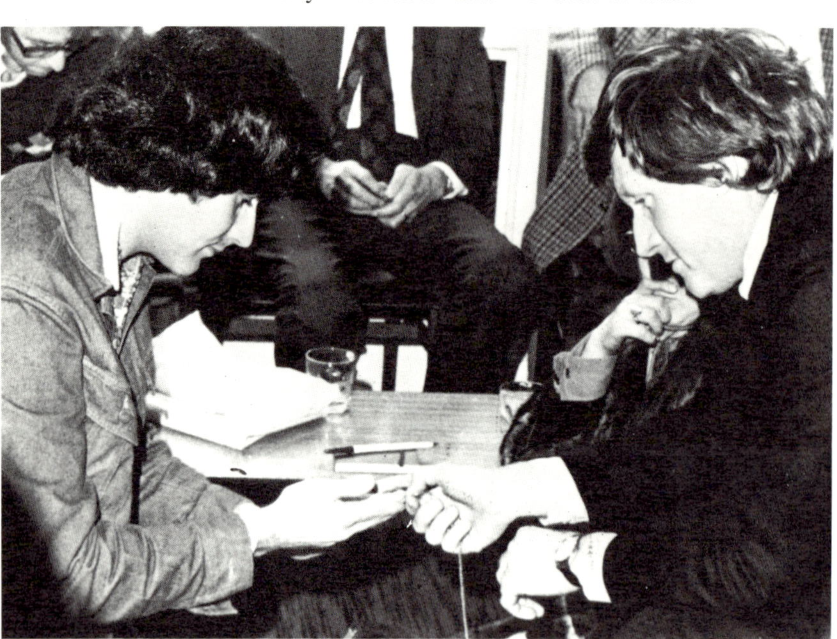

Geller with David Dimbleby, experimenting with a key. Geller's appearance on BBC-TV's *David Dimbleby Talk-in* programme on 23 November 1973 was an outstanding success, and convinced scientists that he was worthy of serious scientific investigation

Now that all the controversy has died down, and Uri Geller is merely another one of those names of the 1970s, a nine days' wonder that no longer causes wonderment, we can look back on his remarkable career, and see that Puharich was right from the beginning. What Geller really needed was to be studied by scientists, not exposed in front of television cameras. A film star or a pop singer has a firm foundation for celebrity; people all over the world are still listening to the records of Bob Dylan and Elvis Presley, or watching old movies of James Dean and Marilyn Monroe. But once you had seen Geller bend a spoon on television, there was nothing more to look forward to – except watching him bend a fork on some other programme. Geller himself was painfully aware of this: he wrote an autobiography; he wrote a novel; he made persistent attempts to star in a film about his own life. And he submitted to hundreds of scientific tests.

The essence of all this investigation is published in a remarkable volume called *The Geller papers*. It makes impressive reading, and demonstrates beyond all doubt that Geller possesses some kind of paranormal powers. Yet because he achieved his main celebrity as a 'magician' on television, Geller has suffered the fate of so many overnight celebrities, and become merely a half-remembered name.

A personal view

My own acquaintance with Geller began when he was at the height of his fame, in 1974. My agent rang me one day and asked me if I would be interested in writing a biography of Uri Geller. I said no. I had just read Puharich's book, which had been one of the major publishing disasters of the year. All his incredible stories about disembodied

Author Colin Wilson with Geller in Barcelona, discussing the nature of Geller's paranormal powers. Geller told him: 'I don't know where they come from or what they mean, or why it should be me and not somebody else'

voices speaking out of tape recorders, and dogs being 'teleported' down the garden, sounded too absurd to be taken seriously. A 'straight' book about Geller's psychic abilities would probably have been a best-seller; but the miracle-working inhabitants of the starship *Spectra* turned the whole thing into farce.

Geller, it seemed, had persuaded the famous impresario Robert Stigwood – producer of *Hair* and *Jesus Christ superstar* (and later of *Saturday night fever*) – to back the idea of a film about his life. First of all, someone had to write the life. When I declined, they suggested that I might like to work on a film script. And as the pay – for an underpaid student of the paranormal – was generous, I decided it might be worth looking into.

I met Geller at Robert Stigwood's offices in London. He seemed a charming and unassuming young man, whose enthusiasm seems to keep his whole personality on rather a high note. As I walked into the office he asked me: 'Are you anything to do with Spain?' I looked blank. 'Just as you walked in that door, a coin jumped out of this tray on the desk – a Spanish peseta – it made me wonder if you had anything to do with Spain.' Stigwood's personal secretary, Rae Knight, verified that this had actually happened, and I later learned to regard her with total trust. They had both been on the opposite side of the room when the coin leapt across it.

At lunch in a nearby restaurant, Geller talked non-stop, made my watch go back several hours by simply holding his hand above it (he changed the date too), bent a spoon, and broke a key I had brought along by simply rubbing it. But he insisted on taking the key to the other side of the room, where there was a radiator – he said he could gain power from metal. On the whole, I was not too impressed. I knew enough about conjuring to know that the spoon bending and watch-changing could have been sleight of hand, and the fact that he had to cross the restaurant to bend a key struck me as suspicious. Yet he performed one feat that left me in no doubt of his genuineness.

What happened was this: Geller turned his back on me, so he looked out over the restaurant (I was in a corner), and asked me to do a drawing on the back of the menu card. I did a sketch of a funny monster I draw for my children. I kept glancing at Geller to make sure he wasn't peeping, or holding a mirror in his hand. Then he made me turn the menu over and cover it with my hand. He turned round again, and asked me to redraw the thing *in my mind*, and try to convey it to him. After a couple of false starts, he suddenly drew a duplicate of the 'monster' on the menu. There was no way in which he could have 'guessed' it, or that Rae Knight might have conveyed it to him – even if she had been an accomplice.

An odd coincidence

A few months later, when asked to write a short book about Geller, I travelled to Barcelona to see him – it struck me only later that his first question to me had been: 'Are you anything to do with Spain?' – an odd coincidence. Again objects fell from the air, and Geller demonstrated metal bending and mindreading. In the office of my Spanish publisher he silenced the sceptical audience by holding up a spoon by its end, and bending it by simply 'tickling' the thin part with his index finger – no kind of pressure would have been possible. He placed his foot against a radiator as he did this.

My own study of Geller has convinced me that his powers are genuine. His mind-reading was particularly convincing. James Randi – who likes to call himself the 'Amazing Randi' – declared that he could easily

Geller undergoing one of a series of tests designed to discover whether his physical make-up is responsible for the powers of his mind

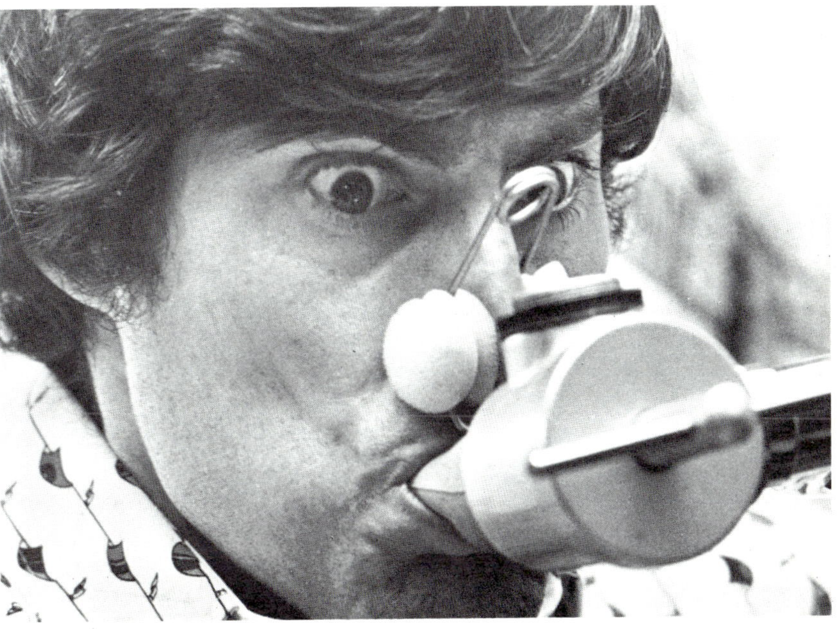

duplicate any of Geller's 'tricks'; but when I met him, he was unable to duplicate the mindreading trick – although he offered to do it for me next day (obviously when he'd had time to prepare it). But Randi *did* bend spoons by stroking them and made my watch go back several hours by rubbing it.

The film on Geller never came off, although I made several 'outline' sketches. I continued to see and correspond with Geller, on and off, for a year or so, but lost touch with him when he moved to New York. In one of his later letters to me he mentioned that he had produced a tremendous impression in Mexico, and was a frequent guest at the home of the president. He also mentioned that he had taken up 'dowsing' for metals from an aeroplane, and made a considerable success of it, working for a mining company. From the financial point of view, I gather he has no reason to complain of the way the world has treated him. And if his spoon bending has ceased to attract much attention, this is hardly surprising. From Geller's point of view, I feel it is a pity it ever did.

And what do I feel about the source of his powers? After a great deal of thought, I am still inclined to believe that Geller is an unconscious 'medium', and that he simply produces more-or-less controlled 'poltergeist effects'. (That other remarkable psychic, Matthew Manning, whom I have also investigated, began his career as the unconscious 'focus' of a series of alarming poltergeist occurrences in his own home.) Geller told me how, at the age of three, he received a bad electric shock from his mother's sewing machine; this, I am inclined to believe, may have started the whole thing. It is surprising how often 'mediums' have had severe traumas or emotional strains in childhood.

'Unconscious mediums'

And what about the 'space men' from the starship *Spectra*? Here again, I believe that Geller's unconscious mind is the basic explanation. But I suspect there was more than that involved. In one of their mysterious 'interviews', the 'space men' told Puharich that he himself had psychic powers. I believe this to be almost certainly true. And the astounding series of events that began when Puharich and Geller got together in Tel Aviv were a kind of wild collaboration between two 'unconscious mediums'. Unlikely? I can only say that the more I have studied the evidence, the more I feel this is the case.

There is one more point. Spiritualists believe that there *are* such things as disembodied spirits, hanging around on the 'earth plane', and often getting into mischief. Such spirits may cause poltergeist effects. And the more I read the weird but inconsequential communications of the 'space beings' from *Spectra*, the more I am reminded of the confused and usually irrelevant material that emerges at so many seances.

These may not, I agree, be the correct explanations. But of one thing I am certain. There *is* something about Uri Geller that demands a deeper and more far-reaching explanation than mere trickery.

Professors John Hasted and John Taylor (above) carried out tests on Geller in 1974. Geller succeeded in bending metal strips sealed in plastic tubes (right). And he was asked to bend a brass strip taped to a letter balance so the pressure he applied could be measured. The scale read only half an ounce (15 grams), and the strip bent upwards, against the pressure of his fingers (far right)

Mind over metal

Few paranormal effects are as controversial as metal bending. But while sceptics dismiss it as fraud or delusion, examples of this bizarre power continue to be recorded and to astonish witnesses

ACCOUNTS OF INEXPLICABLE contortions of metal objects date back at least to the 18th century, when pins were found twisted into 'a vast variety of fantastic figures' during a poltergeist case, while in 1879 victims of an American case reported that spoons 'suddenly twisted out of shape' in their hands. But it was not until 1972, with the arrival of Uri Geller on the international scene, that paranormal or psychokinetic metal bending (PKMB) became a study in its own right.

Over the next four years Geller took part in supervised experiments in 17 different laboratories. Dr George Owen of the New Horizons Research Foundation in Toronto pronounced his abilities as 'paranormal and totally genuine', while Eldon Byrd of the US Navy research centre in Maryland stated that Geller had bent metal under observation 'in a way that cannot be duplicated'. Five professional magicians testified that whatever Geller was doing, it was not conventional magic.

After Geller's first television appearance in Britain in 1973, an epidemic of PKMB broke out in homes over the whole country, especially affecting young children and teenagers. For some it was a new game soon forgotten while other children were encouraged to work at it. In 1974, 18-year-old Matthew Manning, then coming to the end of his period as a poltergeist victim, put on a spectacular display of PKMB in front of 21 scientists, including Nobel Laureate Professor Brian Josephson, and enabled psychiatrist Dr Joel Whitton to identify a hitherto unknown brainwave pattern apparently linked to paranormal activity.

Paperclips dropped into this glass ball were paranormally 'scrunched' into a fantastic shape by one of Professor Hasted's metal bending subjects.

But the first scientist to commit himself to a thorough and long-term enquiry into PKMB was Professor J.B. Hasted, head of the physics department of Birkbeck College, London, who carried out a series of tests with several young subjects, both in his laboratory and in the children's homes. Although in the course of his investigations he introduced more rigidly conventional methodology, he soon realised that successful PKMB depends on many other, more subtle factors: for example, the psychological atmosphere in the laboratory was crucial, the state of mind of both subject and experimenter being a decisive factor. Metal benders, he discovered, had to be treated as *colleagues* rather than as guinea-pigs. In an article he co-authored in *Nature* (10 April 1975), he declared that 'psychokinetic phenomena cannot in general be produced unless all who participate are in a relaxed state.' PKMB was, he assumed, a function of the unconscious mind, and too much conscious effort would upset the process, as would an atmosphere of tension, scepticism or hostility. The PKMB researcher should, he argued, adopt the attitude of a physiotherapist encouraging a patient to regain the use of a damaged limb, rather than telling him it could not be done.

The possibility of trickery had to be eliminated, and to this end Hasted devised experiments in which the metal object was attached to a strain gauge and a chart recorder. And (most important) the subject was not allowed to touch the metal at all. Three of his young colleagues were soon able to produce stress signals on the chart paper under these conditions, signals quite unlike those produced when metal is bent by normal physical force.

'Impossible' tasks

Next, Hasted set his subjects a series of 'impossible' tasks, such as the 'scrunching' together of straightened paperclips inside a glass sphere and the bending of alloy strips that snap rather than bend under normal stresses. Again, the young subjects responded to these challenges, producing a number of remarkable scrunches, while one managed to deform four strips of 'unbendable' alloy merely by leaving them, untouched, in his coat pocket for five minutes. By December 1976, Hasted was able to state categorically, in the *Journal* of the Society for Psychical Research (SPR): 'I therefore report my belief that I have been able to validate the metal-bending phenomenon on a number of occasions by visual witnessing, chart-recording, "impossible" tasks and the bending of brittle metals.'

The following year, in the same journal, he described a series of 13 tests held with 17-year-old Nicholas Williams, the highlight of which was the chart recording of simultaneous strain signals from three different keys hanging from wires, and even from two metal objects 10 yards (9 metres) apart on different floors of the building. Eventually, Hasted was able to add some sequences of videotape to his evidence, in which metal objects can be seen bending without being touched. The PKMB phenomenon had, it seemed, been well and truly validated.

It had also been repeated in several other countries, under the supervision of qualified researchers. At the Péchiney Laboratory in France, metallurgists Professor Charles Crussard and Dr Jean Bouvaist published a detailed report on the abilities of Jean Pierre Girard, the most thoroughly studied of all metal benders. They found that he could induce both anomalous hardening and softening in metal in a manner impossible to explain in terms of conventional metallurgy. Girard, who was born in 1942, developed numerous psychic abilities shortly after being struck by lightning as a child.

He made his début as a metal bender in 1975, in response to a radio appeal from Dr William Wolkowski for people with psi abilities to come forward. He successfully distorted a number of metal samples, including a steel spring, sealed inside glass tubes under Wolkowski's supervision. In one of his most dramatic demonstrations of PKMB, he bent a 3-inch (8-centimetre) screw inside a plastic tube held by Swedish physicist Dr Georg Wikman in about 15 seconds, without touching either the screw or the tube.

In West Germany, Professor Hans Bender of the University of Freiburg studied Girard with the co-operation of William Cox – well-known parapsychologist and magician – and a cameraman, and became one of the first to record PKMB on film. Girard produced more than 10 distinct bends under close scrutiny, but in fairly informal conditions. (Two French magicians, Ranky and André Sanlaville, have testified that his effects are not produced by conventional sleight of hand.) By 1977, Girard had demonstrated his abilities in front of at least 16 scientists.

Professor Bender also filmed an adult Swiss, Silvio Maier, as he bent several spoons by PK alone, breaking some of them in the process, and also bending several heavy forks *upwards* while holding each lightly with only one hand. Meanwhile, in Japan, several children developed PKMB talents after Geller's visit to Tokyo in 1973, and two of them – Masuaki Kiyota and Jun Sekiguchi – were studied at length by several scientists, notably Professor Shigemi Sasaki of the Department of Electro-Communications, Tokyo University, and Dr Matsumi Suzuki of the Aeronautical Instruments Research Institute.

As the evidence from laboratories all over

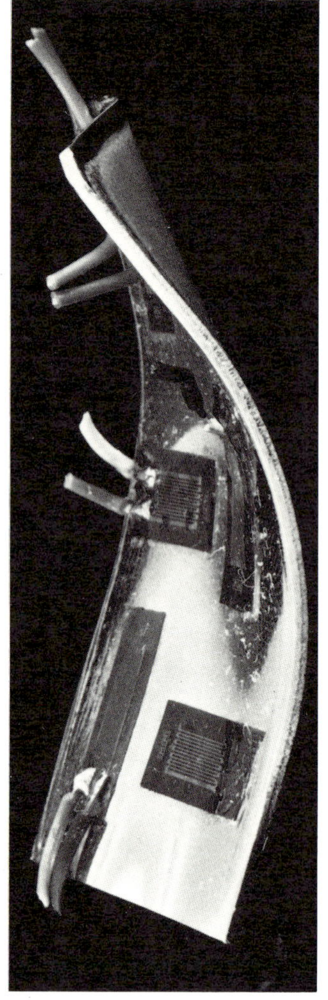

Above: a metal bar fitted with strain gauges and then bent paranormally in Professor Hasted's London laboratory. A chart recorder was also attached to the metal and, to eliminate the possibility of trickery, the subjects were not allowed to touch the metal. It still bent, showing stress signals unlike those produced when attempts were made to bend the bar manually

Right: Professor John Hasted checks strain gauge equipment in the laboratory

Previous page: seven-year-old Mark Shelley bent a spoon and fork after seeing 'that man' – Uri Geller – on television in October 1973. He went on to prove his new skill on more household cutlery before tiring of metal bending. He said: 'It seems a waste of time going around the world like this. I'd rather play football for Ipswich'

the world mounted up, support came from theoretical physicists who found that not only was 'action at a distance' permitted according to the laws of quantum physics, but it could actually be predicted. At a conference on 'Frontiers of Physics' held in Iceland in 1977 it became clear, amid talk of 'collapsing wave functions', 'intrinsic time symmetry' and 'additivity of partial amplitudes', that the human mind had been willingly accepted as a potential influence on physical processes. PKMB had become almost respectable.

The phenomenon has also come to the attention of psychiatrists, and in a lengthy study of young metal benders and their families, Dr Robert Cantor found that most youngsters also showed other paranormal abilities, from telepathy and clairvoyance to healing. Some had also seen tiny lights moving around them, and heard high-pitched whistles. Others reported experiencing headaches while concentrating on bending metal (as did some of their investigators), plus tingling sensations in the arms and face. Cantor also found that PKMB seemed to have no harmful effects, and actually served to increase the children's self-confidence. Most encouraging of all was the fact that all children he questioned insisted that their powers must be used for good. If misused, they felt, they would lose them. The experience of one of them serves as an answer to the often-asked question: 'Who needs bent spoons anyway?'

Belinda H. was only six when she responded to Uri Geller's invitation to bend metal during the transmission of BBC-TV's *Blue Peter* programme. She deformed a spoon through 40° in less than a minute, and later bent an 'unbendable' crystal in the presence of Professor Hasted. (She looked set to win the *Daily Express* £5,000 metal-bending contest until this was mysteriously cancelled.) However, Belinda was more interested in healing. When she was only three years old she had spontaneously tried to cure her ailing grandmother, and on three other occasions she satisfied both her parents that she had been able to relieve severe pain by placing her hands on the affected parts of their bodies.

PKMB has repeatedly been demonstrated to be a fact, and scientists have begun to respond to the challenge it offers. A solution to the age-old mystery of how our minds interact with matter is much nearer than it was when Uri Geller came to public attention in 1972. Jean Pierre Girard feels that PKMB is an evolutionary mechanism necessary for Man's survival that science cannot afford to overlook. From the apparently useless ability to bend spoons there may develop enormously far-reaching effects on the world.

'This power,' says Belinda H.'s mother, 'must have been put there for a reason.'

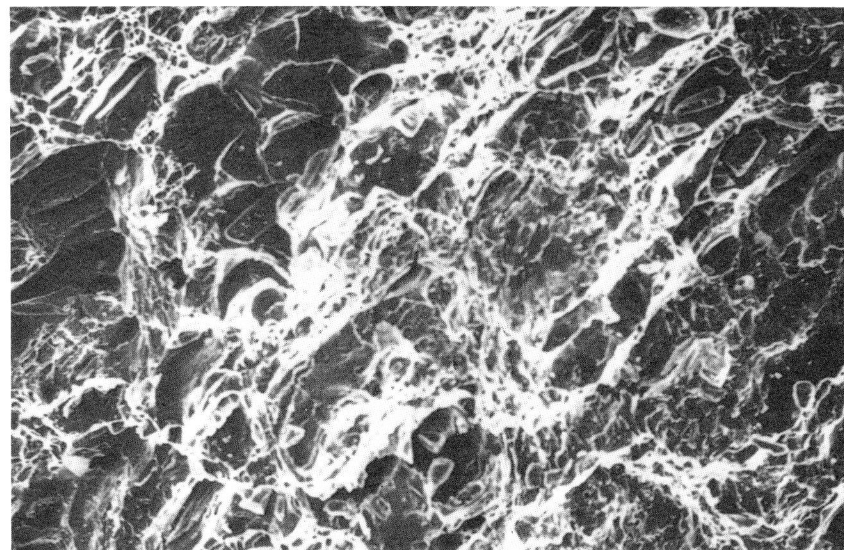

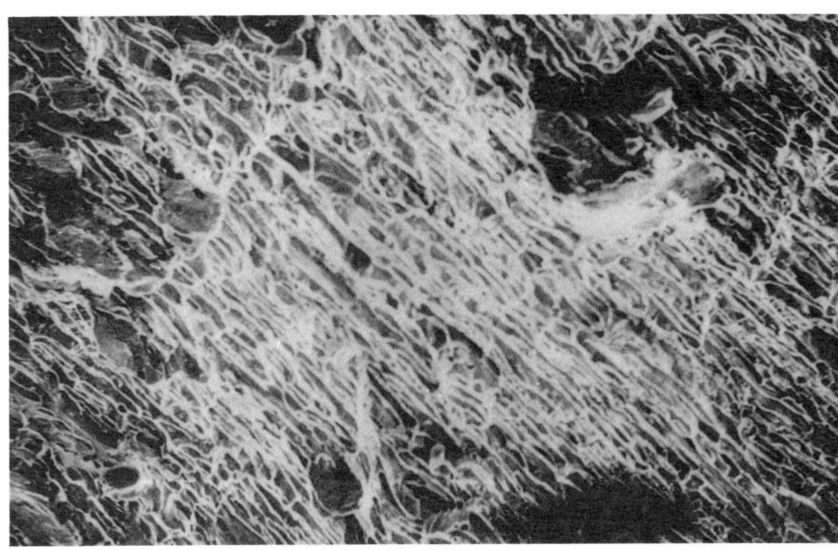

Scanning electron microscope photographs – magnified 750 times – of (top) a section of a Volkswagen key that broke when Geller tried to bend it and (above) of a similar key broken by mechanical means. The paranormally broken key shows a uniform structure, the other key a random pattern

Left: George Porter with some of the objects he bent by PK while listening to Uri Geller on the *Jimmy Young Show* on BBC radio in 1974

Alarms and excursions

Can solid objects dematerialise and reappear at another place? Or pass through other objects without disrupting them? This may be what happens when 'mislaid' items inexplicably 'just turn up'

ON THE MORNING OF 6 MAY 1878 Johann Zöllner, professor of physics and astronomy at the University of Leipzig, sat with the American medium Henry Slade in a room that had been set aside for an experiment in parapsychology. No other person was present. Zöllner held both of Slade's hands in his own on top of the card table at which they sat. After about a minute a small circular beechwood table standing a few feet away began to rock to and fro, its top rising above the edge of the card table as it did so. The circular table then slid slowly towards the card table, tipped over backwards and slid beneath it.

Nothing further seemed to happen for another minute; Slade was about to consult his 'spirit controls' about what they should expect when Zöllner glanced under the card table to check precisely the position of the circular table – only to find that the latter had disappeared! The two men then searched the room, but found no sign of the circular table.

A striking phenomenon

Zöllner and Slade then resumed their places at the card table, with their hands linked on its top and their legs touching, so that Slade could not make any undetected movements. After five minutes' expectant waiting Slade saw lights in the air, as he usually did before psychic events occurred to him. Neither Zöllner nor any of his colleagues ever saw these lights when they participated in sittings with Slade, but Zöllner followed Slade's gaze:

> As I turned my head, following Slade's gaze up to the ceiling of the room behind my back, I suddenly observed, at a height of about 5 feet [1.5 metres], the hitherto invisible table with its legs turned upwards very quickly floating down in the air upon the top of the card table.

The table was no mere hallucination – it gave both men a sharp crack on the head as it descended.

This sober and careful account describes teleportation – the disappearance of matter and its reappearance at the same or another place, with no known cause being involved. Such events are also sometimes called 'disappearance-reappearance' events. A phenomenon that is presumably closely related is the passage of matter through matter – for example, the passage of an object into or out of a sealed container, or the tying of knots

The scientist Johann Zöllner meticulously recorded his teleportation experiments with the medium Henry Slade. In one experiment (right) Zöllner sat with his thumbs pressed down on a loop of string that dangled over the edge of the table. The single knot in the loop was secured with a wax seal. After a few minutes Slade announced that knots had been created in the string, and those shown in the picture were found to have appeared. On another occasion Zöllner requested that wooden rings be linked; the 'spirits' instead transferred them to the leg of a table (below) – a feat that should have involved dismantling the table

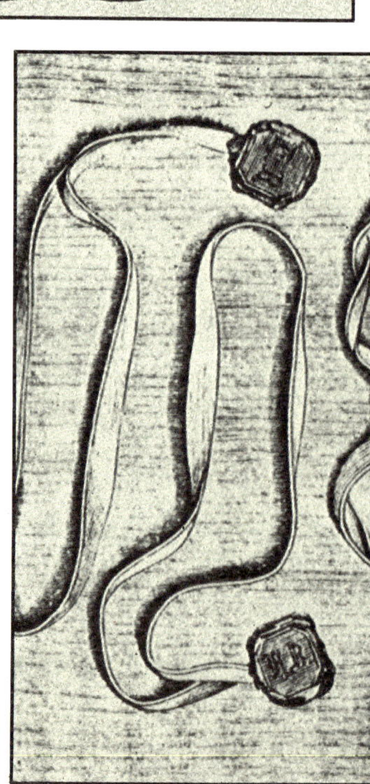

without the use of any normal means.

Such phenomena are reported from some seances, experiments with certain psychokinesis (PK) agents, and in some poltergeist cases. However, they are hardly ever witnessed under 'good' conditions (that is, with parapsychologists in attendance and full experimental controls); so even parapsychologists who seem willing to accept more controllable and 'reasonable' phenomena, such as ESP, join the sceptics in dismissing such tales out of hand as tall stories for the gullible. And because these events exceed most people's 'boggle threshold' (to use the term coined by the author Renée Haynes) and seem to be impossible to reconcile with conventional physics, they have largely been ignored in parapsychology. Zöllner, certainly, was scoffed at, and he was never taken seriously by the parapsychological establishment – for reasons that seem to have more to do with the fantastic nature of the events than with any obscurity in his reports or shortcomings in the conditions of observation. But another contributory factor was that Slade, years later when his powers of mediumship were in decline, was declared by an investigating committee to cheat in the production of 'spirit writing' on slates.

Other sittings by Slade witnessed by Zöllner produced 'impossible' movements of objects: on many of these occasions knots were tied in loops of string, leather or even pig-gut while Zöllner was holding them or otherwise had them under his control. A sitting that was intended to link two wooden rings did not succeed – but it ended with the rings 'impossibly' sitting on the central leg of

Top: capsules used by Julian Isaacs in experiments. The objects inside, intended to be teleported out of the capsules, are as small and light as possible

Above: Julian Isaacs (second from right) with an experimental group. In the boxes are objects that they attempt to teleport. Two boxes have been sealed with sticking plaster, on which a grid of pencil lines has been drawn. Any tampering inevitably disturbs the grid

Left: a pair of leather loops before and after being paranormally linked. The event occurred beneath Zöllner's cupped hands – and he felt the loops move

the circular table whose teleportation has already been described. This table was well out of Slade's range when the event happened, as he was sitting with Zöllner at the other table at the time; to put the rings on the leg, any human agent would have had to take the table to pieces and reassemble it.

Zöllner's work fills a number of weighty volumes, but only a tantalising fraction of this material is available in English translation. Yet if anyone's work deserves an attempt at replication, it is Zöllner's.

Just such an attempt, apparently successful, was reported in the summer of 1932 in the *Journal* of the American Society for Psychical Research (ASPR). The report was written by William Button, then president of the ASPR, who was present at the eight sittings reported and was intimately concerned with the mediumship of 'Margery' – Margery Crandon.

In the experiments the spirit of Margery's dead brother, Walter, ostensibly moved small objects into or out of various kinds of

Spontaneous teleportation of a spanner? There has been a spate of such events in the 'E.' family since the parents, Judy and John, have successfully taken part in a series of metal-bending experiments. The spanner was kept hanging on a hook in a locked garden shed (left). It was last seen there in October 1982 – but thereafter it went missing from the shed and could not be found anywhere, despite a thorough search of the garden and the shed. In March 1983 Mr E. found the spanner – on a wardrobe (below) in his five-year-old daughter's room. It was now rusty, whereas it was formerly in mint condition. All in the family insist: they *didn't* put it there

containers – cardboard boxes sealed with sticking plaster, locked wooden and metal boxes, and so on. This was done many times under apparently good conditions. Poor Margery was bound to her chair with sticking plaster at wrists and ankles; several turns of the plaster were used at each point and it was marked with pencil lines that would show whether the plaster had been taken off and rewound. When objects were teleported out of a container the fact could be checked by shaking the container, when there would be no sound of the object bouncing around inside. Then another object might be teleported into the container – all without the container being opened.

A major problem with these experiments was that Margery's husband, Dr Crandon, was allowed to participate in many of the sittings and in some of them was even allowed to assist in controlling the medium's movements. The possibility of collusion cannot, therefore, be excluded. And Margery did indeed become embroiled in prolonged and bitter controversy in connection with many different manifestations of her physical mediumship.

More recently another highly controversial psychic, Uri Geller, has claimed that a number of spontaneous teleportation events have happened to objects, or even people and animals, connected with him. For example, it is said that Geller suddenly arrived in the glass porch of his friend Andrija Puharich in Ossining, New York, having a moment before been walking in Manhattan, an hour's journey away.

The Indian mystic and religious teacher Sai Baba is the subject of a number of tales brought back by Westerners who have visited him. His speciality is the materialisation of small objects from thin air; the most usual gift is *vibhuti*, a powdery greyish substance often called holy ash and used in healing. The Western parapsychologists who have visited him have never been allowed to impose controls over him. However, Karlis Osis and Erlendur Haraldsson managed to examine one of Baba's robes and found no pockets or other hiding places. Nor did it bear traces of *vibhuti* down the sleeves, which would be expected if Baba were shaking it down them into his hand. But the parapsychologist's judgement on him must remain open because he will not perform under controlled conditions.

Intelligent projectiles

One of the prime occasions of apparent teleportation and the transport of matter through matter is the poltergeist case. In many of these, stones or other missiles apparently arrive from nowhere. Sometimes the missiles do not become visible until they strike an object. A well-known case occurred in 1903. A geologist, W. F. Grottendieck, was conducting a survey in Sumatra. One night he was sleeping in a hut roofed with a layer of large leaves. He was awakened by some small stones falling on and around him. Several more such showers occurred, giving him a chance to investigate their origin. The stones apparently came from the roof, but he could find no gap in the overlapping leaves through which they might have arrived normally. They seemed to fall with unnatural slowness, and when he tried to catch them they seemed to change direction. 'Intelligent' projectiles of this kind are not uncommon in poltergeist cases. However, they are not usually hot – whereas in this case they were warm to the touch.

Very many cases involve the mysterious disappearance of objects, although there is only one very brief account of anyone actually seeing an object vanish in front of them. It happened to a Mrs Kogelnik in London in 1922. The Kogelnik household had been experiencing poltergeist disturbances for months, apparently centred on a maidservant. On this occasion Mrs Kogelnik was working in the loft of the house. Her husband's account records: 'As my wife saw an axe disappearing before her eyes, she quitted the room. All this happened between 10 a.m. and 12 noon, and the light was good for observation.'

Many reasonably well-authenticated disappearance-reappearance events could be cited. There is now accumulating evidence that apparently completely ordinary people may experience minor ones fairly frequently. The replies to the author's enquiries suggest strongly that teleportation may be going on far more frequently, in a minor and usually unnoticed way, than we would ever assume to be possible. The SPR has woken up to this possibility and has started Project JOTT to try to collect a representative selection of such cases. (JOTT stands for 'just one of those things'.)

What does all this mean? A favourite answer has been that space has a fourth dimension, or even more, and that when objects appear and disappear in our world they are actually moving in the fourth dimension.

This is a perfectly reasonable hypothesis. But there are competing explanations, of course. One is the hypothesis that objects become invisible temporarily. But while this is consistent with certain kinds of cases it would not explain the exit of objects from sealed boxes. And hallucination, another frequently proffered explanation, cannot account for cases where permanent structural changes take place – such as the knots in Zöllner's loops of string. Where matter has passed through matter in ordinary three-dimensional space, it may have been taken apart, transported atom by atom and put together again accurately. Or the atoms involved may have been somehow made 'passive' and non-cohesive, so that they did not interact with each other as the objects passed through each other.

'Peter', focus of poltergeist events and apparent teleportations, seems to have been bodily teleported on occasion. Once the author, while at Peter's house, heard a loud thump from upstairs – the usual signal that Peter had 'gone missing'. Mr Isaacs rushed upstairs and pulled open the lower door of the airing cupboard seen here. There was Peter, seemingly in a dazed condition. Had he hidden himself there? In view of other, better witnessed events centred on Peter, the author believes that these teleportations, too, may be genuine

Left: this little yellow idol is a stone buddha belonging to Mr J., a known PK agent who has taken part in the author's experiments. It disappeared after he had spring-cleaned the shelves on which it normally stood. Several days later, there was a crash as the shell seen here fell to the floor, and the buddha seemed to tumble out of the shell – which had been examined in the search for the figure. Was this 'return' triggered by Mr J.'s thoughts? For he was watching a television programme on Buddhism at the time

A process that seems to offer an analogy on the atomic scale to the transport of matter through matter is 'quantum tunnelling', in which an atomic particle 'impossibly' breaks through an energy barrier: the particle is whimsically viewed as tunnelling its way through a barrier that is too high to be jumped. It could be suggested that the transport of matter through matter is a large-scale quantum tunnelling phenomenon. But two daunting questions then arise: first, how can the tunnelling effect, usually operative only over atomic distances, be multiplied to give the kinds of distances encountered in paranormal reports? Second – and this problem is common to all attempts to apply quantum theory to large-scale psi events – how are the billions of atoms in normal-sized objects co-ordinated to make each one simultaneously tunnel to the same place? This problem is enormously more complex than, say, getting tunnels from opposite sides of Mont Blanc to meet in the middle of the mountain.

What is needed is determined research to find people gifted in teleportation, to train them to produce effects under good control, to catalogue the experiences of many ordinary people who also experience similar events, and to use modern electronic technology as a means of exploring the phenomenon. If a fourth dimension really exists it opens up the stunning possibility that there may exist an infinite number of other dimensions – perhaps making up an array of universes in parallel with ours. So the next time you curse an object that has unaccountably disappeared a moment after you have put it down, spare a thought for the possibility that behind this commonplace event there may lurk fantastic realities.

Minds over matter

Psychokinetic effects are notoriously difficult to produce to order – a fact seized upon by sceptics. Yet the SORRAT group of Rolla, Missouri, have succeeded in causing a great variety of paranormal happenings in controlled experiments

THE ENVELOPE MOVED on its own slowly and jerkily from behind the typewriter. It reached the flat top of the typewriter and slid slowly across it. Suddenly it tipped over onto the keyboard – and started to become transparent. Then it vanished completely. This astonishing evidence of psychokinesis (PK) and teleportation was a highlight of one of the most extraordinary 'home movie' shows ever and, not unnaturally, those present asked their host to re-run that particular film. There had been 10 fairly primitive films shown, all shot on standard 8-millimetre film and all showing a wide range of psychokinetic – mind over matter – effects. The most extraordinary thing about these phenomena was that nearly all of them had been filmed inside a locked glass box to which only one person, the experimenter himself, their host for the evening, had the key.

In the weeks that followed, the implications of that evening's 'home movie' session slowly became apparent. If the film had shown genuinely paranormal events – and there was no evidence to prove otherwise – and if they could be reproduced by other groups elsewhere, then parapsychology was on the brink of an enormously significant breakthrough. If PK could be filmed, especially in its more exotic and rare forms, then it could be submitted to detailed study and perhaps give scientists the long-awaited foothold on understanding the elusive physics of psychical phenomena.

Those films shown on a November evening in 1980 in Rolla, Missouri, USA, were the culmination of a long project that had begun in October 1961 with the formation of the Society for Research into Rapport and Telekinesis (SORRAT). This group is probably the USA's most successful producer of long-term, large-scale PK (called 'macro-PK' by parapsychologists).

SORRAT was founded by John G. Neihardt, professor of English literature at the University of Missouri at Columbia. A powerful, charismatic personality and a man of wide interests, he had been fascinated by the paranormal for many years. He was intrigued by the way those people with strong spiritualist beliefs or with a mystical background seemed to attract PK. Neihardt himself was a close friend of the Sioux Indian holy man Black Elk, and as a result was made an honorary member of the Oglala Sioux tribe. Some of the former members of SORRAT believe that he was actually initiated as a Sioux shaman (magician and holy man) and there were even rumours circulating at the time that Neihardt himself handed on this secret initiation to one of the SORRAT members.

This kind of belief may have helped the SORRAT group achieve their remarkable evidence of macro-PK; certainly some of its members were known to possess outstanding psychic gifts. The group, meeting every Friday night at Professor Neihardt's home,

Top, above and right: Dr J. T. Richards (in the striped shirt) and members of SORRAT make a light metal table rise into the air – levitated, they believe, by 'spirits'

Left: the late Professor John G. Neihardt, founder of the SORRAT group. It was rumoured that he was initiated as a Sioux shaman by his close friend, Black Elk; this magical background may have helped him to create the atmosphere of belief that apparently encourages paranormal phenomena

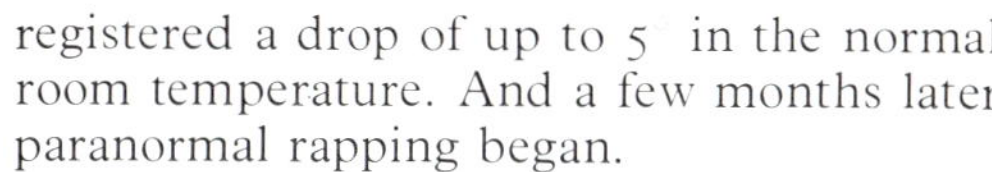

Right: Joseph Mangini, said to be possessed by the spirit of Black Elk during a SORRAT meeting. He is holding a *wichasha wakon*, or holy staff, and embracing Professor Neihardt's daughter Alice

Below right: a hat is levitated a few inches from a desk top

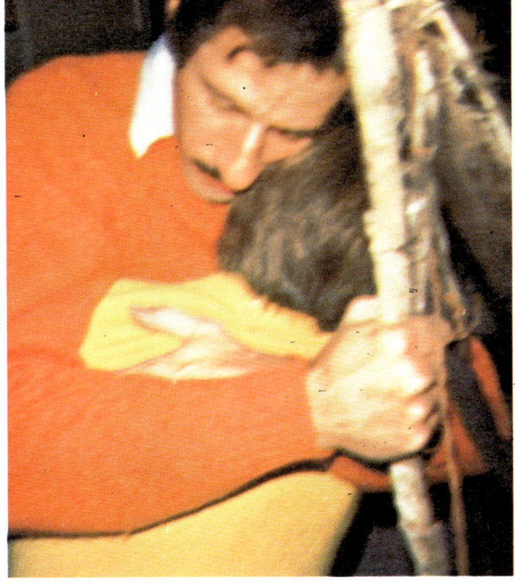

Skyrim Farm, Missouri, grew very close over the 16 years they were together. Originally there were 30 members, but the 'regulars' consisted of 15 to 20 of the more strongly motivated.

The techniques used by SORRAT to induce psychokinetic events were similar to those used by many Spiritualist development circles. Essentially they simply sat around in a group in a carefree and light-hearted manner while waiting for PK to occur. One member of the group, Mr Joseph Mangini, developed the ability to go into a trance – and then PK phenomena were often particularly strong. After meetings had continued for only two months it was found that areas of seemingly paranormal coldness would develop around small target objects laid out on a table top. Thermometers placed near these objects registered a drop of up to 5 in the normal room temperature. And a few months later paranormal rapping began.

These paranormal raps were crucial to the later success of the group mainly because they provided an enormous boost to its confidence and paved the way for other, more complicated, phenomena. But first the group began testing the circumstances surrounding the rapping. For example, raps were still heard when everyone in the group lay down so that their hands and feet were clearly in sight. The raps even occurred outdoors, apparently coming from underground. Indoors they would obligingly move around the room on request, the group sitting quite still meanwhile. And significantly, the raps displayed intelligence, using codes with which to answer questions, even on some later occasions conveying information that was unknown to any member who was present. So the raps, simple or complex, provided audible evidence that the group was getting somewhere and they created a sense of expectancy and excitement. What would happen next?

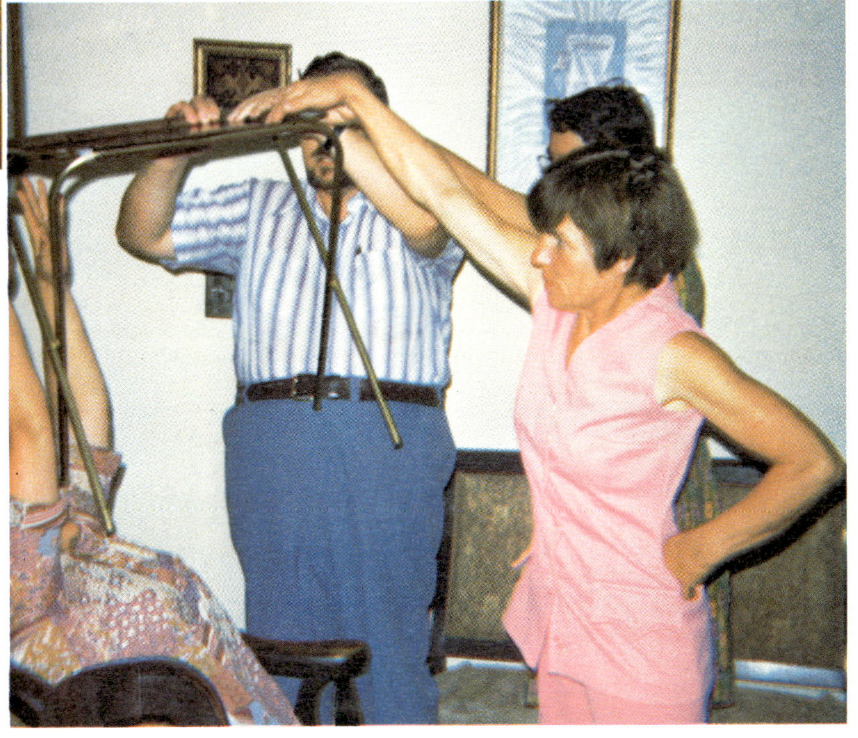

Apart from the positive psychological effects, the raps also served a practical purpose. They opened up a two-way channel of communication between whatever was causing them (called 'the agency' – a deliberately neutral term chosen by William E. Cox, later the group's scientific collaborator) and the group itself. The group used the raps as a code, 'agreeing' with the agency that one, two or three raps would mean 'yes', 'no', and 'maybe' respectively. In this way the group held simple question and answer sessions. The agency could also deliver messages using an alphabetic code – one rap for A, two for B and so on. Once established, this was then used by the group to ask the agency to perform certain PK tasks, which could then be graded.

Groups who aim to achieve macro-PK need to increase the level of difficulty of the tasks they set the agency only gradually – in

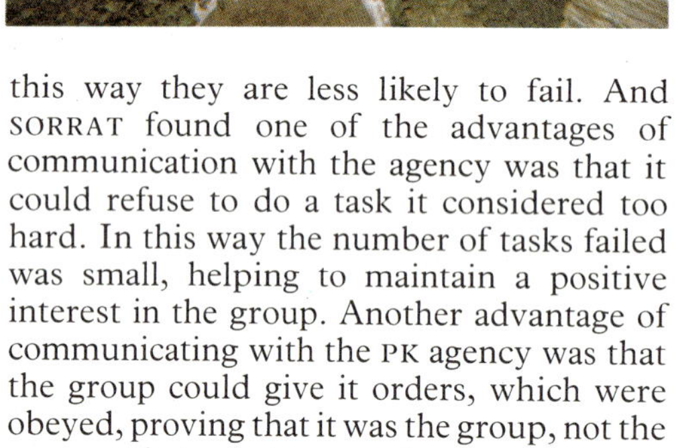

The SORRAT 'spirits' produced a spectacular variety of PK phenomena, which began with paranormal rapping and went on to include a host of levitations (above right and far right) and a 'walking' table (above and right). On another occasion the group managed to levitate a table without touching it (below), and once a tray rose unaided 15 feet (4.5 metres) into the air. The 'Philip' group of Toronto also had a 'walking' table – a star attraction of the Canadian television programme made about Philip– which climbed the steps to the platform on which the group were sitting

this way they are less likely to fail. And SORRAT found one of the advantages of communication with the agency was that it could refuse to do a task it considered too hard. In this way the number of tasks failed was small, helping to maintain a positive interest in the group. Another advantage of communicating with the PK agency was that the group could give it orders, which were obeyed, proving that it was the group, not the agency, that was in control.

One of the most important aspects of the raps was that the agency causing them claimed to consist of a group of spirits. This interpretation was readily accepted by many members of SORRAT who were Spiritualists. From the experimenters' points of view this was a great advantage because these people did not feel personally responsible for trying to make anything happen. And conscious effort – straining to make PK occur – has been proved many times, especially in paranormal metal bending, to be counter-productive, apparently actually preventing it happening.

But the identity of the PK agency remained unclear because, although parapsychologists tend to adopt the humanistic viewpoint – preferring to believe that physical effects are due to the living rather than the dead – the SORRAT 'spirits' later made rather eloquent and striking claims for their independent existence. The SORRAT group's psychokinetic effects gradually became so strong that by late 1965 a small oak table was successfully levitated. Encouraged, they then actually levitated a much more massive table weighing 82 pounds (37 kilograms). Then switching to a light metal tray as their PK target, they managed to levitate it without even touching it. Other highlights of this period included the tray remaining in mid-air for a full three minutes, and its 15-foot (4.5-metre) levitation in the open air.

The SORRAT scrapbooks, kept by Dr J. T. Richards, the group's archivist and photographer, contain many photographs of a host of other objects being affected by psychokinetic forces. And apart from PK, the group induced other psychic phenomena that were, as far as possible, recorded by Dr Richards – such as mysterious lights, apports, teleportation of objects and, on one celebrated occasion, the appearance of a remarkably lifelike full-form apparition on the lawn (which obligingly waited to be photographed). Dr Richards modestly estimates that only one in three of SORRAT's attempts to create PK effects succeeded fully, but these successes were often spectacular compared to the weak PK usually achieved in laboratory experiments.

For many years Professor Neihardt had kept in touch with Dr J. B. Rhine (regarded by some as the father of modern parapsychology) and naturally Dr Rhine was fascinated by the reports of SORRAT's phenomenal successes. Rhine enlisted the help of

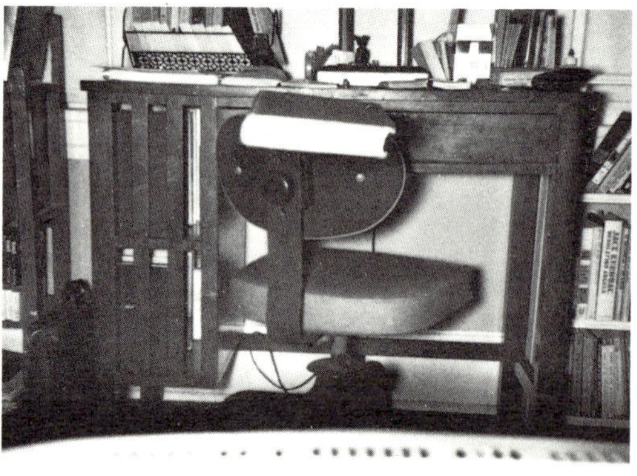

his laboratory's PK specialist William Cox, who, apart from being an original and inventive experimenter, also happened to be an experienced stage magician. Rhine believed he would be invaluable in developing some kind of fraud-proof device inside which SORRAT's PK could be encouraged to take place. A locked box of some sort seemed the obvious answer – in other words a miniature PK laboratory, or minilab.

The prototype minilab, constructed by Professor Neihardt, was a huge glass container, but effects in it were very rare and limited. Cox adapted the idea, making smaller versions out of shallow wooden boxes, which were later called coffee boxes because in the experiments a layer of dried coffee grounds would usually be spread on the box floor. The

equipped with a sheet of carbon paper and a stylus. The agency caused the stylus to write by itself – by pressing down on the carbon paper and leaving scrawls on the white floor. 'Direct writing' (as writing by PK alone became known) resulted in various sorts of communications: sometimes mere scrawls, sometimes whole words, would be written – forerunners of the much more elaborate and coherent messages that were sometimes found in the later minilabs.

In 1977 Cox retired from Rhine's laboratory and devoted himself to the intensive study of the SORRAT PK. He took the opportunity to test the coffee boxes while actually at Skyrim, and made the momentous discovery that PK effects would occur spontaneously, while no one was trying to produce them or, as far as anyone knew, even thinking about them. This totally disproved the common idea that PK requires massive concentration and effort. And the fact that the coffee boxes could be left alone and *still produce PK* was to be exploited in later minilab experiments with astonishing results. It is the phenomenon of spontaneous PK more than anything else that makes the work of the SORRAT group so important.

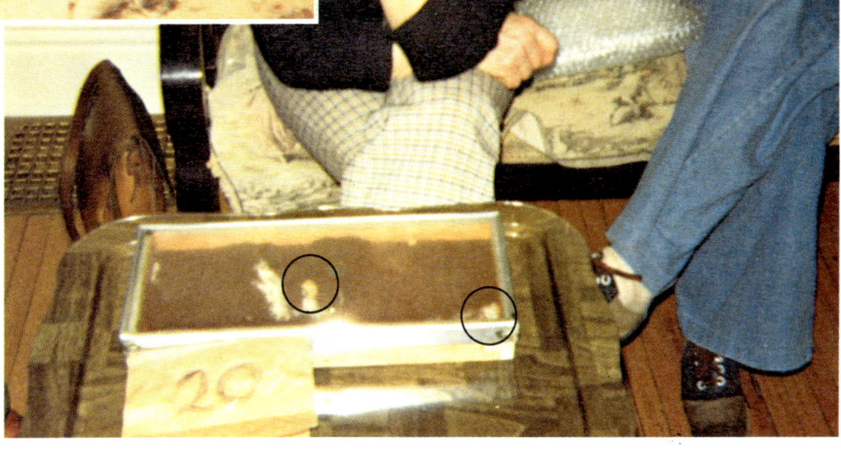

joints of each box and the seal on its glass lid were constructed in such a way that the box could not be opened without disturbing the special markers that had been incorporated into the joints when they were made.

A broken trail

For the experiments, a variety of objects would be placed in the box, and a layer of coffee grounds would be spread on the box floor. Then the agency would be set a specific task. For example, one task consisted of moving one of a pair of dice through the coffee grounds, while leaving the other where it was. The task was specifically devised to prevent the effects being achieved simply by the box tilting – deliberately or accidentally – which would have made both dice move. This particular test was often successful, sometimes providing the added bonus of the moving die leaving a broken trail, as if it had hopped across the coffee grounds. The only conclusion was that the die had actually levitated from place to place.

Sometimes only coffee grounds were placed in the box, and the agency was given the task of producing visible trails in the grounds, exposing the white floor of the box. Other boxes had no coffee grounds and were

Top and above: dice (ringed), moved only by PK, plough a path through a layer of coffee grounds on the floor of a shallow box, exposing the light-coloured timber beneath. Other dice trails were broken – as if the dice had hopped

Below: while in a trance, SORRAT member Joseph Mangini lightly touches a table as it 'walks' up the wall

This preliminary research convinced Cox that SORRAT's effects were genuine. But with the death of Professor Neihardt in 1973 the group began to lose its impetus. However, two SORRAT members, Joseph Mangini and Dr Richards, had already begun to experience spontaneous PK of various sorts as individuals.

Cox settled in Rolla specifically to study PK in the Richards's home. The results of this collaboration have provoked amazement and disbelief among many professional parapsychologists for whom they are simply too good to be true. But despite the criticism and incredulity, the paranormal events at Dr Richards's home were soon to become too astonishing to be ignored.

Cox and box

A pen levitates and writes by itself, leather rings link and unlink, and strange poems suddenly appear – these are only some of the psychokinetic effects in the SORRAT group's minilab. The development of this experiment has exciting implications

THE SORRAT GROUP'S outstanding success in inducing psychokinesis (PK) led parapsychologist William E. Cox to install a minilab at their headquarters at Skyrim Farm, Missouri, USA, in the summer of 1977. The first successful minilab consisted of a perspex box of about one cubic foot (0.03 cubic metres) volume, which was secured to a stout wooden base by steel strips and two padlocks. Cox put various 'toys' inside it for the PK agency to play with. Several minor PK effects happened while the box was at Skyrim Farm, the most outstanding of which was the apparently paranormal arrival of pieces of old Indian beaded leather inside the securely locked and sealed perspex minilab.

The first minilab was then transferred to the home of Dr J. T. Richards in Rolla, Missouri, where Cox also lived. Dr Richards had the double distinction of being both SORRAT's historian and a focus for considerable PK activity, especially paranormal rapping – although he chose to explain it as the work of spirits, rather than of his own subconscious. Various types of PK phenomena took place in the first minilab, and perhaps the most intriguing happened when Cox was present. On this occasion the minilab contained clean paper, a pencil, dried peas dyed white and blue, a small glass, leather rings firmly attached to a point inside the box, a set of six spools strung on a wire with twisted ends, and miscellaneous other small objects.

Several friends of Dr Richards who were interested in psychic matters had met at his house and gathered around the minilab, which was on a coffee table in the sitting room. They turned out the light and waited. Suddenly they heard noises from inside the box; PK activity was taking place. Cox was telephoned and he arrived at the farm in time to hear what he construed as the dried peas jumping about inside the minilab. Then there was silence and the light was turned on again. On investigation, the group discovered that the locks were still secure, but some surprising changes had taken place inside the box. One of the six spools was missing and the

Above: the locked and sealed minilab in the basement of Dr J. T. Richards's home in Rolla, Missouri. A die has moved – apparently of its own volition – leaving a white trail where it has ploughed through a layer of coffee grounds on the floor of the minilab, exposing the white wood beneath. An unidentified white object has also levitated above the raised tin in the centre

Left: consecutive frames from one of the Rolla 'home movies' showing the paranormal linking of two seamless leather rings outside the minilab

Far right: a white envelope moves smoothly out of its outer envelope – which *remains sealed*

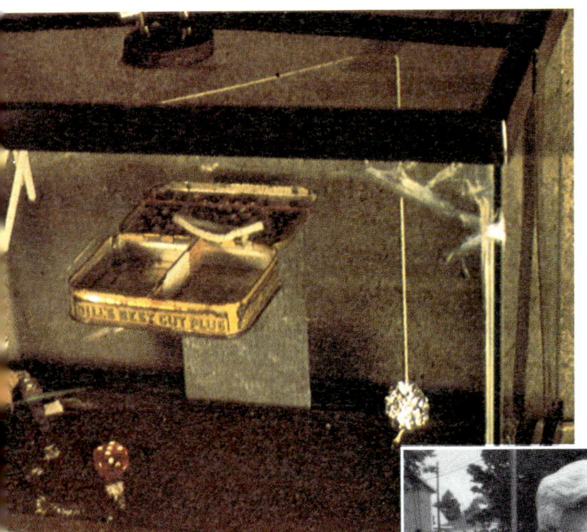

Below: W. E. Cox with some metal objects that bent while secured in the minilab. The aluminium bar, which is ½ inch (1.2 centimetres) thick, was bent 11°. The round white object is what remained of a plastic thermometer after it partially melted while in the minilab. The spoon bent after being sealed in the minilab by a locksmith – who swore that the lock remained secure

Above: this sealed bottle acted as a kind of 'minilab'. Various objects were placed in it: a couple of pipecleaners, a pencil stub, a piece of paper and a safety pin. Acted upon by PK the pipecleaners became the 'man' who wrote 'Freedom, love, faith' on the paper with the pencil stub

ring of wire on which they had been strung had had its ends re-twisted differently. Thirty blue peas had apparently jumped into the glass, two straight pipe-cleaners were now twisted into linked rings and the leather rings had been dislodged.

Shortly before this, Cox met a Mr S. C. who rapidly became a valued collaborator; he suggested and helped to set up ciné camera facilities so that any PK inside the second and third minilabs could be filmed while it was happening. Target objects for PK action were linked to special switches so that whenever an object moved the switch was triggered. The switches were wired to a timing device that in turn automatically switched on two lights and triggered a ciné camera to shoot a 30-second sequence of film showing whatever was happening inside the locked minilab. A 12-hour clock was also set in front of the camera so the timing of any PK activity would be shown (the later British minilabs use 24-hour clocks that also show the date, thus pinpointing the events precisely). This is how all later film of PK activity in minilabs has been shot. Cox's first set-up was crude – the ciné camera was clockwork so it sometimes ran down, the lights were not very powerful so that definition was poor and the standard 8-millimetre film added to the problems of obtaining good quality pictures. The timer was also triggered falsely on several occasions.

Sceptics will, in view of the extraordinary nature of the events filmed at Rolla, simply write off all minilab PK as 'impossible' and therefore fraudulent. But reports of telekinesis and teleportation have a long history and have persistently cropped up in the literature of psychical research; for example there are accounts of well-witnessed teleportation in Professor John Hasted's *Metal-benders* (1981). Viewed from an historical perspective Cox's results are by no means unique, although the fact that they are recorded on film adds to their significance.

Cox's second and third minilabs were set up in a small room in the basement of Dr Richards's home in Rolla. They were fish tanks turned upside down onto a thick wooden board. They differed only in that the third was larger than the second and in minor details regarding the position of the locks. A strip of steel was wrapped tightly round each minilab, then passed through two slits in the baseboard and under the base. The ends of the band were secured together by a high-quality padlock. The minilabs were then locked onto their baseboards and the narrow slit between each tank and its board was sealed with a rubber gasket; this effectively

stopped anyone being able to slip anything through the gap. To improve security further, Cox used some special plastic string, obtainable only from Germany, which he tied tightly round the ends of the steel strip; the ends of the string were then melted together and bound with adhesive tape. Lastly, Cox impressed the insignia of his notary's ring into the melted plastic while it was still warm. Cox had sole charge of the two keys to each padlock and had complete control over how the objects were set up inside the minilabs.

So if one wanted to assume that the minilab PK events were fraudulent two questions would have to be asked: who is doing the cheating – and how? Given Cox's background of more than 30 years' PK research and a few years' successful work with minilabs it seems most unlikely that he would have failed to detect any fraud perpetrated by others in the group. Cox's record also speaks powerfully against his being in collusion with others; in 30 years in J.B. Rhine's laboratory there was never any occasion to doubt his honesty and integrity.

A box of tricks?

Shifting their ground, sceptics might then point out that the objects inside the minilabs could easily be manipulated with fine threads, but judging by the evidence of all film shot at Rolla it becomes obvious that the activity in the minilabs was far too complex and co-ordinated to be produced in that way. Another accusation is that the films were animated. Animation would involve taking a series of single frame shots of the minilab and its contents, the objects being moved very small distances between each shot – so that when the film is shown at the normal speed of 18 frames per second the objects appear to be moving on their own and continuously. This would be an enormously time-consuming task and a dummy minilab would have to be set up secretly to avoid detection, for the real minilab is frequently visited and is in a busy domestic environment. Of course it is possible to maintain the fraud hypothesis by assuming that everybody concerned was in collusion, or that Cox and Richards have a secret film studio somewhere. But once other groups of researchers start to reproduce the Rolla results the fraud hypothesis will become increasingly less tenable.

The first filmed events were obtained in May 1979 and showed a levitating pen. Shortly afterwards further sequences were filmed of this pen engaged in 'direct writing' inside the locked and sealed minilab. Among the words written the name 'John King' was prominent – King being the control claimed by several mediums, notably the famous Italian Eusapia Palladino and 'he' figures as one of the group of ostensible spirits associated with minilab experiments. On 4 July 1979 a pen was filmed writing the words 'Glorious Fourth' on some paper outside of, and in front of, the minilab. As with much of the direct writing, the motion of the pen was extraordinarily rapid – Cox estimates a writing speed of more than double his own. A slower example of PK from this early period is that of an aluminium film canister 'walking' inside the locked minilab. It can be seen slowly edging its way across the width of the tank, stumbling a little over a minor obstruction near the middle.

It was in May 1979 that Cox unexpectedly obtained hard evidence of teleportation connected with the minilab. On the floor of the basement he found a green felt-tipped pen that he knew he had safely locked inside the minilab the night before.

Comings and goings

The tally of teleportation events is now a long one. Pipecleaners, water, matchbooks, peas, pens, delicate mica sheets, string, small toys, jewellery, film, metal objects, and paper have all passed into or out of minilabs.

A classic experiment in this area is the paranormal linking of two rings. Cox has obtained more than six of these events on film, the first in the summer of 1979. The film clearly reveals that the rings are indeed interlinked – but only for a brief period before they separate again. The actual interlinkage happens between frames so no pictures exist of the 'halfway' situation. Irritatingly, the rings (made of several grades of

Part One (abbreviated) of a 1,900-word Notarized Deposition from Mr. R. Henson of Abel Lock & Key, Rollo, Missouri:

County of Phelps

City of Rolla, Mo.

I have been asked to examine an aquarium tank by Mr. W. E. Cox of this city, and the security of its attachment to a solid wooden base...

...I have inserted my own lock into the hasp, and have permanently plugged it... If serious alterations of the objects in it later occur, I am quite willing to testify to it in the presence of a public notary, since I do not believe this is in fact possible without first destroying my lock. Its keyway I chose also to seal with superglue and then tape.

Signed: Ronnie Henson Witnessed: W. E. Cox 5/8/81

Part Two (abbreviated):

At my shop on May 12, 1981, Mr. Cox brought to me the same container...I could not find any evidence that the plugged and permanently-glued Master Lock had been opened, nor had the sealed paper cover over the keyway (bearing my imprint) been punctured or torn...

...We could see that various changes had now occurred inside... I certainly cannot understand how these things have taken place...

Signed: Ronnie Henson
ABEL LOCK & KEY
117 So. Bishop A[illegible]
Rolla, Mo. [illegible]

Witnessed: Mary Dellinger
" W. E. Cox

I, Leona Biddle, a Notary Public, do certify that Mr. Ronnie Henson and Mr. W. E. Cox appeared before me on May 14, 1981, and that Mr. Henson has declared that both Part One and Part Two of this document to which my signature is affixed is true and correct in every particular.

5/14/81 Leona Biddle
My com. exp. 6-25

Above: the abbreviated form of a deposition signed by a Rolla locksmith who declared that the lock he fitted to 'an aquarium tank . . . with a solid wooden base' (the minilab) was not tampered with in any way, yet 'various changes have occurred inside' and he 'certainly cannot see how these things have taken place'. However, security was only gradually imposed after PK was achieved reasonably frequently; an experiment that is over-secure in the early stages often has the effect of discouraging PK completely

leather) have always unlinked again so that no permanent linkages have been left as evidence. In their written messages to the alleged spirits co-operating in the minilab research Cox and Richards have laid much stress on the importance of permanent linkages. Amusingly, one of the 'spirits' replied: 'We've tried, but we can't make the damn leather rings stay linked – sorry. John King.'

The variety and frequency of minilab PK have continued to grow, and later events filmed in the locked and sealed minilab have included the sorting of dyed peas into single-colour groups, the sorting of cards into suits and the blowing up of balloons. Paranormal metal bending has taken place inside the minilabs; spontaneous combustion has also occurred, and the variety of telekinetic actions recorded is extremely wide.

The freedom with which material objects have apparently passed through the minilab walls has led the Rolla group to use it as a paranormal 'postbox'. The disappearance of letters has been filmed and a few days later these letters have been delivered through the normal postal service. As this 'PK post' practice grew, the envelopes were left open in the minilab and a motley selection of objects surrounding them would be telekinetically popped inside before the letters were teleported. It was noticed very often that foreign stamps would somehow find their way on to the envelopes so that the letters would arrive bearing dated Australian, Italian or South American stamps. The PK takes the path of least resistance since the postmarks invariably read 'Rolla' and the letters seem to spend little time between disappearing from the minilab and arriving at the Rolla sorting office. In the UK Dr John Beloff and the author have received several of these letters.

Many of the classic phenomena repeatedly described in the literature of psychical research have also been reported as happening in the minilab. These include the abrupt and mysterious appearance (an 'apport' in Spiritualist terms) of a piece of typing and direct writing (left); the swift levitation of two leather rings (above) and the spontaneous combustion of a piece of paper on the floor of the box (above right). On another occasion the glass at the top right hand side of the minilab cracked – when a candle inside spontaneously ignited. If these and other reported examples of minilab PK are authentic then they represent a breakthrough in PK experimentation

One of the exciting potentialities of minilab research for the future is the teleportation of small devices containing electronic sensors and radio transmitters or some very compact form of cassette recorder. Using 'space probes' of this sort might allow physicists to obtain information about what happens to objects when they disappear.

Meanwhile, perhaps the last word should be left to those immaterial minilab jokers. The following verse is one of several that have appeared in the basement at Rolla. This specimen was typed, apparently paranormally, on a typewriter deliberately supplied with paper and left outside the minilab, but similar offerings have been produced within it. It is certainly a fitting tribute to the pioneer of minilab research:

A clever man, W.E. Cox,
Made a really remarkable box;
In it, we, with PK,
In the usual way,
Wrote, spite of bands, seals and locks!

Lights...cameras...action!

Claims for PK in the American minilabs have met with severe criticism but the British minilab programme is specifically designed to provide positive proof for or against the controversial phenomenon

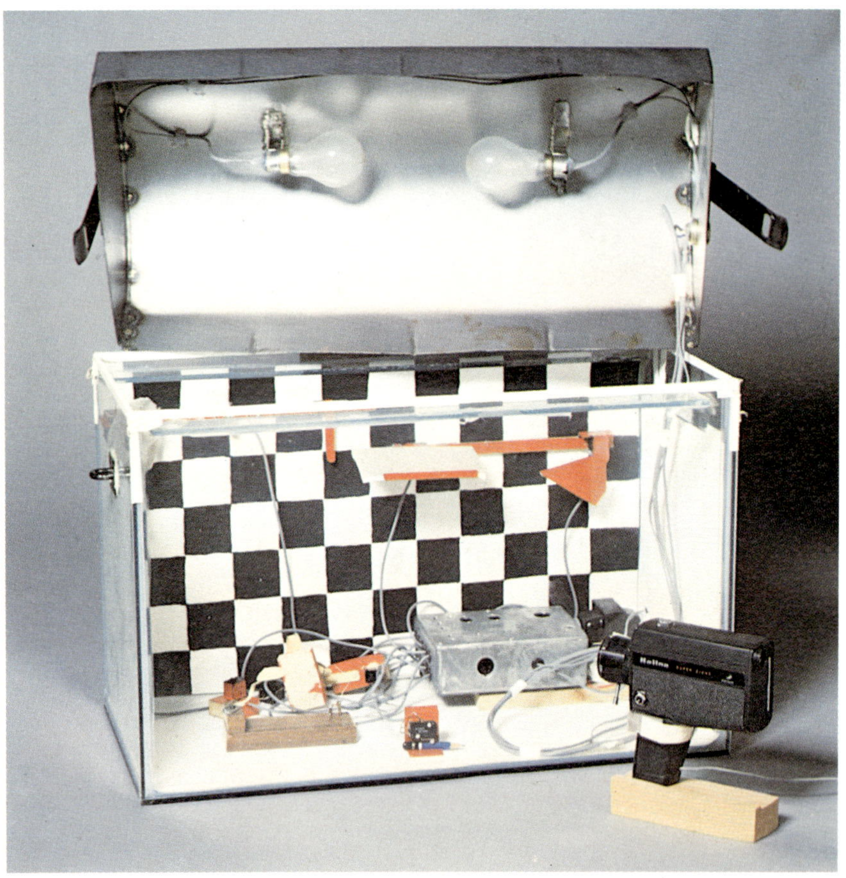

THE AMAZING PK effects produced in the first American minilabs were the result of 16 years' regular meetings of the SORRAT group, but when the British minilab programme began in 1980 it was hoped to obtain PK almost immediately. The idea was to use subjects who had already experienced PK in their lives *before* taking part in the experiment.

The author based the programme on an assumption that seems, at first sight, startling to say the least. This was that at least some people were experiencing teleportation (the paranormal disappearance and reappearance of objects) sporadically and spontaneously in their everyday lives. This form of 'domestic PK' (paranormal happenings in the home) often goes unnoticed or is discounted because it is 'impossible'. Even gifted psychics usually tend to ignore odd disappearances or reappearances as 'silly' and meaningless because there is no rational explanation for them. It is only if events become overwhelming (such as in poltergeist cases) or if the person experiencing them is familiar with the concept of teleportation that the phenomenon tends to be acknowledged. And for the less psychic the chances of recognising it are even slimmer.

After seeing the SORRAT film and discussing the events filmed with W.E. Cox and Dr J.T. Richards the author set out to achieve similar effects – but much faster – by choosing his subjects carefully. The British minilab programme began, therefore, with a series of three lectures given to a selected audience in the English Midlands in May 1980. It consisted entirely of convinced Spiritualists. They were to be screened as potential minilab agents because they already accept the existence of psi, are often psychically gifted and practised – and they are more likely to experience and recognise teleportation than others.

Spectacular stories

The Spiritualists were also shown some of the SORRAT ciné film to interest them in the programme and perhaps to stimulate some memories of 'background PK' they might have experienced but dismissed at the time. Then they were asked if they had any personal experience of teleportation. The harvest of stories was quite spectacular.

Although an indeterminate number of reported teleportation events can be ascribed to faulty memory, misperception (not seeing something that is there), absentmindedness and so on, these people related stories that were backed with so much circumstantial evidence that it was difficult to categorise them as other than truthful accounts – or

Left: the first British minilab, designed and built by Julian Isaacs at Aston University, Birmingham. The chequerboard pattern is to facilitate the computation of the speed of objects that move by PK alone. The red bar supports two arms that hold letters. If a letter levitates, an arm rises, releasing a microswitch, which activates the lights and camera – resulting in 30 seconds of filmed PK. One of the arms has been bent by PK

Below left: some of the 'toys' donated for the minilab's PK agent to act on

Top: a brass spoon mounted so that, should it bend, it would make contact with the silver wire. It did bend, but only after the minilab became non-functional owing to an electrical fault

Above: two yellow-painted aluminium strips, mounted in a U shape so that they each press down a microswitch. If they bent through PK, they would release their microswitches and instantly initiate filming. They bent and actually intertwined – but irritatingly the event was not filmed because of an electrical malfunction in the minilab

deliberate lies. For instance, the teleported object may have gone missing very shortly after being put in a specific place, too soon to have been forgotten, and when found would be in a different and very obvious place. Members of the audience who reported instances of teleportation were then invited to a fourth lecture to which non-Spiritualist psychics were also invited. This combined audience was requested to swap teleportation stories and was encouraged to attempt some preparatory minilab experiments at home.

The rationale behind the 'telling a yarn' procedure is that PK tends to be highly responsive to suggestion. Even talking about paranormal happenings is a potent way of encouraging them to happen. And as the SORRAT group proved, maintaining interest is the key to obtaining striking results.

At this stage no one can tell whether the agents actually need to be members of PK groups before producing PK in the minilab at home. Unfortunately some PK groups do not manage to maintain the optimistic and positive approach needed to be successful and therefore the individual members may never have a chance of developing as agents. However, the British programme represents a step into the unknown and it may be that a pattern emerges upon which future minilab research can be based.

The American minilab project possesses two great advantages in encouraging PK. One is the presence of an interested and concerned investigator, William E. Cox, who has been assiduous in attending his minilab and in maintaining the high level of interest in the group. The other advantage is that, although instances of PK in the Rolla minilab are not witnessed as they happen, they are always automatically recorded on film. This means that the effects can be seen by a wider audience than just the SORRAT group and wherever they are seen they inspire new people with an interest in the subject. There may well be a snowball effect whereby the film sparks off enough motivation in the viewers that there will be a rapid rise in the generation of PK.

In the British project, the preparatory minilab experiments, which are very simple and non-technical, are described on a set of information sheets; these are given to anyone who reports frequent teleportation and who is interested in controlling the phenomenon. Target objects – preferably ones that have been acted upon by PK before – are put in specific places and a written log is kept recording their movements, including any disappearances and reappearances; this effectively sidesteps faulty memory. The objects are checked every few days.

The next step involves the use of two shoeboxes that are called 'coffee boxes'. A thin layer of coffee grounds or used tea leaves is spread upon the bottom of each box and a variety of small objects – such as marbles or small ornaments – are put in the box. The shoeboxes are then labelled on the lid and the base and put where they are unlikely to be disturbed (except by PK). A record is kept of which items are in the box and their position. The boxes and their contents are inspected every few days. The objects may move around inside the boxes or may even teleport from one box to the other.

If PK does start to happen more varied PK tasks are set. But the important thing at this early stage is to forget about security, the guiding principle being to concentrate on obtaining the PK first and only employing secure conditions once the phenomena start to happen reasonably often. The experimenter takes care to keep in touch with the subjects and when the frequency and extent of PK is satisfactory a fully equipped minilab is substituted for the shoeboxes. Even so, full security is applied only once a number of ostensibly paranormal events have been filmed inside the unlocked minilab.

But what causes the PK to happen? Although there are no straight answers the experimenter suggests that Spiritualists, or any others to whom the idea appeals, make contact with any spirits they believe will help and ask them to assist the minilab programme by causing PK. Requests for specific PK effects can be written down and the messages left near the target objects as they were at Rolla, along with pens, pencils and paper for any 'direct writing' replies. But if the idea of 'spirits' is too implausible appeals can be made in the same way to one's own subconscious, for it is generally accepted by parapsychologists that the subconscious often acts separately from the conscious mind. But if the subconscious is invoked it must be addressed as if it were a separate entity, for it will act only if kept dissociated from one's consciousness.

By mid 1980 the first British minilab was in the home of 'Peter', a former poltergeist focus, in the Midlands. His exuberant and spontaneous PK had started after he discovered his very powerful metal bending ability. Besides this, Peter has apparently generated a large number of telekinetic and teleportation events including the teleportation of £25 in notes, which were put into an envelope that was folded in half and then taped many times all over the sides and joins. It was treated in this way because the wad of money had already disappeared and reappeared several times. The taped envelope was put into the zipped compartment of his mother's purse, which she carried in her pocket. She suddenly felt the purse go flat. On inspection the envelope was found to be taped exactly as before – but all the money was missing.

Above: the second British minilab, which was built almost exclusively for detecting paranormal metal bending, although it was also fitted with two leather rings hanging from supports that were connected to microswitches. The metal objects were set up so that if they bent they would touch the bare wires arranged round them, which would in turn trigger off the lights and camera (not seen here). The matt black background makes it easier to see any movement of the metal objects. By late 1981 the most successful examples of British minilab PK were of paranormal metal bending

Left: a Spiritualist couple from Coventry, England, with a brass ornament that they believed to have teleported while they attended one of Julian Isaacs's lectures

Right: 'Peter' with some of his bent metal. He is one of the very few paranormal metal benders who is also a poltergeist focus (another is Matthew Manning). The substantial metal bar he is holding in his left hand bent during a 30-minute period of meditation, while his sister remained in the same room. The bar proved too strong for the author to bend manually

Left: a note pad bearing a message in 'direct writing'. It reads, 'Hi, fooled ya, it ain't pluged (*sic*) in' and is signed 'Quazer' – one of the other-dimensional 'super heroes' chosen by Peter, a Marvel Comic fan, to help him produce minilab PK. The message refers to the fact that the minilab that had been installed in Peter's home was set up, but not plugged in, nor was the lid secured. The pencil in the holder depresses a microswitch; if the pencil moved it would trigger the switch, which would activate the lights and camera

Peter also claims to have been teleported bodily from place to place more than once. There is some supporting evidence for this but unfortunately none of the occasions was adequately witnessed. But there are several accounts of people being teleported in the literature of psychical research – Mrs Samuel Guppy's apparently paranormal transportation across London for instance or the occasion of Uri Geller's sudden shocked arrival at Ossining, New York, from New York city, as alleged by investigator Dr Andrija Puharich. There are also reports of animals being teleported without harm.

Musical chairs

But one teleportation event did happen in Peter's presence that was witnessed and is of potentially great significance. Peter and his sister were sitting in the lounge of their parents' home when an electronic calculator – the kind that plays a series of notes held in its memory – vanished from under a pile of papers and magazines: the calculator's tune was suddenly heard, apparently coming from under a chair. They immediately tipped the chair up and checked underneath but no calculator was to be seen. However a few minutes later the tune was heard again, this time coming from under the settee. Peter and his sister looked under it but there was nothing there. This sequence happened several times, with the invisible calculator apparently moving about under the various pieces of furniture in the room, playing its tune. There is no reason to doubt the sister's word, for in all other incidents her testimony has proved to be impeccable.

This story presents us with the intriguing idea that objects might become invisible while they are still audible. Of course this is by no means the only paranormal explanation for the calculator story – it may, for example, have moved from place to place too rapidly to have been found. But it does suggest that devices that transmit both radio waves and sound (perhaps ultrasonic sound) would be worthwhile trying to teleport in case it is still possible to keep track of them by sound alone when they are invisible. So possibly the calculator story has opened up important new lines of investigation.

Peter has achieved a limited success with his minilab. Although by late 1981 his powers had declined, he did generate some authentically paranormal metal bending inside the minilab and the tank itself was seen shaking and moving from place to place.

Other minilabs were, by late 1981, being equipped to be set up in the homes of potential agents. And the search for PK 'stars' goes on.

It may be that the work of the SORRAT group proves to be a turning point in parapsychology; certainly it has inspired a major PK programme in Britain, which may produce far-reaching results.

Sometimes PK in the home of potential minilab agents is uncontrollable. A bedroom is turned upside down (above) by an invisible agency and the PK prankster enjoys a pun by tying an upended bed with red tape (right). Perhaps this was a wry comment on the stringent security precautions that surround minilab experiments

Tricks of the mind

A young woman is tormented by a solid-seeming apparition of her father, a traveller in the East learns to project 'thought forms', and an American claims to record the pictures in his mind on film. Are such manifestations merely the delusions of unbalanced minds, or do thoughts have a life of their own?

Stalked by a nightmare

As a child Ruth had been sexually assaulted by her father. But the horror really began when, years later, his hallucination started to plague her. Her case provides investigators with unique and fascinating insights into the very nature of reality

'WE ARE SUCH STUFF as dreams are made on,' wrote Shakespeare. Perhaps because, as T. S. Eliot said in *Burnt Norton*, 'human kind/Cannot bear very much reality.'

But what is 'reality' and what are dreams? To the natural scientist things are real when they can be communicated by the senses or by instruments that are extensions of the senses, when their measurements can be taken and their behaviour observed, when deductions can be made about them and scientific laws established. In the realms of thought sane men distinguish, mainly without difficulty, between fantasies and imagination and 'real' concepts.

Research has shown that there are, indeed, 'realities' beyond those generally perceived by our five senses, such as the notes whose pitch is too high to be heard by human ears. And there may be yet another 'reality' – affirmed by the experiences of mystics while in their ecstasies. But the fact remains that 'sanity' for most of us is the common ground of shared sensory perception; on the whole the cat sits on the mat and not vice versa.

Above: actress Connie Booth plays Ruth in the BBC's dramatised documentary *The story of Ruth* in 1982. Ruth, an American living in London with her husband Paul, was of average intelligence and perfectly normal – except for one thing: a three-dimensional hallucination of her father (who was still living in the USA) followed and tormented her, reviving the hell she had been through when, as a 10-year-old, she had been sexually molested by him (left)

But what if our mind betrays us, not in casual mistakes but by completely misinterpreting the data supplied by our senses? What of Sybil Isabel Dorsett who, among her 16 personalities, saw herself in the mirror variously as a sophisticated blonde, brown-haired, a tall willowy redhead, a dark brown-eyed man, a blue-eyed man, a timid ash-blonde, a small slim brunette – with widely differing characters to match. She even bought clothes to suit one personality that were utterly unsuitable for her 'real' physical self – their choice bewildered her other selves when they inhabited her body.

And what of Ruth, a 25-year-old American woman, married to Paul and living in London with their three children, the patient of Dr Morton Schatzman, psychiatrist? Her experiences narrated in Schatzman's book, *The story of Ruth*, and dramatised on television by the BBC in 1982, needed no fictional embellishments.

Ruth described her symptoms to Dr Schatzman: sex with Paul seemed dirty, she was scared of doors, avoided company, panicked in crowds and hated going shopping;

she had no appetite, felt negative towards her children, and that her brain was going to explode. She was third of a family of four, the youngest born 10 years after her. While her mother was having the last baby, Ruth's father attempted to rape her – and nearly succeeded. That the assault was likely to be real, not imagined, is supported by the facts that the father was an habitual drunkard and regularly took drugs; he was violent – once he actually fired a gun at Ruth (but missed); he had forged cheques; he was a frequent inmate of mental homes and jails.

'Sickening hatred'

Ruth told her mother about her father's assault, but she professed not to believe her, and packed her off immediately to the children's home she had lived in before, whenever her father deserted the family. Ruth married at 17, never lived with her parents again and felt a 'sickening hatred' towards her father.

What Ruth did not immediately tell Schatzman was that she had been almost daily seeing an hallucination of her father that appeared as real and solid as any living person. He had begun to appear a year after the birth of her youngest child. Sometimes she saw his face superimposed on Paul's or on her baby's; and even when she did not see him she felt his presence in the house. She believed he wanted her dead and was prompting her to suicide. Once he sat with her at a friend's dining table looking so solid and ordinary that if Ruth had been at home she felt she would have offered him coffee. On another occasion he occupied a chair between two visitors. She heard him speaking and watched him following their conversation – although he was invisible and inaudible to the others present.

Ruth became an in-patient at the Arbours Crisis Centre that Dr Schatzman and some colleagues had set up in London in 1971. There she continued to see her father and feel, for example, her bed moved by his legs knocking against it (although it did not really move). She saw him very clearly – 'I can see each tooth' – heard him laughing and even smelt the sweat on him while in the doctor's presence.

Schatzman saw that Ruth thought rationally; her overall pattern of behaviour was not that of a psychotic, and he knew that it was statistically common for mentally healthy people in the West to have some experience of hallucinations. Having read that the Senoi, a Malayan tribe, thought dream life so important that they taught children to face,

There are many legends in which hapless victims are pursued – and sometimes confronted – by paranormal beings, ghosts or, perhaps, hallucinations. The most famous of these were the Furies of Greek legend, who hounded Orestes (below). Caesar's ghost was widely believed to have appeared to Brutus, the 'friend' who struck the final, mortal blow (right). Guilt, in the form of the apparition of a 'wronged lady', warned Lord Lyttelton of his approaching death (above right). Ruth's 'father' pursued her as relentlessly as the Furies, mocking her terror, stalking her as she walked down the street, or suddenly appearing among a group of friends. He persecuted her in this way, he said, because when she was a child he 'hadn't hurt her enough'

master and use whatever caused terror in their nightmares, he suggested to Ruth that she follow their example and confront her father's apparition.

The victory was not immediately, nor easily, won. Ruth continued to see her father, sometimes superimposed even onto complete strangers, to hear and smell him; she felt that he read her thoughts and sensed that he was trying to master her and to take her over. The psychiatrist told her to send the apparition packing, which she eventually did – but on at least one occasion his distinctive smell remained.

A very real father figure

On her sixth day at the centre Ruth saw Paul change into her father, wearing the same clothes, and when he lightly touched her hand she felt it squeezed until it hurt. She refused to sleep with her husband that night because she felt he was her father. The next day she saw her father's face superimposed upon Dr Schatzman's. The doctor suggested she *try* to change him into her father because confronting something makes one fear it less and it would prove to Ruth that she had control; if she could summon the apparition at will, she could also will it away. This achieved, the next step was to create it on its own – without using a real body as a 'model' – and dismiss it; this she managed to do.

Further advance was made when Ruth again superimposed her father on Schatzman, but he appeared to be wearing different clothes from the doctor. When Schatzman moved towards her the apparition did so also, and when Schatzman lightly laid his hand upon Ruth's she again felt her hand being painfully squeezed. She succeeded in dismissing the appearance, but the experience left her very tired.

When Ruth left the centre after 11 days, Schatzman suggested that, far from being 'crazy', she was gifted in being able to summon and dismiss apparitions at will. Her family history suggested to him that the gift might be hereditary. At this point the doctor had to go to New York for two and a half weeks, during which time Ruth's father appeared to her at least eight times. She heard the rustle of his clothes and the popping of his cigarettes out of a packet, and was awoken once by his sitting on her bed. She managed to send him away once, confused him on another occasion by casual reference to coffee and on a third, when he appeared while she was having a bath, by asking him to pass her a towel. The apparition then ceased for 19 days, its longest continuous absence, but then suddenly reappeared superimposed upon Paul in bed.

On his return, Schatzman suggested that Ruth try to create a friendlier apparition as an experiment in controlling them. After some effort she projected a complete image of her best friend Becky, and held mental conversations with her. Ruth's apparitions usually behaved normally (although occasionally they walked through closed doors), but she also hallucinated the consequences of their actions, feeling a draught of air through a door opened by them and seeing Becky squeezing toothpaste onto a brush and handing it to her, though door, paste and brush had not really moved. The duration of the appearances varied from seconds to 15 or 20 minutes, and their creation both excited and drained her. She found that her apparitions had personalities – although she could finally dismiss them, she could not always make them do what they did not want to do.

Ruth next 'doubled' Dr Schatzman in his presence, creating, in effect, a *doppelgänger* (wraith or double) sitting in a chair on his

In a scene from the television drama, Ruth feels repelled by Paul's sexual advances – for it was not her husband (played by Colin Bruce) whom she saw lying beside her, but her father. However, later in her course of treatment she found she could not only summon up an hallucination of Paul when he was absent, but make love with 'him' – an experience she found sexually satisfying

left. When Schatzman made to sit in his double's chair, the latter sat in *his*, and when he passed in front of his apparition he blocked it from Ruth's sight. She saw both reflected simultaneously in a mirror, and when Dr Schatzman held out his arms to thin air Ruth saw him actually dance with his double!

Ruth made further advance when she produced an apparition of *herself* with which she established mental communication, although she found the experience exhausting. She repeated the experiment in Dr Schatzman's presence, her head hurting and heart pounding with the effort.

A twilight world

By this time Ruth had changed from patient to co-researcher with the psychiatrist. When she observed that an apparition's legs cast a shadow, experiments were carried out with light and darkness. Ruth could hallucinate the darkening and lighting-up of a room, yet failed to be able to make out the words on a bookcover in a room that was actually dark but she 'saw' as lit. She could walk round an apparition, seeing it from every angle, feel it (it was a little colder than a living being), and see and feel it moving parts of her body, though these did not really move, or only very slightly. The apparitions could write messages that Ruth could read but the paper remained blank to everyone else, and they did not appear in photographs of chairs in which she saw them, nor did their voices register on tape recorders – thus proving they had no objective reality.

Ruth next discovered she could create her father's apparition superimposed upon her own reflection in a mirror, and did so with Dr Schatzman sitting by to prevent her being 'taken over'. She 'felt' her father's emotions and this frightened her, but 'he', in reply to the psychiatrist's questions, gave information about himself. For Ruth the experiment resulted in considerable discomfort, but, although she felt her father's fear, anger and sexual desire, she was not taken over by him. The experience was akin to trance, with some similarities to mediumistic trances. However, whether the information that was given by her 'father' was true – and whether Ruth had ever known it – could not be determined.

During several such sessions, a number of facts connected with her father's previous history and Ruth's childhood emerged. She felt his and her feelings simultaneously, and the more she learned about him, the more she pitied him. She found she could create him and merge with him without using the mirror, and still sense his feelings as before. 'The more I relaxed,' she said, 'the less I saw him and the more I became him.' Schatzman discovered that he could talk directly to the father through Ruth and found a plausible personality consistent with itself but not with Ruth's. Schatzman wondered whether this could have been a buried aspect of herself; perhaps she identified herself with her father as aggressor.

A startling development occurred when Ruth visited the USA and spent some time with her father. She created an apparition of Paul in her car – and her father apparently *also saw it*. Perhaps even more startling was her success in twice making love with apparitions of Paul whom she 'created' on nights when he was absent. Both experiences were, she reported, sexually very satisfying.

Above left: Dr Morton Schatzman, the psychiatrist whose imaginative and sympathetic approach to Ruth's distress finally eradicated the nightmare element from the hallucinations she saw – and actually helped her control and even create them at will

Left: Ruth confides in Dr Schatzman, played by Peter Whitman in the television programme

Other experiments, however, failed. For example, Ruth tried to describe some new underpants Paul had bought by envisaging his apparition clad in them – but they were not the same as the real ones. And in an attempt to elicit information about Dr Schatzman's life from his apparition, the 'misses' far outweighed the 'hits'.

Gradually the limits of Ruth's strange ability became apparent. Apparitions could not convey information about objects out of Ruth's own real line of vision. Her children could not see them. And although three adult subjects who had themselves hallucinated more than once tried to see Ruth's apparitions and sensed, even glimpsed, figures, they did not describe what she saw.

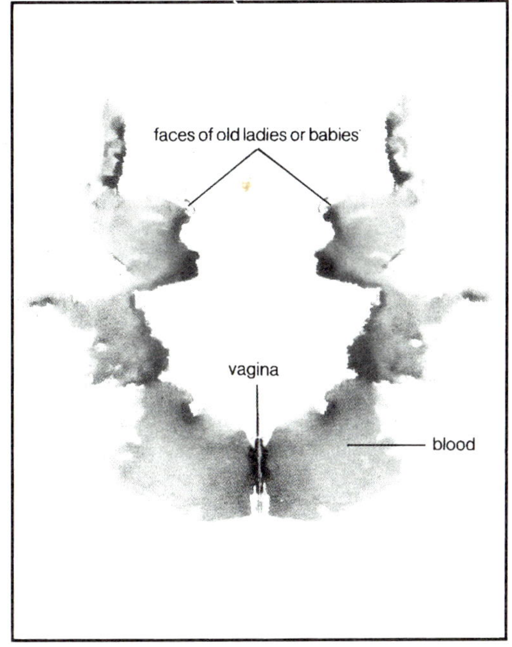

Once, however, Paul saw a self-image of Ruth she had created sitting on a sofa. He heard it speaking and saw its lips moving, then found the real Ruth sitting elsewhere, where she had been for some time. But most of these tests revealed only the subjectivity of Ruth's apparitions, while presumably some form of extra-sensory perception must have occurred with her father and Paul when they had seen their fleeting apparitions.

The final breakthrough in Ruth's therapy was when she succeeded in making a double of herself. Perhaps this doppelgänger – which brought to her recollection forgotten incidents from her youth – was simply a mechanism that enabled her to tap her subliminal memory. Whatever the explanation, Ruth recalled incidents from her past in great detail, many of which were confirmed by her mother. Sometimes she could merge with her own apparition, enabling her to go into 'memory trances', which in some respects were like those of spirit mediums and in others like hypnotic regression. In time she learned to use this 'trance' technique without having to create her double, but she did need someone else to be present to tell her what she had said, because she did not remember it.

Psychiatrists frequently make use of the Rorschach inkblot tests to gain some insight into the minds of their patients. The tests use randomly produced inkblots; the patients are asked what the shapes remind them of. Ruth, both as her adult self and when hypnotically regressed to her teens, was shown several of the inkblots. One (left) was shown to the 'teenage' Ruth, who saw in it the heads of two babies, both of whom were bleeding. At another session she saw two old women and a vagina in the same inkblot – an identification that anyone might make. The other blot reproduced here (right) reminded the hypnotised Ruth of a vicious animal with pincers – or a penis. Asked if she had ever seen her father's penis the 'teenage' Ruth replied primly: 'No, never. He was very careful never to do that sort of thing.' Yet when the notes of the session were read back to her 'normal' self Ruth said that was a lie: 'He would wave it at you when he was drunk.' What seems to have emerged from these sessions was that the 'teenage' Ruth had disliked psychiatrists intensely and said anything in order to be as unco-operative as possible. And her general level of association when faced with the inkblots was not that of a psychotic

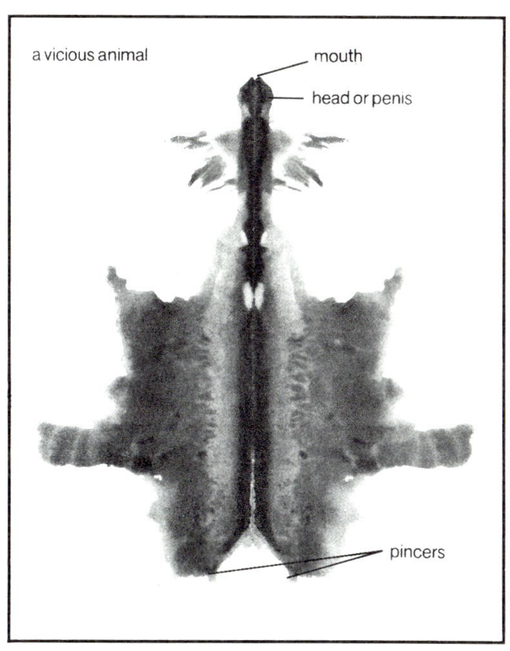

In her regressions Ruth talked and behaved like a child or an adolescent. Given a number of psychological tests while regressed to various ages, she performed in them as girls of those ages would have been expected to do. They showed that she *was* reliving her life as child and adolescent. Other tests proved that Ruth's apparitions affected her sight and hearing as flesh and blood entities would have done, summed up by the psychiatrist and neurophysiologist who conducted the tests in the words, 'You've produced the appearance of a real person.' Yet more tests to see if an apparition's actions could affect Ruth physically succeeded in some measure. Dr Schatzman concluded that, far from being 'crazy' or having a damaged brain, Ruth showed evidence of an extraordinary capacity for creativity and projection.

Why did the hallucinations come when they did? In 1976, when they began, her elder daughter was three years old, the age at which Ruth first entered the children's home, and her eldest child seven, her age when her father returned to the family after his first period of desertion. These recollections of childhood traumas, perhaps subconscious, allied to the loneliness of living overseas in England – another Ruth amid the alien corn – could have triggered her experiences.

What of Ruth after the therapy? For Ruth apparitions are now entertainment. When driving alone she can put one in the passenger seat for company, or converse with another silently at a boring party. But the implications of her story for psychical research are far-reaching indeed.

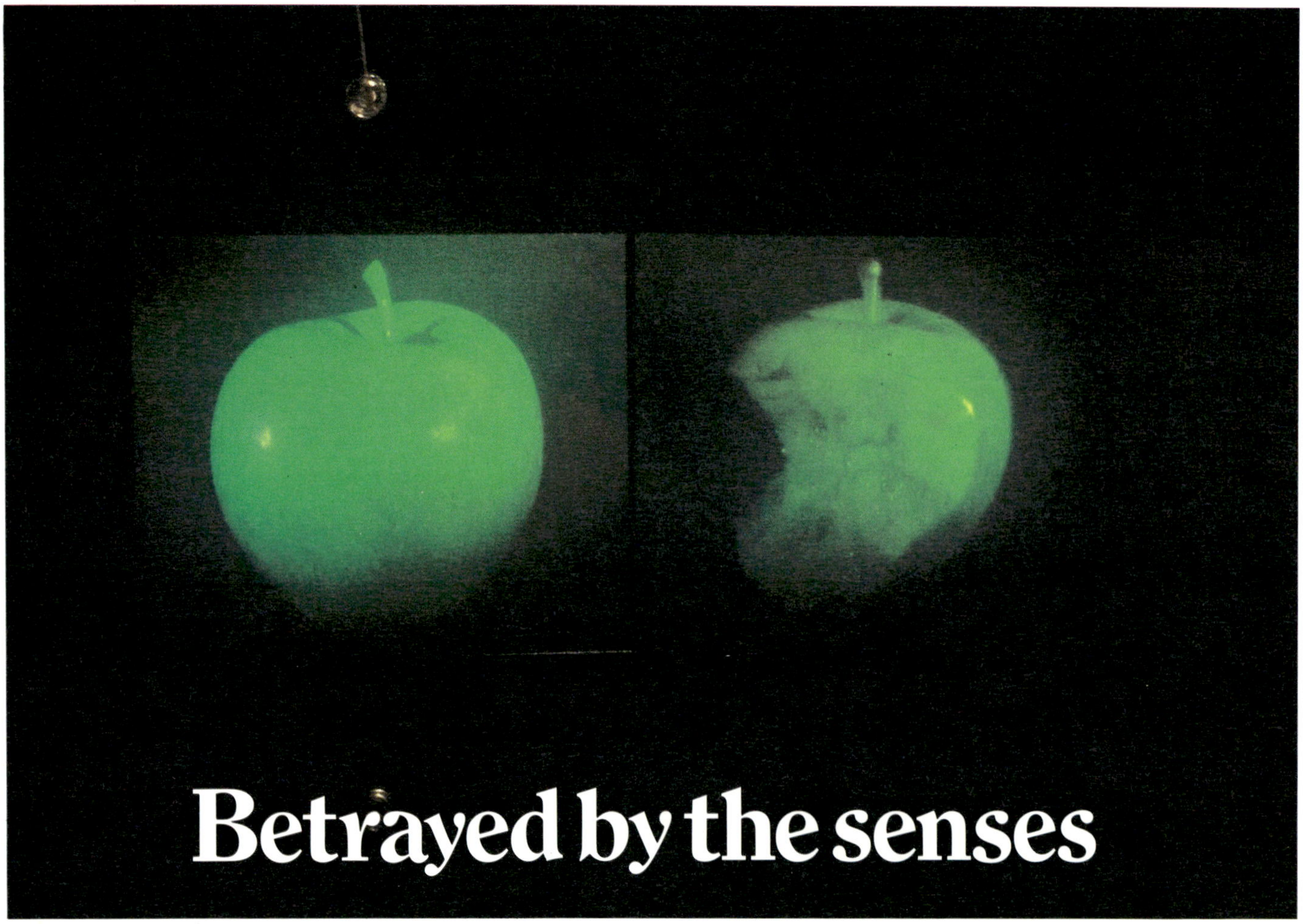

Betrayed by the senses

The more we learn about the mind, the less sure we can be that our senses convey the truth – even hallucinations seem 'real' enough to a witness. Our ideas of reality may need to be revised dramatically

RUTH'S ASTONISHING STORY is by no means unique in the history of abnormal psychology. In psychiatric literature there are numerous examples of normal people who have for a period experienced hallucinations that they knew to be illusory yet that behaved as if they were real. The viewer walking round them saw their backs, they blocked out light and objects, were reflected in mirrors and appeared in double images when the side of the observer's eyeball was pressed, as real objects do. Having no objective reality, however, there was no way in which light could travel from them and affect the eye so as to register an image in the brain.

Yet in such cases the image is there – for at least one person. In the case of realised, waking hallucinations this must mean that, instead of light travelling from a real object, registering on and being interpreted by the viewer's brain, the brain itself must create an image and in some way 'project' it to the spot where it is seen. Similar processes must occur in hallucinations affecting the other senses, such as in auditory hallucinations.

A subject experiencing hallucinations

Our perception of the world is not always what it seems. A hologram of an apple (above) looks 'real' enough, yet it is only an image created by laser light. And even the concept of the apple's greenness would be quite meaningless to a person blind from birth. Animals also see the world differently: a bee might see the eye of a bird as huge and segmented (right); and dolphins (far right) use sonar with which to 'see' – and even, it is believed, possess a form of X-ray vision

may feel that he or she is going crazy, seek psychiatric help and eventually, if lucky, be cured. There are, however, many types of hallucination – waking, sleeping, trance, hypnotic and semi-waking-sleeping – which seem so real that the subject cannot believe they do not 'really' exist.

Perchance to dream

Everyone experiences the hallucinations of dreams. Much of what we dream consists of unimportant fragments of memory, dramatisations of anxieties or desires escaping from subconscious repression, and sometimes simply the communication of physical discomfort – such as a dream of being suffocated when a pillow has slipped across one's face. Many apparently ordinary dreams are insignificantly precognitive, as J. W. Dunne argues in his *An experiment with time* (1927). Extraordinary dreams, marked out as veridical because of their startling vividness and impact on the dreamer, may sometimes be significantly precognitive. These are picture-shows inside the dreamer's mind and correspond to no external reality that his or anyone else's physical senses can apprehend at the time. Yet, if they prove precognitive, they are the shadows of coming events, as real as the shadow of a man overtaking you when the evening Sun is at your back.

In medieval times there was great fear of *incubi* and *succubi* – respectively male and female demons who had sex with sleeping women and men. These could be blamed for the sexual dreams that most people have from time to time. But modern psychiatry is discovering that some *somnambules* (such people are extremely susceptible to hypnotic suggestion) – a small number of females and a rather smaller number of males – can have such vivid sexual fantasies that they can reach orgasm. Phantom pregnancies are also known, one historical example being that of Mary Tudor who so yearned for a child that for a full nine months she showed all

Queen Mary I (1516–1558), whose marriage to Philip of Spain resulted in an hysteric, or 'phantom', pregnancy. In such cases all outward appearances indicate the progress of pregnancy; the woman ceases to menstruate and may suffer from morning sickness and other allied conditions – but there is no baby. It seems that the intense desire of the frustrated mother creates the cruel illusion of motherhood

A welcome visitor

Some years ago author David Christie-Murray was invited to lecture on psychical research at a school and was given dinner before the talk by the housemaster who had arranged the lecture. Another guest was the mother of two boys at the school, who told Mr Christie-Murray this story:

The woman had always longed for a daughter and, when her two sons were in their teens, she adopted a baby girl whom she came to adore. But when the girl was still only a toddler she was killed in a car crash. What was worse, the woman said, she herself had been driving the car, and the accident had been entirely her fault.

The loss of the child and the sense of crushing guilt made life doubly agonising for the grieving mother. One night, some time after the tragedy, she suddenly woke up and, overwhelmed by sorrow and feeling the need of comfort and companionship, tried to wake her husband. But it was impossible: he seemed to be in some kind of coma. In the end she gave up and in utter desolation went into what had been the child's bedroom and sat on her bed.

Then, quite suddenly, the little girl was standing in front of her. She held out her hands and said 'Mummy'. The mother opened her arms to the child, who climbed onto her lap and laid her head on her shoulder. She was solid and warm, flesh and blood – a 'living' child whose hair could be felt against her mother's cheek and heart-beat sensed against her breast. They sat in their joyful embrace for a short time. Then the little girl clambered down from her mother's lap and said 'Mummy, I have to go now' – and vanished.

The experience left the mother with a sense of joy as great as her previous desolation – and a total conviction of the survival of bodily death.

David Christie-Murray said: 'There was no doubt about the emotion and sincerity with which she told her story and, if she was a pretender trying to hoodwink a psychical researcher of long standing, she was a very convincing actress. If the experience was genuine, as I do not doubt it was, at least it shows that not all "otherworldly" encounters are hostile, sinister or sick.'

This story will confirm the Spiritualist belief that spirits can materialise in solid form (below: the alleged materialisation of Katie King at a seance in Rome in 1974). Yet others may dismiss such phenomena as tricks of the mind – which explains nothing. Ruth and many others will testify that the mind can play some very extraordinary 'tricks' indeed.

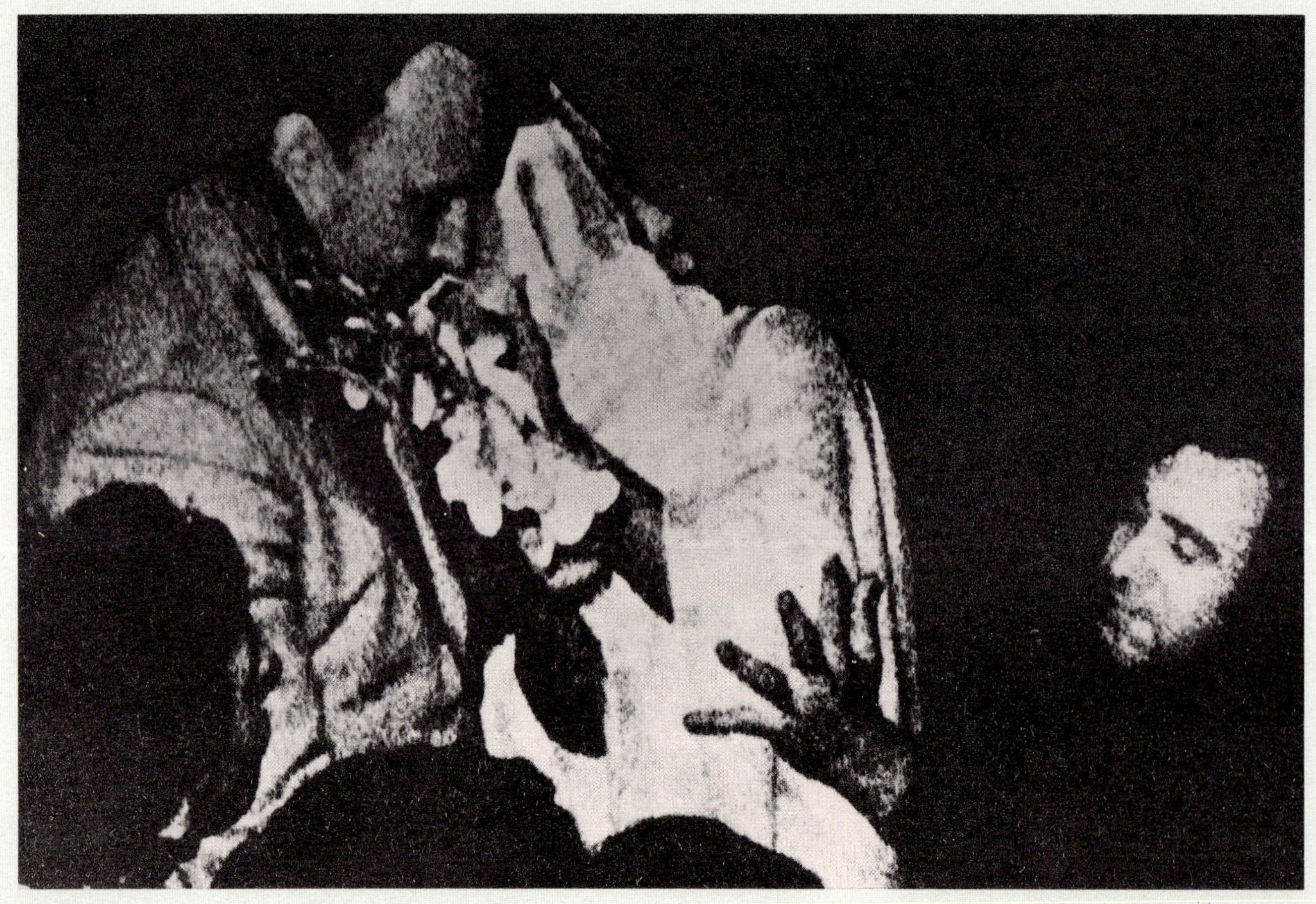

the signs of a developing pregnancy.

What is more astonishing – yet equally true, if psychiatrists are to be given more credence than medieval legend – is the incidence of 'spectral rape', defined by some as a 'serious phenomenon'. A significant number of women have reported having experienced this, both while sleeping and while waking, developing during the ghostly assault bruises, scratches and bites that could not possibly have been self-inflicted, even as a result of the hysteria induced by sexual repression and guilt – the usual medical explanation of such experiences. And there are instances where members of the victim's family claim to have seen a ghostly attacker dissolving before their eyes.

Flogging oneself to death

Even here the human mind may be the agent. A knife-slash can appear on the face of a man reliving a brawl under the influence of drugs or hypnosis. A girl believing herself to be the reincarnation of a slave flogged to extinction may collapse on what she thinks was the place of her death, whiplashes appearing spontaneously across the back. Such wounds are patently not self-inflicted physically yet may be so mentally, as much the 'stigmata' of a disturbed mind as those of a saint. As for the shadowy rapist seen by others, he could be an hysteric vision created and communicated by the victim to others.

Some of these phenomena are experienced while falling asleep, and some during the process of waking. These are the two twilight times in everyone's day, when we are particularly open to hallucinations or perhaps even visitations from another dimension. These occur when wakefulness is merging into sleep or sleep into wakefulness, called respectively *hypnagogic* and *hypnopompic* states. Some of the images experienced at these times seem so overwhelmingly real that even the most hardened sceptic experiencing them finds it impossible to believe that they do not correspond to some reality.

It is said that what mystics see and feel while in their ecstasies is so different from everyday reality that there are no words to describe their experiences. The fourth-century St Anthony, having cut himself off from the world, was constantly beset by demons (above) or seductive women. He believed them to be 'real' enough to see and communicate with but, drawing on his faith, could dismiss them at will. A more modern mystic was the 19th-century writer Emily Brontë (right), whose ecstatic trances contrasted sharply with her everyday world of baking bread and supervising her down-to-earth Yorkshire household

Cultural expectations often dictate the content of hallucinations. Somnambules have always existed, and in ages of greater superstition – or simple faith – assisted by herbal drugs, fasting, mortification of the flesh, meditation and cultural conditioning, have experienced either the orgies of witchcraft sabbats, or visions and communications from angels, the Virgin and the Christ. In our age, a similar kind of cultural conditioning may explain the hallucination of the woman who, while remaining seated beside her friends in a car, gave a running commentary of being taken on board a UFO and examined by its occupants.

Her experience is akin to the hallucinations of hypnosis where good subjects can be made to see people and objects that are not there and not to see others that are. And how 'real' is the chocolate or mustard that is tasted by both subject and hypnotist – although only the hypnotist has put them in his mouth? Or the pinprick or pinch felt by the subject but inflicted on the hypnotist?

The evidence points to the existence of many kinds of reality. One that is quite different from our workaday world is that of the mystic or visionary who, when in an altered state of consciousness, suddenly becomes at one with the whole of the Universe and its source. He or she remembers this moment of insight with a clarity that makes day-to-day reality seem as nebulous and insignificant as a dream.

But whether these other levels of reality are halfway houses between the commonplace world and the mystics' 'ultimate' reality, or whether at least some manifestations of them – such as hallucinations – are merely the aberrations of sick minds is a question that, at present, we cannot answer.

Ted Serios in focus

Can thoughts really be photographed? Chicago bell-hop Ted Serios believes they can, and has produced hundreds of pictures as proof. Many claims have been made by, and for, this psychic photographer – and numerous sceptics have attempted to expose him

TED SERIOS SAT DOWN in the hotel room and pointed a Polaroid camera at his face. The flashbulb fired and Dr Jule Eisenbud immediately took the camera from him and pulled the print from the back. Instead of showing Serios's face the unmistakable image of a building appeared.

For Serios, a chain-smoking, alcoholic Chicago bell-hop, it was just another of his strange psychic photographs that he calls 'thoughtographs'. But for Dr Eisenbud, an associate professor of psychiatry at the University of Colorado Medical School, it was such an impressive demonstration of paranormal power that he went on to study Serios for several years and write a book about him.

When he flew to Chicago for the first experimental session with the hard-drinking psychic photographer in April 1964, Eisenbud was almost certain that he was about to witness 'some kind of shoddy hoax'. Because of his interest in the paranormal, Eisenbud was aware that there had been many so-called psychic photographers over the years who had been caught cheating, usually by tampering with the film. The appearance of the Polaroid camera had changed that, making it easier to control the production of such 'thoughtographic' prints as well as giving results in seconds.

Investigators who have worked with Serios supply their own film and cameras;

Right: one of the few colour 'thoughtographs' produced by Serios. He was aiming at a target picture of the Hilton hotel at Denver, but obtained this image of the Chicago Hilton instead

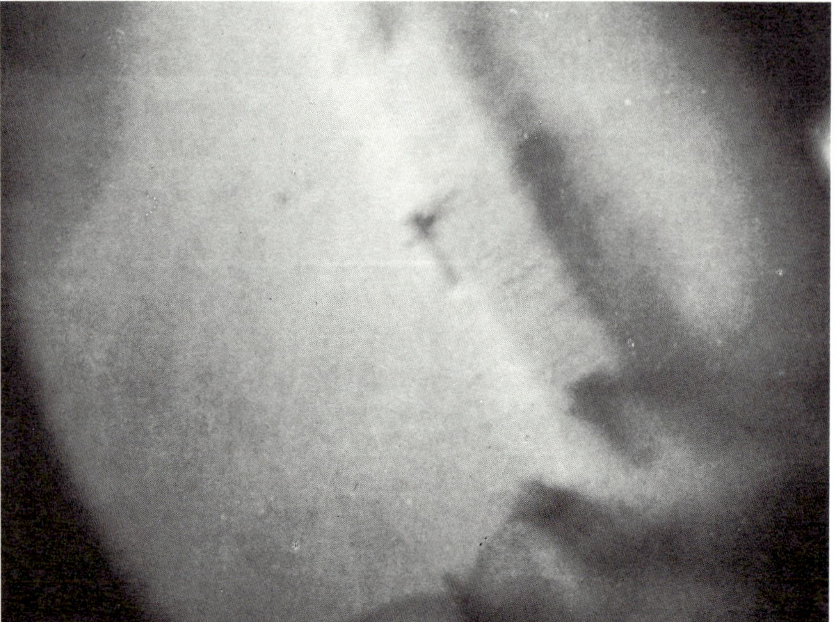

Below: the first picture of a 'recognisable structure' that Serios produced for researcher Dr Jule Eisenbud. It was immediately identified by one of the observers at the session as the Chicago Water Tower (below right)

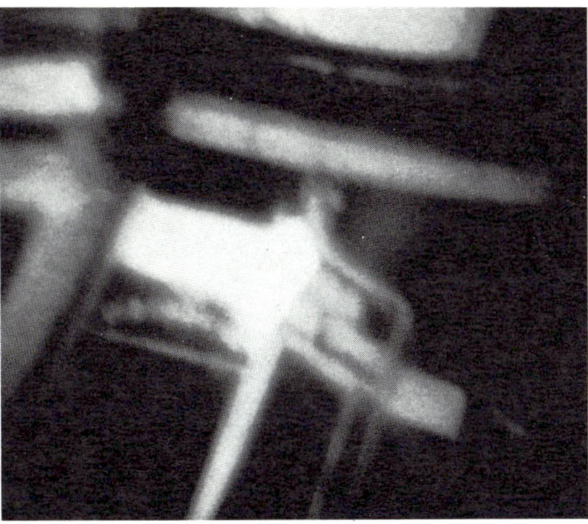

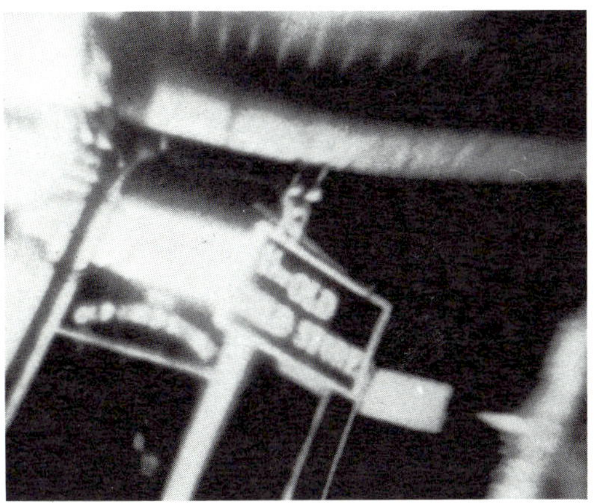

Above: one of eleven views of a shop front in Central City, Colorado, produced by Serios (left) in 1965. At that time the building was used as a tourist shop called the 'Old Wells Fargo Express Office', but several years before it was 'The Old Gold Store', no photographs of which were known to exist. In one of the pictures (top), the billing reads 'The Wld Gold Store': to create this effect fraudulently, Serios would have had to use two transparencies

sometimes they even take the pictures themselves, with the camera pointing at the Chicago psychic – and yet, the results that emerge are frequently very strange indeed. Not all the photographs carry images; some are unusually white while others are totally and inexplicably black, even though the room lighting and other factors remain constant. Occasionally, the image that emerges from the Polaroid covers the whole area of the print while at other times it obliterates only a portion of Serios or identifiable items in the room where the experiment is being conducted.

Can Serios really impress his thoughts on photographs? It is so unlikely that the possibility of a cunning fraud has to be looked at from the start, and sceptics do not need to look very far to have their suspicions aroused. In his early days, Serios just looked at the camera to produce his startling pictures, but later he introduced a 'gismo', which he holds in front of the lens while concentrating. Sometimes he uses a small plastic cylinder, one end of which is covered with plain cellophane, the other with cellophane over a piece of blackened film; on other occasions he simply rolls up a piece of paper.

The purpose of the 'gismo', says Serios, is to keep his fingers from obscuring the lens. His critics, however, see it as having a far more sinister purpose. It could very easily conceal a 'gimmick' containing microfilm or transparency, they argue, and for them it is as suspicious as a conjuror's hat.

Two reporters, Charles Reynolds and David Eisendrath, constructed a small device that could be hidden in a 'gismo' and that produced similar-looking results to those of Serios. Their account, published in *Popular Photography* in October 1967, gave the sceptics the 'evidence' they needed.

Secrets of the 'gismo'

Eisenbud and other researchers, on the other hand, are satisfied that the 'gismo' contains no hidden equipment, nor does Serios slip anything inside it just before an exposure is made. They are all aware of the hidden microfilm hypothesis and have evolved an experimental protocol to overcome it. Serios is usually given the 'gismo' when he feels he can produce a paranormal print. It is then taken from him immediately and examined. It is probably in his hands for no longer than 15 seconds at a time and throughout that period it is under close scrutiny.

Serios usually wears short-sleeved shirts or strips to the waist, making it impossible for him to conceal anything close to his hands. Besides, say the researchers, they are frequently close enough to the action when Serios tells them to fire the camera that they can actually see through the 'gismo' and *know* that it contains no hidden devices.

On numerous occasions images appeared when someone else was holding the 'gismo' and the camera, and able to examine both freely. Two eminent American psychical researchers, Dr J. G. Pratt and Dr Ian Stevenson, who conducted numerous tests with Serios, have stated: 'We have ourselves observed Ted in approximately 800 trials and we have never seen him act in a suspicious way in the handling of the gismo before or after a trial.' Quite apart from the fact that Serios has never been caught with any hidden transparencies or microfilm, Dr Eisenbud argues that the very nature of the images that Serios produces rules out the 'gimmick' theory.

Serios invited investigators to bring with them target pictures concealed in envelopes, which he tried to reproduce on Polaroid film paranormally. On the first occasion that

Top: the blurred lettering on this 'thoughtograph' enabled researchers to identify the building as a hangar belonging to the Air Division of the Royal Canadian Mounted Police (above). The picture bears the unmistakable stamp of Ted Serios in the misspelling 'CAINADAIN'

Eisenbud saw Serios produce a paranormal picture, in a Chicago hotel room, the psychiatrist had taken with him two views of the Kremlin buildings, each hidden in a cardboard-backed manila envelope.

One of the images that Serios produced at this session was of a tall, thin building, which one of the witnesses immediately identified as the Chicago Water Tower – a landmark that would have been familiar to Serios. Though this seemed to be totally off target, Eisenbud was very impressed, partly because some of the images and symbols in the picture were relevant to a line of thought that was in his mind at the time.

Two years later, however, Eisenbud came across another view of the Kremlin buildings and this time Ivan's Bell Tower, which was only partly visible in one of the two target pictures, was prominent. It was only then that he realised that it has 'an easily discernible resemblance' to the Chicago Water Tower. Serios, it seems, scored a hit after all.

But stranger things have happened. In May 1965 Serios produced 11 slightly different versions of what appeared to be a plate glass store front. On two of them the name 'The Old Gold Store' is clearly visible in bold block lettering. Two years later the place was recognised as a tourist shop in Central City, Colorado, which is now the 'Old Wells Fargo Express Office'. The name change, says Eisenbud, must have occurred no later than 1958 and possibly earlier, and research has failed to unearth any photographs of the store in its earlier days.

But, although Serios's paranormal picture corresponds perfectly (but for the name) with the present-day store, there is a curious substitution in one picture of the letter 'W' for 'O' so that it reads 'The Wld Gold Store'. And the 'W' is exactly where it would be if 'Wells Fargo' had been spelled out.

Something similar happened with a picture that showed two storeys of a building and some slightly out-of-focus lettering that was, nevertheless, discernible. The building was ultimately acknowledged by the Royal Canadian Mounted Police as one of their Air Division hangars, but they pointed out a curious misspelling, which other observers had also noted. The words in Serios's picture read 'Air Division *Cainadain* Moun——'.

If Serios were somehow using concealed transparencies to produce his pictures then he was also having to tamper with the originals in an expert way to come up with such bizarre images. Another very clear picture showed Williams's Livery Stable, across the street from the Opera House in Central City. But there were strange distortions. The brickwork had changed: in Serios's picture it was like embedded rock whereas the building is in fact constructed of pressed brick. Also, the windows in the paranormal print were bricked up.

Because of such pictures, in which Serios seems to be photographing the past (and distorting reality, too), Eisenbud and some fellow researchers arranged an experimental session on 27 May 1967 at the Denver Museum of Natural History where, surrounded by neolithic and palaeolithic artefacts, it was hoped his powers might capture on film something that was several thousand years old.

Serios felt confident of success and began by drawing a mental impression he had received of a man lighting a fire. Strange images were recorded on several of the

Hidden in the hand?

James Randi, professional stage magician and debunker of things paranormal, is convinced that Ted Serios is a fraud and that his so-called 'thoughtographs' are produced not by his mind but by the device Serios calls a 'gismo'.

A 'typical Serios gimmick', described by Randi in his book *Flim-flam! – the truth about unicorns, parapsychology and other delusions*, consists of a small magnifying lens, about ½ inch (1.2 centimetres) in diameter and with a focal length of about 1½ inches (4 centimetres), fixed to one end of a cylinder about 1½ inches (4 centimetres) long. A circle cut from a colour transparency (a 35-millimetre slide, for example) is glued to the other end of the cylinder. To avoid detection, the device can be wrapped loosely in a tube of paper.

By holding the 'gismo' – lens end towards the palm – close to the lens of a Polaroid camera focused to infinity, and snapping the shutter, the image on the transparency will be thrown onto the Polaroid film. After use, Randi explains, the 'gismo' will slide easily out of the paper (to be disposed of later) and the paper tube can be offered for inspection.

It is possible to take photographs in this way, although the pictures that result will usually be of poor quality, just as those 'taken' by Serios were. However, showing how the images *could* have been produced is very different from using such an optical device undetected in hundreds of demonstrations. And neither Randi nor any other of Ted Serios's critics has done that.

pictures, the most impressive of which shows a Neanderthal man in a crouching position. But Serios's camera lens had *not* delved into time to record this image. It was realised immediately by one witness, Professor H. Marie Wormington, of the Department of Anthropology, Colorado College, that it resembled very closely a well-known life-size model of a Neanderthal man group in the Chicago Field Museum of Natural History, postcards of which were readily available.

The final curtain

So, was Serios faking the photographs? Subsequent studies show that the man in Serios's pictures is shown at different angles and in the opinion of several professional photographers and photogrammetric engineers, these paranormal prints 'could not have been produced from a single microtransparency, but would have required at least several and perhaps eight different ones, most of which could not have been produced from a simple photographic copying of the Field Museum photograph or of a photograph taken by Ted himself.'

Soon after this session, Serios's psychic powers waned and within a year, although he continued to submit to experiments, all he could produce were 'blackies' or 'whities' without discernible images, leaving psychical researchers still baffled about just what paranormal forces had been at work to produce his astonishing pictures.

Serios had lost his powers at other times – the longest period being for two years – and it seemed to happen without warning. He said: 'It is as if a curtain comes down, ker-boom, and that's all, brother.'

But perhaps there was a warning. The last supervised full-frame thoughtograph he produced was in June 1967 . . . and it showed the image of a curtain.

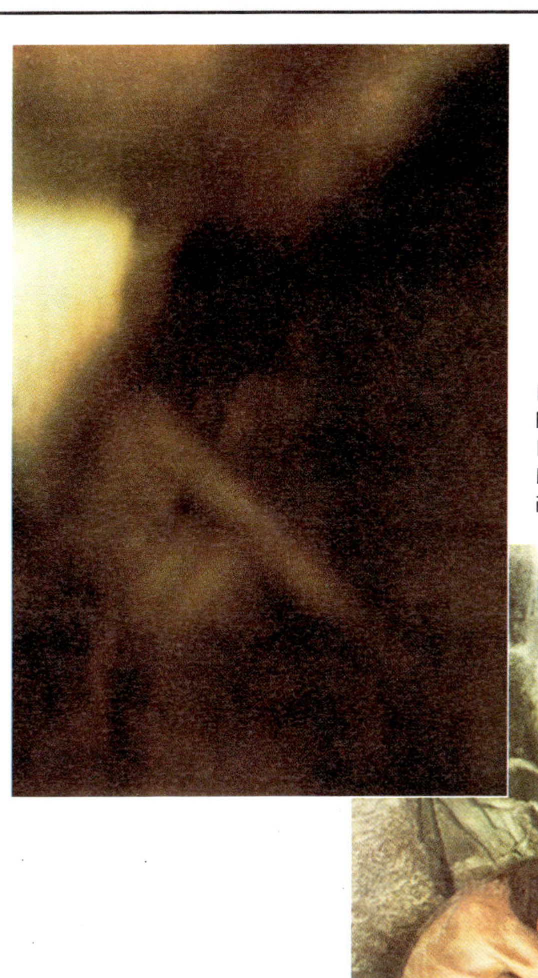

Left: Serios's version of a life-size model of a group of Neanderthals in the Field Museum of Natural History in Chicago (below)

The word made flesh

Apparitions, many researchers believe, exist only in the human mind. But what of the art, allegedly practised by Tibetan adepts, of making thought forms materialise so strongly that they can even become visible to other people?

CONDITIONS ON THE ROAD from China to Lhasa, the forbidden capital city of Tibet, were even worse than usual in the winter of 1923 to 1924. Nevertheless, small numbers of travellers, mostly pilgrims wishing to obtain spiritual merit by visiting the holy city and seeing its semi-divine ruler, the Dalai Lama, struggled onwards through the bitter winds and heavy snow. Among them was an elderly woman who appeared to be a peasant.

The woman was poorly dressed and equipped. Her red woollen skirt and waistcoat, her quilted jacket, and her cap with its lambskin earflaps, were worn and full of holes. From her shoulder hung an ancient leather bag containing barley meal, dried bacon, compressed tea, rancid butter, and a little salt and soda.

With her black hair coated with grease and her dark brown face, she looked like a typical peasant woman. But her hair was really white, dyed with Chinese ink, and her complexion took its colour from oil mixed with cocoa and crushed charcoal. For this Tibetan peasant woman was in reality Alexandra David-Neel, a Frenchwoman who, 30 years before, had been an opera singer of note who had been warmly congratulated by Jules Massenet for her performance in the title role of his opera *Manon*. In the intervening years Mme David-Neel had travelled to strange places and had undergone even stranger experiences. These had included meeting a magician with the ability to cast spells to hurl flying rice cakes at his enemies, and learning the techniques of *tumo*, an occult art that enables its adepts to sit naked amid the Himalayan snows. Most extraordinary of all, she had constructed, by means of mental and psychic exercises, a *tulpa* – a phantom form born solely from the imagination, and yet so strongly vitalised by the adept's visualisation and will that it actually becomes visible to other people.

To understand the nature of the tulpa one has to appreciate that, as far as Tibetan Buddhists (and most Western occultists) are concerned, thought is far more than an intellectual function. Every thought, they believe, affects the 'mind-stuff' that permeates the world of matter in very much the same way as a stone thrown into a lake makes ripples upon the water's surface.

Usually these thought ripples have only a short life. They decay almost as soon as they are created and make no lasting impression on the mind-stuff interpenetrating the physical plane. If, however, the thought is particularly intense, the product of deep passion or fear, or if it is of long duration, the subject of much brooding and meditation, the thought ripple builds the mind-stuff into a more permanent thought form.

Tulpas and other thought forms are not considered by Tibetan Buddhists to be 'real' – but neither, according to them, is the world of matter that seemingly surrounds us. Both are illusory. As a Buddhist classic from the first century AD expresses it:

All phenomena are originally in the

Below: pilgrims approach the holy city of Lhasa, the forbidden capital of Tibet, in a photograph taken in the 1930s; this modern photograph (below right) testifies to the continuing practice of this arduous form of religious devotion. One of the most remarkable pilgrims to have undertaken this journey was Alexandra David-Neel (right, with a companion, the lama Yongden) who, in the 1920s, travelled throughout Tibet and learned many of the secrets of the Tibetan Buddhists – including the art of making thought forms materialise

mind and have really no outward form; therefore, as there is no form, it is an error to think that anything is there. All phenomena merely arise from false notions in the mind. If the mind is independent of these false ideas, then all phenomena disappear.

If the beliefs about thought forms held by Tibetan Buddhists, by mystics and magicians, are justified, then many ghostly happenings, hauntings, and cases of localities endowed with a strong 'psychic atmosphere' are easily explained. It seems plausible, for example, that the thought forms created by the violent and passionate mental processes of a murderer, supplemented by the terror stricken emotions of a victim, could linger around the scene of the crime for months, years, or even centuries. This could produce intense depression and anxiety in those who visited the 'haunted' spot and, if the thought forms were sufficiently vivified and powerful, 'apparitions', such as a re-enactment of the crime, might be witnessed by people possessed of psychic sensitivity.

Sometimes, it is claimed by students of the occult, the 'spirits' that haunt a particular spot are tulpas, thought forms that have been deliberately created by a sorcerer for his own purposes.

The existence of extremely potent thought forms that re-enact the past would explain the worldwide reports of visitors to old battlefields 'witnessing' military encounters that took place long before. The sites of the battle of Naseby, which took place in the year 1645 during England's Civil War and of the 1942 commando raid on the French port of Dieppe, are among battlefields that enjoy such ghostly reputations.

A tulpa is no more than an extremely powerful thought form, no different in its essential nature from many other ghostly apparitions. Where, however, it does differ from a normal thought form is that it has come into existence, not as a result of an accident, a side effect of a mental process, but as the result of a deliberate act of will.

The word tulpa is a Tibetan one, but there are adepts in almost every part of the world who believe they are able to manufacture these beings by first drawing together and coagulating some of the mind-stuff of the Universe into a form, and then transferring to it some of their own vitality.

In Bengal, home of much Indian occultism, the technique is called *kriya shakti* ('creative power'), and is studied and practised by the adepts of Tantrism, a religio-magical system concerned with the spiritual aspects of sexuality numbering both Hindus

and Buddhists among its devotees. Initiates of 'left-handed' Tantric cults – that is to say, cults in which men and woman engage in ritual sexual intercourse for mystical and magical purposes – are considered particularly skilled in *kriya shakti*. This is because it is thought that the intense physical and cerebral excitement of the orgasm engenders quite exceptionally vigorous thought forms.

Many Tibetan mystical techniques originated in Bengal, particularly in Bengali Tantrism, and there is a very strong resemblance between the physical, mental and spiritual exercises used by the Tantric yogis of Bengal and the secret inner disciplines of Tibetan Buddhism. It thus seems likely that Tibetans originally derived their theories about tulpas, and their methods of creating these strange beings, from Bengali practitioners of *kriya shakti*.

Students of tulpa magic begin their training in the art of creating these thought beings by adopting one of the many gods or goddesses of the Tibetan pantheon as a 'tutelary deity' – a sort of patron saint. It must be emphasised that, while Tibetan initiates regard the gods respectfully, they do not look upon them with any great admiration. For, according to Buddhist belief, although the gods have great powers and are, in a sense, 'supernatural', they are just as much slaves of illusion, just as much trapped in the wheel of birth, death, and rebirth, as the humblest peasant.

The student retires to a hermitage or other secluded place and meditates on his tutelary deity, known as a *yidam*, for many hours. He combines a contemplation of the spiritual attributes traditionally associated with the *yidam* with visualisation exercises designed to build up in the mind's eye an image of the *yidam* as it is portrayed in paintings and statues.

To keep his concentration upon the *yidam*, to ensure that in every waking moment there is a single-pointed devotion to that being, the student continually chants traditional mystic phrases associated with the deity he serves.

He also constructs the *kyilkhors* – literally circles, but actually symbolic diagrams that may be of any shape – believed sacred to his god. Sometimes he will draw these with coloured inks on paper or wood, sometimes he will engrave them on copper or silver, sometimes he will outline them on his floor with coloured powders.

The preparation of the *kyilkhors* must be undertaken with care, for the slightest deviation from the traditional pattern associated with a particular *yidam* is believed to be extremely dangerous, putting the unwary student in peril of obsession, madness, death, or a stay of thousands of years in one of the 'hells' of Tibetan cosmology.

It is interesting to compare this belief with the idea, strongly held by many Western occultists, that if a magician engaged in 'evoking a spirit to visible appearance' draws his protective magical circle incorrectly, he will be 'torn in pieces'.

Below: a Buddhist monk with drum and incense stick. The rigorous mental and physical discipline taught by Buddhism enables some of its followers to attain paranormal powers; in her book *Initiations and initiates in Tibet* Alexandra David-Neel tells of a man (right, standing on left) who was reputed to be able to hypnotise and cause death at a distance

Wolf at the door

In her book *Psychic self defence* (1930), the occultist Dion Fortune (left) relates how she once 'formulated a were-wolf accidentally'.

She had this alarming experience while she was brooding about her feelings of resentment against someone who had hurt her. Lying on her bed, she was thinking of the terrifying wolf-monster of Norse mythology, Fenrir, when suddenly she felt a large grey wolf materialise beside her. She was aware of its body pressing against hers.

From her reading about thought forms, she knew she must gain control of the beast immediately. So she dug her

Eventually, if the student has persisted with the prescribed exercises, he 'sees' his *yidam*, at first nebulously and briefly, but then persistently and with complete – and sometimes terrifying – clarity.

But this is only the first stage of the process. Meditation, visualisation of the *yidam*, the repetition of spells and contemplation of mystic diagrams is continued until the tulpa in the form of the *yidam* actually materialises. The devotee can feel the touch of the tulpa's feet when he lays his head upon them, he can see the creature's eye following him as he moves about, he can even conduct conversations with it.

Thoughts made visible

Eventually the tulpa may be prepared to leave the vicinity of the *kyilkhors* and accompany the devotee on journeys. If the tulpa has been fully vitalised it will by now often be visible to others besides its creator.

Alexandra David-Neel tells how she 'saw' a phantom of this sort which, curiously enough, had not yet become visible to its creator. At the time Mme David-Neel had developed a great interest in Buddhist art. One afternoon she was visited by a Tibetan painter who specialised in portraying the 'wrathful deities'; as he approached she was astonished to see behind him the misty form of one of these much feared and rather unpleasant beings. She approached the phantom and stretched out an arm towards it; she felt as if she were 'touching a soft object whose substance gave way under the slight push'.

The painter told her that he had for some weeks been engaged in magical rites calling on the god whose form she had seen, and that he had spent the entire morning painting its picture.

Intrigued by this experience, Mme David-Neel set about making a tulpa for herself. To avoid being influenced by the many Tibetan paintings and images she had seen on her travels, she decided to 'make', not a god or goddess, but a fat, jolly-looking monk whom she could visualise very clearly.

elbow into its hairy ribs and exclaimed, 'If you can't behave yourself, you will have to go on the floor,' and pushed it off the bed. The animal disappeared through the wall.

The story was not yet over, however, for another member of the household said she had seen the eyes of the wolf in the corner of her room. Dion Fortune realised she must destroy the creature. Summoning the beast, she saw a thin thread joining it to her. She began to imagine she was drawing the life out of the beast along this thread. The wolf faded to a formless grey mass – and ceased to exist.

Two Tibetans dressed as gods. Tibetan Buddhists regard their gods with reverence, but believe that they are no less trapped in the cycles of birth, death and rebirth than any human being – and even attempt to make the gods materialise by a sustained effort of concentration

She began to concentrate her mind.

She retired to a hermitage and for some months devoted every waking minute to exercises in concentration and visualisation. She began to get brief glimpses of the monk out of the corner of her eye. He became more solid and lifelike in appearance – and eventually, when she left her hermitage and started on a caravan journey, he included himself in the party, becoming clearly visible and performing actions that she had neither commanded nor consciously expected him to do. He would, for instance, walk and stop to look around him as a traveller might do; sometimes Mme David-Neel even felt his robe brush against her, and once a hand seemed to touch her shoulder.

Mme David-Neel's tulpa eventually began to develop in an unexpected and unwished for manner.

He grew leaner, his expression became malignant, he was 'troublesome and bold'. One day a herdsman who brought Mme David-Neel a present of some butter saw the tulpa in her tent – and mistook it for a real monk. It had got out of control. Her creation turned into what she called a 'day-nightmare' and she decided to get rid of it. It took her six months of concentrated effort and meditation to do so.

If this, and many similar stories told in Tibet, are to be believed, the creation of a tulpa is not a matter to be undertaken lightly. It is a fascinating example of the power of the human mind to create its own reality.

Think of a number...

The phenomenal feats of mental computation achieved by a few remarkable people have astonished observers as being far beyond the normal human capability for calculation. What is the secret of these star performers.

IN TODAY'S AGE of the cheap pocket calculator many of us are in danger of losing whatever arithmetical skill we may once have possessed. In former times a shop assistant confronted with six similar items at 25p each would make an instant mental calculation that 25p × 6 = £1.50 and would punch that figure on the cash register. Nowadays in the same situation the shop assistant will solemnly punch 25p six times. Whereas children once mastered the 12 times table as a basic skill, they now use their trusty calculator to discover, say, what 4 × 9 equals.

Compared with previous generations most of us are arithmetically illiterate. But in past centuries there have been human beings whose calculating ability has so far outshone that of their contemporaries and predecessors that mathematicians, scientists and psychologists have been astounded. Appearing at random like meteors these 'lightning calculators' demonstrate that the human brain is capable of feats that remain largely unexplained.

Some of these lightning calculators have been exceptionally gifted in other spheres of human activity; others, in contrast, have exhibited a stupidity that threw their strange talent into bizarre relief. The only thing common to most of them is that they demonstrated their extraordinary gift in early childhood. With some it lasted throughout their lives; with others it departed after a few years. Like the infant musical prodigies Chopin and Mozart, who played brilliantly and composed at an early age, the mathematical prodigies seem to have been either self-taught or simply endowed with their ability.

The Irish mathematician Sir William Hamilton (1805–1865) is a good example of someone with exceptional all-round ability. He began to learn Hebrew at the age of three, and by the time he was seven a fellow of Trinity College, Dublin, said that he showed a greater knowledge of the language than many candidates for a fellowship. By the age of 13 he knew at least 13 languages. Of his early mathematical ability a relative said, 'I remember him a little boy of six, when he would answer a difficult mathematical question, and run off gaily to his little cart.'

The German mathematician and scientist Carl Friedrich Gauss (1777–1855) demonstrated an exceptional early ability to carry out mathematical calculations in his head. A story is told of the first day he attended the arithmetic class of his school, when he was aged nine. Almost as soon as the teacher had finished dictating some problems young Gauss threw down his slate with the remark, 'There it lies.' At the end of the hour the slates were checked: only Gauss's answers were correct. By the time he was 13 he was excused from further mathematics lessons; and many of his most important mathematical discoveries were made between the age

Skill in mental arithmetic was once vitally important to scientists. Sir William Hamilton (below left) and Carl Friedrich Gauss (right) were many-sided scientific geniuses who were also mathematical prodigies. After the death of Gauss anatomists pronounced his brain to be far more complex than that of a labourer (below)

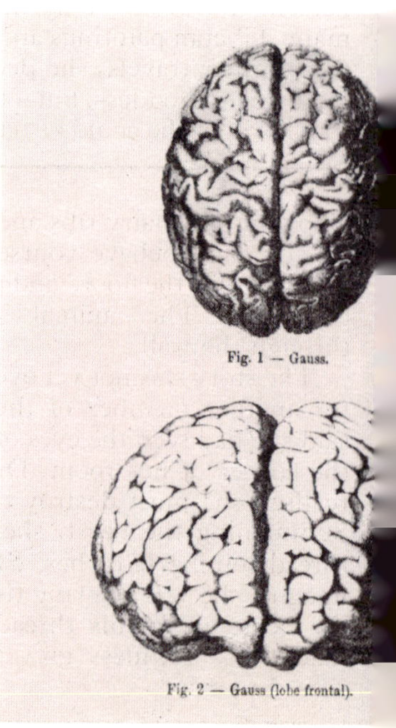

of 14 and 17. He became the foremost mathematician of his age, publishing his book on the theory of numbers when he was 24; he also made notable contributions to astronomy. Throughout his life he demonstrated an astounding ability to remember numbers and to carry out calculations in his head at uncanny speed.

The multi-faceted brilliance of Hamilton and Gauss tends to obscure their extraordinary arithmetical skill. When we examine such people as Tom Fuller, Jedediah Buxton and Zacharias Dase however, the real mystery of this peculiar power becomes evident.

Some of the 18th-century African slave-dealers seem to have surprised the Europeans with whom they traded by their mental agility in calculating intricate deals. However one of their victims, Thomas Fuller, outshone the best of them. He was shipped as a slave to America, to the state of Virginia, where he became known as 'the Virginia calculator'. In 1780, when he was 70, he was tested by William Hartshorne and Samuel Coates; among the questions they asked him were the following.

'How many seconds are there in a year and a half?' Fuller gave the correct answer in about two minutes.

'How many seconds has a man lived who is 70 years, 17 days and 12 hours old?' In a minute and a half Fuller supplied the answer. When his questioners told him he was wrong, he pointed out that they had not taken into account leap years.

Fuller died in 1790. He never learned to read or write.

Another 18th-century illiterate who was nevertheless a mathematical prodigy was Jedediah Buxton, the son of an English village schoolmaster. In spite of his father's occupation, Jedediah steadfastly refused to be educated, and as an adult he could not even scrawl his own name. He seemed to have no interest in anything apart from calculating. In 1725 he remarked that he was drunk with reckoning. This was scarcely surprising for he had just answered, after a labour of one month (and without pen or paper), the following mammoth question. How many barley corns, vetches, peas, beans, lentils and grains of wheat, oats and rye would fill a space of 202,680,000,360 cubic miles? And also how many hairs, each an inch long (and taking 48 hairs laid side by side to measure one inch across) would fill the same space?

His ability to solve this and similar problems earned him a certain fame and in 1754 he was taken to London to be examined by

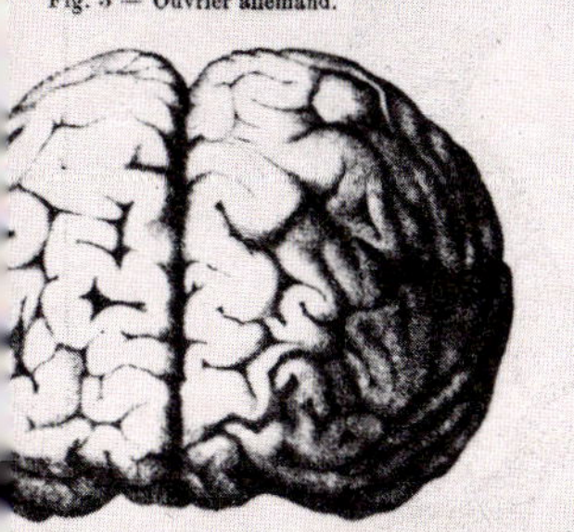

Fig. 3 — Ouvrier allemand.

Fig. 4 — Ouvrier allemand (lobe frontal).

Tricks of the trade

Much of the labour of arithmetical calculations can be reduced by the use of a few simple tricks, and there can be little doubt that many of the famous lightning calculators used these. Those who professed not to know how they obtained their results may have used such methods subconsciously.

The following are some examples. If you want to test how much time and trouble they save, you should try solving the problems the long way – and time yourself!

What is the square of 97?
Instead of multiplying 97 by 97 in the conventional way, proceed as follows:

$$97 \times 97 = (100-3) \times (100-3) = 10{,}000 - 300 - 300 + 9 = 9409.$$

Multiply 197 by 104

$$197 \times 104 = (200-3) \times (100+4) = 20{,}000 - 300 + 800 - 12 = 20{,}488.$$

What is the square root of 3249?
Try approximate appropriate numbers:
$50^2 = 2500$ (too small)
$60^2 = 3600$ (too big)
Only 3^2 or 7^2 will give 9 in the last place.
Try:

$$53^2 = (50+3) \times (50+3) = 2500 + 150 + 150 + 9 = 2809 \text{ (wrong)}$$

Therefore the answer must be 57.

What is the square root of 92,416?
The required number must lie between 300 and 310, since 300^2 (90,000) is too small, and 310^2 (96,100) is too big. Looking at the last two digits, we find the number that gives 16 when squared (4). So the square root must be 304.

What is the square root of 321,489?
To find the appropriate numbers (in hundreds) around which to test, look at the first two digits (32). The square of 5 is 25 and the square of 6 is 36, so the square root will lie between 500 and 600. Looking then at the last two digits, we ask what number squared ends in 89? The answer is 67. So the square root must be 567.

Mnemonic devices can be used to remember numerical formulas that crop up frequently, such as the value of π (the ratio of the circumference of a circle to its diameter) to 12 figures. This is $\pi = 3.14159265359$.

The formula can be memorised by means of the following couplet, in which the number of letters in each word gives the number of each digit:

See, I have a rhyme assisting
My feeble brain its chore resisting.

Although dodges such as these have undoubtedly helped lightning calculators, they do not explain the astonishing ability demonstrated by many of them at such an early age.

The son of a village schoolmaster, Jedediah Buxton (left) refused to learn to read and write but showed an extraordinary talent for mental computations. He excelled in very long problems that took weeks to solve, all without benefit of pen and paper. Archbishop Whately (below) was also a calculating prodigy, but his powers deserted him when he started school

the Royal Society. He visited Drury Lane theatre to see Shakespeare's play *Richard III*, but his response to this theatrical experience was to count the number of times each actor appeared and left the stage and the number of words each one spoke.

Travelling genius

A 19th-century mathematical wonder was Zacharias Dase, who was born in 1824. His extraordinary ability in mental arithmetic became evident quite early in his life, and as his fame grew he travelled extensively throughout Europe, becoming acquainted with eminent scientists such as Gauss and the German astronomer Johann Encke. Dase seems to have had wider intellectual horizons than Buxton and Fuller, and wished to use his calculating genius in the service of mathematics and science. Since he was able to multiply and divide large numbers in his head, he was able to create mathematical tables at incredible speed. By 1847 he had calculated the natural logarithms for every number between 1 and 1,005,000 to seven figures. The length of time he required for any mental calculation was dictated by the size of the numbers involved. In one test he multiplied together the numbers 79,532,853 and 93,758,479: it took him 54 seconds. Multiplying two numbers each of 20 figures took him 6 minutes; two numbers each of 40 figures took 40 minutes; and two of 100 figures each took him $8\frac{3}{4}$ hours! And all this was done without writing anything down.

Although he was anxious that his talent should be used to further the cause of science, he had, unfortunately, no ability beyond his gift. Many people thought he was stupid. One teacher tried for six weeks without success to teach him the basics of mathematics. Geometry was a closed book to him. And yet in spite of all this he did in some sense achieve his ambition. In 1849, on the recommendation of Gauss, the Hamburg Academy of Sciences gave Dase financial support to create tables of factors and prime numbers between 7 million and 10 million. He was still at this colossal task when he died in 1861.

Other lightning calculators were Richard Whately (1787–1863), archbishop of Dublin, whose powers left him when he went to school, Vito Mangiamele, the son of a Sicilian shepherd, and the American boy Zerah Colburn.

Vito Mangiamele was aged 10 when he was tested by the astronomer François Arago before the French Academy in 1837. To the question, 'What is the cubic root of 3,796,416?' the child gave the correct answer in half a minute. It took him less than a minute to provide the answer (which is 5) to the question, 'What satisfies the condition that its cube plus five times its square is equal to 42 times itself increased by 40?' On being asked to supply the 10th root of 282,475,249, the little boy gave the answer '7', which is correct.

Zerah Colburn's talent seems to have appeared almost overnight. At first considered backward, he showed no sign of arithmetical ability at his village school; then one day his father heard him reciting the multiplication tables to himself without error. Soon his father was exhibiting young Colburn at various places in the United States, and he took him to England in 1812. Now eight years old, Zerah was bombarded with questions such as, 'What is the square root of 106,929?' Without hesitation he could

The American child prodigy Zerah Colburn at the age of eight. He was exhibited by his father as a mathematical marvel, and astounded observers by his seemingly magical ability to answer the calculating problems with which he was bombarded

The human slide rule

Born in 1806, George Bidder (right) was the son of an English stonemason. While still quite young, he was taken about the country by his father to exhibit his calculating prowess. People would test him with complicated questions such as: 'How many drops are there in a pipe of wine, if each cubic inch contains 4685 drops and each gallon contains 231 cubic inches, and assuming there are 126 gallons in a pipe?'

Bidder was highly intelligent, and his fate was quite different from that of other lightning calculators such as Buxton, Colburn and Dase. He not only went to school but subsequently attended Edinburgh University, where he won the mathematical prize in 1822. He became one of the foremost engineers in Britain, working both for the Ordnance Survey and later for the Institution of Civil Engineers, of which he became president. He is regarded as the founder of the London telegraphic system and is credited with the design of the Victoria Docks in London. An expert in civil engineering in an era when England's railway system was being created, Bidder was much sought after.

Unlike Archbishop Whately, who lost his outstanding calculating abilities at an early age, Bidder's powers actually improved as he grew older. According to a fellow of the Royal Society, he had 'an almost miraculous power of seeing, as it were, intuitively what factors would divide any large number . . . given the number 17,861 he would instantly remark it was 337×53.' He was not, apparently, able to explain how he did this; 'it seemed a natural instinct to him.'

Bidder passed on his gift to his son, George Bidder QC. Although not as brilliant a reckoner as his father, Bidder junior was a noted mathematician who could multiply a 15 figure number by another 15 figure number in his head. Two of Bidder's granddaughters also showed considerable dexterity in mental arithmetic.

The theory that the right hemisphere of the brain (the one less used by most, right-handed, people) might be more active in lightning calculators was put forward in 1903 by the psychical researcher Frederic Myers. As evidence for this he cited the fact that both Bidder QC and Edward Blyth, another 19th-century engineer and lightning calculator, were left-handed, indicating that their dominant hemisphere was the right one. However it is not possible to determine now whether any of the earlier lightning calculators were left-handed; nor is it possible to say with certainty that the gift can be inherited. The mystery remains, one facet of the larger mystery of the human brain.

answer '327'. To the question, 'What is the cube root of 268,336,125?', he could give the answer '645' just as readily. He was also able to say whether a large number was a prime number (one that cannot be evenly divided) or, if it was not, he could give its factors (the numbers that multiplied together give the original large number). For example, if he was given the number 4,294,967,297, he said that it was equal to 641 × 6,700,417.

Zerah Colburn never seems to have excelled in any other activity; he died at the early age of 35.

Common denominators

Dr E.W. Scripture made a study of such lightning calculators, and collected accounts of many more than those described here. As a psychologist he was naturally interested in trying to discover how such arithmetical prodigies achieve their astounding results. While his studies do not clear up the mystery completely, they do give us a glimpse behind the curtain, so to speak.

Scripture pointed out that in order to carry out their calculations and to store a multitude of numbers in their memories for long periods of time the lightning calculators need to have exceptional memories. Buxton, Fuller, Dase and Colburn all gave evidence of possessing remarkable memories, often in areas other than computation. Possession of total recall would also enable the results of past calculations to be available for future operations, in much the same way that the 12 times table, once learned, is available to the ordinary mortal. Various conversion constants, such as the number of seconds in a year, or the number of inches in a mile, once assimilated, would be readily available for future calculations.

Mathematical prodigies are not all male. In 1981 ten-year-old Ruth Lawrence won an open scholarship to Oxford University in competition with over 500 students almost twice her age. She was assessed by the university as being possibly the most brilliant maths student ever seen in Britain

Scripture also suggested that other characteristics of the lightning calculator were rapid recall, a love of arithmetical computations and arithmetical short cuts, mathematical precocity and a good visual imagination. He concluded that a combination of these factors in a human being will produce a lightning calculator.

What he did not explain is why such characteristics are found in particular individuals such as Colburn, Mangiamele, Dase and Bidder (see box). If it is a question of heredity, what special constellations of genes would be necessary to create such persons? How is it that a few brains can perform supernova feats of computation that make the ordinary person's mathematical skills appear primitive? At almost any level of consideration, the lightning calculator remains an unexplained phenomenon.

The mind and the future

The past and the present are known to us, but the future remains mercifully hidden – or does it? Most of us know what it is to have a vague feeling of premonition, but increasing evidence suggests that lucid glimpses of the future are experienced more commonly than we think.

The sinking of the *Titanic*, the assassinations of the Kennedy brothers and the Aberfan disaster – all these have been subjects of premonitions. Those with the fascinating gift of precognition can achieve some spectacular successes

The warning voice

AT 5 O'CLOCK one morning in 1979 a knock at her apartment door woke Helen Tillotson from a deep sleep. She heard her mother calling, 'Helen, are you there? Let me in!' Helen hurried to the door to find out what was wrong. Her mother, Mrs Marjorie Tillotson, who lived in a Philadelphia apartment block across the street, demanded to know why Helen had been knocking on *her* door minutes earlier.

Helen, 26, assured her mother that she had retired at 11 o'clock the previous night and had not woken up until she heard her mother knocking at the door. 'But I *saw* you. I *spoke* to you,' said Mrs Tillotson. She said Helen had told her to follow her home immediately without asking questions.

Suddenly there was a loud noise from outside. Both women rushed to the window: across the street a gas leak in Mrs Tillotson's block had caused an explosion, and her apartment was gutted. 'If she had been asleep there at the time,' said a fire chief, 'I doubt whether she would have got out alive.'

Had Helen been sleep-walking? Or did her mother have a psychic vision? Whatever the explanation, either mother or daughter had apparently sensed the danger of an explosion, and saved Mrs Tillotson's life. Such incidents are known as premonitions; although they are rare, enough cases have been documented to suggest that some people are able to catch a glimpse of the future.

Early in 1979 Spanish hotel executive Jaime Castell had a dream in which a voice told him he would never see his unborn child, which was due in three months. Convinced that he would die, Castell took out a £50,000 insurance policy – payable only on his death, with no benefits if he lived. Weeks later, as he drove from work at a steady 50 mph (80 km/h), another car travelling in the opposite direction at over 100 mph (160 km/h) went out of control, hit a safety barrier, somersaulted and landed on top of Castell's car. The drivers of both cars were killed instantly.

After paying the £50,000 to Castell's widow, a spokesman for the insurance company said that a death occurring so soon after such a specific policy was taken out would normally have to be investigated thoroughly. 'But this incredible accident rules out any suspicion. A fraction of a second either way and he would have escaped.'

Sometimes a number of people have dreadful forebodings of the same event. Many of them have no direct connection with the tragedy they foresee, but some, like Eryl Mai Jones, become its victims. On 20 October 1966, this nine-year-old Welsh girl told her mother she had dreamed that when she had gone to school it was not there. 'Something black had come down all over it,' she said. Next day she went to school in Aberfan – and half a million tons of coal waste slithered down onto the mining village, killing Eryl and 139 others – most of them children.

After the disaster, many people claimed to have had premonitions about it. They were investigated by a London psychiatrist, Dr John Barker, who narrowed them down to 60 he felt were genuine. He was so impressed by the evidence for premonitions of the tragedy that he helped set up the British Premonitions Bureau, to record and monitor predictions. It was hoped the Bureau could be used

Above: the terrible events of 21 October 1966, when the entire Welsh mining village of Aberfan was obliterated by coal waste, were foreseen by many people. Among them was nine-year-old Eryl Mai Jones (inset), who became one of the victims

to give early warning of similar disasters and enable lives to be saved. Unfortunately it has not yet proved to be of very much practical use.

A similar attempt to harness predictions is now in operation in the United States. An earthquake is expected on the San Andreas fault in the near future and it is hoped it will be possible to predict its date by monitoring premonitions so that a mass evacuation can be made before the event.

When Dr Barker analysed the Aberfan premonitions he noticed that there was a gradual build-up during the week before the Welsh tip buried the school, reaching a peak on the night before the tragedy. Two Californian premonition bureaux – one at Monterey, south of San Francisco, the other at Berkeley – are now sifting through predictions from members of the public in the hope of detecting a similar pattern.

Sceptics often point out that information about premonitions is published only after the event, and that the vast majority of such predictions are discarded when they are found to be wrong. This may be true in many cases, but there are exceptions.

Prophet arrested

A Scottish newspaper, the *Dundee Courier & Advertiser*, carried a story on 6 December 1978, headlined 'Prophet didn't have a ticket'. It told of the appearance of Edward Pearson, 43, at Perth Sheriff Court, charged with travelling on the train from Inverness to Perth on 4 December without paying the proper fare.

Pearson – described as 'an unemployed Welsh prophet' – was said to have been on his way to see the Minister of the Environment to warn him about an earthquake that would hit Glasgow in the near future. The *Courier's* readers doubtless found it very amusing. But they were not so amused by the earthquake that shook them in their beds three weeks later, causing damage to buildings in Glasgow and other parts of Scotland. Earthquakes in Britain are rare. Prophets who predict them are even rarer.

The most remarkable prophecy ever made must surely be the story of the *Titanic*, the great ocean liner which sank on her maiden voyage in 1912 with terrible loss of life. In 1898 a novel by a struggling writer, Morgan Robertson, predicted the disaster with uncanny accuracy.

Robertson's story told of a 70,000-tonne vessel, the safest ocean liner in the world, which hit an iceberg in the Atlantic on her maiden voyage. She sank and most of her 2500 passengers were lost because, incredibly, the liner had only 24 lifeboats – less than half the number needed to save all the passengers and crew on board.

On 14 April, 1912, the real-life tragedy occurred as the 66,000-tonne *Titanic* was making her maiden voyage across the Atlantic. She, too, hit an iceberg; she, too, sank. And, like the liner in the novel, she did not have enough lifeboats – only 20, in fact – and there was terrible loss of life. Of the 2224 people on board the luxury liner, 1513 perished in the icy waters. Robertson even came close to getting the vessel's name right – he called it the SS *Titan*.

Another work of fiction about a similar tragedy had appeared in a London newspaper some years earlier. The editor was a distinguished journalist, W. T. Stead, who added a prophetic note to the end of the story: 'This is exactly what might take place, and what will take place, if liners are sent to sea short of boats.' By an ironic twist of fate, Stead was one of the passengers on the *Titanic* who died for that very reason.

Such cases are rare, however, and for every prediction that is fulfilled there are perhaps a thousand that are not. In 1979 the Mind Science Foundation of San Antonio, Texas, USA, came up with a novel experiment to test how accurately people could predict an event. The American Skylab space station had begun to fall out of orbit and, although it was known for certain that it

Far right, below: the *Titanic*, the 'safest ocean liner ever built', which sank on her maiden voyage in 1912. Journalist W.T. Stead (right), one of the many who drowned, had published a strangely prophetic story a few years earlier about a similar tragedy

Above: Nostradamus, the 16th-century seer, is credited with having prophesied the atom bomb attacks on Nagasaki and Hiroshima (above left) in 1945. But his writings are couched in such general terms that it is difficult to tell precisely what they predict

would eventually fall to Earth, scientists did not know when this would occur or where it would land. The Foundation invited people known to have psychic powers – and anyone else who wanted to participate – to predict the date of Skylab's fall and the spot on Earth where its remains would land. It called the exercise Project Chicken Little, and over 200 people responded to the appeal. Their predictions were analysed and published before Skylab fell – and they were virtually all wrong: very few came close to the date of Skylab's return (11 June) and even fewer guessed that it would land in Australia.

Bombs and assassinations

While experiments to prove that the future can be predicted have not been very successful, some individuals nevertheless seem to excel at prophecy. Nostradamus, for example, the 16th-century seer, made many prophecies that have apparently come true. Not everyone agrees with their interpretation, however. Take this one, for example:

> Near the harbour and in two cities will be two scourges, the like of which have never been seen. Hunger, plague within, people thrown out by the sword will cry for help from the great immortal God.

What does it predict? Nostradamus's followers say it is a prediction of the atom bomb attacks on Nagasaki and Hiroshima in 1945. But no one could have used his prophecy to foretell the events. In other words, it is hindsight that gives credibility to Nostradamus' writings.

A modern seer is Jeane Dixon, who predicted the assassinations of President John F. Kennedy, his brother Robert Kennedy, and civil rights leader Martin Luther King. Her premonition of the American president's murder came 11 years before the event and before he had even become President.

A devout woman, she had gone to St Matthew's Cathedral in Washington one morning in 1952 to pray, and was standing before a statue of the Virgin Mary when she had a vision of the White House. The numerals 1 – 9 – 6 – 0 appeared above it against a dark cloud. A young, blue-eyed man stood at the door. A voice told her that a Democrat, who would be inaugurated as President in 1960, would be assassinated while in office.

She predicted his brother's death in 1968 – in an even more startling way – while addressing a convention at the Ambassador Hotel, Los Angeles. She invited questions from the floor and one woman asked if Robert Kennedy would become president. Suddenly, Jeane Dixon saw a black curtain fall between her and the audience, and she

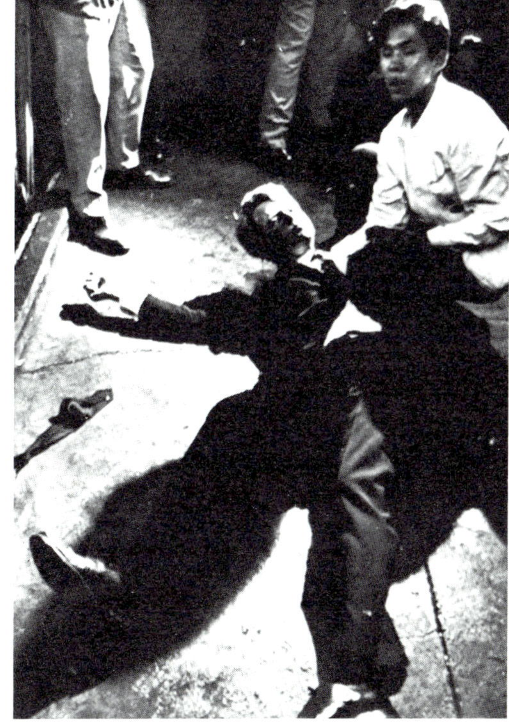

Below: Jeane Dixon, the modern American seer who predicted the assassinations of President John F. Kennedy, his brother Robert Kennedy (left) and civil rights leader Martin Luther King

told the questioner: 'No, he will not. He will never be President of the United States because of a tragedy right here in this hotel.'

A week later Robert Kennedy was gunned down in the Ambassador Hotel.

But even Jeane Dixon doesn't get all her predictions right. In fact, even the best seers claim no more than a 70 per cent success rate, and sceptics argue that it appears so high only because their predictions are vague.

Sceptics, of course, will argue that it is impossible to look into the future. Many of them feel that, until the existence of precognition is proved in the laboratory, it cannot be taken seriously. But, although it may not be easy to look ahead at will, there remain on record some extraordinary stories of premonition that are difficult to explain according to the laws of conventional science – unless there is something wrong with our concept of space and time.

A first-class example of this is the experience of Mark Twain. Before he became a famous writer – and while he was still known by the name Sam Clemens – he worked as an apprentice pilot on a steamboat, the *Pennsylvania*, which plied the Mississippi river. His younger brother Henry worked as a clerk on the same boat. Sam went to visit his sister in St Louis, and, while he was there, he had a vivid dream. He saw a metal coffin resting on two chairs. In it was his brother and, resting on his chest, a bouquet of white flowers with a crimson one in the middle.

A few days later, back on the boat, Sam had an argument with the chief pilot of the *Pennsylvania* and was transferred to another boat, the *Lacey*. His brother stayed aboard the *Pennsylvania*, which was travelling up the river two days ahead of the *Lacey*. When Sam reached Greenville, Mississippi, he was told that the *Pennsylvania* had blown up just outside Memphis with the loss of 150 lives. His brother Henry, however, was still alive, though badly scalded, and Sam spent six days and nights with him until he died. Exhausted, he fell into a deep sleep; when he awoke, his brother's body had been removed from the room, so he went to find it.

He found it just as he had seen it in the dream. Henry was in a metal coffin, which was resting on two chairs. But there was one detail which was missing – the flowers. As Sam watched, an elderly woman entered the room carrying a bouquet of white flowers with a single red rose in the centre. She placed them on Henry's body and left.

Mark Twain's glimpse of the future was fulfilled in every detail.

Samuel Clemens (1835–1910), better known as the writer Mark Twain, who had a remarkable premonition about his brother's death in a steamboat accident on the Mississippi River

A nightmare comes true

On the evening of Friday, 26 May 1979 the world was shocked to learn that an American Airlines DC-10 airliner had crashed – a mass of flames and twisted wreckage – on take-off from Chicago's O'Hare International Airport. The lives of 273 people were lost in the worst disaster in the history of flying in the United States.

In Cincinnati, Ohio, 23-year-old office manager David Booth sat slumped in horrified disbelief in front of his television. For 10 consecutive nights before the disaster he had had the same terrible nightmare. First, he heard the sound of engines failing, then looked on helplessly as a huge American Airlines airplane swerved sharply, rolled over and crashed to the ground in a mass of red and orange flames. Not only did he see the crash and hear the explosion, he also felt the heat of the flames. Each time he awoke in terror and was obsessed all day by the memory of the hideous dream. He was sure it was a premonition: 'There was never any doubt to me that something was going to happen,' he said. 'It wasn't like a dream. It was like I was standing there watching the whole thing – like watching television.'

After several nights he could no longer keep his terrible premonition to himself and, on Tuesday, 22 May 1979, he telephoned the Federal Aviation Authority at the Greater Cincinnati Airport. Then he called American Airlines and a psychiatrist at the University of Cincinnati. They listened sympathetically, but that didn't make David Booth feel any better. Three days later, almost out of his mind with worry, he heard the news of the DC-10 crash.

The Federal Aviation Authority had taken David Booth's call seriously enough to attempt – in vain – to match up the details of his nightmare with some known airport or airplane somewhere in the country. When they heard the news of the crash, the details tallied all too well. 'It was uncanny,' said Jack Barker, public affairs officer for the southern region of the FAA. 'There were differences, but there were many similarities. The greatest similarity was his calling [naming] the airline and the airplane . . . and that [the plane] came in inverted.' Booth had mentioned a 'three-engine aircraft' resembling a DC-10, and the crash site he described was similar to the airport at Chicago.

David Booth stopped having nightmares once the disaster had happened, but he continued to feel disturbed by the whole affair. 'How can you make sense of something like that?' he asked. 'There's no explanation for it. No meaning. No conclusion. It just doesn't make sense.'

Dreams that come true

Why do we dream? Do dreams show us aspects of the real world that we cannot see in waking life? And can they really reveal the future? The significance of premonitory dreams has long been widely acknowledged

OTHER WORLDS SEEM to open to us in sleep. Often our dreams take us to remote times and places; often we find ourselves among people and things that are familiar, yet strangely transfigured. We do things that are impossible in waking life, or find ourselves paralysed and unable to perform the simplest actions. Sometimes we have a sense that we possess profound knowledge that could give meaning to our whole lives – knowledge that is forgotten on waking, or seen to be nonsense. And sometimes, perhaps, we are given real knowledge in dreams – a glimpse of the future as it will really happen.

The nature of dreaming has puzzled civilised mankind from the earliest days, and countless strange beliefs and cults have grown up around dreaming. This need not surprise us when today no single theory of sleep and dreaming is generally accepted.

Above: *Jacob's ladder* by William Blake. Jacob's dream of the ladder and of God's promise to him is one of the most important prophetic dreams in Jewish history

Ancient beliefs about dreaming were usually based on the assumption that they predicted future events, and elaborate means of interpreting them were devised. One of the oldest surviving manuscripts, an Egyptian papyrus 4000 years old, is devoted to the complex art of dream interpretation.

A dream experienced by the Pharaoh Thutmose IV about 1450 BC was deemed sufficiently important to be engraved on a stone tablet that he erected in front of the Great Sphinx at Giza. It tells how, while he was still a prince, Thutmose took a midday nap and dreamed that the god Hormakhu spoke to him, saying: 'The sand in the district in which I have my existence has covered me up. Promise me that thou wilt do what I my heart wish; then will I acknowledge that thou art my son, that thou art my helper. . . .' When he became Pharaoh, Thutmose cleared the sand that had drifted over the Sphinx, which was sacred to Hormakhu, and his reign was long and fruitful, as the god had promised in the dream.

Dreaming of feet of clay

A dramatic story concerning a dream of Nebuchadnezzar, king of Babylon during the following century, is recounted in the book of Daniel. The king awoke one morning certain that he had had a dream, but unable to remember it. Sure that it was of divine origin, he called upon his wise men to tell him the dream and what it meant. They insisted that they could not tell what the dream had been, but Nebuchadnezzar imperiously threatened them with instant death if they failed to do so.

Daniel, already noted for his understanding of visions and dreams, saved the day. He prayed that God should reveal the dream to him, and that night he had a vision. He saw an image whose head was of gold, breast and arms of silver, belly and thighs of bronze, calves of iron and feet partly of iron and partly of clay. The image was destroyed by a stone, which then grew into a mountain and filled the whole Earth. The king recognised this as his dream, and Daniel interpreted it: the gold head represented the king's rule, and the other parts of the image represented the decline of the kingdom under succeeding rulers, ending in its destruction. The kingdom that followed would be set up by God and would last for ever. The king paid homage to Daniel, and raised him to high office.

The Old Testament patriarch Jacob, while fleeing from his murderous brother Esau (whom he had tricked out of his birthright), slept in the wilderness and while he slept, he had a dream. A ladder reached from earth to heaven, which the angels of the Lord ascended and descended while the Lord himself stood at the top. God told Jacob that

Right: Daniel reveals King Nebuchadnezzar's forgotten dream of 'an image with feet of clay' and interprets it as a symbolic prophecy about the kingdom. Impressed, the King pays homage to Daniel

Above left: the Sphinx and stone tablet telling of Thutmose IV's dream of the god Hormakhu. The god promised him a prosperous reign if he cleared away the sand from the Sphinx

Above: Alexander the Great, whose punning dream was correctly interpreted as a prophecy of victory by his official dream interpreter, Aristander

he would give him the land upon which he lay, and promised him 'in thee and in thy seed shall all the families of the Earth be blessed.' The dream, which inspired awe and terror in Jacob, came true, for he became the ancestor of all the tribes of Israel.

Generals, as well as patriarchs, conducted their affairs according to the supposed meanings of dreams. Alexander the Great, while besieging the Phoenician city of Tyre in 332 BC, dreamed of a satyr dancing on a shield. His dream interpreter Aristander recognised it as a clever pun: *satyros*, the Greek for satyr, could be taken as *sa Tyros*, meaning 'Tyre is yours'. Alexander continued with the campaign and captured the city.

This early example of a dream containing a pun interestingly foreshadows Freud's theory that the unconscious mind is a master jester, which expresses repressed impulses in multiple puns, creating coded dream messages that can slip past the censorship of the conscious mind.

But among the speculative thinkers of the ancient world there were some voices raised in opposition to the generally accepted views of dreams. Cicero, Rome's greatest orator, argued fiercely in the first century BC that those who claimed to be able to interpret dreams did so by conjecture and not from well-founded knowledge. And though among Muslims dream divination was accepted as a genuine way of gaining knowledge of the future, Mohammad forbade it in the sixth century AD because it had reached excessive proportions among the people.

It is now, of course, highly unorthodox to regard dreams as communications with the gods or spirits. There is a split between those academic psychologists who believe that dreams are reflections of subconscious activity expressing our hopes and fears, and those who believe that they merely embody the 'junk' that the brain has accumulated during the day and no longer needs.

Undoubtedly some dreams – especially nightmares – are caused by complex psychological influences whose roots lie in the past rather than in the immediate surroundings. But there is yet another class of dreams – those striking ones that seem to provide a prevision of future events and probably led to the ancient beliefs about divination.

One often-quoted prophetic dream concerns the assassination of the British Prime Minister, Spencer Perceval, on 11 May 1812. Eight days earlier a person living in Cornwall dreamed that he saw a small man enter the lobby of the House of Commons, dressed in a blue coat and white waistcoat. Then he saw another man draw a pistol from under his coat, which was brown with ornate yellow metal buttons. He fired at the first man, who fell to the ground with blood issuing from a wound just below his left breast. Some other gentlemen who were present grabbed the assassin. When the dreamer asked who had been shot, he was told it was Mr Perceval.

The dreamer was so impressed that he wanted to warn the Prime Minister, but his friends dissuaded him, saying that he would be dismissed as a fanatic. Later, during a visit to London, he saw pictures of the assassination in print shops, drawn from accounts by eyewitnesses. He recognised many details of his dream, including the clothes the two men were wearing.

Although that incident is said to have been carefully studied at the time and confirmed, it is far from constituting good evidence, because the dreamer is not identified. By contrast, the following dream was described by a great writer, Charles Dickens:

> I dreamed that I saw a lady in a red shawl with her back towards me. . . . On her turning round, I found that I didn't know her and she said 'I am Miss Napier.'
>
> All the time I was dressing next morning, I thought – what a preposterous thing to have so very distinct a dream about nothing! and why Miss Napier? For I have never heard of any Miss Napier. That same Friday night I read. After the reading, came into my retiring-room Miss Boyle and her brother, and *the* lady in the red shawl whom they present as 'Miss Napier'!

Dreams of death and disaster

Such dreams, as Dickens remarks, are usually very distinct, or have a special quality of their own. Dr Walter Franklin Prince, an American clergyman and historian who became a noted psychical researcher, said that during his life he had experienced four dreams compared with which all his other dreams were 'as the glow-worm to the lightning flash': the imagery in these dreams was exceptionally vivid and the emotions they aroused usually intense. This is his account of one of those dreams:

> I dreamed that I was looking at a train, the rear end of which was protruding from a railway tunnel. Then, suddenly, to my horror, another train dashed into it. I saw cars crumple and pile up, and out of the mass of wreckage arose the cries, sharp and agonized, of wounded persons . . . And then what appeared to be clouds of steam or smoke burst forth, and still more agonizing cries followed. At about this point I was awakened by my wife, since I was making noises indicative of distress.

The following morning a railway disaster occurred in New York. When Dr Prince read the newspaper accounts he was struck by many 'coinciding particulars': the trains had collided at the entrance of a tunnel; in addition to those killed and injured by the impact, others perished or were severely wounded when steam pipes burst and the wreckage caught fire; and the disaster occurred no more than six hours after the dream and just 75 miles (125 kilometres) away from Dr Prince's home.

Below: Cicero, the famous Roman orator, was intensely sceptical about the claims of dream interpreters. He argued that they relied on conjecture

John W. Dunne, a British pioneer aeronautical engineer, was intrigued by his own dreams, which often seemed to glimpse future events. Dunne proposed theories on time that endeavoured to explain dream precognition. His book *An experiment with time*, published in 1927, is one of the most famous studies of the subject.

Dunne made meticulous records of his dreams. The following, which occurred in the autumn of 1913, was a typical example:

Above: the British Prime Minister, Spencer Perceval, is assassinated by John Bellingham on 11 May 1812. Eight days before, an unknown Cornishman dreamed of the event in extraordinary detail – even down to the type of buttons on the assassin's sleeve

> The scene I saw was a high railway embankment. I knew in that dream – knew without questioning, as anyone acquainted with the locality would have known – that the place was *just north of the Firth of Forth Bridge*, in Scotland. The terrain below the embankment was open grassland, with people walking in small groups thereon. The scene came and went several times, but the last time I saw that a train going north had just fallen over the embankment. I saw several carriages lying towards the bottom of the slope, and I saw large blocks of stone rolling and sliding down.

He tried to 'get' the date, but all he could gather was that it was the following spring. His own recollection is that he thought it was mid April, though his sister believed he mentioned March when he told her of the dream next morning. They agreed, jokingly, to warn their friends against travelling by rail in Scotland during the next spring.

On 14 April 1914 the 'Flying Scotsman' mail train jumped the parapet near Burntisland station, 15 miles (24 kilometres) north of the Forth Bridge, and fell on to the golf links 20 feet (6 metres) below.

In recent years several bureaux have been set up to collect premonitions from the public in an attempt to overcome the often-made objection that such reports surface only after an event. The Toronto Premonitions Bureau received the following account of a premonition, which, like so many others, came in a dream.

A Canadian woman, Mrs Zmenak, dreamed that police telephoned her. They told her that her husband would not be home for a while because someone had been killed; then she saw a body without legs. When she woke she was sure her husband would not die, but that someone else would be killed if he went out next day. He ignored her warning. What happened next is described in the journal of the New Horizons Research Foundation, which ran the bureau:

> On the way home his car failed electrically and came to a standstill; he walked to a telephone to ask his wife to pick him up. A police car stopped to ask what he was doing, and as he was explaining another car drew up on the other side of the road and the driver, who was lost, crossed over to ask his way. The police gave him directions, and as the driver went back to get into his car he walked into the path of another car and was killed instantly. His legs were doubled up underneath him, they looked as if they were cut off. The police telephoned Mrs Zmenak . . . and told her that her husband would not be returning home yet because a man had been killed and her husband was needed to make a statement as a witness.

When a prophetic dream coincides with reality to such a remarkable extent, it would seem to suggest that in sleep the usual barriers of time and space can be breached. And since we all sleep and dream, we all have the opportunity to pass through those barriers on occasion.

The Archduke Ferdinand, just before his assassination by Serbian nationalists. The murder shattered the already fragile relations between the European powers and ushered in the carnage of the First World War

A portent of war

During the night of 27 June 1914 a Balkan Bishop, Monseigneur Joseph de Lanyi, had a terrifying dream. In it a black-edged letter lay on his study table, bearing the arms of Archduke Ferdinand (heir-presumptive to the Austro-Hungarian throne, and to whom the Bishop was tutor). When he opened the dream letter, the Bishop saw a street scene at the head of the paper. The Archduke was seated in a motor car with his wife at his side, facing a general. Another officer sat at the side of the chauffeur. Suddenly two men stepped forward and fired at the royal couple.

The text of the letter read: 'Your Eminence, dear Dr Lanyi, my wife and I have been victims of a political crime at Sarajevo. We commend ourselves to your prayers. Sarajevo, 28 June 1914, 4 a.m.'

The next day the shaken Bishop received news of the assassination. And within weeks all Europe was at war.

Below: John W. Dunne dreamed vividly of a train falling over an embankment near the Forth Bridge. Some months later the 'Flying Scotsman' crashed there

Science and the dream makers

Psychologists studying dreams in the experimental laboratory have found examples of telepathy and precognition. Attempts to produce dream ESP to order have met with startling results

THE ARTIST'S DREAM puzzled him. It began with images of a number of posts. Then he had the impression of a prize fight. 'I had to go to Madison Square Garden to pick up tickets to a boxing fight,' he recalled, 'and there were a lot of tough punks around – people connected with the fight around the place.' Why should he have such a dream? He had no interest in boxing and had never been to a fight.

But there *was* a reason for the dream. The artist was a guinea pig in the dream laboratory at Maimonides Medical Center, State University of New York. He had allowed himself to be wired up to a machine that monitored his brain activity during sleep; as soon as it showed that he had been dreaming, the researchers woke him up and asked him to describe his dream.

In another part of the Maimonides laboratory a woman was looking at a picture that had been chosen at random from a pool of 12. She concentrated on trying to communicate it to the sleeping artist. And the target picture on this occasion was a painting that showed Jack Dempsey being knocked out of the ring at Madison Square Garden.

When independent judges were shown a verbal description of the sleeper's dream impressions, together with the 12 pictures in the target pool, they had no difficulty in matching it with the painting of Dempsey's fight. The dream was a spectacular hit.

Above: Luis Angel Firpo knocks Jack Dempsey out of the ring. This picture, transmitted telepathically to a sleeper, triggered a dream about boxing

Below: Dr Montague Ullman monitors the brain waves of a sleeper in his dream lab

The experiments at the Maimonides dream laboratory were conducted for over 15 years from the early 1960s, and were designed specifically to look for telepathy between dreaming subjects and waking agents who 'transmitted' pictures to them. They found a particularly good subject, Dr William Erwin, and an equally good agent, Sol Feldstein, who was a doctoral student. The research team were able to conduct telepathy-in-dream experiments with them that yielded results far better than chance could be expected to produce; the odds were in fact 1000 to 1 against chance being responsible.

But every so often the researchers came upon cases where, instead of receiving someone else's thoughts, a dreamer would apparently have a glimpse of a future event. This came as no surprise to Dr Montague Ullman, the New York psychiatrist who led the Maimonides team. He had himself experienced a premonition of the future in one of his dreams.

One night Dr Ullman dreamed that he met a fellow dream researcher, Dr Krippner, and was surprised to see that he had a massive, bleeding lesion on his face. The dream startled him so much that he awoke 'with a sinking sense of terror'. Later that day Dr Ullman visited a part of New York city with which he was unfamiliar. He was surprised to see a man whose walk – 'a kind of hunched-over shuffle' – reminded him of Dr Krippner. Convinced that it was his colleague, but puzzled that he should also be in that part of the city, Dr Ullman crossed the road to speak to him. As he approached, however, he realised it was not Dr Krippner – but the man had 'the same, horrible, ulcerating lesion

An experiment in mass telepathy. For six nights in 1971 the Grateful Dead's audiences were enlisted as 'senders'. The 'receiver' was Malcolm Bessent (above), sleeping at the dream laboratory. One night the audience 'sent' this picture of the seven spinal chakras (right). In yoga these are claimed to be bodily energy centres. Bessent's dream description referred to: using natural energy; an 'energy box' to catch sunlight; someone levitating; and a spinal column. Note the figure's halo, which could have stimulated the idea of sunlight

The dreamer observed

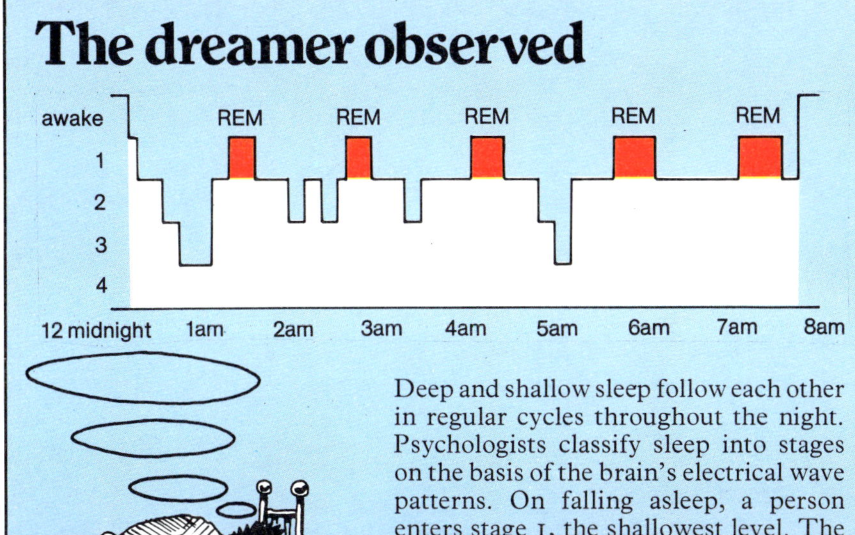

Deep and shallow sleep follow each other in regular cycles throughout the night. Psychologists classify sleep into stages on the basis of the brain's electrical wave patterns. On falling asleep, a person enters stage 1, the shallowest level. The brain wave pattern is similar to that of wakefulness. As sleep deepens into stages 2, 3 and 4 the brain waves become slower, though their voltage increases. Some muscles, such as those of the limbs and the jaw, relax while others, such as those that push food along the digestive tract, continue normally. After about $1\frac{1}{2}$ hours the brain waves suddenly return to the stage 1 pattern, while the body becomes yet more relaxed and completely immobile – except for the eyes, which begin quick, jerky movements behind the closed eyelids. It is difficult to rouse the sleeper from this REM (rapid eye movement) sleep, but when this is done the sleeper nearly always has a dream to report, which may be vivid and full of action. Typically, REM sleep lasts about 20 minutes; the whole cycle is then repeated. Later cycles are shallower than earlier ones. Volunteers have been deprived of their dreams by being woken when REMs begin. Even after months of this, there is usually little effect on waking life, but the volunteers compensate by spending much more of the night dreaming, as soon as this is again permitted by the experimenters.

around his mouth' that he had seen in his dream the night before.

This was a spontaneous dream experience, but Dr Ullman found the same shift in time occurring in the laboratory, too. In early 1971 the rock band the Grateful Dead took an interest in the Maimonides telepathy research and visited the dream laboratory. The research team decided to enlist the musicians' help in an experiment designed to discover whether telepathic communication is stronger if more than one agent is involved. The band was giving six concerts in New York, 45 miles (70 kilometres) from the research unit, and agreed to ask each night's 2000-strong audience to act as telepathic agents.

On the evening of each concert an English psychic, Malcolm Bessent, went to sleep at the Maimonides laboratory under the watchful eye of the research team. At the concert a picture of Bessent was briefly projected onto a screen. Then another picture, selected at random, was shown for 15 minutes while the Grateful Dead played their music, and the audience tried to transmit the picture.

When Bessent's dreams were analysed, it was found that he had succeeded in scoring four 'hits' out of six. And the story does not end there: it has an unexpected twist. The researchers wondered if it would be possible for someone else to 'intercept' the telepathic communication and describe the pictures. They asked another of their laboratory subjects, Felicia Parise, to try to tune into the concert audience's thoughts, but the audience was not told she was doing so. Taken at face value her results were disappointing, because there was only one hit. But the team noticed a remarkable displacement effect.

On three nights Miss Parise's impressions bore no resemblance to the picture that was being shown to the audience at that time. But they were impressive descriptions of images that either had been shown on earlier nights or were still to be randomly chosen and projected. She seems somehow to have seen into both the past and the future.

Psychical researchers have long been aware that dreams provide a wealth of paranormal information. There were apparently many dream warnings of the Aberfan disaster of 1966. The tiny Welsh village was overwhelmed when a coal tip subsided, killing 144 people. When Dr John Barker analysed 31 supposed premonitions of the tragedy, he found that 28 occurred in dreams.

Detection of dreaming

Until the 1950s the problem for investigators of dream premonitions was that most people have no recollection of their dreams, or rapidly forget them. But then it was found that, by waking a person after a period of 'rapid eye movement' sleep (see box), an account of a dream was almost always forthcoming. The technique also enabled researchers to time 'transmission' of mental images to a sleeper to coincide with a dreaming phase.

Dreams vary in nature, and studies of one kind in particular – the lucid dreams – are exciting a great deal of interest. The name might suggest merely a particularly vivid dream, but the term is in fact used to describe experiences in which the sleeper *knows* he is dreaming and can look at his dream objectively, even critically, and perhaps even control its content.

Lucid dreams have been the subject of study and discussion for many years. A Dutch investigator, Dr van Eeden, began recording his own dreams in 1896, and after three years started to distinguish lucid dreams from the others, recording 352 in all. The following had a great impact on him:

> In May, 1903, I dreamed that I was in a little provincial Dutch town and at once encountered my brother-in-law, who had died some time before. I was absolutely sure that it was he, and I knew that he was dead. . . . He told me that a financial catastrophe was impending for me. Somebody was going to rob me of a sum of 10,000 guilders. I said that I understood him, though after waking up I was utterly puzzled by it and could make nothing of it. . . .
>
> I wish to point out that this was the *only* prediction I ever received in a lucid dream in such an impressive way. And it came only too true, with this difference, that the sum I lost was 20 times greater. At the time of the dream there seemed not to be the slightest probability of such a catastrophe. I was not even in possession of the money I lost afterwards. Yet it was just the time when the first events took place – the railway strikes of 1903 – that led up to my financial ruin.

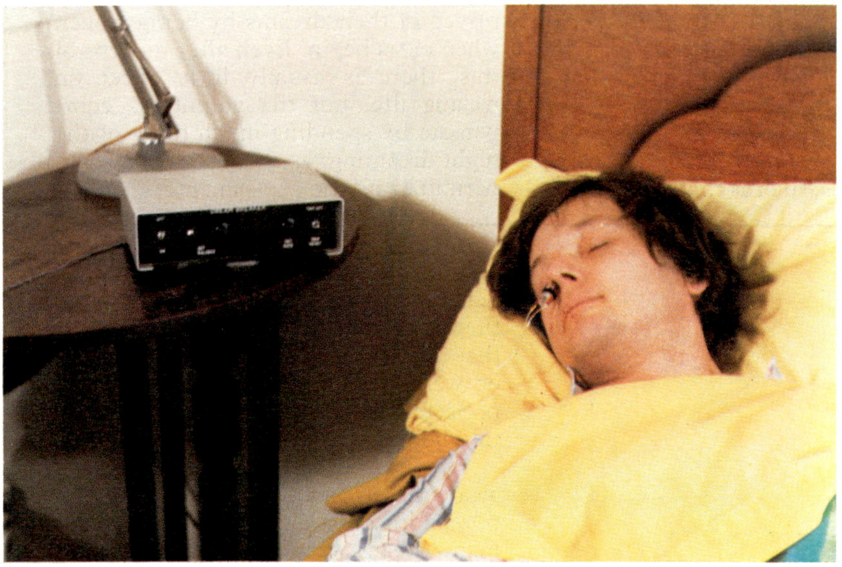

Top: Dr Keith Hearne, who has developed means by which sleepers can gain control over their dreams. His dream machine (above) uses a nose-clip to monitor breathing. When the rate and depth of breathing show a lucid dream is possible, weak electrical shocks indicating the fact are delivered to the subject, who can then become the director of his own 'dream movie'

Dr Keith Hearne, a research psychologist at Hull University, is pioneering a new approach to dream research through lucid dreaming, and he is coupling his study with experiments in ESP. He makes the point that every night something like 400,000 people in the United Kingdom experience nightmares; it would be very easy to find similarities between some of these and later events and conclude that they were premonitions.

When a sleeping person is dreaming, not only does he experience rapid eye movements, but his muscles become virtually paralysed. So, even though the dreamer is having a lucid dream and therefore knows he is dreaming, he cannot signal this fact to the researcher by, for example, switching a button, because his fingers will not move. Dr Hearne decided to see if communication could take place between sleeper and researcher using eye movements as signals.

By pre-arrangement with a subject, Alan Wordsley, it was agreed that eight left-right movements of the eyes would indicate that a lucid dream was happening at that moment. The first such communication was recorded in the Hull dream laboratory in April 1975. Since then the communication has become more sophisticated. Using a pre-arranged code, Wordsley can signal that he is doing some other deliberate act in his dream.

It was, however, very laborious work since, after spending 45 nights in the laboratory, Dr Hearne had recorded only eight lucid dreams. So he devised a 'dream machine' that provides 'conscious controllable dreams'. It detects that a sleeper has begun to dream and then signals to the sleeper by applying a small voltage to his wrist. The sleeping mind then knows that it is dreaming, and the dream becomes a lucid one.

Dream telepathy

Dr Hearne also discovered that the lucid dreamer can signal to the waking world by altering his breathing pattern. He has used this fact in a novel way in order to test ESP. When a sleeper realises he is dreaming, he makes rapid breathing movements. A bedside black box responds to this and immediately sets off an automatic dialling machine. When the other participant in the experiment receives a telephone call and there is silence on the line, he or she knows that the subject is having a lucid dream at that moment. A picture card is selected at random by the recipient of the call and a mental picture is sent to the dreamer just as in the telepathy experiments at Maimonides Medical Center. Dr Hearne's work on ESP in lucid dreams continues.

Since ancient times dreams have been regarded as channels of occult or otherwise extraordinary knowledge. It may indeed be that in the dreaming state human beings are at their most sensitive to every subtle influence impinging on them – from other minds, from the wider Universe, and even from the past and future. Psychic activity during dreaming is now being investigated.

The new work on lucid dreaming suggests that a great advance in our understanding of this aspect of the paranormal is imminent, thanks to the active participation of the dreamer. As Kenneth Hearne says:

> Lucid dreams are the ideal state for testing psi because the dreamer knows he is dreaming and is taking part in a psi experiment, so he can look for a number or an image. Lucid dreams may well be the royal road to a knowledge of psychic phenomena.

The bookies' nightmare

Few precognitive dreams are as useful as those that give accurate descriptions of future winners at horse races – yet sometimes even non-gamblers have such dreams. Is it possible to control this profitable talent?

IT IS A COMMON BELIEF that no one can, or should, make money out of his or her paranormal abilities. Indeed many sensitives believe that, their talent being a gift from God, it would be immoral in the extreme to use it to further their own fortunes. If they did so, they say, the gift would be removed or, worse still, the fortune they acquired would bring with it tragedy and disaster.

H. E. Saltmarsh, the British psychical researcher, made a number of studies of ostensible precognition cases published in the *Proceedings* and *Journal* of the SPR. A careful, cautious and experienced researcher, Saltmarsh found it necessary to accept the reality of precognition. In his book *Foreknowledge* (1938) he gives, among other cases, two that he felt implied the precognition of winners of horse races.

One of them involved a Mr John H. Williams, a Quaker, about 80 years of age, and a staunch opponent of gambling. On 31 May 1933, at 8.35 a.m., Mr Williams woke from a dream about the Derby. In the dream he had been listening to a running commentary on the race on radio. The commentator gave the names of the first four horses. Mr Williams remembered two of them, Hyperion and King Salmon.

The Derby was to be run that day at 2 p.m. Mr Williams told a neighbour whom he met on a bus that morning about his dream. He

Above: Dr Samuel Johnson (1709–1784), who said: 'By pretension to second sight no profit was ever sought or gained.' But this is not always the case – considerable sums have been won at the races (below) as a direct result of dreams

also told it to a business acquaintance.

That afternoon, although so strongly antagonistic towards gambling, he listened to the radio commentary on the race and heard his dream over again, the commentator using identical expressions and giving the same names.

Saltmarsh states that he corresponded with Mr Williams and the two men he had told his dream to that morning. They confirmed Williams's account.

Dame Edith Lyttleton, a member of the SPR and herself a gifted sensitive, collected a number of such cases in her book *Some cases of prediction* (1937), all but one of them sent to her by people who had heard a radio broadcast she made on precognition in 1934.

From the large number of letters she received, she selected some of the most promising for investigation. Every case in the collection was corroborated by at least one person, sometimes by two or three, who had heard of the prediction before fulfilment. Dame Edith stated: 'That some predictions are cases of definite precognition I personally have no doubt at all.'

Among these cases are no less than eight where the result of a horse race or a football match was predicted.

A Mr Freeman dreamed that he visited Lincoln and remained so long in Lincoln Cathedral that on arriving at the racecourse he feared he had missed the first race, the Lincoln Handicap. He was told that he had; it had been won by Outram. On waking Mr Freeman related his dream to some friends. This was in November and the list of entrants in the race was not published until

Above: Hyperion, winner of the 1933 Derby. On 31 May – the night before the race took place – John H. Williams, a Quaker and a staunch opponent of betting, woke from a dream about the Derby. In the dream he had been listening to a running commentary about the race on the radio. The dream commentator gave the names of the first four horses. Mr Williams remembered only two of them: Hyperion and King Salmon. That afternoon, although he would not normally do so, he listened in to the radio commentary on the Derby and heard his dream over again, the commentator using identical expressions and giving the same names. Mr Williams had obviously not benefited from his dream and had no interest in, and indeed a strong objection to, horse racing – so why did he have that dream? Are many more precognitive dreams similarly wasted?

January of the following year. In March the race was won by Outram with rather long odds laid against it.

It is of course possible that such cases could be attributed to chance. G. N. M. Tyrrell has argued:

> The number of dreams and impressions occurring to people is legion and among so vast a number there must be a few chance hits which taken alone would seem very striking. Those only are remembered while the rest are forgotten; and so you get a set of cases which you falsely imagine to be precognitive, but which are really only the cream of the coincidences which are due to natural chance.

This of course is a strong argument, often put forward, and may account for a number of seemingly striking and ostensible precognitions. But even Tyrrell – among other investigators – has pointed out that other factors must be taken into account. For example, in the literature there is a close correlation between the dream or impression that subsequently correlates with a future event and elements of extraordinary vividness and feelings accompanying that dream or impression. These features compel the percipient to do something about it, to tell his circle of friends, to take some action.

A run for his money

The following case, however, is one for which the corroborative evidence is quite remarkable. It concerns John Godley, later Lord Kilbracken, and it began on 8 March 1946 when he was an undergraduate at Balliol College, Oxford. This strange chapter in his life ended 12 years later.

Godley found that he could dream precognitively. Moreover, the subject matter of his precognitive dreams was the winners of horse races. The punters' dream – or the bookies' nightmare – seemed to have homed in on Godley.

On the night of 8 March, he dreamed that in Saturday's evening paper he read the racing results and noticed that two horses Bindal and Juladin had both won at starting prices of 7-1. Godley woke up. He went to a café in town where he met a friend, Richard Freeman. He told him of his dream, they looked at *The Times* and found that Bindal was running at Plumpton that afternoon. Later that morning, he found in the *Daily Express* that Juladin was running at Wetherby.

The undergraduate was now understandably excited. He told some of his friends, who placed bets. Godley himself backed

Win some, lose some

J. H. Jung-Stilling, writer, physician and psychical researcher (right), told the story of Dr Christopher Knape who, in 1768, dreamed that he received the winning numbers of the State lottery. He bought some tickets and won some money. About eight years later the dream recurred – but unfortunately a noise woke him up and he was able to remember only the first two digits. Nevertheless he bought a few tickets and made 20 dollars.

A year later his dream returned. Encouraged by his earlier successes he felt he was on to a certainty. However, although the number did come up he won nothing: a short time before the draw his ticket money was returned, for all the tickets had been sold.

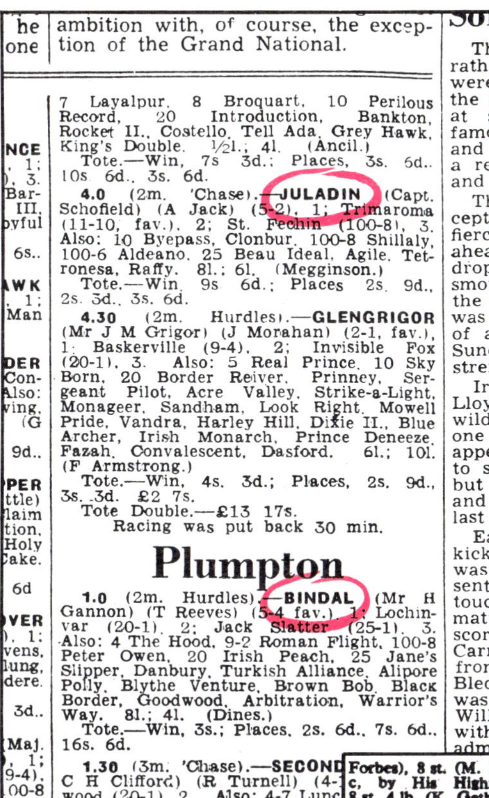

ambition with, of course, the exception of the Grand National.

7 Layalpur. 8 Broquart. 10 Perilous Record, 20 Introduction. Bankton. Rocket II., Costello, Tell Ada, Grey Hawk, King's Double. 1½l.; 4l. (Ancil.)
Tote.—Win, 7s 3d.; Places, 3s. 6d., 10s 6d., 3s. 6d.

4.0 (2m. 'Chase).—JULADIN (Capt. Schofield) (A Jack) (5-2), 1; Trimaroma (11-10, fav.), 2; St. Fechin (100-8), 3. Also: 10 Byepass, Clonbur, 100-8 Shillaly, 100-6 Aldeano, 25 Beau Ideal, Agile, Tetronesa, Raffy. 8l.; 6l. (Megginson.)
Tote.—Win, 9s 6d.; Places 2s. 9d., 2s. 3d., 3s. 6d.

4.30 (2m. Hurdles).—GLENGRIGOR (Mr J M Grigor) (J Morahan) (2-1, fav.), 1; Baskerville (9-4), 2; Invisible Fox (20-1), 3. Also: 5 Real Prince, 10 Sky Born, 20 Border Reiver, Prinney, Sergeant Pilot, Acre Valley, Strike-a-Light, Monageer, Sandham, Look Right, Mowell Pride, Vandra, Harley Hill, Dixie II., Blue Archer, Irish Monarch, Prince Deneeze, Fazah, Convalescent, Dasford. 6l.; 10l. (F Armstrong.)
Tote.—Win, 4s. 3d.; Places, 2s. 9d., 3s. 3d. £2 7s.
Tote Double.—£13 17s.
Racing was put back 30 min.

Plumpton

1.0 (2m. Hurdles).—BINDAL (Mr H Gannon) (T Reeves) (5-4 fav.), 1; Lochinvar (20-1), 2; Jack Slatter (25-1), 3. Also: 4 The Hood, 9-2 Roman Flight, 100-8 Peter Owen, 20 Irish Peach, 25 Jane's Slipper, Danbury, Turkish Alliance, Alipore Polly, Blythe Venture, Brown Bob, Black Border, Goodwood, Arbitration, Warrior's Way. 8l.; 4l. (Dines.)
Tote.—Win, 3s.; Places, 2s. 6d., 7s. 6d., 16s. 6d.

1.30 (3m. 'Chase).—SECOND C H Clifford) (R Turnell) (4-wood (20-1), 2. Also: 4-7 Lunc 11-2 Blue Steel, 100-8 Su (Pullen.)
Tote.—Win, 9s. 9d.; Place £1 5s. 6d.

Above right: Lord Kilbracken (seen here with American film actress Jayne Mansfield) who, as John Godley, had an astonishing run of successful dream predictions about the outcome of races. It began on 8 March 1946 when he dreamed that he read the racing results and noticed that two horses, Bindal and Juladin, had both won their respective races at starting prices of 7–1. The next day he discovered that horses of those names were running and he backed them to win. They did (above), but at different odds from those he had dreamed. On 4 April he had a similar dream – and another win. And on 28 July of that year he dreamed he telephoned his bookmaker; he was told that Monumentor had won at 5–4. On waking he consulted the papers and discovered that the horse with the most similar name was Mentores. He backed it and it won at 6–4 (right). Godley's 'gift' stayed with him, on and off, for 12 years – then it left him abruptly, never to return (much to his chagrin)

Forbes), 8 st. (M. Beary), 2; BRAMHALL PRINCE, gr c, by His Highness—Caramid (Mr. W. Satinoff), 8 st. 4 lb. (K. Gethin), 3.
Also ran:—Safety Curtain, V.E. Day, Tuberose. (Whiteman, at Upper Lambourn.) 1½l., 2l.
STARTING PRICES.—11 to 8 agst Irish Dance, 11 to 4 Safety Curtain, 4 to 1 Bramhall Prince, 5 to 1 Farman Hill, 10 to 1 Tuberose, 33 to 1 V.E. Day. TOTE.—Win 5s. 3d.; places, 3s., 3s. 6d.

6.0 (5.3).—MAIDEN PLATE (£138) (1m. 3f.).
MENTORES, gr f, by Ximenes—Tormentil (Mr. F. N. Gee), 4yrs, 8 st. 12 lb. (K. Gethin), 1; INTRUDER, br c, by William of Valence—Her Awakening (Mr. J. Worthington), 4yrs, 8 st. 12 lb. (M. Beary), 2; COUP DE DIABLE (Mrs. L. Montagu), 5yrs, 9 st. (T. Bartlam), 3.
Also ran:—Daikiri, June Jinks, Skookum Joe, Michael Collins, Puck Star, Shaun, Mahfil. (Chamneys.) Nk., 3l.
STARTING PRICES.—6 to 4 agst Mentores, 7 to 2 Intruder, 4 to 1 Skookum Joe, 10 to 1 Coup de Diable, June Jinks, 25 to 1 others. TOTE.—Win, 5s. 9d.; places, 3s., 2s. 9d., 3s. 9d.
DAILY DOUBLE.—SAXTON and IRISH DANCE; £37 12s.; 64 winning tickets.

both horses. Bindal won at 5-4. Godley put his winnings on Juladin, which in due course won its race.

Not unnaturally, the news spread through the undergraduate community. For a fortnight after the event many were the morning enquiries made of Godley as to whether he had had any racing dreams. Godley was worried. He suspected, probably with good reason, that if he did dream any more horse names and they did not win, he would never be forgiven by those friends and acquaintances who had put their shirts on them.

But it did happen again, on Thursday, 4 April 1946, when Godley was at home in Ireland. Again in his dream he was looking at a list of winners. The only horse he remembered was Tubermore. He told his family at breakfast. At that time, the family lived in such isolation that on a Thursday they would get Tuesday's edition of *The Times* and Wednesday's *Irish Times*. Godley telephoned the local postmistress, who checked the daily papers and found that a horse called Tuberose was running in the Grand National. The name seemed close enough and he and members of his family backed it. The BBC news at 6 p.m. that day told them that Tuberose had won.

By now Godley took the matter seriously. He kept records of his dreams when he returned to Oxford, but it was only on 28 July 1946 that he dreamed that special sort of dream again. In it he telephoned his bookmaker from a telephone box in the Randolph Hotel in Oxford to ask him for the result of the last race. The dream was so vivid that Godley even felt how stuffy the box was. He was told that Monumentor had won at 5-4. Next morning he checked the runners. There was a horse named Mentores. He backed it. It won at 6-4.

The fourth time Godley had one of these dreams, a year later, he dreamed he was at a race meeting. He noticed not only that a horse had an easy win but also that it carried the colours of the Gaekwar of Baroda: not only that but he recognised the jockey, the Australian Edgar Britt. The next race found everyone shouting for the favourite – The Bogie. In fact the excited clamour woke Godley up.

In a fine state of excitement he went downstairs and consulted *The Times*. The Gaekwar of Baroda's horse – called Baroda Squadron – was being ridden by Edgar Britt at Lingfield that afternoon. In the next race the favourite was The Brogue.

Godley backed both horses. And also told a number of people, including his girlfriend Angelica Bohm, and his friend Kenneth Harris. He wrote a statement about his predictions, had it dated and witnessed by three people, took it to the post office where it was placed in an envelope – which, after sealing, was stamped by the postmaster with his official time stamp and locked up in the post office safe. Both horses won.

Fame came to Godley as newspapers all over the world got hold of the story and, perhaps as a result, he was given the post of racing correspondent on the *Daily Mirror*. Predictably, he also became inundated with mail from those who hoped he would share his good fortune with them (or at least give them a few winners), those willing to pay him a percentage of their winnings for information, those seemingly in dire need, and those obviously of unsound mind.

His episodic and unpredictable gift stayed with him. On 29 October 1947 he dreamed of a horse called Claro. He backed it. It was unplaced. However, on 16 January 1949 he dreamed again of the racing results. On waking he recalled that one of the winners had been a horse called Timocrat. Godley backed it – and it won.

On 11 February of the same year, he dreamed of two winners, Monk's Mistake and Pretence. Pretence won – but Monk's Mistake lost.

Nine years later, Godley dreamed that a horse called What Man? won the Grand National. He backed the horse with the most similar name – Mr What – and won the largest amount of money in his career as a dream punter.

Godley's astonishing case is supported by a large number of testimonies. Many of his predictions were told to his fellow undergraduates before the races were begun; at least one was written down, witnessed and sealed away, namely the occasion of his double prediction of Baroda Squadron and The Brogue. He had no idea why he should have demonstrated such a gift in such a way except that he was mildly interested in horses and, like all impecunious students, had a strong motivation to back winners.

Even if we accept that his case, and some of the others described above, shows evidence of a precognitive faculty at work, the idea of people predicting and backing winners may still make us dismiss these cases as somehow 'wrong' or 'frivolous'. However, they too are worthy of study for in their effects clues regarding the mysterious nature of time and that of the human psyche may be ultimately discerned.

Below: Mr What wins the 1958 Grand National, the most popular British Classic (bottom). Godley had dreamed that a horse called What Man? had won the race; he chose the horse with the nearest name – and won the largest sum of money since he had become a dream punter

Crime and psi

Never do psychic powers attract more attention than when they are employed in the investigation of sensational crime. Can the guilty really be detected paranormally, and should the police be more willing to enlist the aid of psychics?

Does Peter Hurkos have any genuine telepathic skills? To the Hollywood celebrities who queue up to see him the answer is a resounding 'yes'. But when the great man's claims were investigated some surprising conclusions emerged

Less sensitive by half?

THE MEDIA LOVE PETER HURKOS – and so do the many Hollywood stars who go to him for paranormal counsel. 'That Hurkos ranges from 87 per cent to 99 per cent accuracy in his psychic projections is irrefutable,' the jacket of Norma Lee Browning's admiring biography *The psychic world of Peter Hurkos* proclaims. These figures – however they were arrived at – certainly look impressive. But what is the truth behind the statistics? Parapsychologists – with the exception of the remarkable Dr Andrija Puharich – rarely mention his name. Unlike his countryman Gerard Croiset, Peter Hurkos has never had the unqualified support of prominent university professors. What, then, is his record of success?

Peter Hurkos was born in the Netherlands as Pieter van der Hurk, but changed his name on emigrating to the United States, of which he is now a citizen, in the 1950s.

Many sensitives recall having had mysterious and inexplicable experiences since early childhood. Hurkos, however, was not born psychic. He acquired his sixth sense only in 1943, as a result of an accident. While he was painting an army barracks he fell from a ladder and had to be taken to a hospital in the Hague. When he regained consciousness he discovered that he now could see events that other people could not see, in distant places and in the future.

His first such vision concerned a fellow patient who was about to be released from the hospital in which Hurkos was staying. Hurkos just *knew* that the man was a British secret agent and would be shot by the Nazis on a crowded street, the Kalverstraat, within a couple of days. He tried frantically to warn the stranger, but the hospital staff thought he was hallucinating. But of course, everything happened as Hurkos had foreseen. The patient, who was indeed a British agent, was shot by the Gestapo on the street named by Hurkos, two days after the vision.

At least, that is what Hurkos and his biographers claim. And here we encounter the perennial problem in assessing anecdotal evidence for ESP. Some incidents seem inexplicable as reported. But can we rely on the reports? In the case of the doomed secret agent, there are compelling reasons for taking the story with a pinch of salt. No independent confirmation of the claim has ever been published. And the State Institute for War Archives in Amsterdam has no record of any British agent having been shot by the Germans in Kalverstraat between 10 July and 5 August 1943, in which period the incident must have occurred. It is scarcely conceivable that such an event would have escaped the notice of the state archivists. 'It is very improbable that this incident really took place,' the Institute replied to enquiries made in 1982.

Hurkos the hero

In his autobiography *Psychic: the story of Peter Hurkos*, the sensitive claims to have distinguished himself by all kinds of heroic acts as a member of the anti-fascist underground movement in Nazi-dominated Holland. His most spectacular feat concerns a friend in the Resistance, Yap Mindemon, who had been arrested by the Germans and taken to a camp in Vught. Hurkos disguised himself as a German officer, went to Vught, introduced himself – in 'flawless German' – as 'Wehrmachtkapitan Robert Fischner' and told the camp commandant that the prisoner was needed at headquarters for questioning. The Germans swallowed this story, and took the psychic to Mindemon. Then, the fake Wehrmacht officer received an ESP warning. Mindemon would assume that Hurkos had really gone over to the enemy side and denounce him as a traitor, thereby giving the game away. Hurkos had no choice except to play the part of the beastly Nazi. Cursing, he hit and kicked Yap until the poor fellow

Above: the Kalverstraat in Amsterdam, circa 1941. This was the scene of the events of Hurkos's first vision when, in 1943, he foresaw the murder of a fellow hospital patient by Nazi soldiers. Hurkos tried to alert hospital staff but the nurses ignored him, thinking he was hallucinating. Perhaps he was – since, despite the claim that his vision became reality two days later, no such incident is on record at the State Institute for War Archives in Amsterdam

Above: the camp where Hurkos, disguised as a German officer, allegedly succeeded in freeing a Dutch prisoner. Although the incident remains undocumented, Hurkos's own dramatic account of the adventure and the brilliant way in which he apparently carried off the impersonation suggests he was cut out for the stage, even Hollywood. This is, indeed, where he has ended up

Top: Peter Hurkos, in the room in which movie star Sharon Tate was murdered, helping police with their investigation. Charles Manson was later convicted of the massacre, which claimed the lives of Sharon Tate and four of her friends. Hurkos said three men were responsible – in fact, three women and one man were involved

became unconscious. The soldiers carried the prisoner to the staff car that the camp commandant had kindly put at 'Robert Fischner's' disposal. 'Arrogantly I slid behind the wheel and drove through the gates of the camp as fast as I could,' the psychic recalls.

There are good reasons for dismissing this story as fictitious. First, because it is contrary to everything we know about how the highly organised and bureaucratic Nazi war machine operated. Second, because the files of the Vught camp, which are preserved at the State Institute for War Archives, do not contain the slightest indication that such a sensational escape ever took place. And third, because a Dutchman whose German was sufficiently 'flawless' to fool a German camp commandant would not have introduced himself as 'Wehrmachtkapitan'. In the German Wehrmacht, such people were not called 'Kapitan', but 'Hauptmann'!

At the end of the war, Hurkos started to give clairvoyant stage performances in the Hague, assisted by his brother, a professional showman. His specialities were 'object readings' – psychometry – and describing pictures blindfold. It is alleged that he made many striking 'hits'. However, a magician would be unlikely to find these successes inexplicable. And Hurkos failed miserably when, around 1947, he was tested by the Belgian scientist Professor Albert Bessemans, a critical investigator of paranormal claims and an expert in several forms of legerdemain.

From the many verbatim accounts of Hurkos's stage performances, it is obvious that he employs the sleight-of-hand of the stage clairvoyant. Subjects are confronted with ambiguously worded (and, thanks to Hurkos's thick Dutch accent, ambiguously pronounced) general statements in such circumstances that they will inevitably project a 'meaningful' interpretation onto them. Afterwards, the 'good sitters' selectively remember what went on.

His clairvoyance explained?

In an article in the *Skeptical Inquirer* Ronald Schwartz presents and analyses transcripts of a typical Hurkos seance that formed part of a radio broadcast. This example demonstrates his technique.

> Hurkos: 'One, two, three, four, five – I see five in the family.'
> Sitter: 'That's right. There are four of us and Uncle Raymond, who often stays with us.'

Another example is as follows:

> Hurkos: 'One, two, three, four, five – how many people are in the family, sir?'
> Sitter: 'Six.'
> Hurkos: 'Five besides you.'
> Sitter: 'Five besides me, yeh.'

Childish as this may seem, it is a very effective technique. 'One, two, three, four, five' applies to a great many different situations. Hurkos does not specify what he means. The specification is provided by the sitter, and the psychic gets the credit. A couple with five children? A hit. A couple with three children? A hit. A couple with four children? That is 'five besides me', also a hit. A couple with two children plus a dog? Well, Hurkos even saw that we have a dog! If the number of actual members of the family is too small, the sitter may help Hurkos by mentioning dead relatives, lodgers or frequent visitors. Or Hurkos may smile and intimate that another child is on the way. If even that does not work, the psychic may indicate that, in fact, he was referring to the sitter's parental home – with or without an Uncle Raymond! In the unlikely case that nothing can be made to fit, Hurkos will simply change the subject.

Around 1950, Peter Hurkos made a vain attempt to conquer Britain. His psychic show was previewed by experienced psychical researchers, notably Dr Eric John Dingwall, who saw nothing suggesting paranormal powers.

The British were amused, but hardly impressed, with Hurkos's attempts to solve the riddle of the theft of the Stone of Scone from Westminster Abbey in December 1950. It had been suspected from the start that the stone had been stolen by Scottish nationalists and taken away to Scotland. Hurkos was of the same opinion. Clairvoyance told him that the stone was hidden in Glasgow. He went there, but did not find it. Small wonder, for the Stone of Scone turned out to have been hidden in a ruined abbey in Arbroath, some 80 miles (130 kilometres) from Glasgow. Hurkos and his biographer, Norma Lee Browning, have repeatedly claimed that, in the Stone of Scone case, the psychic scored a number of striking hits that were later 'covered up' by the embarrassed authorities. Scotland Yard has formally denied that Hurkos or any other clairvoyant was of any help. The Dutch newspapers were able to have a good laugh at Hurkos's expense when, returning from Britain, Hurkos ran into unforeseen trouble. At Schiphol Airport, the Dutch customs searched his luggage and discovered a fair amount of contraband. 'My powers never seem to work when I try to use them on my own behalf,' the psychic sheepishly admitted when, 13 years later, something similar happened in the United States.

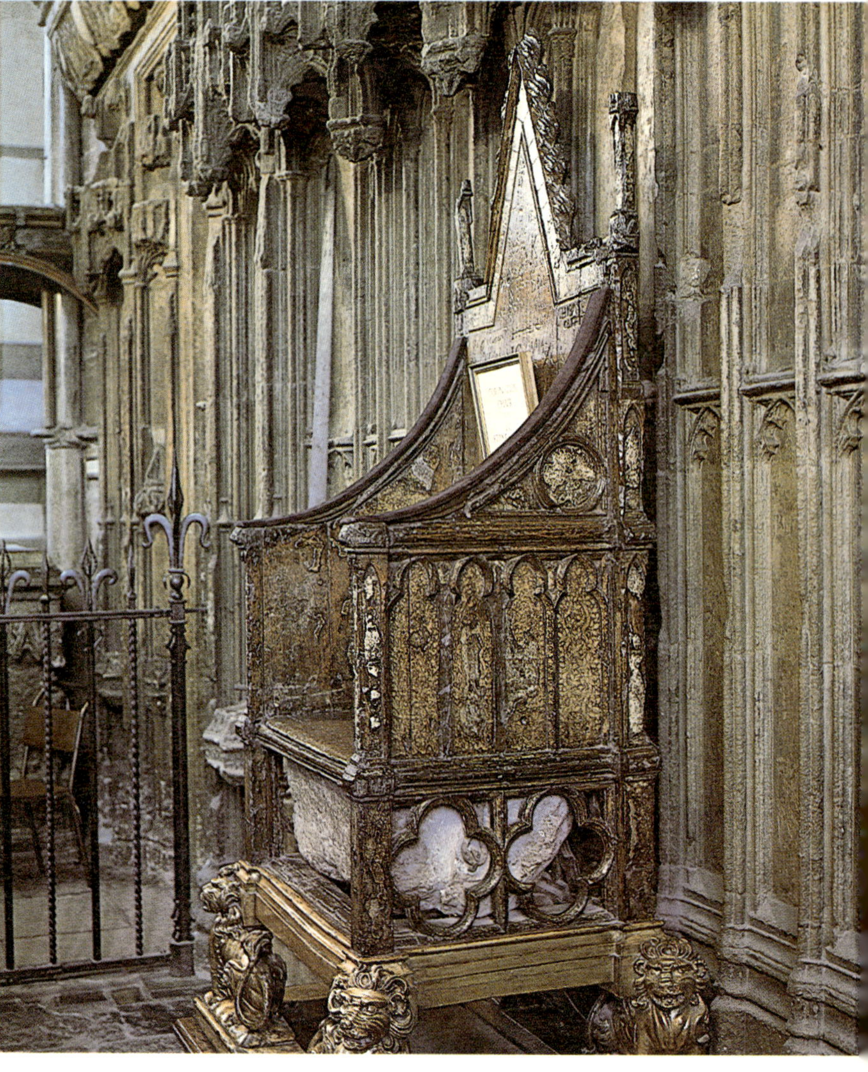

When the Stone of Scone was stolen from its resting place beneath the Chair in the Chapel of Edward the Confessor (above) in Westminster Abbey (right), the incident generated a great deal of public interest. The police were besieged with calls from psychics and clairvoyants who claimed to know where the relic had been hidden. Peter Hurkos came to Britain and, using his psychic powers, suggested the police try looking in Glasgow. The Stone was eventually found some 80 miles (130 kilometres) from there in Arbroath

The million dollar question

These facts prompt the question, does Peter Hurkos have any paranormal powers at all? The author has investigated several of his supposed prize cases. The results of this research throw suspicion on the claim that he ranks 'from 87 per cent to 99 per cent accuracy in his psychic projections'.

Consider the following case, reported in Nat Freedland's *The occult explosion*:

> Peter received a written commendation from the Pope for helping solve the murder of a priest in Amsterdam – and, incidentally, for not revealing that the murderess was mother of the priest's illegitimate child.

No date is given. We know, however, that Hurkos began his career as a psychic detective after the Second World War. In January 1982 I discussed the case with the Reverend Rector Solleveld, who was from 1945 to 1964 secretary to the Roman Catholic diocese of Haarlem, of which Amsterdam is a part. Rector Solleveld told me that the claim could not possibly be true, for the simple reason that no priest had been murdered in Amsterdam since the war. 'As the secretary to the bishop I would certainly have heard of such an incident,' he told me. 'It is also highly unlikely that the Pope would have written a commendation without having informed the diocese.' The Reverend Landsdaal, Rector Solleveld's successor as diocesal secretary, confirmed this. And so did the Amsterdam police, who knew nothing about a murder in which the victim had been a priest.

His greatest triumph

By all accounts, Peter Hurkos's most impressive single feat has been, as Nat Freedland put it, that of 'psychically detecting a rich young firebug who'd been considered above suspicion in the investigation of a rash of arsons.' This case features in almost every book or article ever written about Hurkos. The facts – as reported – are astonishing indeed. The account in the autobiography is as follows. In August 1951, the farmers in the area around the Dutch city of Nijmegen were terrorised by an outbreak of arson. The cost of the damage soon amounted to a total of over £100,000. Two hundred men continually patrolled the countryside, but they could

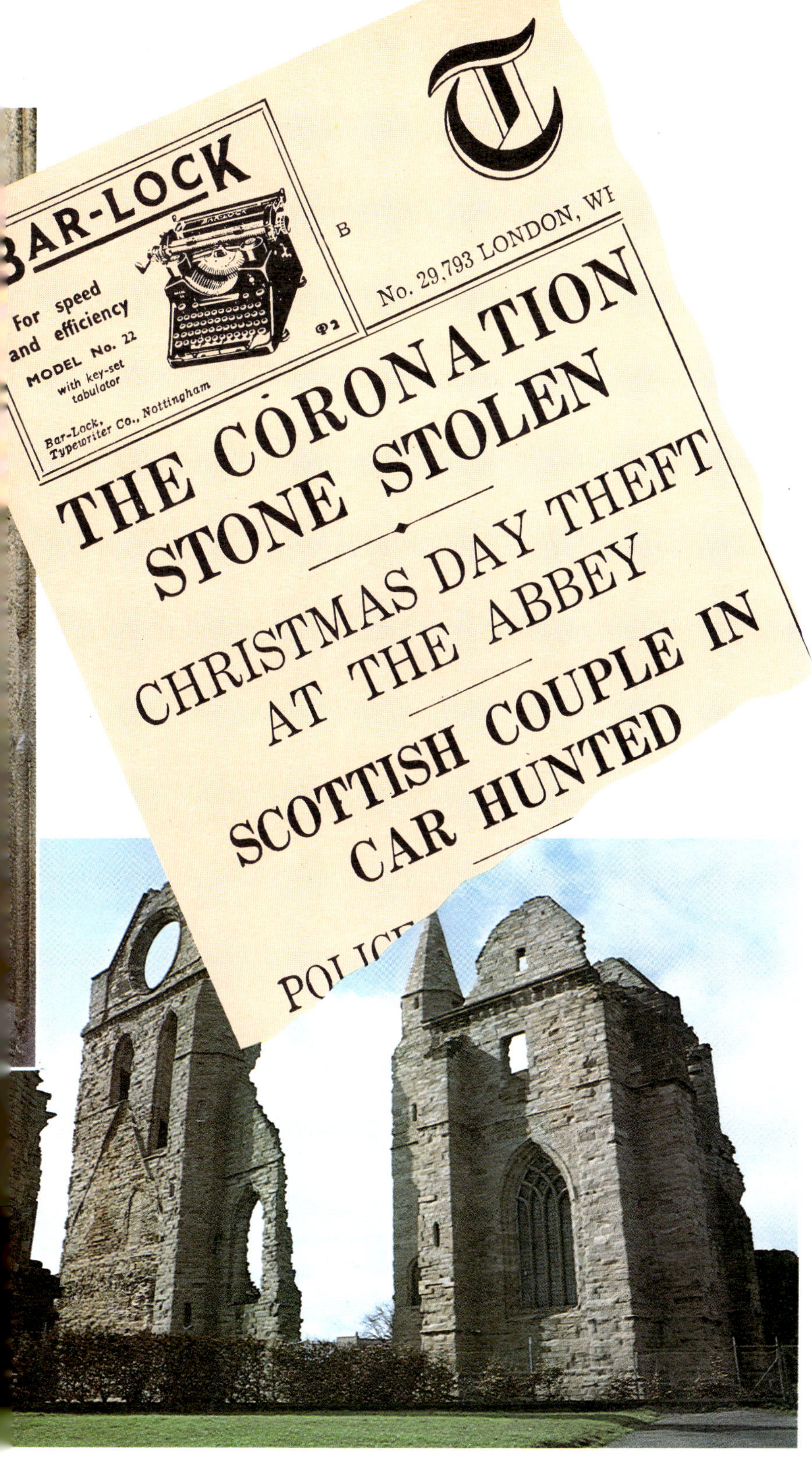
Bar-Lock
For speed and efficiency
MODEL No. 22
with key-set tabulator
Bar-Lock, Typewriter Co., Nottingham
No. 29,793 LONDON, W
THE CORONATION STONE STOLEN
CHRISTMAS DAY THEFT AT THE ABBEY
SCOTTISH COUPLE IN CAR HUNTED

Top: the front page headlines carried by the *Daily Telegraph* on 27 December 1950. It would have been an excellent publicity coup if Hurkos had managed to pinpoint where the Stone had been taken. In fact, he and his biographer claim he came very near to doing just that but, they say, the authorities later, in their embarrassment, 'covered up' the fact

not prevent the mysterious pyromaniac striking time and again. Peter Hurkos offered his assistance. At first, the police were reluctant to co-operate. They had second thoughts when Hurkos proved his talent by accurately describing the contents of police chief Cammaert's pockets. The psychic was taken to the burnt-out farms. In one of these he found a key. The moment he touched it he had a crystal-clear vision of the perpetrator of the crimes: a tall boy, 15 to 16 years of age, a former employee of a baker's shop.

The police asked him if he could pick out the suspect if they showed him pictures of all the town boys. At the police office, Hurkos was given 'the high-school yearbooks' of the Nijmegen schools for the preceding five years. When he pointed to the suspect he had 'seen' psychically the police refused to believe him. Hurkos had selected the portrait of Piet Vierboom, the 17-year-old son of a rich and respected Nijmegen family. 'It can't be,' the police chief exclaimed. 'The family is one of the finest in Nijmegen!' Nevertheless, Piet Vierboom was brought in for interrogation. He denied the charges until Hurkos took over the questioning. The boy could not resist the psychic's piercing glance. 'I cannot lie to *you*. Yes, I did it,' he cried.

The only problem with this remarkable account is that it is not true. The original documents that I have been able to consult tell a very different story.

The prime suspect

The police actually started to suspect Piet Vierboom, the mentally deranged son of an Ooijpolder farmer, soon after the arson attacks began. Piet was a likely suspect because two months previously a mysterious fire had raged at Van Mook's bakery in the village of Bemmel, where the boy was employed. On that occasion, however, the evidence against Piet was not strong enough to warrant an arrest. However, the police remembered the incident on 12 August, when the rash of arsons in the Ooijpolder area broke out. They discovered that the fires coincided with Piet's holiday, which he spent at his parental home. Moreover, on 14 August they found sweet-wrappings at the site of one of the fires. Investigation revealed that Piet had recently bought a considerable quantity of that particular brand of sweets at the local confectioner's shop.

The public prosecutor, Baron Speijart van Woerden, had Piet arrested on 17 August. After the first interrogation, little doubt remained about the boy being responsible for the arson attacks that had been reported throughout the area.

As for Peter Hurkos's contribution: his attempts to help solve the case began only on 18 August, a day after Piet Vierboom's arrest. At his own request, he was allowed to give a demonstration of 'psychic powers' at the Nijmegen police office. A policeman (who had been present at the interrogation of the suspect!) showed Hurkos a photograph of the Vierboom family. Hurkos picked out Piet all right. ESP? The well-known technique of 'muscle reading' – reading the tiny muscular movements that indicate involuntary reactions – seems perhaps a more likely explanation. Baron Speijart was not impressed. 'I cannot imagine that Peter Hurkos's performance had any scientific value whatsoever,' he wrote afterwards. Time and again, the Nijmegen arson affair has been hailed as Peter Hurkos's clairvoyant masterpiece. But the real facts of the case are less than worthy of a psychic superstar.

Croiset: the psychic detective

The Dutch clairvoyant and healer Gerard Croiset was often successful in locating missing persons – dead or alive – and frequently made the headlines for his work with the police. The work of this remarkable psychic has achieved widespread recognition

EIGHT WEEKS after his 24-year-old daughter Carol had disappeared, Professor Walter E. Sandelius was prepared to try anything to find her. Carol had disappeared from a hospital in Topeka, Kansas, USA, and although photographs of the attractive young woman had been circulated throughout the country she was still missing.

Walter Sandelius, a professor of political science at the University of Kansas, had read about the Dutch clairvoyant and healer Gerard Croiset, who had a reputation for finding missing people – dead or alive – and solving crimes with his psychic powers.

So, on 11 December 1959, with no other immediate hope of finding his daughter, he telephoned Utrecht University. He spoke to Professor Willem Tenhaeff, the parapsychologist who had spent many years studying Croiset, and arranged to call again the following day when the clairvoyant would be in Tenhaeff's office.

When he did so, Croiset told the Kansas professor: 'I see your daughter running over a large lawn and then crossing a viaduct. Now I see her at a place where there are stores, and near them a large body of water with landing stages and many small boats. I see her riding there in a lorry and in a big red car.'

'Is she still alive?' asked the anxious father.

'Yes, don't worry,' said Croiset. 'You will hear something definite at the end of six days.'

On the sixth day, as arranged with Croiset, Professor Sandelius went downstairs at 8 a.m. to telephone Tenhaeff. As he picked up the telephone he glanced towards the living room and was astonished to see his daughter sitting on the sofa! Subsequent questioning of the Dutch clairvoyant proved that he had successfully 'seen' across nearly 5000 miles (8000 kilometres) and described Carol's movements with impressive accuracy.

This is one of hundreds of such cases that were investigated and kept on file at Utrecht University. Many were described in Jackson Harrison Pollack's book, *Croiset, the clairvoyant*. But not all had such happy endings. Croiset was often the first person to break the news to relatives that a missing person was dead. Sadly in many of the cases they were children who had fallen into Holland's waterway system and drowned.

The father of five children, Croiset was

Left: Croiset using an electronic version of the Zener card experiment, designed to test the powers of precognition. Croiset's guesses were often significantly above average

Below: Croiset tells the Dutch police in 1963: 'The body is there – you can look for it.' He had located the body of a missing boy in the Vliet canal through psychic means alone

always eager to help distraught parents whose sons or daughters had disappeared, and he refused to take any money for his psychic work.

In the case of one missing boy, Wimpje Slee, Croiset told an uncle over the telephone that he had fallen into the water and drowned, and that his body would be found near a bridge. Then, on Friday 19 April 1963, in order to get stronger impressions, he met the boy's uncle and was able to tell him that Wimpje had drowned near a small house with a slanted weather-vane. But, he added, his body was no longer there. It would be found, however, on Tuesday, between two bridges near the house described.

Newspapers in The Hague heard of the story and published Croiset's prediction the following day, enabling their readers to check for themselves. On Tuesday, 23 April – just as Croiset had foretold – Wimpje's body was discovered floating on the Vliet canal, precisely where the clairvoyant had said it would be found. Not surprisingly, the *Haagsche Courant* headlined its story: 'Croiset proved right once more'.

Pictures of Croiset's craggy features and wiry hair frequently appeared in European and Scandinavian newspapers. He assisted the police to look for missing persons in half a dozen countries and co-operated in tests conducted by leading psychical researchers. But it was to Professor Tenhaeff that he was particularly loyal.

Professor Tenhaeff of Utrecht University and the Utrecht Chief of Police are pictured here with Gerard Croiset. They were a regular team, Croiset helping the police in their search for missing persons and Professor Tenhaeff monitoring the clairvoyant's progress. Few psychics have been as rigorously tested as Croiset

A star performer

Of the 47 psychics and sensitives tested by the professor, Croiset was undoubtedly the star performer. Unlike other clairvoyants who shun research work, Croiset moved to Utrecht in 1956 in order to be closer to the university and to make himself more readily available. And when grateful individuals offered him money for helping to find lost friends or relatives he always declined, saying the only 'reward' he wanted was for them to file a report of what happened with Professor Tenhaeff. As a result, the Utrecht archives must contain some of the best authenticated accounts of clairvoyance on record.

Despite the research work, however, Croiset never really knew how his psychic power functioned. He once described it as like seeing a fine powder, which formed first into dots and then lines. Out of these lines shapes and scenes would form, first in two dimensions then in three. Usually his clairvoyance was in black and white, but if a corpse was involved he would see pictures in colour.

Croiset's involvement in police investigations tends to make his popular image a distorted one. Although he was undoubtedly a brilliant psychic detective, he was hesitant about working on certain cases of murder and theft for fear that he would wrong an innocent person. For example, at the site of a murder he might describe a person in great detail who was not the murderer, but an innocent passer-by. In fact, Croiset said that in 90 per cent of criminal cases he found it difficult to discover the culprit, though he was able to give police valuable clues. On the other hand, in cases of accidental disappearances it is claimed that Croiset had an 80 per cent success rate.

But it was not necessary for Croiset to wait for crimes to be committed or for people to vanish in order to prove that he possessed extra-sensory powers. Instead, Professor Tenhaeff devised a 'chair test', which was repeated with astonishing accuracy over 20 years or more. It demonstrated that Croiset could apparently see into the near future.

It worked like this: a week or more in advance of a large public meeting, Croiset would be asked to make written statements about the person who would sit in a specific seat. On the day of the meeting, individuals would be allowed to sit where they wanted (no one knowing which chair had been selected) or were given numbered tickets at random as they arrived directing them to sit in certain seats. Then Croiset's predictions would be read to the audience. Time and again, the unsuspecting person sitting in the pre-selected seat confirmed that the majority of the statements Croiset had made were correct. These would often consist of the person's sex, a physical description and details of their work, people around them, or descriptions of specific incidents in their life. Occasionally, Croiset could get no advance impressions – in which case it was usually discovered that the seat was left unoccupied on the night.

Gerard Croiset died on 20 July 1980, at the age of 71. But the records on file at Utrecht University of the world's most tested psychic will continue to intrigue and baffle scientists for many years to come.

The story of medium Robert James Lee and his 'vision' of Jack the Ripper seems, on the surface, a perfect example of impeccable psychic sleuthing. But how reliable is that macabre story?

THE MURDEROUS EXPLOITS of Jack the Ripper in the East End of Victorian London excited the avid interest of many mediums and clairvoyants who claimed that their psychic powers enabled them to determine when and where the Ripper would commit his next foul deed. It has even been claimed that the case was eventually solved by the timely intervention of a gifted medium – Robert James Lees (1848–1931).

This claim rests on a document that, according to the *Daily Express*, was 'dictated by the medium', and released after his death in 1931. Its validity is strengthened by the further claim that his story has never been contradicted by the police.

According to the Spiritualist movement, Robert Lees developed his psychic powers during boyhood, and they were so outstanding that Queen Victoria consulted him when he was a mere 13 years old. Other royal consultations followed. By the time of the Ripper murders Lees' sensitivity was at its

The murders and the medium

peak and it led unexpectedly to a loathsome clairvoyant experience.

Lees's posthumous statement records that, shortly after the third Whitechapel murder, while writing in his study, he became convinced that the Ripper was about to strike again. He had a vision of an East End location – a narrow court with a gin palace nearby. He could see the name of the court clearly, he could even see that the clock on the wall of the gin palace stood at 12.40 a.m. A man and a woman entered a dark corner of the court. The man was cold sober, the woman the worse for drink. In her drunken state she leaned against the wall for support and the man quickly closed her mouth with his hand, drew a knife and slit her throat. Then he let her drop to the ground, stabbed her repeatedly, coolly wiped the blade on her dress and walked off into the night.

All this was seen in full harrowing detail. Shaken, Robert Lees hurried to Scotland Yard to warn the police, but he was treated as a harmless lunatic – though to humour him the duty officer wrote down the time and place of the 'forthcoming murder'.

The following night, the Ripper slew a prostitute in the very manner, at the very time, and in the very court named by Lees.

The news of this murder greatly disturbed Lees and he found himself unable to sleep at night. His health suffered so much that his doctor advised a holiday abroad, so Lees moved for a while to the Continent. During that period, the Ripper murdered four more women – but Lees was untroubled by visions and he returned home renewed in health.

A vision of the victim

About one year later Lees had another premonition. This time the vision was far less clear than his first, but he was able to see the murdered woman's face. He also noted the peculiarity of the mutilations – one ear was completely severed, the other was left clinging to the face by a mere strand of flesh.

On recovering from the trauma of this trance, Lees visited Scotland Yard again. There he insisted on seeing the chief inspector of police and poured out the story to him. This time his tale was received with awe, and from his desk the inspector drew out a shabby postcard and handed it to Lees. It was written in red ink and adorned with two bloody fingerprints. It read:

> Tomorrow night I shall again take my revenge, claiming, from a class of women who have made themselves most obnoxious to me, my ninth victim.
> JACK THE RIPPER
> P.S. To prove that I am really Jack the Ripper I will cut off the ears of this ninth victim.

The inspector now looked on Lees's story as a warning sent from heaven, since no one but himself knew of the postcard message. Extra police were drafted into Whitechapel and by the next day the alleys and courts of the area were swarming with plainclothes men. But, despite these precautions, the Ripper struck again. As in the vision, he left his victim with one ear severed and the other hanging.

Robert Lees suffered a further breakdown in health and left London for the Continent once more. While he was abroad, the Ripper killed his sixteenth prostitute and informed Scotland Yard that he would go on until he reached a score of 20.

A grim tally

Shortly afterwards the medium returned to London and dined at the Criterion restaurant in Piccadilly with two Americans. Half-way through the meal Lees cried out: 'Great God! Jack the Ripper has committed another murder.' They checked the time – it was 7.49 p.m. – then all three went post-haste to Scotland Yard.

The police there knew nothing of any such murder but, before Lees had finished dictating his statement, a telegram arrived stating that a body had been found in Crown Court. The time of discovery was given as 8.10 p.m.

At once an inspector drove to Crown Court with the medium. On arriving, Lees pointed to a dark corner and said, 'Look in the angle of the wall. There is something written there.' The inspector ran forward, struck a match and saw that chalked on the wall were the words 'Seventeen, Jack the Ripper.'

The inspector needed no more convincing. According to Lees's posthumous document, he now seemed to see the medium as 'an instrument of Providence' and he became determined to make use of his 'marvellous

Above left: the medium Robert James Lees (1848–1931), who is said to have had precognitive visions of Jack the Ripper's murders

Above: a contemporary newspaper sketch showing the discovery of one of Jack the Ripper's victims. The murders created enormous public interest – and still fascinate researchers today

Left: Brick Lane, Whitechapel, in the East End of London, at the time of the Ripper murders. One of his mutilated victims was discovered in an alley off this thoroughfare

Right: alley leading to Durward Street – formerly Buck's Row – where the Ripper killed Polly Nichols on 31 August 1888

though incomprehensible powers'. Lees 'consented to try to track the Ripper much in the same way as a bloodhound pursues a criminal. There seemed to be some magnetic wave connecting him . . . with the fugitive.'

All that night Lees allowed that strange 'magnetic' influence to guide him. He moved swiftly through the London streets, followed by the inspector and his detectives. At last, at 4 a.m., Lees stopped. He pointed suddenly to the gates of a West End mansion and gasped, 'There is your murderer – the man you are looking for.'

The Ripper at home

The inspector was dismayed for he recognised the house as the residence of one of the most celebrated society physicians. It was unthinkable to link such a distinguished man with the East End slaughter. But the medium insisted that the Ripper was inside. Lees's insistence made the inspector waver and he set the medium a new task. 'Describe to me the interior of the doctor's hall and I will arrest him, but I shall do so at the risk of losing my position.' Without hesitation Lees said, 'The hall has a high porter's chair of black oak on the right hand as you enter it, a stained glass window at the extreme end, and a large mastiff is at this moment asleep at the foot of the stairs.'

The police waited until the servants rose at 7 a.m., then they rang the door-bell. The door opened to reveal a hall exactly as described by Lees, except for one thing – there was no dog in sight. But, as the servants explained, there was a mastiff in the house and it did sleep at the foot of the stairs, but every morning it was let out into the garden as soon as they rose.

'This is the hand of God,' whispered the inspector and he asked for the doctor's wife to be called. She poured out an incredible story. Her husband was a dual personality: to the outside world he was always a kindly and sympathetic man, yet she knew that at times he became a brutal and uncontrollable sadist. Occasionally she had even locked herself and the children into a bedroom to escape his vicious side. Then came the most horrible part of all. The Ripper murders began and she 'noticed with heart-breaking dread that whenever a Whitechapel murder had occurred her husband was absent from home'.

After hearing the wife's account the inspector called in two experts on insanity and the doctor was sent for. When confronted the doctor admitted that his mind had been unbalanced for some years and there were times when he had complete lapses of memory. Once he had found his shirt-front soaked with blood, but he attributed this to a nosebleed during one of his stupors.

A search of the house brought proof that the Ripper had been found at last and the doctor's 'respectable' personality was overcome by horror and remorse. He begged to be killed at once, since he 'could not live under the same roof as a monster'. But this was never seriously considered. Instead, 12 doctors were summoned to constitute a Commission in Lunacy – the Ripper was declared insane and all parties to the proceedings were sworn to secrecy.

The mad doctor was promptly removed to a private asylum for the insane in Islington, north London, where he was lodged under an assumed name. But in order to account for the doctor's disappearance a sham death and burial was arranged – and the public was convincingly duped. Even the asylum keepers and inspectors never dreamed that they had custody of the infamous Jack the Ripper. To them, he was simply inmate number 124 – until the day he died.

This detailed and elaborate account gained a massive circulation when it was

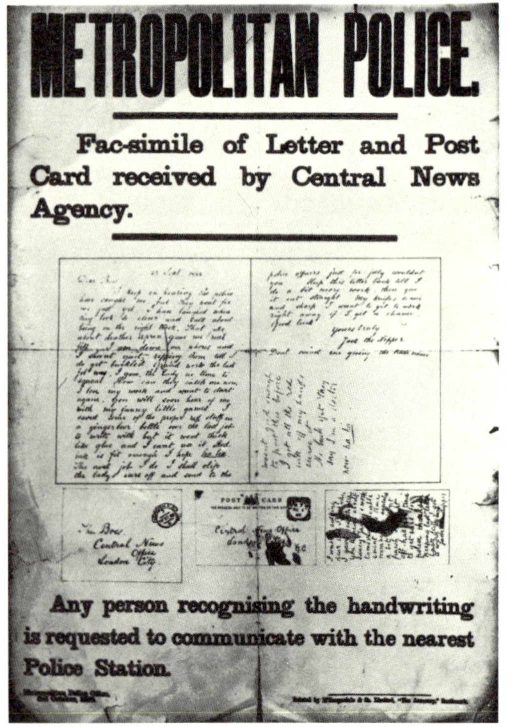

Above: the Duke of Clarence (left) with his father, the Prince of Wales (right) and the rest of his family. Clarence has been cited by more than one writer as a central character in the Ripper story, if not the murderer himself. Certainly his death in 1892 – allegedly from natural causes – conveniently rid the Royal Family of the greatest threat to their reputation

Left: Scotland Yard's search for Jack the Ripper included an unprecedented poster campaign, which used postcards said to be addressed to the police by the Ripper

Left: formerly 'The Ten Bells', this East End pub was the haunt of some of the Ripper's victims

Right: Sir Melville Macnaghten, head of CID at Scotland Yard during the time of the Ripper murders

Below right: Miller Court, where Jack the Ripper butchered his last victim, Mary Kelly

Bottom: Hereward Carrington, the American psychical researcher who was inclined to treat seriously the *Daily Express* story of Lees and the Ripper

published in the *Daily Express* in March 1931. From then on it was repeated in newspapers, magazines and books throughout the world. Its very wealth of detail made it look authentic. It was treated seriously by investigators of standing, such as Hereward Carrington and Dr Nandor Fodor. And leading Spiritualist editor Maurice Barbanell often retold it and never had any doubts about its accuracy. Yet, for all that, this story is completely untenable. There is no possible way of matching it up with the real facts of the murders and their subsequent investigation.

Too many murders

To begin with there were not 17 murders but five. It is true that some earlier and later murders were at times confused with the Ripper's – but that was solely due to a circulation-hungry press and a sensation-seeking public. Sir Melvile Macnaghten, head of CID at Scotland Yard, was adamant that 'The Whitechapel Murderer had *five* victims and five victims only.'

Then the murders were not spread over a period of years, as in the document, but took place over a period of a mere 10 weeks – beginning on 31 August 1888 and ending on 9 November.

Police records show that none of the murders took place at the times quoted and no murder took place at Crown Court. And no postcard was ever received bearing the quoted message. There *was* a postcard written in red ink with red smudges, but this was posted in London on 1 October *after* the double murders of 29 September, and after details of these murders had become public knowledge. The writer of this card and of a previous letter was, in fact, the first to use the name 'Jack the Ripper'. It was believed to have been the work of some sensationalist reporter.

Lastly, the police *have* denied that Lees was involved with the Ripper hunt. In fact, Robert Lees's own diary entries contradict this part of the tale. They show that he did not approach the police until 2 October 1888 – three days after the murders of the 29th.

And remember, at this late stage there was only one more murder to come – that of Mary Kelly. This last killing took place not at 7.49 p.m. in the open, at Crown Court, but in the early hours of the morning, in a sordid room in Miller's Court off Dorset Street.

In that case, what prompted Lees to dictate his absurd statement? The answer is simple: there was no statement! That claim can now be shown up merely as a journalistic device used to sell the story. The truth is that the *Daily Express* report of 1931 turns out to be nothing more than a slightly modified reprint of an article that first appeared in the *Sunday Times-Herald* of Chicago as long ago as 28 April 1895.

The Chicago piece was 'inspired' by the alleged remarks of 'Dr Howard, a well-known London physician . . . who sat on the commission in lunacy.' Despite this, it was simply a few facts coloured by fiction.

What remains true, however, is that Lees did independently state that he himself had cornered the murderer. But others made similar claims. Robert Clifford Spicer for one claimed that *he* had arrested the Ripper; while Dr Lyttleton Stewart Forbes asserted that it was his actions alone that had brought the murders to a halt. Those killings bred a good many illusions and delusions. And in the case of Robert Lees there is not a scrap of proof to show that his firm belief was anything more than one such cherished delusion.

The hunt for the Yorkshire Ripper

For five long years, the Yorkshire Ripper eluded all attempts to track him down. Many psychics, however, were convinced they had the key to the Ripper's identity. Was any of their information of value?

ON 5 JULY 1975, Anna Patricia Rogulskyj was murderously attacked and left for dead near her home in Keighley, West Yorkshire. No one knew it at the time, but this was the first in a terrible series of vicious killings and attempted killings by a man who would elude almost every effort of the police to bring him to justice, and who for five long years was known only by the chilling nickname of 'the Yorkshire ripper'.

The police hunt for the Ripper was one of the most intense, prolonged and, at a cost of several million pounds, one of the most expensive in British history. As the gruesome catalogue of murders grew, and the Ripper began to make headlines all over the world, the mystery increased.

The Ripper killed his 13th and last victim in November 1980. In the years between, thousands of letters and telephone calls offered the police assistance and advice. A good number of these came from people who claimed to have special insights given them by 'the spirits' or by 'psychic powers'.

One of the most dramatic forecasts ran in the *Sunday People* of 1 July 1979. It was given front-page space, and its headline, set dramatically in large type, read: 'FACE OF THE RIPPER'. Alongside was a large sketch of 'the Ripper', drawn by artist Bob Williams.

The account had it that 'famous clairvoyant Doris Stokes has seen the face of the Ripper'. The 'remarkable sketch' was based on her description – the Ripper had a 'scar below his left eye which twitches when he gets agitated'; Doris Stokes had 'got through' to his mother, Molly or Polly, who told her that the killer was married but that his wife had left him. The Ripper was 5 feet 8 inches (1.7 metres) tall, called Ronnie or

Sunday People

JULY 1, 1979 No. 5083 16p

What woman psychic 'saw' for The People

FACE OF THE RIPPER

Mrs. Stokes: He's scared

FAMOUS clairvoyant Doris Stokes has "seen" the face of the Ripper.

And last night she described the most vicious killer of the century so that our artist Bob Williams could draw this remarkable sketch.

Mrs. Stokes also "names" the Ripper.

She says his first name is Johnny or Ronnie and she has given police a choice of three surnames. Mrs. Stokes, who has just returned home after helping Los Angeles police solve a murder riddle, gives a remarkable description of the killer.

She says he is aged between 31 and 32, slightly built, 5ft. 8in. tall, with lank mousy hair which covers his ears.

He parts his hair on the right where there is a small bald patch which he tries to cover up.

Check

He has a distinctive scar on his left cheek, a mark – possibly a mole – on his right cheek bone, and a

The Ripper – as Doris Stokes "saw" him for the Sunday People.

One of the most promising leads given to the police by psychics during the hunt for the Yorkshire Ripper appeared on the front page of the *Sunday People* on 1 July 1979. The famous clairaudient Doris Stokes (right) claimed to know what the Ripper looked like, and the article was accompanied by an artist's impression of her description (below). The police took the information she supplied very seriously – but unfortunately, it led nowhere

Johnnie, and his surname began with the letter M. He lived in a street named Berwick or Bewick.

As shown in the sketch, 'the Ripper' is clean-shaven with long, straight hair, 'mousey hair which covers his ears'. The hair is parted on the right, where 'there is a small bald patch which he tries to cover up.'

As to his background, Doris Stokes believed that 'the Ripper' had received treatment at a hospital, 'possibly Cherry Knowle Hospital at Ryhope, near Sunderland, which specialises in mental cases'.

Mrs Stokes, who is a clairaudient – one who hears voices, rather than a clairvoyant (as she was inaccurately described in the *Sunday People*), who sees things – repeated this information on Tyne Tees television.

But her description caused some annoyance to long-distance lorry driver Ronnie Metcalf of Berwick Avenue, Downhill, Sunderland, who closely resembled it. 'It's not me, so just lay off,' he announced. 'I seem to fit the bill exactly. At first I didn't mind having my leg pulled, but really this is no laughing matter. There are bound to be people who take this clairvoyant stuff seriously and who will be pointing the finger at me.'

These vivid impressions came to Doris Stokes after she had heard a broadcast of the tape recording said to have been made by the killer. Her experience led her to conclude that the Ripper lived on Tyneside or Wearside.

The police were impressed. Northumbria's Assistant Chief Constable, Brian Johnston, was even quoted as saying that the police would be checking on all places with

Above: Gerard Croiset, the Dutch psychic who announced in the *Sun* that the Ripper lived in this area of Sunderland (top), possibly in the flats marked in the photograph with the figure 7

the names Berwick and Bewick in their region.

Five months later, the Dutch psychic detective Gerard Croiset pronounced, and seemed to agree broadly with Mrs Stokes. In the *Sun* of 28 November 1979, he said that the Ripper had 'long hair cut straight across the neck'. He limped due to a damaged right knee, and he lived in the heart of Sunderland in a large block of service flats over a garage. When about six years old, the Ripper had been in 'a kind of institution for psychologically disturbed children'.

Clairvoyant Flora MacKenzie reached quite different conclusions – she forecast that the killer would live in the Barnsley-Sheffield

Information received

In response to a request in the magazine *The Unexplained*, the editor received a large amount of psychic information about the possible identity of the Yorkshire Ripper. He was able to pass on some of this material to the Yorkshire police.

Many of the premonitions, however, were too vague to be of much help in tracking down the Ripper; one anonymous writer, for example, claimed that the Ripper 'will be cornered by police and a violent struggle will take place when he is found' – an event that can be expected whenever a criminal with a known record of violence is apprehended. Other predictions came close to the truth, but not quite close enough: T. A. Ennis of Lancaster forecast that the Ripper would have claimed '14, or it could be 17, victims' before he was caught (the true number was 13), and M. S. Breakspear of Aldershot, writing on 2 December 1980, forecast that he would kill a nurse, possibly called Mary, possibly on the 14th of the month (by this time the Ripper had killed his final victim).

This sketch of the Ripper was sent to *The Unexplained* by London psychic Philip Rowe

There were other premonitions that came extraordinarily close to the truth. One John Pope, of Barnet, Hertfordshire – who gained his information from a crystal ball he had inherited from his aunt – claimed that the Ripper was in his 30s, with black hair that stuck upwards as if it were held in place by a permanent wave, and that he had a small goatee beard. And Ian Johnson of Market Drayton, Shropshire, wrote that a news broadcast had triggered a vision of 'a man with curly black hair and a beard. His features were indistinguishable. He was wearing a blue garage uniform.'

The premonitions sent in by readers had one thing in common with those published in the national press before the arrest of Peter Sutcliffe: even the most detailed of them were too vague to provide useful clues for the police to work on. Many experts believe that clairvoyance is a gift that can be improved by training; perhaps the first aim should be greater accuracy.

area. But Patrick Barnard produced his own conflicting forecast – one much more detailed than anyone else's.

Mr Barnard's story took over the front page of the Southend *Evening Echo* on 24 November 1980. He described how he had looked down on the Ripper 'as if from my bedroom window'. The killer was a man of average build with dark hair, and

> . . . on the shoulders of his black duffel coat were the white letters RN. It seemed he was walking out of a submarine dockyard. I felt it was in Scotland and I got the impression he was working on a nuclear submarine. Wouldn't that explain everything? A crewman on a sub, at sea for months at a time, while the police are chasing their own tails looking for him ashore?

In his visions, Mr Barnard saw an old and abandoned green railway coach in an overgrown and disused siding. This was the place where the Ripper came after each murder to change his clothes. The Ripper's home was also close to a railway – a top flat in a dilapidated grey house over a railway tunnel.

Mr Barnard had no doubts whatever about the accuracy of his telepathic vision. 'I have seen these things as plainly as slides projected upon a screen,' he said. But the Leeds police were not impressed. They first reacted by saying, 'We get thousands of people like this, all ringing up and telling us something different.' They added 'Railway coaches in these parts don't have green livery.'

Above: Patrick Barnard, who produced by far the most detailed forecast of the Ripper's identity. His prediction, published in the Southend *Evening Echo* of 24 November 1980, claimed that the Ripper was a crewman on a submarine

Below: the 'amazing dossier' of information supplied to the *Daily Star* by an anonymous medium

Yet two days later, an *Evening Echo* reader reported that he had seen green railway coaches on a disused line close to 'a remote coastal road near Hull'. Inspector Terry Lamb of the Hull police took this report seriously enough to send out officers to trace the coaches – but later reports showed that the searches led nowhere.

Days after Patrick Barnard's disclosure came a crop of forecasts. The *Daily Star* ran a front-page lead story and devoted a double-page spread to what it called an 'amazing dossier' from an anonymous medium. The Ripper was now alleged to be between 40 and

DAILY STAR SPECIAL—AN AMAZING DOSSIER THAT COMES FROM BEYOND THE GRAVE

THE WORLD OF THE RIPPER

Each person here knows the identity of the maniac—perhaps without realising it

by ELLEN PETRIE

THE DAILY STAR yesterday handed the police an astonishing dossier from beyond the grave on the world of the Ripper.

Readers should note that if only one detail proves correct—and there is a wealth of information—it could provide the clue that finally traps the savage killer.

One remarkable suggestion made is that "the Yorkshire Ripper" actually lives in neighbouring Lancashire — possibly in the Bolton area.

He is also said to have already been questioned by police during routine inquiries on the Ripper.

The dossier includes the seven drawings on these pages carried out by a famous psychic artist following instructions from her spirit guide.

Supremo

Conscience

HOW YOU CAN HELP

MOTHER Elderly — probably in her 80s — domineering and religious. The Ripper, is very much under her influence, one reason he has never married.

THE MOST SAVAGE KILLER OF OUR TIME

- CLAIRVOYANT information handed to police by the Daily Star claims that the killer is 40-45 years old, of stocky build, 5ft. 3ins. tall. Fair hair, could recently have been dyed. Eyes blue. Moles on face.
- HANDS, large and powerful; feet small. There is something wrong with his right toes.
- PROBABLY a plumber by trade who once worked as a miner. Dresses in quiet check shirts and blue overalls.
- LIVES in Lancashire, possibly in the Bolton area, and drives a blue van.
- BORN in London, an only child, he moved North when six years old. Hobbies, shoe repairing and wood carving.
- NEVER married. Extremely kind to children. Has a dog — probably black — and may keep a parrot.
- RECEIVED psychiatric treatment in the early 70s. Has already been seen by police during routine inquiries in the Ripper investigation.
- ENJOYS a game of dominoes, but basically a loner. Victims are not chosen at random but watched for days, sometimes weeks, before an attack.

NEIGHBOUR Visits public house called The Crown. Passes time of day with the killer in the park where they both walk their dogs. Connections with Labour club and a nearby poster showing huge ice cream cone.

CAR mechanic in garage, also does private work, possibly for Ripper. Plays darts, sometimes watched by the killer. Public houses: Swan, Anchor, Queen's Head. Fair-haired. Does car with number 297 mean anything?

FRIEND of mother, possibly neighbour. Works in shop or factory connected with baking. Also knowledge of pub trade; possibly works as a part-time barmaid.

HUSBAND of woman on left? Connections with a public house called The Swan. There is a cracked mirror and juke box. He owns an alsatian.

HOME HELP May have visited Ripper's home. Links with an old people's home. Visits second hand clothes shop and also has a prison connection.

NAME of Jack? Night watchman, but previously held a managerial position in an engineering firm. May be a member of a photographic club.

45 years old, of stocky build with blue eyes, moles on his face, and fair hair that 'could recently have been dyed'. He was born in London but moved north when six years old. He was probably a plumber by trade, but once worked as a miner. He was unmarried, partly owing to the influence of his mother – a domineering and religious woman 'probably in her 80s'.

A list of 12 'psychically supplied' names of acquaintances was included, together with other fine details – one being the remarkable fact that the Ripper possibly owned a parrot!

The 'amazing dossier that comes from beyond the grave' was illustrated by seven drawings supplied by a 'famous psychic artist'. An eighth drawing, of the Ripper himself, was held back in case it hindered police investigations.

The next development came when medium David Walton went into print, in *Psychic News* of 6 December 1980. His information included the tit-bit that the Ripper 'sometimes disguises himself as a woman'. Walton also believed that he had contacted the Ripper's dead father, and had homed in on a terraced house, where the killer occupied a small back room.

True or false?

Nella Jones, a Kent clairvoyant, agreed with Walton's hunch that the Ripper was a transvestite. 'That's right. I told the police about that months ago. He could also appear as a priest,' she said. When the Ripper was finally tracked down in January 1981, it became clear that this – and all the other descriptions by psychics – were wide of the mark. But, in another series of predictions, Mrs Jones had been absolutely accurate.

Between October 1979 and January 1980, Mrs Jones gave a series of interviews to journalist Shirley Davenport, who passed on her premonitions to the police. Mrs Jones said the killer's name was Peter, that he lived in a large house, No. 6 in the street, on an elevated site in Bradford, Yorkshire. 'Peter', she said, was a lorry driver, and his cab bore the name of the company he worked for; the name began with the letter C. She said that 'Peter' had been a tearaway in his youth, and added that he had committed other crimes. In an interview in early November 1980 she told Miss Davenport that the next murder by the Ripper would be on 17 November.

The Yorkshire Ripper is called Peter Sutcliffe. He lived with his wife Sonia in a large house on an elevated site; the address was No. 6, Garden Lane, Heaton, Bradford. He worked as a lorry driver for a haulage company named Clarks. He had been a tearaway in his youth and had been charged with a number of offences. On 17 November he killed Leeds student Jacqueline Hill.

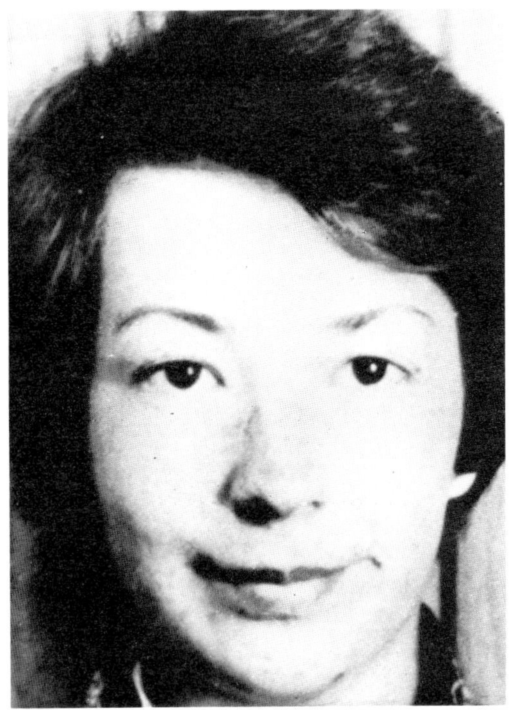

The only psychic to give a really accurate description of the Ripper was Kent clairvoyant Nella Jones (left). In an interview given in early November 1980, Mrs Jones stated that the Ripper was called Peter, that he worked as a lorry driver for a firm whose name began with the letter C, and that he would kill his next victim on 17 November. The Ripper (right) is called Peter Sutcliffe; he worked as a lorry driver for a firm named Clarks (above), and he claimed his final victim, Leeds student Jacqueline Hill (below left) on 17 November. There is an interesting connection with the original Jack the Ripper: Mrs Jones thought – erroneously as it turned out – that the Yorkshire Ripper might be a transvestite. There had also been a suggestion that the Victorian Ripper might disguise himself as a woman – or, indeed, even be one

In the footsteps of the Ripper

Many of the psychic descriptions of the Ripper supplied to the police turned out to be wrong. There is however a chilling possibility that these predictions refer to another murderer – whose grim career was mysteriously intertwined with the Ripper's.

AS WITH every major criminal case where the perpetrator of the crimes cannot be found, the Yorkshire Ripper investigation attracted hordes of psychics, seers, mystics, an assortment of cranks, armchair detectives, and members of the public who honestly believed that they had vital information about the killer's identity. Reviewing these claims in the light of what is now known about Peter Sutcliffe, the Ripper, it can be seen that few of these people came anywhere near the truth. This is particularly true of those people whose proclamations were based on dreams, visions, divinations, tea-leaf readings and crystal-ball gazing – with the one exception of Nella Jones.

The psychic prophecies in the Ripper case raise the serious question of the value of psychics in police investigations. There are frequent claims that the police either ignore or do not acknowledge the often remarkable success of psychics, that extra-sensory abilities are not taken seriously. Where accepted investigative procedures have failed to produce any leads, it is argued, the police should call on the help of psychics.

But how far is this point of view justified? Can psychics be depended upon to the extent that it is reasonable to instruct policemen to follow up their leads?

There are several impressive stories about people whose extra-sensory powers have led to the arrest of criminals or the finding of missing persons. One of the most remarkable psychic sleuths is Peter Hurkos, a psychometrist – somebody who divines details about a person through contact with, or proximity to, something belonging to that person. And Gerard Croiset, who died on 20 July 1980, was a clairvoyant whose reputation as a finder of missing children remains without parallel.

Extra-sensory abilities that are of use in criminal detection can only rarely be described as true clairvoyance: in almost every case of clairvoyance there is somebody involved in some aspect of the investigation who has the required information, so telepathy could be taking place.

Two of the current first-division psychic detectives are women: 55-year-old New

Above: Peter William Sutcliffe, the Yorkshire Ripper, is conducted under police escort into Dewsbury Crown Court on 6 January 1981, to be charged with the murder of student Jacqueline Hill – the last of the 13 horrific Ripper murders. As the list of victims grew, the police received hundreds of messages from psychics who believed they had the clue to the Ripper's identity. After the Ripper's capture, it seemed that a number of descriptions had been fairly accurate – but none had provided any fresh leads. Even Peter Sutcliffe's wife Sonia (right) claimed that she did not know her husband was the Ripper

Jersey grandmother and housewife Dorothy Allison and attractive Californian Kathlyn Rea. Both have a significant number of failures, but their track record in locating missing persons is nonetheless staggeringly successful.

St Louis, Missouri, USA, is the base of the PSI squad – a group of psychics licensed as private detectives, who operate from the $80,000 home of Bevy Jaegers. The home was a gift from Pete Dixon, a St Louis commodities broker who made more than a million dollars after acting on advice given by Mrs Jaegers. She began making her reputation when she accurately described the location of the body of a murdered mission woman, said where her car could be found, and described the way in which she had been killed.

However, even though the United States police have openly sought the help of psychics and publicly acknowledged their services, all but the most enlightened police departments seem happier with the tried and trusted police methods. Psychics claim that the police fear ridicule from those who do not believe in ESP phenomena, or of being accused of not doing their job properly. The real reason, however, seems to be that for every impressive story about people whose extra-sensory powers have brought a criminal to justice, there are countless others in which psychics, seers and mystics have led the police on a wild goose chase, too much of their information being of a vague variety – such as 'The man you are looking for lives alone and has a mole on his left knee.'

One of the problems that confronted the West Yorkshire police in their hunt for the Yorkshire Ripper was the sheer volume of information they had to deal with, much of it consisting of useless snippets of information. The divinations of psychics simply threatened to blow the fuse of a system that was already overloaded.

Above: Bevy Jaegers, leader of the Missouri 'PSI squad' – a group of US psychics licensed as private detectives

Alex Sanders, self-styled King of the Witches, announced that the Ripper lived alone in a flat near some railway arches in South Shields. It remains a matter of speculation how many policemen it would have taken to locate every single man living in a flat near railway arches in South Shields. Peter William Sutcliffe lived in the Heaton area of Bradford.

A Dutch engineer, Wim Virbeek, said the Ripper was a washing-machine mechanic from Aberdeen. How long would it have taken to question all the washing-machine mechanics in and from Aberdeen?

Dutch clairvoyant Dono Meijling toured the murder sites and gave the police eight specific leads, one of which was that the killer was related to Detective Chief Superintendent Jim Hobson, one of the policemen leading the hunt for the Ripper. None of the leads proved helpful.

Reginal du Marius, an astrologer who lives in Manchester, where two of the murders took place, confidently announced on 26 July 1979 that the Ripper would strike the following day. The Ripper didn't. So much for astrology.

These psychic pronouncements did not inspire confidence in extra-sensory perception. But they *did* raise a disturbing question in the minds of many people. Were the

Right: Alex Sanders (left), the self-styled King of the Witches. He believed that the Ripper lived by himself, in a block of flats near some railway arches, in South Shields. How long would it have taken police to check the identity of every single man living in such a flat?

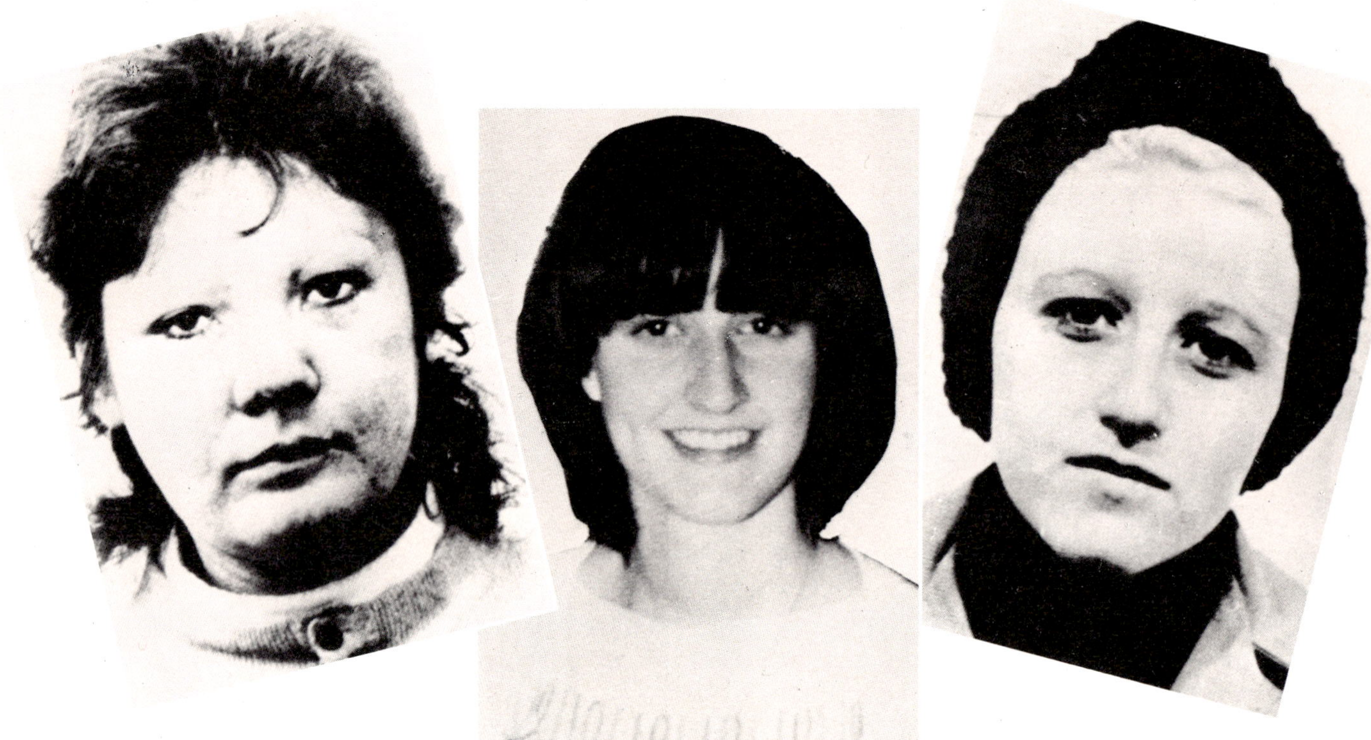

Some of the Ripper's victims: Josephine Whitaker (centre) and Yvonne Pearson (right). Peter Sutcliffe denies killing Joan Harrison (left), with whose murder he was charged. If he did not, who did? Could it be that the psychic descriptions of the Ripper that were dismissed as inaccurate actually refer to someone quite different – the murderer of Joan Harrison?

psychics describing the Yorkshire Ripper – or were they tuning into someone else entirely?

In 1975 a Preston prostitute named Joan Harrison was found murdered. Shortly before she died, she had had sex with a man. Forensic tests revealed that his blood group was B and that he was a 'secretor' – someone who secretes minute particles of blood into his semen and saliva. B secretors are rare, amounting to around 6 per cent of the population.

It was some time before the police officially accepted Joan Harrison as a Ripper victim. In other killings, the Ripper used a knife, but Joan Harrison was not stabbed, and there was no evidence that the Ripper had had sex with his victims – yet Joan Harrison had had sex shortly before she died, presumably with her killer.

Doubt about the Ripper

In the course of 1978 and 1979 the police received a total of three letters and a tape recording purporting to be from the Ripper, and claiming responsibility for the Harrison murder. They also contained information that the police believed could have been known only to themselves and to the killer. Forensic tests on the envelopes revealed that the sender was a B secretor.

Although the blood group of the sender connected him with only one murder, that of Joan Harrison, he did make a number of remarks that convinced the police that he was the Ripper. But when Peter Sutcliffe finally admitted to being the Ripper, he denied killing Joan Harrison or sending the Ripper letters and tape. Since he was not a B secretor – he was, however, of blood group B; an interesting coincidence – the police had no alternative but to believe him.

Who, then, killed Joan Harrison? A man living alone in a flat near some railway arches? A washing-machine mechanic from Aberdeen? It remains possible that this man could have confused the psychics. He certainly confused other people. There are many coincidences about the Ripper case that are Fortean in the extreme.

On Joan Harrison's left breast there was a bite-mark made by somebody with a gap between their upper front teeth. A similar mark was found on the left breast of Ripper victim Josephine Whitaker. Peter Sutcliffe has a gap between his upper front teeth. He denies killing Joan Harrison and categorically denies biting Josephine Whitaker's left breast. Who or what, then, left the mark?

Ripper victim Yvonne Pearson was last seen alive on 21 January 1978. Her body was not found until 26 March 1978. Beneath the body, positioned in a way that convinced the police that it could only have been put there deliberately, was a copy of the *Daily Mirror*. It was dated 21 February, one month to the day after Yvonne Pearson was last seen alive. The only explanation is that Peter Sutcliffe put it there, but he denies having done so. So who did? By coincidence – perhaps – one of the letters purporting to be from the Ripper was posted to the *Daily Mirror*.

Somebody else is connected with the Ripper killings, even if only insofar as he wrote the letters, sent the tape – and possibly murdered Joan Harrison. There remains a chilling possibility: did *he* confuse the psychics? Whoever he is, he is still at large.

Up and away

To Man – an earthbound species – the ability of birds to fly has always been a potent symbol of freedom. Did our ancestors have the ability to master levitation or even to achieve astral projection – the flight of the soul?

Defying the law of gravity

The power to overcome the force of gravity may be the product of long training, or may occur spontaneously, amazing levitator and onlookers alike. There have been many famous cases of this extraordinary talent

THREE NOTABLE MEMBERS of London society witnessed, on 16 December 1868, an incident so extraordinary that it is still the focus of controversy. Viscount Adare, the Master of Lindsay and Captain Wynne saw the famous medium Daniel Dunglas Home rise into the air and float out of one window in a large house in fashionable London and then float in at another – over 80 feet (24 metres) from the ground it is claimed. D. D. Home became known primarily for his levitations, of himself and of objects – on one occasion a grand piano – but he was not alone in having this 'impossible' ability to defy the law of gravity.

St Joseph of Copertino (1603–1663) flew into the air every time he was emotionally excited. Being of an excitable nature, he often made levitations, and they were well witnessed. A simple peasant – some say he was actually feeble-minded – this boy from Apulia, Italy, spent his youth trying to achieve religious ecstasy by such means as self-flagellation, starvation and wearing hair-shirts. He became a Franciscan at the age of 22, and then his religious fervour 'took off' quite literally.

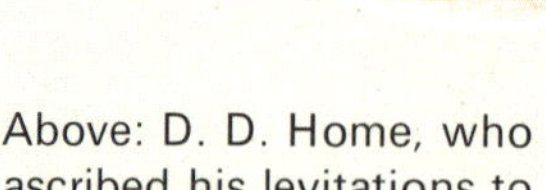

Above: D. D. Home, who ascribed his levitations to the work of spirits

Above right: Home floats into the air with no visible means of support

Below: St Joseph of Copertino owed his canonisation to his ability to levitate

St Joseph and his 'giddiness'

Joseph became something of an embarrassment to his superiors. During mass one Sunday he rose into the air and flew onto the altar in the midst of the candles; he was quite badly burned as a result.

For 35 years Joseph was excluded from all public services because of his disconcerting habits, but still tales of his levitations spread. While walking with a Benedictine monk in the monastery gardens he suddenly flew up into an olive tree. Unfortunately he couldn't fly back down, so his fellow-monks had to fetch a ladder.

A surgeon, at least two cardinals and one pope (Urban VIII), among many others, witnessed Joseph's extraordinary spells of weightlessness – which he called 'my giddinesses'. He spent his entire life in a state of prayer, and the Church concluded the levitations must be the work of God.

Another levitating saint was St Teresa of Avila, who died in 1582. This remarkable mystic experienced the same feelings as many people feel during the common 'flying dreams'. She described how she felt about her levitations:

> It seemed to me, when I tried to make some resistance, as if a great force

> beneath my feet lifted me up. . . . I confess that it threw me into great fear, very great indeed at first; for in seeing one's body thus lifted up from the earth, though the spirit draws it upwards after itself (and that with great sweetness, if unresisted) the senses are not lost; at least I was so much myself as able to see that I was being lifted up. After the rapture was over, I have to say my body seemed frequently to be buoyant, as if all weight had departed from it, so much so that now and then I scarce knew my feet touched the ground.

So insistent were her levitations that she begged the sisters to hold her down when she felt an 'attack' coming on, but often there was no time for preventive measures – she simply rose off the floor until the weightlessness passed.

Most levitators are believers in one particular system, be it Christianity, Hindu mysticism, ancient Egyptian mysteries or Spiritualism. It was to this last category that D. D. Home belonged.

Born in Scotland and brought up in America, Home was a puny, artistic child. At the age of 13 he had a vision of a friend, Edwin. Home announced to his aunt's family that it must mean that Edwin had been dead for three days. This was proved to be true. Home's career as a medium had begun – but it was not until he was 19 that he was to defy the law of gravity.

Ward Cheney, a prosperous silk-manufacturer, held a seance at his home in Connecticut in August 1852. D. D. Home was there to provide the usual 'Spiritualist' manifestations – table-turning, rappings, floating trumpets and mysterious lights.

Home was quite capable of keeping the guests entertained in this fashion but something happened, completely unannounced, that made his name overnight. He floated up into the air until his head was touching the ceiling. Among the guests was the sceptical reporter, F. L. Burr, editor of the *Hartford Times*. He wrote of this bizarre and unexpected incident:

> Suddenly, without any expectation on the part of the company, Home was taken up into the air. I had hold of his hand at the time and I felt his feet – they were lifted a foot [30 centimetres] from the floor. He palpitated from head to foot with the contending emotions of joy and fear which choked his utterances. Again and again he was taken from the floor, and the third time he was carried to the ceiling of the apartment, with which his hands and feet came into gentle contact.

Home's career advanced rapidly; he was lionised in seance parlour and royal court alike. He came back to Europe to inspire adoration and scepticism (Robert Browning's

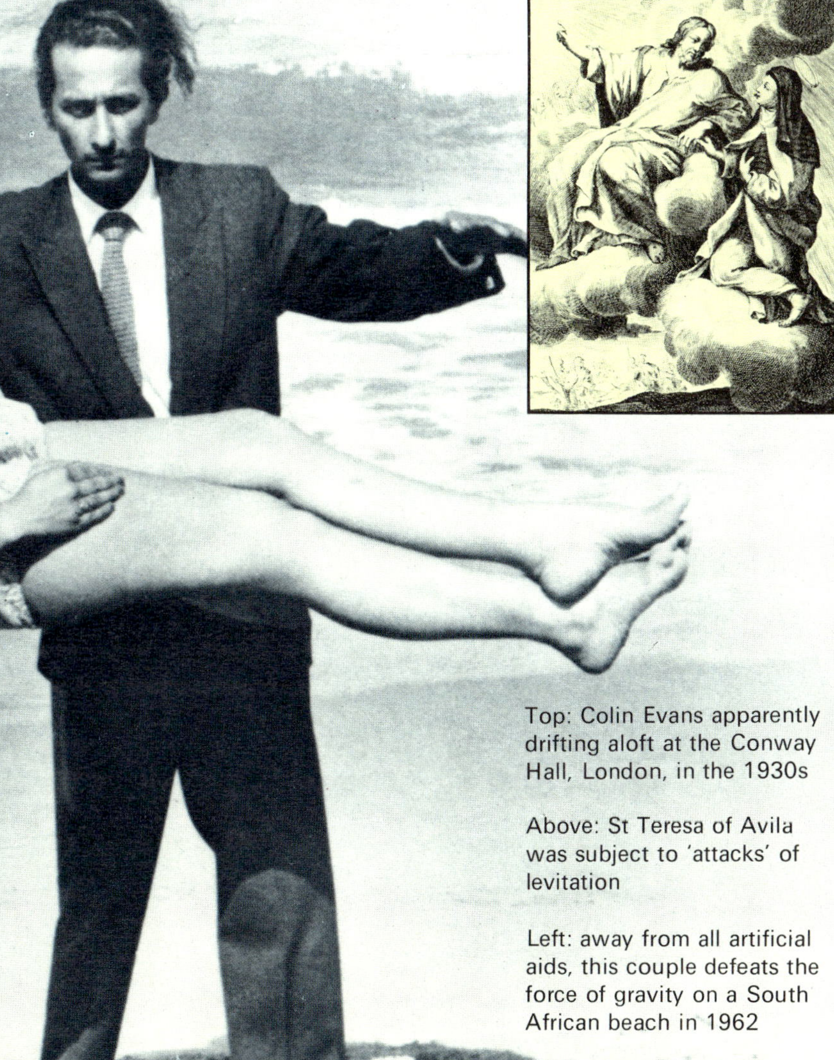

Top: Colin Evans apparently drifting aloft at the Conway Hall, London, in the 1930s

Above: St Teresa of Avila was subject to 'attacks' of levitation

Left: away from all artificial aids, this couple defeats the force of gravity on a South African beach in 1962

satirical poem 'Mr Sludge' was based on his own biased view of the medium). Wherever he went there were bizarre phenomena – winds howled in still rooms, apports of fresh flowers fell from the ceiling, doors opened and shut, fireballs zigzagged around the room – and Home levitated.

The famous occasion already mentioned when he floated out of one window and in through another, is still the subject of heated debate, particularly since the incident was documented by respectable witnesses. One of them, the Master of Lindsay (later the Earl of Crawford) wrote:

> I was sitting with Mr Home and Lord Adare and a cousin of his [Captain Wynne]. During the sitting Mr Home went into a trance and in that state was carried out of the window in the room next to where we were, and was brought in at our window. The distance between the windows was about seven feet six inches [2.3 metres], and there was not the slightest foothold between them, nor was there more than a 12-inch [30-centimetre] projection to each window, which served as a ledge to put flowers on. We heard the window in the next room lift up, and almost immediately after we saw Home floating in the air outside our window. The moon was shining full into the room; my back was to the light, and I saw the shadow on the wall of the windowsill, and Home's feet about six inches [15 centimetres] above it. He remained in this position for a few seconds, then raised the window and glided into the room feet foremost and sat down.

Sceptics such as Frank Podmore or, more recently, John Sladek, have tried to disprove this levitation, although neither of them was among the witnesses. Sladek attempts to discredit the three who were present by comparing the details of their stories – such as how high the balconies were from the street, or indeed, whether there were any balconies at all.

Podmore, on the other hand, is more subtle in his sceptism. He mentions the fact that a few days before the levitation, and in front of the same witnesses, Home had opened the window and stood on the ledge outside. He had pointedly drawn their attention to himself standing on the narrow ledge some considerable distance from the ground. Podmore remarked drily 'the medium had thus, as it were, furnished a rough sketch of the picture which he aimed at producing.' On another occasion Home suddenly announced 'I'm rising, I'm rising', before proceeding to levitate in front of several witnesses.

Podmore implied that Home's levitations were nothing more than hallucinations produced by his hypnotic suggestion, rather in the same manner that the Indian rope trick is said to be a mass hallucination, the secret being in the magician's patter.

But even in the face of extreme hostility, Home remained a successful levitator for over 40 years. Among his witnesses were Emperor Napoleon III, John Ruskin and Bulwer Lytton – and many hundreds more, not all of whom were as inconsistent in their testimonies as Adare, Wynne and Lindsay. Moreover during that long span of time and mostly in broad daylight, Home was never proved to be a fraud. And despite Podmore's accusations Home never went out of his way to build up an atmosphere heavy with suggestibility. In fact, he was one of the few

Top: the classic stage levitation. The girl, Marva Ganzel, is first hypnotised into a cataleptic trance while balanced on two swords. When one is taken away, she somehow remains suspended in mid-air

Above: Frank Podmore, who suggested that D. D. Home's most famous levitation was merely an hallucination

Right: accounts of levitation and other manifestations of the seance room did not impress *Punch*, which in 1863 published this lampoon, showing that some surprises, at least, could be administered by all too explicable means

Ridicule has long been poured on the notion that people can free themselves from the force of gravity: this cartoon (left), entitled *The day's folly,* was published by Sergent in 1783. But Alexandra David-Neel (below) came back from 14 years in Tibet with no doubt that adepts could achieve weightlessness

mediums who actively eschewed 'atmosphere' – he preferred a normal or bright light to darkness and encouraged the sitters to chat normally rather than 'hold hands and concentrate'.

Although in his mature years Home could levitate at will, he apparently also levitated without being aware of it. On one occasion, when his host drew his attention to the fact that he was hovering above the cushions of his armchair, Home seemed most surprised.

Stage illusionists frequently pride themselves on their *pièce de résistance*: putting their assistant into a 'trance', balancing her on the points of two swords – then removing the swords so that she hangs in the air without apparent support. Sometimes she is 'hypnotised' and seen to rise further into the air – still without visible means of support. One of two things must be happening: either she does not rise into the air at all (that is, we all suffer a mass hallucination) or she rises aided by machinery invisible to us.

Of course, Home and other Spiritualists would also attribute their feats of apportation or levitation to 'machinery invisible to us' – but in their case the machinery would be the agency of spirits. To the end of his life, Home maintained that he could only fly through the air because he was lifted up by the spirits, who thus demonstrated their existence. But he described a typical levitation as follows:

> I feel no hands supporting me, and, since the first time, I have never felt fear; though, should I have fallen from the ceiling of some rooms in which I have been raised, I could not have escaped serious injury. I am generally lifted up perpendicularly; my arms frequently become rigid, and are drawn above my head, as if I were grasping the unseen power which slowly raises me from the floor.

The gravity enigma

And yet we do not refer in this spiritualistic way to the 'unseen power' that keeps us *on* the floor. Every schoolboy knows about Newton and his discovery of the law of gravity. But psychical research points to the relative ease with which certain sensitives can turn this law on its head.

In her book *Mystère et magique en Tibet* (1931), Madame Alexandra David-Neel, the French explorer who spent 14 years in and around Tibet, told how she came upon a naked man, weighed down with heavy chains. His companion explained to her that his mystical training had made his body so light that, unless he wore iron chains, he would float away.

It would seem that gravity does not necessarily have the hold on us we have been taught it has. Sir William Crookes, the renowned scientist and psychical researcher, had this to say about D. D. Home:

> The phenomena I am prepared to attest are so extraordinary, and so directly oppose the most firmly-rooted articles of scientific belief – amongst others, the ubiquity and invariable action of the force of gravitation – that, even now, on recalling the details of what I have witnessed, there is an antagonism in my mind between *reason*, which pronounces it to be scientifically impossible, and the consciousness that my senses, both of touch and sight, are not lying witnesses.

So we conclude that in some *special* cases – such as saints or particularly gifted mediums – levitation exists. But there is a growing body of thought that puts forward the idea that anyone can do it, providing he or she has the right training – students of transcendental meditation claim to do it all the time.

The art of levitation

It is claimed that many ancient peoples knew the secrets of levitation. But it is not, apparently, a lost art: some people today claim to be able to attain weightlessness at will. Is there any truth in these stories?

A UNIQUE SERIES of photographs appeared in the magazine *Illustrated London News* on 6 June 1936. They showed the successive stages in the levitation of an Indian *yogi*, Subbayah Pullavar – thus proving that, whatever else it was, this phenomenon was not a hypnotic illusion.

A European witness of the event, P. Y. Plunkett, sets the scene:

> The time was about 12.30 p.m. and the sun directly above us so that shadows played no part in the performance. . . . Standing quietly by was Subbayah Pullavar, the performer, with long hair, a drooping moustache and a wild look in his eye. He salaamed to us and stood chatting for a while. He had been practising this particular branch of yoga for nearly 20 years (as had past generations of his family). We asked permission to take photographs of the performance and he gave it willingly. . . .

Plunkett gathered together about 150 witnesses while the performer began his ritual preparations. Water was poured around the tent in which the act of levitation was to take place; leather-soled shoes were banned inside the circle, and the performer entered the tent alone. Some minutes later helpers removed the tent and there, inside the circle, was the fakir, floating on the air.

Plunkett and another witness came forward to investigate: the fakir was suspended in the air about a yard from the ground. Although he held on to a cloth-covered stick, this seemed to be for purposes of balance only – not for support. Plunkett and his friend examined the space around and under Subbayah Pullavar, and found it innocent of any strings or other 'invisible' apparatus. The yogi was in a trance and many witnesses believed that he had indisputably levitated,

Photographs taken of a levitation performance carried out by an Indian yogi, Subbayah Pullavar, before a large number of witnesses. The photographs were taken by the Englishman P. Y. Plunkett and a friend, and published in the *Illustrated London News* of 6 June 1936. The first photograph (below) shows the yogi before levitation, lying inside a tent. He is grasping a cloth-wrapped stick, which he continues to hold throughout the performance. The tent is then closed (right) for some minutes during the mysterious act of levitation itself

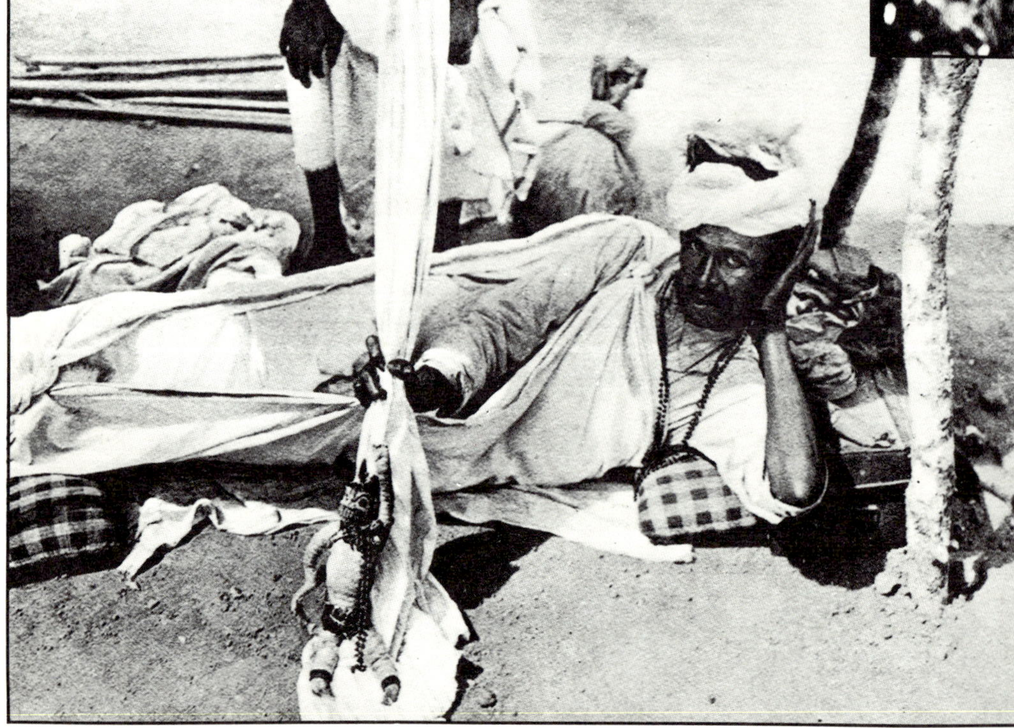

As the levitation performance continues, the curtains of the tent are drawn back and the yogi appears, floating in mid-air (top). Plunkett and his friend examined the space beneath and around the yogi, but were unable to find any evidence of strings or other supporting apparatus. Although some sceptics have claimed that the yogi was, in fact, not levitating but merely in a cataleptic trance, the relaxed position of the hand on the post suggests that the body of the yogi was indeed very nearly weightless during the performance. After levitation (above right) the yogi's body was so stiff that five men could not bend his limbs

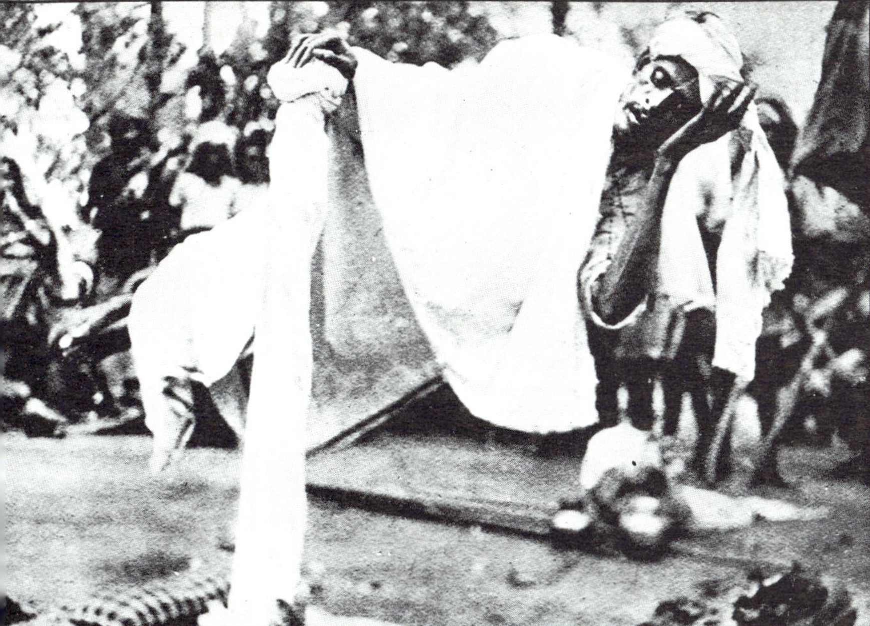

although it has been suggested that he had, in fact, merely passed into a cataleptic trance. The famous photographs were taken from various angles during the four minutes of the performance, and then the tent was re-erected around the fakir. Evidently the 'descent' was something very private, but Plunkett managed to witness it through the thin tent walls:

> After about a minute he appeared to sway and then very slowly began to descend, still in a horizontal position. He took about five minutes to move from the top of the stick to the ground, a distance of about three feet [1 metre] . . . When Subbayah was back on the ground his assistants carried him over to where we were sitting and asked if we would try to bend his limbs. Even with assistance we were unable to do so.

The yogi was rubbed and splashed with cold water for a further five minutes before he came out of his trance and regained full use of his limbs.

The swaying motion and horizontal position that Plunkett witnessed seem to be essential to true levitation. Students of transcendental meditation (TM) are taught, under the supervision of the Maharishi Mahesh Yogi at his headquarters in Switzerland, to levitate. One student described this 'impossible' achievement:

> People would rock gently, then more and more, and then start lifting off in to the air. You should really be in a lotus position to do it – you can hurt yourself landing if you've got a dangling undercarriage. To begin with it's like the Wright brothers' first flight – you come down with a bump. That's why we have to sit on foam rubber cushions. Then you learn to control it better, and it becomes totally exhilarating.

So can *anyone* induce levitation? The TM

Right: the Transcendental Meditation movement claims that this photograph shows students levitating. It is alleged that, under the supervision of tutors, the students achieve weightlessness through meditation

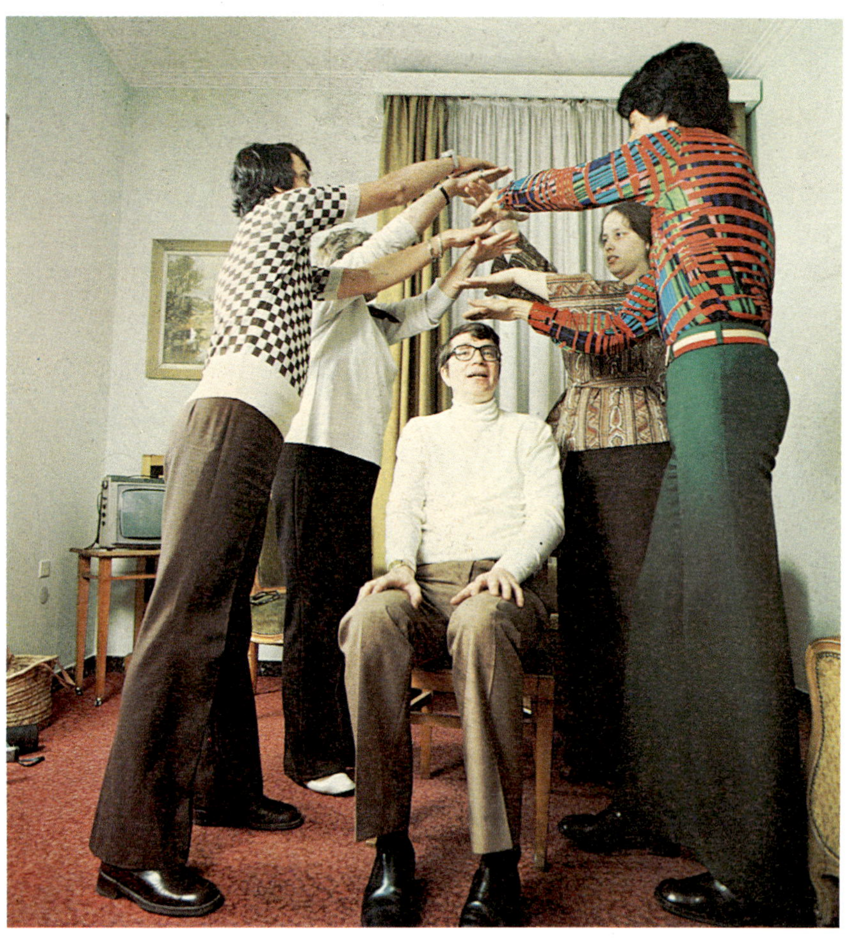

dowser's rod, intervenes to achieve the miracle of nullifying the force of gravity.

It seems that religious fervour may have something to do with the phenomenon; there are many reports of levitation by both Christian and Buddhist monks. In 1902 Aleister Crowley met his compatriot Alan Bennett, who had become a Buddhist monk, at his monastery in Burma in 1902; he, too, had become so weightless that he was 'blown about like a leaf'.

Alexandra David-Neel, the French explorer of the early 20th century, describes witnessing an extraordinary kind of long-distance running by a Tibetan lama: 'The man did not run. He seemed to lift himself from the ground proceeding by leaps. It looked as if he had been endowed with the elasticity of a ball and rebounded each time his feet touched the ground. His steps had the regularity of a pendulum.' The lama is said to have run hundreds of miles using this strange form of locomotion, keeping his eyes fixed on some far-distant goal.

The famous Russian ballet dancer Nijinsky, too, had the extraordinary ability of appearing to be almost weightless. He would jump up high and fall as lightly – and slowly – as thistledown in what was known as the 'slow vault'.

Like many inexplicable phenomena, levitation seems to be singularly useless. The distance covered is rarely more than a few

students believe they can, after a stringent mental training; the disciplines, both spiritual and physical, of the yogis seem to prepare them to defy gravity. It is fairly easy to induce a state of semi-weightlessness, as this account of a fat publican – a perfectly ordinary person – being raised in the air as a party trick shows.

The fat man sat on a chair and four people, including his small daughter, demonstrated the impossibility of lifting him with their index fingers only, placed in his armpits and the crooks of his knees. They then removed their fingers and put their hands in a pile on top of his head, taking care to interleave their hands so that no one person's two hands were touching. The four concentrated deeply for about 15 seconds; then someone gave a signal, and quickly they replaced their fingers in armpits and knees – and the fat publican floated into the air.

Sceptics might point to the intervention of non-spiritual spirits, bearing in mind the location of the event, but the phenomenon has been witnessed hundreds of times in pubs, homes, and school-yards. If it works – and one must assume it does – then how is it possible?

The sudden burst of concentration of four people with a single, 'impossible' target could, some people believe, unlock the hidden magic of the human will. Or it has been suggested that a little-known natural force, perhaps the same one that guides the

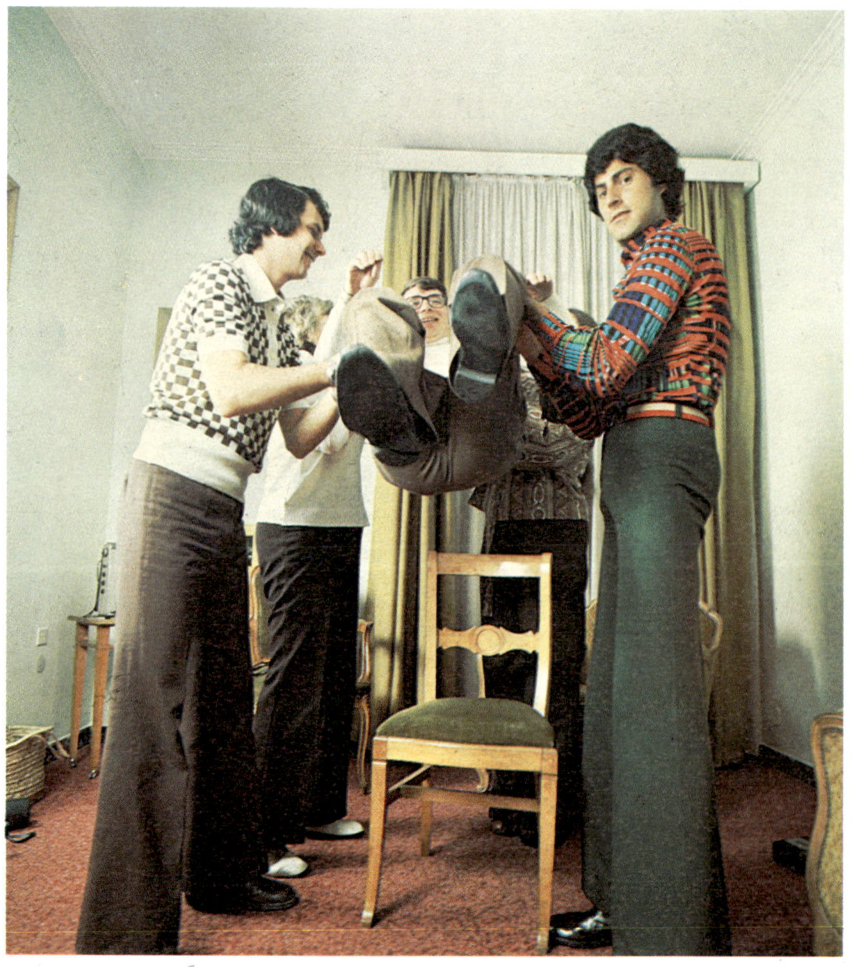

Left: an aerial view of the white horse at Uffington in Oxfordshire. The terrain on which it is carved is so hilly that its true shape can only really be appreciated from the air – a fact that has led some to speculate that the people who carved it were able to levitate and inspect their work from above

Opposite page: Uri Geller and some friends conduct a levitation session with Colin Wilson as subject. First (top) the experimenters place their hands on top of the subject's head, in such a way that no one person's two hands are touching. Then, on a command from Geller, they remove their hands from the subject's head and place their index fingers under his arms and knees. The subject immediately rises into the air (bottom)

feet or, at the most, the height of a room – useful only for dusting or decorating the home. But some people believe that the ancients could levitate quite easily, and did so to design certain enormous earthworks that can be appreciated only from the air, such as some of the white horses of the chalk downland in England and the desert patterns in Peru.

Ancient flight

The limitations of modern levitation need not have applied to the ancients – perhaps they had developed the art to a high degree and could soar into the sky at will. Like other psychic faculties, it appears that levitation is an art, once almost lost, that is now being re-learned by determined students. Perhaps one day, modern levitators will be able to 'fly' as the ancient Druids supposedly could.

The reported 'flights' of the ancients suggest to some researchers that they might have constituted out-of-the-body-experiences or astral travel, rather than flesh-and-blood transportation. Certainly, many accounts of levitation or flying read like lucid dreams – and dreams of flying are very common experiences. Some dreamers wake up convinced they *can* fly; fortunately, the sights and sounds of the real world generally bring them to their senses before they can experiment.

With a few exceptions, it seems that one can levitate only after long periods of training and discipline: in this way, the body is mysteriously 'given permission' to defy the law of gravity. Perhaps there is a law of levitation with a secret formula – an 'Open, Sesame' – which the initiate uses before rising off the ground.

This theory would explain the unusual cases of spontaneous or random levitation that fascinated Charles Fort. One such case was 12-year-old Henry Jones from Shepton Mallet who, during the year 1657, was observed on several occasions to rise into the air. Once he was able to put his hands flat against the ceiling, and on another occasion he took off and sailed 30 yards (27 metres) over the garden wall. The phenomenon lasted only a year – but this was long enough for the rumour to spread that he was 'bewitched'.

Certainly levitation is a rare phenomenon, but when considered with other accounts of equally rare and bizarre human attributes, such as incombustibility, elongation and superhuman strength, it must be taken seriously. Mothers who lift cars off their trapped children, those who can walk on fire and the sleepwalkers who perform 'impossible' feats pose profound questions about the nature of Man's physical and psychical potential. Perhaps we are intended to be able to defy gravity at will. Until we understand the nature of the phenomenon it must remain one of the mysterious hidden powers that many suspect man could develop.

KELLAR
LEVITATION.

The disembodied self

Many people have suddenly found themselves in the peculiar position of existing outside their own bodies, looking at the world from some detached, external point. In what circumstances do such out-of-the-body experiences take place?

ASTRAL PROJECTION, ESP projection and spontaneous projection are just some of the terms that refer to the same phenomenon – an out-of-the-body experience (OOBE). This is an experience in which a person leaves his physical body and appears to view the external world from a position that is completely divorced from his material body. It has been widely reported in both psychic and medical journals and it appears to be a relatively common experience.

The circumstances in which an OOBE occurs vary considerably. Stress seems to be a significant factor and many people have reported experiencing the sensation of leaving their bodies when undergoing an operation, after an accident or when seriously ill. But there are numerous cases of people who were asleep or going about everyday tasks, such as shopping or gardening, when the experience occurred.

From accounts given by those who have had an OOBE, the general sensation is at first indistinguishable from the ordinary physical state, except for a feeling of buoyancy and positive well-being. Some subjects have mentioned that their 'phantom' or 'astral' body seemed to remain attached to their physical body by a thin cord, enabling them to return to their normal state.

The word 'astral' is used to describe a second body within the physical one. It is an exact copy of the flesh and blood version, but is made of finer material and has a luminous appearance. It is apparently capable of separating itself from the physical body and travelling about, passing through solid objects. The astral body exists in what is called the astral plane, which includes the everyday world, but extends beyond it. It is also said to survive death.

References to the astral body abound in ancient literature. Ancient Indian writings tell of eight *siddhis* (supernormal powers) that can be acquired through meditation. The sixth *siddhi* is 'flying in the sky', presumably indicating astral projection. A religious belief common to some cultures is that

Above: the ancient Egyptians thought of the astral body, or *ba*, as a bird with a human face. At death, the bird would leave the physical body, but hover close to it

Opposite page: a 19th century magician advertises his sensational stage act. One common theory is that 'levitation' is simply a hallucination produced in the observer by hypnotic suggestion, yet those who have levitated themselves describe the sensation as very similar to that of an OOBE. Are the two phenomena related?

Left: in his second Epistle to the Corinthians, St Paul refers to a man who had had an out-of-the-body experience

Below: the great mystic poet and painter William Blake portrays the reunion of the soul and the physical body in this illustration of Robert Blair's poem, *The grave*, published in 1813

the *shaman* (a kind of priest-doctor) is able to leave his body at will and escort the souls of the dead to the land of tribal ancestors.

It appears from drawings that the ancient Egyptians believed that the astral plane was entered by 10 gates and seven doors. They thought of the soul or astral body as a bird, independent of gravity (a puny soul was symbolised as a mouse!).

Among the many Biblical references to astral projection, St Paul describes a man he knew who 'whether in the body or out of the body, God knoweth, was caught up into paradise and heard unspeakable words, which it is not lawful for a man to utter' (2 Corinthians 12:3).

Widespread beliefs

The modern idea that it is wrong to awaken a sleepwalker may be traced back to the primitive belief that to do so would prevent the soul, or astral body, from returning. Even more frightening is the belief, common in Haiti, that the soul can be stolen by evil beings and its owner subsequently enslaved – the zombies of Haiti are deemed to be bodies without souls.

In 1978, Dean Shiels, Associate Professor at the University of Wisconsin, USA, published the results of his cross-cultural study of beliefs in OOBEs. He had collected data from nearly 70 non-Western cultures and this revealed that the belief in OOBE occurred in about 95 per cent of them. Despite the need for further research, Professor Shiels remarked that 'the near-universality of OOBE beliefs and the *consistency* of the beliefs is striking.'

The notion of the astral body has a continuous history in the West, too – medieval scholars wrote of the soul as the *anima divina* or *anima humana*. Dante's *Purgatorio* (canto 25), written in the 14th century, says that after death the soul 'around it beams its own creative power, like to its living form in shape and size . . . the circumambient air adopts the shape the soul imposes on it.'

One of the few men whose ability to travel astrally was acknowledged by the Roman Catholic Church was St Anthony of Padua (1195–1231). St Anthony was a Portuguese Franciscan friar who won a great reputation as a preacher in southern France and Italy. He is the patron saint of the poor and is often called upon for the return of lost property.

It is said of St Anthony that one day in 1226, when he was preaching in a church in Limoges, he suddenly remembered that he was supposed to be reading a lesson at another church on the other side of town. St Anthony stopped his sermon, pulled his hood over his head and knelt silently for several minutes. During that time, monks in the other church saw the saint suddenly appear in their midst, read the lesson, then

The near-death experience

Many people have experienced an OOBE for the first time through being involved in a serious accident. In 1964 David Taylor and a friend were spending the last few weeks of their tour of East Africa in northern Tanzania, when they had a serious collision with a lorry. David nearly died as a result of his injuries.

'We had been driving through the game park and had just turned on to the main road to Moshi. It was dusk and I was sitting half-asleep in the passenger seat.

'I was suddenly woken by my friend, who was delighted to see the first vehicle we had come across in six hours, driving down towards us. Either my friend or the other driver must have been half-asleep, too, for within seconds the two vehicles drove smack into each other.

'As the two vehicles collided, I suddenly found that I was watching the scene from several yards up in the air, as if I were suspended above the road. I saw our own Land-Rover colliding with a large lorry. I watched as I was thrown from the Land-Rover and my friend then climbed out unhurt and came back to examine my body. I also saw the lorry drive off. I remember thinking that I looked a terrible mess lying there on the road and could well be dead.

'The next thing I knew was coming to in Moshi Hospital. I had been unconscious for two days with serious injuries. I told my friend what I had seen and he confirmed that it was indeed a lorry that had run into us and that it had driven on. I had only been saved because another car had come down the road soon afterwards and taken me to the hospital.

'The whole experience, even after all these years, has left me completely unafraid of death.'

Below left: the astral body lying above the physical body at the start of an OOBE. The 'cord' that connects the two bodies has been mentioned by some subjects as the means by which they can return to a normal state

Bottom: St Anthony of Padua's ability to leave his physical body enabled him to preach to two congregations at once

just as suddenly disappear again. St Anthony returned to his kneeling body and continued his sermon.

During recent centuries, many notable writers have described their own experiences of spontaneous projection or those of colleagues, among them Walter de la Mare, T. E. Lawrence, Jack London and Guy de Maupassant. Ernest Hemingway experienced the sensation of quitting his body when he was hit by shrapnel during the First World War. He later described it as

> . . . my soul or something coming right out of my body, like you'd pull a silk handkerchief out of a pocket by one corner. It flew around and then came back and went in again, and I wasn't dead any more.

The phenomenon of OOBE raises considerable problems for philosophers and psychologists. Many sceptics maintain that any suggestion of an OOBE should be dismissed as an hallucination or delusion. But people who have had such experiences are adamant that they have, indeed, taken place. Even when unconscious at the time of the experience, some people have later described what was going on around them and those present have confirmed their accounts. Subjects who experience this phenomenon are fully aware that they are in an out-of-the-body state.

Many subjects who have had an OOBE while on the operating table or after a serious accident say that the experience has profoundly changed their view of life and dispelled any fears about dying. An interesting theory on this type of projection, or 'near-death experience' (NDE) has been put forward by Doctor Carl Sagan, director of the Laboratory for Planetary Studies in New York. He describes the phenomenon of NDE in these terms:

> Every human being has already had an experience like that of travellers who return from the land of death; the sensation of flight and the emergence from darkness into light; an experience in which the heroic figure may be dimly perceived, bathed in radiance and glory. There is only one common experience that matches this description. It is called birth.

In times of mortal danger or acute emotional stress, perhaps one is able to retrieve these memories of birth and, once again, leave the darkness – the suffering body – and rise towards freedom and the light.

Left: a detail from William Blake's depiction of the Valley of Death, painted as an illustration for Robert Blair's poem *The grave*. Blake was convinced of the immortality of the human soul

Below: Lord Geddes, who presented a detailed report of an out-of-the-body experience in 1937

A matter of life and death

Out-of-the-body experiences frequently occur when the body is on the point of dying, and those who have come back bring extraordinary accounts of timelessness and mystic well-being. Does this mean that there is conclusive evidence for a life after death?

ALTHOUGH MANY PEOPLE have claimed to be able to achieve an out-of-the-body experience (OOBE) at will, whenever they want to, most experiences seem to take place spontaneously and without any conscious effort. However, as we have seen, the circumstances in which an OOBE occurs are often unusual – on the operating table, for instance, or when the body undergoes a severe shock as in a car crash. And it is not, apparently, an occurrence that is restricted to the mystical, the sensitive or the adept. In 1975 a survey of 1000 students and residents of Charlottesville, Virginia, revealed that 25 per cent of students and 14 per cent of the residents claimed to have had an OOBE – figures that confirmed earlier reports that the experience occurs to about one person in four.

This doesn't mean, of course, that the experience happens very often to that quarter of the population. For most people an OOBE happens when it is least expected, though it can certainly have a profound effect on the individual concerned. Robert Crookall relates such a case in his book *The study and practice of astral projection*. It was first reported in 1937 by Sir Auckland (later Lord) Geddes in a paper presented to the Royal Medical Society of Edinburgh. Here is the doctor's own account, taken up just as he realised that he was suffering from acute poisoning:

'I wanted to ring for assistance, but found I could not, and so placidly gave up the attempt. I realized I was very ill . . . thereafter at no time did my consciousness appear

to me to be in any way dimmed, but I suddenly realised that my consciousness was separating from another consciousness, which was also "me". . . .

'Gradually I realised that I could see not only my body and the bed in which it was, but everything in the whole house and garden, and then I realised that I was seeing not only *things* at home, but in London and in Scotland, in fact wherever my attention was directed. . . . And the explanation which I received (from what source I do not know, but which I found myself calling to myself *my mentor*) was that I was free in a time dimension of space, wherein *now* was equivalent to *here* in the ordinary three-dimensional space of everyday life.

'I next realised that vision included . . . things in the four or more dimensional place that I was in.

'Just as I was beginning to grasp all these, I saw "A" enter my bedroom. I realised she got a terrible shock and I saw her hurry to the telephone. I saw my doctor leave his patients and come very quickly and heard him say and saw him think, "He is nearly gone." I heard him quite clearly speaking to me on the bed, but I was not in touch with the body and could not answer him.

'I was really cross when he took a syringe and rapidly injected my body. . . . As my heart began to beat more strongly, I was drawn back, and I was intensely annoyed, because I was so interested and was just beginning to understand where I was and what I was seeing. I came back into my body, really angry at being pulled back, and once back, all the clarity of vision of anything and everything disappeared, and I was just possessed of a glimmer of consciousness which was suffused with pain.'

Added the doctor: 'I think that the whole thing simply means that but for medical treatment . . . I was dead to the three-dimensional world.'

Losing the fear of death

Others, undergoing an OOBE at a point when they seemed physically dead, have said that the experience has removed any fear of dying they might have had. As one put it: 'It appeared I had a choice to re-enter my body or go ahead and die. I knew I was going to be perfectly safe whether my body died or not.' And another, experiencing an extraordinary joy in his out-of-the-body state, was *told* to return to his body – at that moment lying on an operating table suffering cardiac arrest – because 'my work wasn't done on earth'. There are many like this case on record, and the similarities between the accounts lead inevitably to the question: does the out-of-the-body experience provide evidence for the reality of one of Man's deepest and oldest desires – the survival of physical death?

What most authorities who have studied OOBEs agree on is that the experience seems to indicate that life is *more* than merely physical. Yet it is not only during a crisis or at the point of death that an OOBE may take place. Pat, a 20-year-old florist, shared a flat in Canterbury, England, with her cousin, who was a musician. In April 1970, she says,

> I had been lying on the sofa for a few hours, listening to my cousin playing the piano. I was completely relaxed and felt as if I were going to sleep. I felt a weight pressing down on my face and suddenly I was aware that . . . I had actually risen to ceiling height. I turned over and seemed to hover. . . . I could see everything in the room quite clearly, even myself lying on the sofa. . . . Then I got what I can only describe as a coloured door floating in front of me. A voice within me seemed to say, 'Open the door to seek knowledge.' And as I moved toward it the door swung open to reveal a different coloured door. I remember thinking to myself that if I were to find an answer (but to what I didn't know) I had to

A patient undergoing surgery. Out-of-the-body experiences often occur when the physical body suffers a severe shock – such as that caused by a general anaesthetic – or when it is on the point of death

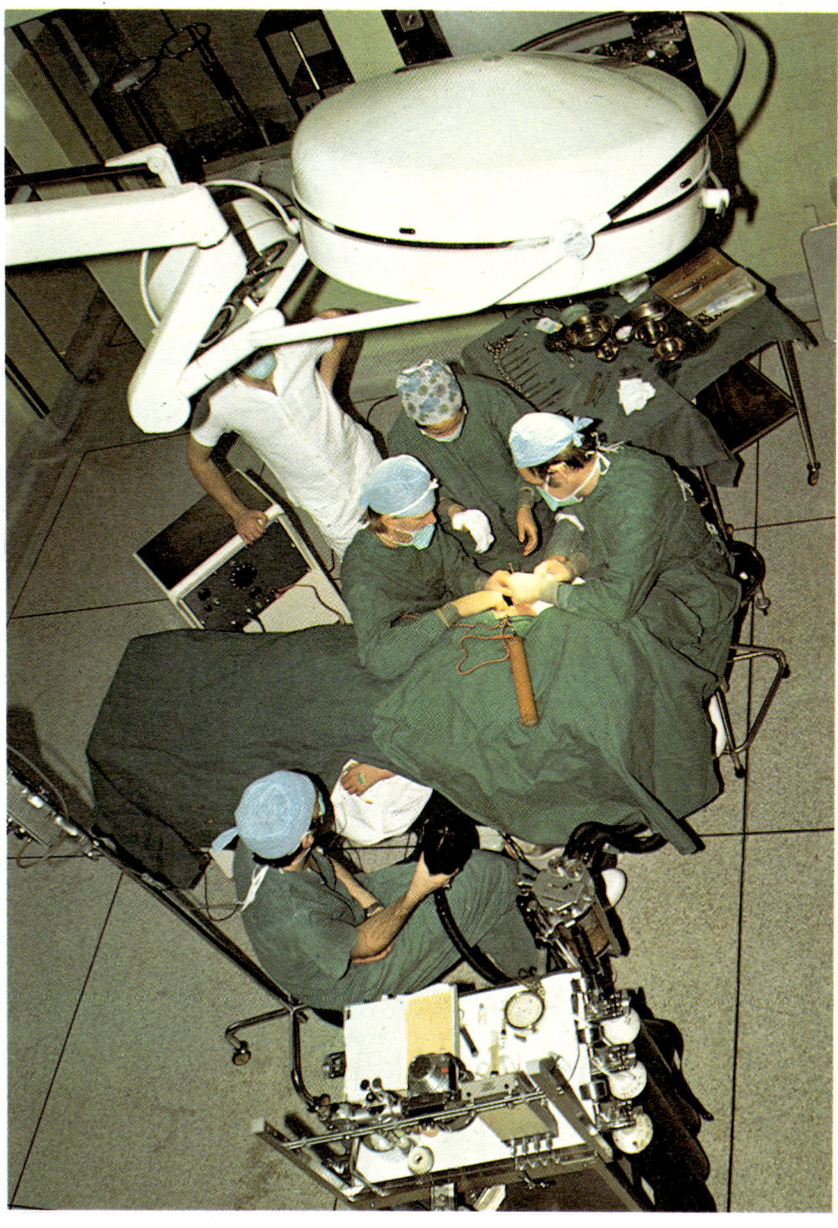

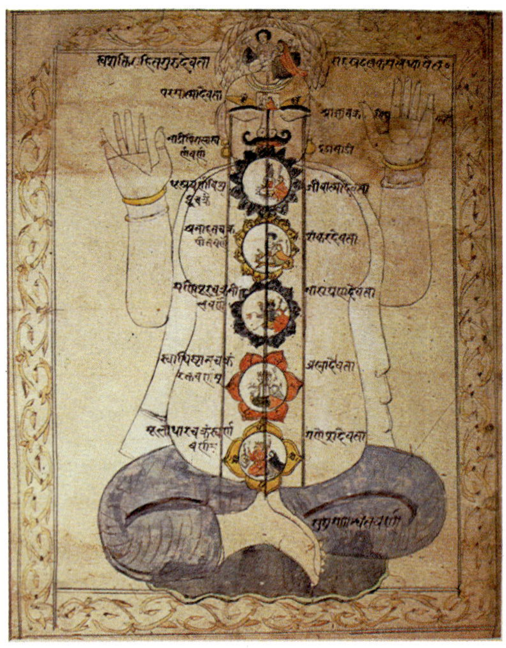

Right: this 19th-century Tantric watercolour shows the spiritual centres – *chakras* – that Laya Yogo adepts believe to be a link between the physical body and the soul, or 'subtle body'. Stimulating the *chakras* may induce a mystical state remarkably similar to that experienced during an OOBE

Above: the Arizona State Penitentiary, rated one of the four toughest jails in the USA. Here Ed Morrell's consciousness departed from his body when under excruciating torture. Jack London based his book *The star rover* on Morrell's experiences in prison

> travel on. I lost count of how many doors I went through but I suddenly found myself way up in the sky hovering over Canterbury. Only it wasn't April any more; it was a summery day. I didn't want to return, indeed I had a great sense of elation. But I had slight feelings of trepidation. What would happen if I travelled on into the unknown? As I was thinking about this I found myself staring down at my body again. I decided that I couldn't do it. Funny really – as soon as I had made my decision I was back in my body before you could say 'Jack Flash'.

The astral body, or soul, or detached consciousness, does seem to be made aware of other dimensions of existence through the OOBE. In June 1974 Mrs 'T' was in hospital in Libya, recovering from a major operation, when she left her physical body:

> I seemed to get the knowledge that the answer to absolutely everything is within reach of every one of us. I also had the feeling that . . . if I did not return to my body I would have to move on. . . . I was told that it was not time for me to go, I must return for a little while longer as there was something else I had to do. I was not told what that might be. While out of my body I gained the understanding that time was non-existent, eternity or a fraction of a second could be the same.

Such accounts also suggest that the extra-physical dimensions of existence are perhaps more important than the physical ones. And this 'further' state of being acts as a kind of haven when the physical body is pushed to intolerable limits.

In *The twenty-fifth man* Ed Morrell described his experiences in the Arizona State Penitentiary – an account vouched for by author Jack London, who knew Morrell intimately. While in prison Morrell was repeatedly tortured: he was trussed up in two strait-jackets, and then water was poured over him so that they shrank. He said it was like being 'slowly squeezed to death' before he found himself floating free of his agonised body. In that state Morrell saw not only his immediate surroundings, but travelled across the world and, apparently, in time: among many people he saw during OOBEs was a woman whom he later married.

Mankind's deepest wishes

Time travel, a sense of timelessness, survival of the individual after death, a deep sense of purpose and meaning to existence – these, it may be objected, are all *wishes* that have been nursed by mankind since the dawn of time. And it has been argued – by Dr Susan Blackmore for example – that an OOBE is perhaps a creation of the mind, a world of thought and imagination. It springs, in other words, from the same deep sources as our most ancient desires, and is another expression of the longing to be free of the limitations of earthly existence.

Yet this will not explain such phenomena as the ability to travel 'astrally' – under laboratory conditions – and accurately read a number out of sight of the physical body. Yet this happened during an experiment conducted by Charles Tart: against massive odds the subject read the number 25132 while being monitored.

So the out-of-the-body experience remains an enigma. The psychological theories do not account for the abilities of an Ingo Swann to leave his body and describe distant places. And such scientific data as we have – for instance that changes in brain waves are registered by EEG devices when an OOBE takes place – are descriptions of events and not explanations for them.

Points of view

Descriptions of death in many ancient religious texts read very like out-of-the-body experiences – OOBEs. Can this mean that, during an OOBE, it is possible to visit the land of the dead?

IT IS OFTEN THOUGHT that if one has an out-of-the-body experience – an OOBE – there remains no doubt about survival after death; that, in fact, an OOBE is a kind of mini-death, but with the difference that one has the option of returning to the body afterwards. Certain passages in religious literature seem to confirm the similarity between death and OOBEs. Some parts of the Bible can be interpreted to describe death as the breaking of a silver cord that joins the 'other' body to the physical body – as in the famous passage from Ecclesiastes 12: 'Remember also your Creator in the days of your youth, before the evil days come . . . before the silver cord is snapped, or the golden bowl broken.' Saint Paul can be interpreted to give support to the notion that we have two distinct bodies: in I Corinthians 44, writing of the resurrection of the dead, he remarks, 'If there is a physical body, there is also a spiritual body.' And in II Corinthians 12:3–4, he tells of a man who 'was caught up into Paradise – whether in the body or out of the body I do not know, God knows – and he heard things that cannot be told, which man may not utter.' The pioneering 'psychic' writers of the 19th and 20th centuries seized on these references, and similar passages in ancient Hindu scriptures such as the Upanishads, to lend weight to their descriptions of their own OOBEs in terms of the soul in another body made of some subtle material as yet unknown to western science, moving out of coincidence with the physical body, and travelling away from it.

Until a few years ago, I myself thought that an OOBE would be an experience of great significance in which it would perhaps be possible to see dead relatives, converse with them, and bring back information that could be checked. All this would be of enormous help and significance in answering the ancient question of whether there is life after death.

With this in mind, I tried hard, with various methods, to experience an OOBE myself. A book by S. Muldoon and H. Carrington, *The projection of the astral body* (1929), sets out a number of different methods of inducing an 'astral projection', as it was called in those days. All the procedures involved lying in bed on one's back, and using the will and imagination in various ways. The principle was to loosen the grip of the physical body on the astral body by, for instance, imagining oneself, in the astral body, consciously rotating about an axis from head to feet, observing first the ceiling, then the wall, then the floor and the other wall. (Try to imagine this, while lying on your back with eyes closed! It is not at all easy.) Other methods involved imagining oneself going up in a lift at the moment of

Previous page, bottom: *The mourning*, by George Elgar Hicks (1824–1914), shows parents grieving over their little girl while her soul – which looks very similar to the 'astral body' described by people who experience OOBEs – flies heavenwards. In William Blake's illustration from Robert Blair's poem *The grave* (above), the soul of the dying man is, intriguingly, shown as a woman: 'How wishfully she looks/On all she's leaving now no longer her's (*sic*)!'

Previous page, top: an illustration of astral travel from Muldoon and Carrington's book *The projection of the astral body*. The astral body is joined to the physical body by a silver cord, through which flow 'vital forces'. When the astral body is far from the physical body, the cord is stretched and becomes very thin, cutting down the supply of vital force; the astral body is then able to move around freely

sleep, telling oneself that at a particular point in the dream one would wake up in a full astral projection. A third method involved going to bed very thirsty and imagining oneself going to the kitchen tap for a drink of water, pre-programming oneself to awaken, in an astral projection, on arrival at the tap.

Floating in the air

For one hour every night for a month I tried these methods on retiring to bed. At last I had success. The first sign was that, in accordance with the book, I found myself in a cataleptic state – unable to move a muscle. This was stated by Muldoon and Carrington to be the normal precursor to the experience. I used my will – or was it my imagination? – to make myself float upwards, and the experience was quite fascinating. I felt as though I were embedded in the mud at the bottom of a river, and the water was slowly seeping into the mud and reducing its viscosity, so that eventually I was borne upwards by the water. Slowly I floated upwards, still cataleptic, like an airship released from its moorings. I reached the ceiling and floated through it into the darkness of the roof space. Then I passed through the roof tiles, and the sky, clouds and Moon became visible. I increased my 'willing' (or 'imagining'), and my velocity of ascent up into the sky increased. I have the memory of the wind whistling through my hair clearly to this day. From the moment of getting into bed to this point up in the sky I had no break of consciousness. Eventually, it all died down, and I was back in bed. I immediately wrote full and detailed notes on my experience, and recollected that I had read an account by a French writer, Yram, of similar experiences of travelling up into the sky.

Thinking it over, it seemed a quite useless experience. Any sensible person would say that I had dreamed the whole episode. So I resolved that next time would be different – and it certainly was! The book stated that the catalepsy would disappear when the projection from the body exceeded 'cord activity range', and the projector would be free to walk about. 'Cord activity range' meant that, according to Muldoon, the distance from the body was great enough to reduce the 'silver cord' connecting the astral and physical bodies of the experimenter to a fine thread. The 'vital forces' (whatever they were) flowing through it would then be reduced to a low level and the catalepsy would disappear. If this occurred, it would be possible to walk into town, examine a shop window never seen before, memorise the contents, return to the body, write it all down, and carefully check the description the following day. If this worked, surely no one would suggest that the whole experience had been a dream – especially if they were given the description before checking, and, even better, if they had themselves chosen the shop window to be 'astrally' visited immediately before the experiment.

So I tried again. This time it took only three or four nights to repeat the projection. However, on this occasion I stopped the vertical movement at ceiling height and changed direction. Still cataleptic, I floated horizontally, feet first, towards the first-floor window of the room. Floating smoothly through the top of the window frame, I was aiming to describe a smooth parabola down onto the lawn where, I hoped, I should be outside 'cord activity range' and the real work of acquiring evidence could begin. It did not happen like that. As I cleared the window and started the descent to the lawn I had one of the most intriguing experiences to date. I felt two hands take my head, one hand over each ear, move me (still cataleptic) back into the bedroom and down into the body. I heard no sound, and saw nothing.

At this point I found I was so tired during the day because of insufficient sleep that I had to discontinue the experiments, and have never had the opportunity to repeat them.

The experiences I have described took place in the 1950s. Since then I have learned a great deal. First, I would say that lying on one's back in bed and concentrating on a particular idea is a recipe for producing an auto-hypnotic trance. I have no doubt that I put myself into a trance. Secondly, as I was expecting – and therefore suggesting to myself – that my experience would be what the book described, I entered a cataleptic state. Had I not anticipated that, I believe it probably would not have occurred. Thirdly, as I was expecting to float vertically upwards, that is the experience I had. Other experimenters, with different ideas of what will happen to them, do not enter a cataleptic state, and sometimes 'leave the body' horizontally, through the head, or sideways. A suggestion, to a good enough subject in a deep enough trance, that he or she will move around in a subtle body to other parts of the physical world, near or far, will often be enough to produce that effect. Many people are capable of having an OOBE as a result of suggestion under hypnosis. So, do they see the ordinary physical world? Well, hardly! They do not have their physical eyes with them and clearly cannot. So what do they experience? Surely, they experience a dramatised reconstruction of a memory of the physical world; can it be anything else?

Sometimes the physical world seen in an OOBE does not quite match reality. There may be symbolic additions like bars on the windows to prevent escape. Objects may have a kind of luminosity. Muldoon suggests that it is possible to awaken, projected, from an ordinary dream by observing an incongruity in the surroundings, for example, by observing that the paving stones do not have their long edges in the correct direction. There are often vital differences from the experiences of the physical world, the whole surroundings changing to those of the spiritualists' 'summerland' (early stage of the afterlife) and including 'discarnate' people.

Above: Peter Pan leads Wendy, John and Michael in their flight to Neverland, in an illustration by Mabel Lucie Attwell from J.M. Barrie's famous children's book. Some people see the story as a classic description of shared OOBES

Right: two souls, dying at the same moment, make their departure from the body: 'Together freed, their gentle spirits fly/To scenes where love and bliss immortal reign'

Projecting the double

One of the best cases of a 'normal' projection into a 'duplicate physical world' involved Englishwoman Eileen Garrett, the famous psychic. She describes in her autobiography how she projected her 'double' from a room in New York to a place in Newfoundland, the home of the well-known doctor who had designed the experiment. She could 'see', she wrote, the garden and the sea, the flowers and the house, smell the salt in the air and hear the birds. Entering the house, still quite conscious of her body lying in the room in New York, and able to speak to the experimenters there, she observed the doctor descending the stairs and entering his study. He also was psychic and appeared to be aware of her presence. She obeyed his instructions and described the objects on his table to the experimenter in New York. She also described a bandage on the Newfoundland doctor's head which, he told her out loud, was the result of an accident that morning. He then walked to the bookcase and she knew telepathically, she says, that he

When after the long vernal day of life,
Enamour'd more, as more remembrance swells
With many a proof of recollected love,
Together down they sink in social sleep;
Together freed, their gentle spirits fly
To scenes where love and bliss immortal reign.

method. An important and apparently real experience he had involved his projection to the location (unknown to him) of a woman friend, whom he found talking to two girls. He could attract the attention only of the woman and she told him (mentally) that she knew of his presence – but all the time she was talking to the girls. Though she stated that she would remember his visit, he nevertheless pinched her at about waist level – not expecting that she would feel anything. To his surprise, she cried out. After the experiment, when she returned to her home, Monroe asked her (normally) what she was doing at the time of his projection. She described what he had observed. She remembered nothing of his 'visit'. Exasperated, he said 'Did you not feel the pinch?' Very surprised indeed, she did – and could not understand how this could have happened. She showed him the marks on her skin at the right position. At the time, she had apparently thought that her brother-in-law crept up behind to surprise her. The pinch hurt! An interesting feature of some of Monroe's OOBES was that he occasionally felt that he was partly or wholly 'someone else'. This is distinctly different from the reports of many other experimenters, who talk of having dual consciousness – that is, consciousness both in the projected form and in the reclining physical body – and sometimes even of discussions between the two.

was thinking of a certain book. He took it down, held it up for her to read the title and then read a paragraph, chosen by him at random, silently to himself. She received his impressions telepathically. (The book was about Einstein.) So the experiment continued. All this was written down, she explains, in New York and sent by post that evening to Newfoundland. Next morning a telegram was received from the doctor in Newfoundland to describe the accident he had had before the experiment, explaining the bandage. All this, says Eileen Garrett, was accurate. The critical scientific reader will ask for a reference to the refereed published report and, as far as this writer knows, that is not available. However, Eileen Garrett was well known to all psychical researchers of standing and, again, as far as I know, was never accused of dishonesty. It seems that, by and large, the experiences she had, and the results that were obtained, were as she described them. Similar results have been obtained by other experimenters.

Another person who experienced OOBES regularly was Robert Monroe. His 'projections', however, were not as wide ranging as those of Eileen Garrett, and different in some ways. Monroe analyses the preliminaries he experienced and gives sufficient detail to enable others to experiment, using his

Above: a miniature from an early 19th-century Bhagavata Purana from India. It tells the story of Usha, who experienced spontaneous 'dream flights'. The information she obtained on them could later be checked by visiting the places she described

Right: 'the causal body of an Arhat', an illustration from *Man visible and invisible* by C.W. Leadbeater. Leadbeater believes that we have at least three bodies besides the physical – the emotional, the mental and the spiritual. The latter is seen here as it would allegedly appear to a trained seer

Fact, imagination, or psi?

What happens when someone's 'astral body' visits a place during an out-of-the-body experience? Does anything actually leave the physical body – or is an OOBE simply a dramatised form of telepathy or clairvoyance? To solve this problem, scientists have conducted a fascinating series of experiments

The astral body leaves the physical body at death, in this illustration of 1829 by the French artist Corbould. People who experience OOBEs often describe them in terms of a journey undertaken by the 'astral body'. What actually happens during an OOBE is still the subject of debate

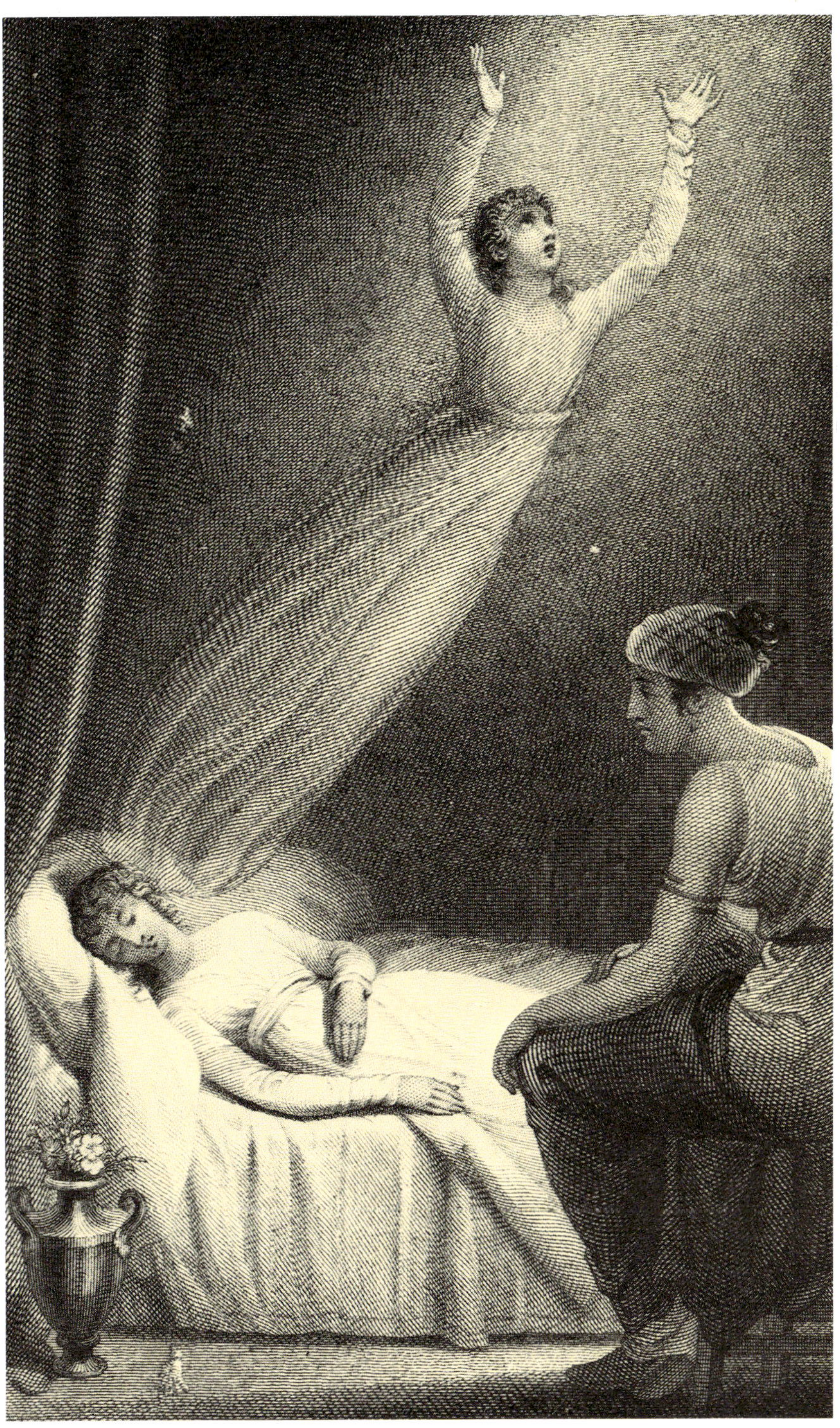

ONE OF THE MAJOR DIFFICULTIES in psychical research is how to eliminate the suspected intervention of telepathy – precognitive or coincidental. The problem is especially acute in the investigation of OOBEs. The obvious way to test an OOBE is to ask the person undergoing the experience to 'visit' a place he or she has never seen when awake, and then ask for a detailed description of the surroundings, which can later be checked. But it seems that there is no way of knowing whether a real OOBE is involved, or whether the subject is using pure clairvoyance to gain the information – that is, 'knowing' facts about the physical world independently of the senses. Another interesting suggestion has been made: that having an OOBE may act as a trigger to make overt information that is lying passive in the subject's subconscious. Indeed, it could be that seeing, hearing, touching, smelling and tasting are mere illusions, and that we in fact sense the physical world by clairvoyance.

To combat this problem as it relates to OOBEs, Profesor A. J. Ellison built a box containing some fairly sophisticated electronic circuitry. With the subject of the experiment in an OOBE state, Ellison could, by pressing a button on the machine, make a three-digit random number appear at the back – out of his sight. He would then ask the subject to tell him the number at the back of the machine, and enter that number on another dial positioned at the front of the machine. The machine would tally the numbers on the two dials and note whether or not the subject had been successful in stating the original number correctly. This procedure could be repeated any number of times to give a run of experiments. At the end of a run, the dials could be set to display the number of successes. (The machine could also indicate how many of the separate digits corresponded on each occasion, if this information was required.)

The important point about this method is that since at no time – before, during or after the experiment – are the random numbers in the mind of the experimenter, telepathy of any kind is ruled out. The next step was to use the box to test a number of subjects who, previous experiment had showed, were able to have OOBEs when this was suggested to them under hypnosis; this ability is fairly common among good hypnotic subjects.

This test started with several trial runs in which, for speed, Ellison looked at the numbers at the back while the first subject was attempting to tell him what they were. These runs were remarkably successful. On two or three occasions, the subject was completely accurate. So they started a run of 25 tries in which Prof. Ellison did not look at the

Professor Arthur Ellison (left), professor of electrical engineering at City University, London, has devised a method for investigating the nature of OOBEs. A figure produced by a random number generator appears – seen by no one – at the back of a box (below); the subject of the experiment is then asked to go, in his 'astral body', and 'read' the number. The number he 'sees' is recorded on the dial at the front of the machine (bottom), and the machine checks whether or not the reading is correct. At no time is the original random number seen, in the ordinary sense, by anyone; thus a successful reading by the subject indicates that his OOBE is *not* a kind of dramatised telepathy

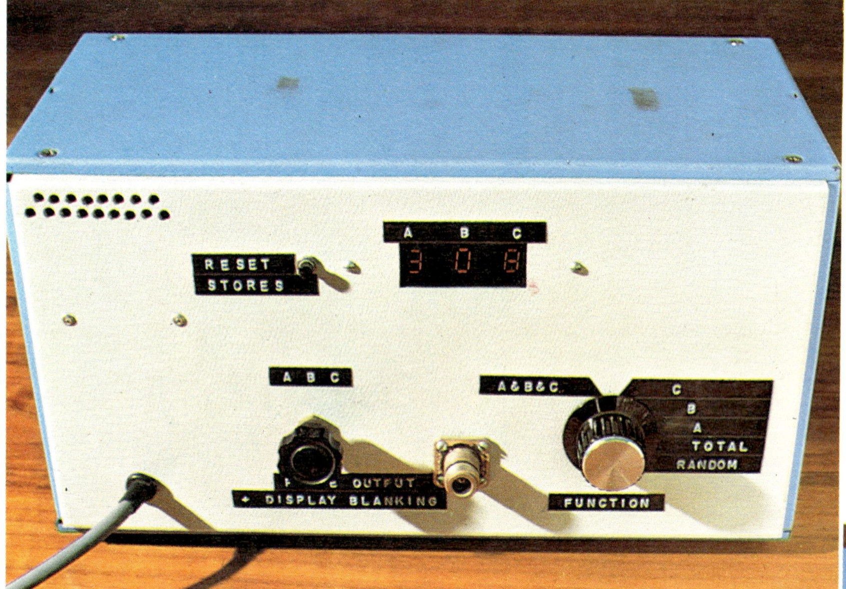

numbers at the back, but used the method described above. Almost at once, the subject seemed to be in difficulty, and said that she was finding it impossible to 'read' the numbers clearly, as they were 'too small'. It was suggested that she practise with small numbers set up by a friend at home (and looked at afterwards, for the recording of 'right' or 'wrong'), then return in a month or two to continue the more rigorous experiments using the box. Ellison was not surprised however, when she did not reappear.

A second hypnosis subject proved unable to read the figures at the back of the box under any conditions, and did not continue the experiments.

Ellison's third subject was an American psychic who came to his laboratory during a visit to Britain and was told about the machine. He volunteered to try a run immediately – unfortunately not allowing time to check that the box was functioning properly. He indicated that the numbers would 'just appear' in his mind, and the OOBE experience was not necessary in his case. This, of course, raises some interesting questions about the nature of OOBEs – as already mentioned, it is possible that an OOBE can be considered to be a dramatised reconstruction of a memory of certain surroundings, incorporating information – such as the number on the dial on the back of the box – that is obtained by 'pure clairvoyance'. This is, of course, no explanation – what, after all, is 'pure clairvoyance'? – but there is certainly plenty of evidence that information can appear in the mind without any particular procedure, such as inducing an OOBE, being necessary. The psychic ran through a series of around 20 'guesses'. Ellison then turned the dial to see how many he had got right, expecting to find a zero score – and, to his astonishment, the window indicated eight.

But the following morning Ellison did a run himself, also scoring eight. Clearly, there was something wrong. Careful examination indicated a non-visible fault in a micro-circuit, resulting in all seven bars of the units digit being illuminated, forming the figure eight. Careful cleaning of the component in question reduced Ellison's score on a subsequent run to its usual zero.

Beating the odds

The fourth subject to use the box was a famous British psychic. This time, the experiment was planned and the box carefully checked for correct operation. Ellison and his research assistant did a run or two each and obtained typically low scores. After allowing plenty of time for the circuitry to warm up and stability to be established, and a final check, the visiting psychic made the first run

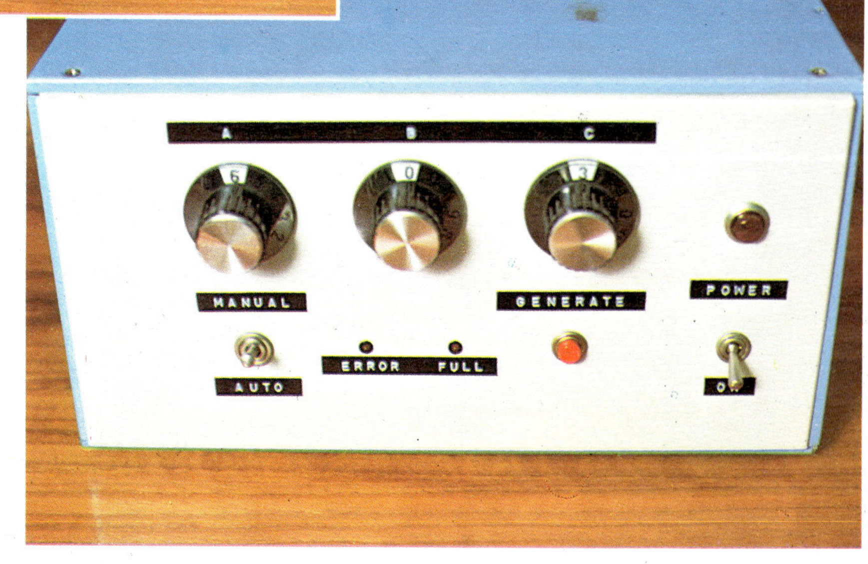

of 20 tries. A score of eight! But a check by Ellison also gave a score of eight. Again, there had to be something wrong with the equipment – and, sure enough, careful cleaning of the microcircuit again restored the box to normality. Again, the professor and his assistant did a run – both resulting in the usual low scores. Everything was working correctly. The psychic did another run – and obtained another score of eight. But when they recleaned the equipment and tried again they obtained their average low scores. Had the equipment again been at fault? It was impossible to tell.

A sceptical observer would say that it was mere chance that a fault appeared in the equipment on two occasions when well-known psychics were the subjects of experiment. An experienced psychical researcher, however, might observe that this kind of thing often happens. It is as though the unconscious mind of the psychic, knowing that a high score was required, achieved this by the easiest available method – by using PK on the microcircuit rather than clairvoyance. But it is impossible to prove this contention: it merely remains a possibility. Meanwhile, the random number box test of whether or not a psychic having an OOBE can 'observe' the normal physical world in any way when the possibility of using telepathy is eliminated awaits available opportunity and subjects for further research.

Research conducted at the Psychical Research Foundation in Durham, South Carolina, USA, appears to indicate that animals may be able to detect the presence of astral bodies. Psychic Stuart Blue Harary (below) was able to 'go', while in an OOBE state, and calm a pet kitten (bottom). An objective measure of the kitten's distress was provided by placing it in a box marked into squares, and noting how much it moved

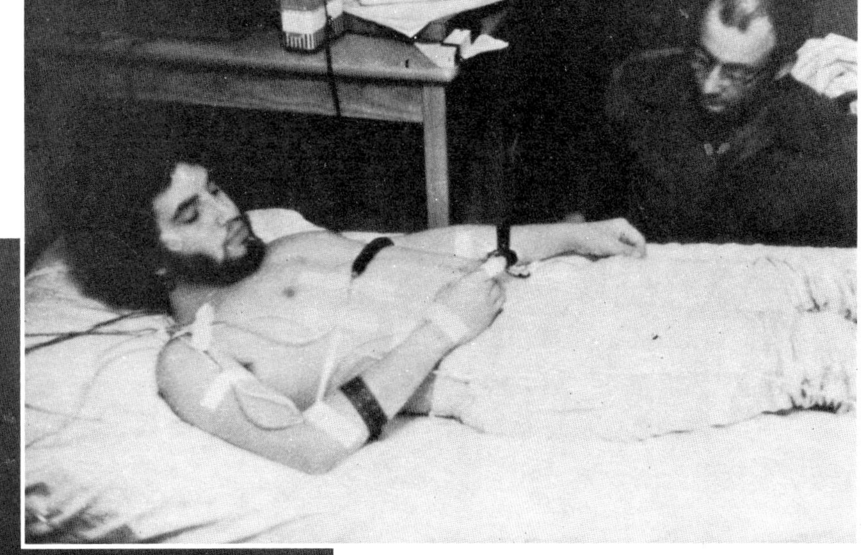

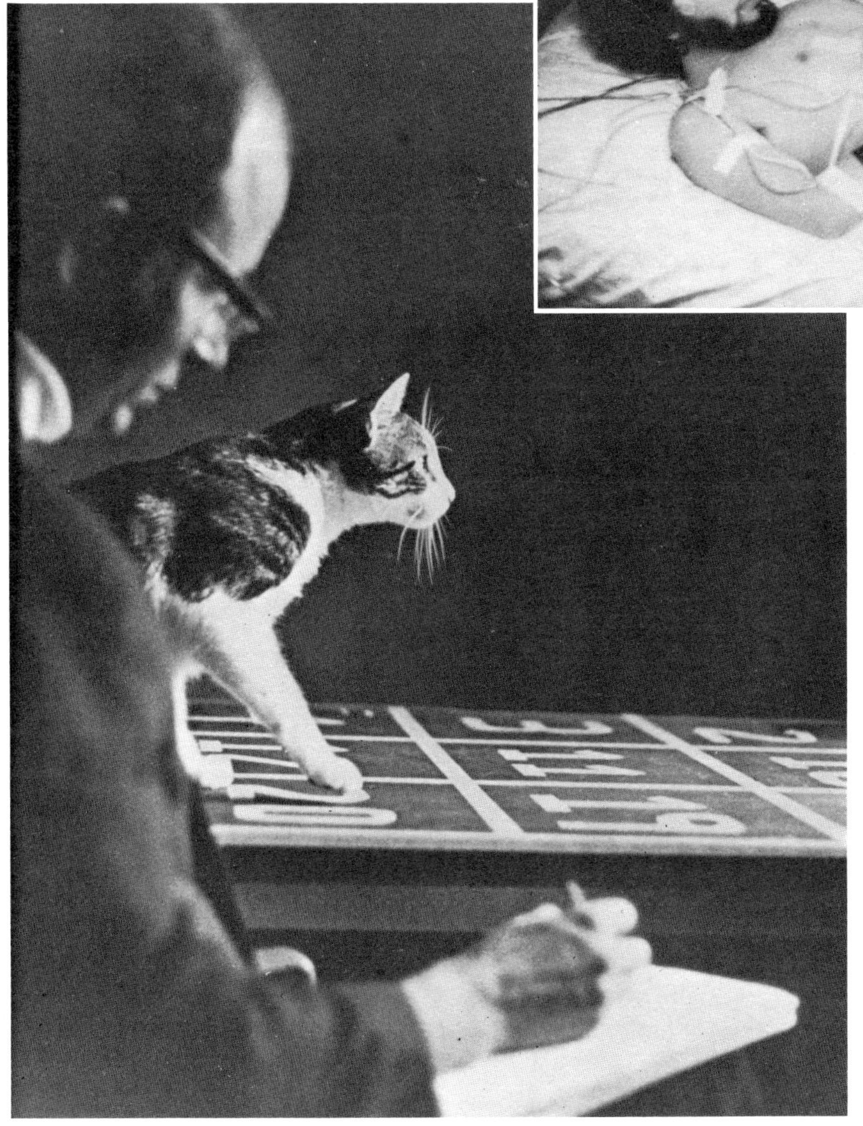

Dr Karlis Osis, the Research Officer of the American Society for Psychical Research, has conducted some interesting experiments with Alex Tanous to try to determine whether the observations conducted during OOBES are performed with something similar to the human eye. Osis required Tanous, in his OOBE state, to 'look' through the window of a box in which was an optical system superimposing images that gave a certain appearance to normal sight when viewed from a certain point in space. This appearance was in effect an illusion – something that did not physically exist – and the experiment was designed to answer the question of whether OOBES can be regarded as a kind of dramatised clairvoyance, or whether something (perhaps the 'astral body') actually travels from place to place during an OOBE. Osis claims that his results indicated some support for the idea of a presence in the physical space in front of the box. There are, however, problems in the interpretation of his results: the limits of clairvoyance are, after all, unknown and, even though it was possible to choose the target patterns randomly so that no one knew what their appearance to the human eye would be, it may be possible for the unconscious mind of the subject to deduce the appearance from clairvoyant knowledge of the relative positions of the components in the box, and to dramatise the experience to produce the correct result. Osis claims that later experiments in which he placed physical sensors (strain gauges) in front of the window of the optical box seemed to indicate that some kind of physical object might be there during

Miss Z and the hidden number

The first fully controlled laboratory experiment to investigate the nature of OOBES was conducted by Dr Charles Tart (left) of the University of California. Dr Tart's subject was a Miss Z, who reported having experienced OOBES since childhood. Wiring her up to an electroencephalograph, Dr Tart asked Miss Z to put herself into an OOBE state. On a shelf above her head was a slip of paper on which was written a number selected by Dr Tart from mathematical random number tables before the beginning of the experiment. The wires from Miss Z's head to the electroencephalograph were designed to be of such a length that she could not physically get up and look at the number on the shelf without causing an interruption in the pattern on the electroencephalograph print-out.

Nothing significant happened on the first night of the experiment. On the second night, Miss Z was successful in experiencing an OOBE, in the course of which she said she saw a clock on the wall above the shelf – she could not have seen this while lying down – and had 'read' the time as 3.15 a.m. A check on the electroencephalograph print-out revealed unusual brainwave patterns at that time. The third night she had a similar experience.

It was not until the fourth night that she attempted to read the figure on the slip of paper – and did so with complete success. She reported the time of her experience – by the laboratory clock – as between 5.50 and 6.00 a.m. At 5.57 a.m. on the electroencephalograph tape her brainwave patterns showed a disturbed output.

Dr Tart's experiment seemed to show that *something* paranormal was going on during Miss Z's OOBES. Professor Ellison's experiment is designed to answer the question, what?

OOBE observations: there seemed to be a tendency for more 'hits' on the optical targets when the gauges indicated activity.

Some interesting experiments using experimenter and psychic Stuart Blue Harary were conducted at the Psychical Research Foundation in Durham, North Carolina. The aim was to observe the behaviour of small rodents, snakes and kittens in the presence of an 'astral projection'. The kittens were put in a large open test box marked into squares. The normal random activity of the kittens could be expressed in terms of the number of squares occupied by a kitten in a given period of time. In normal experimental conditions, the kittens tended to be frightened, cry and move about a great deal. Harary 'went', in an OOBE state, to the kittens' box and tried to calm them. One of the kittens did indeed change in behaviour, its movement and activity both decreasing during the times when Harary was having an OOBE. The other kitten took no notice. Later experiments were not very significant, but it appears from the work done by Harary and other researchers that it might be worthwhile to investigate whether animals are better than machines as detectors of subjects having OOBES.

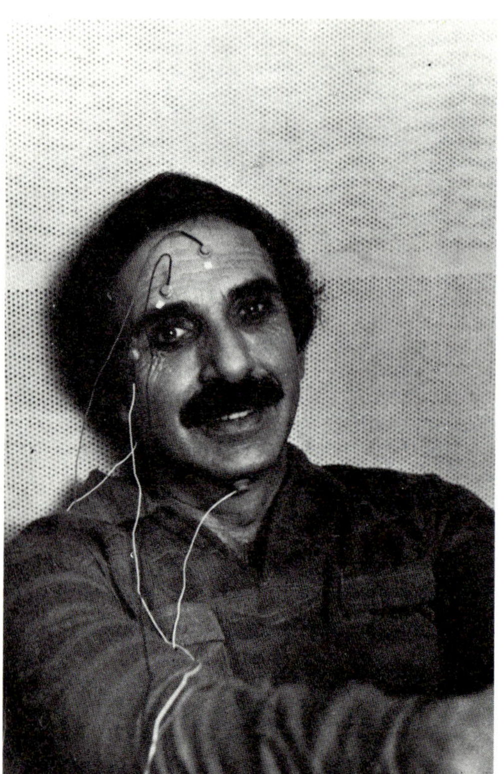

Does anything actually leave the physical body during an OOBE? Dr Karlis Osis (above), of the American Society for Psychical Research, has conducted experiments in which he places strain gauges in front of the site that the subject, psychic Alex Tanous (left, shown wired up to an electroencephalograph as he is during the experiments) is asked to visit

Worlds of illusion?

One can reasonably conclude from all this that it may not be meaningful to take subjects' descriptions of their own experiences of OOBES too literally. An OOBE may be a mental construction consisting of memories of the physical world, with some information obtained through telepathy or clairvoyance superimposed on it. Eastern scriptures suggest that the 'astral world' to which many people believe we go after death (and which we visit in the 'astral body' in an OOBE) is a 'world of illusion', based perhaps on a combination of our memories of this world and our desires, both conscious and unconscious. As Professor H.H. Price has pointed out, such a world of mental images would be just like the world described by mediums and psychics, with all the individual differences one would expect. However, as Professor Price also pointed out, such a 'next world' would not be at all dissimilar from what some philosophers say *this* world is like. Perhaps a study of the OOBE will help us to a better understanding of ourselves and our perceptions and mental processes.

Inspiration and genius

Many great artists and thinkers describe their insights as coming to them suddenly, fully-formed, and some of us have experienced such 'flashes' on a more mundane level. What is the source of these inner promptings and how much do they contribute to the workings of genius?

Dreams of discovery

The powers of the mind can be extraordinarily enhanced during the hours of sleep. What kind of inspirations come to artists and thinkers in their dreams and where do they come from?

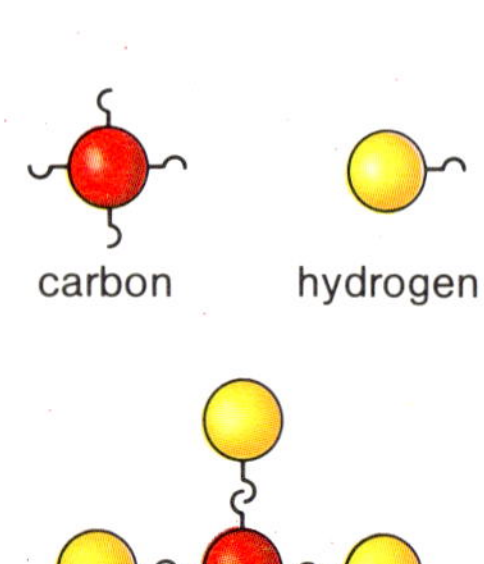

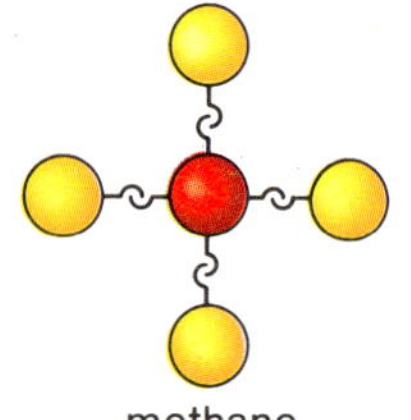

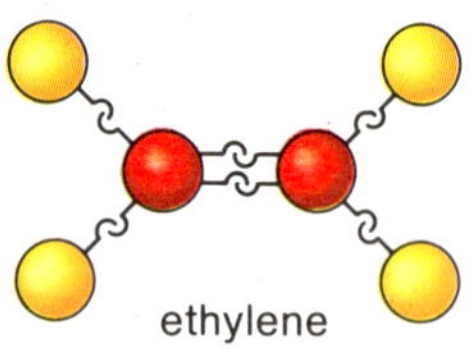

The structure of benzene was discovered by August Kekulé (right) in a dream. Kekulé wanted to work out how the hydrogen and carbon atoms in benzene linked together. Carbon atoms have four 'hooks', or valence bonds (above), while hydrogen has one. Four hydrogens can link with one carbon to form the methane molecule, or with two carbons to form the ethylene molecule. But in benzene, six carbons are linked with six hydrogens. When Kekulé tried to imagine them forming a chain (below left), some unattached 'hooks' were left over. In a dream (below centre) he saw a snake swallowing its own tail, then the carbon and hydrogen atoms swirling in a circle, and finally a ring-shaped structure (below right), now known to be the correct form of the benzene molecule

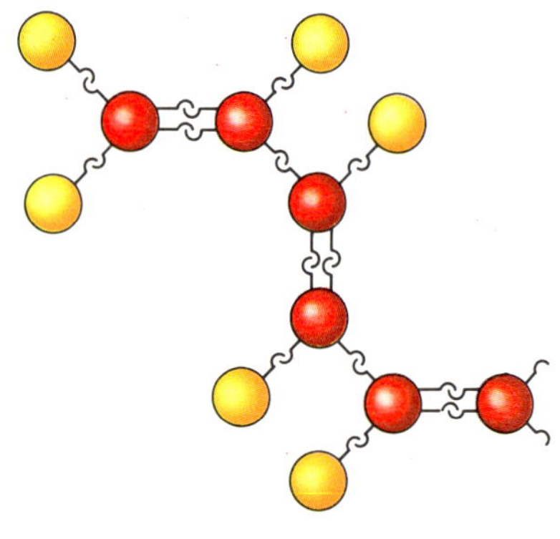

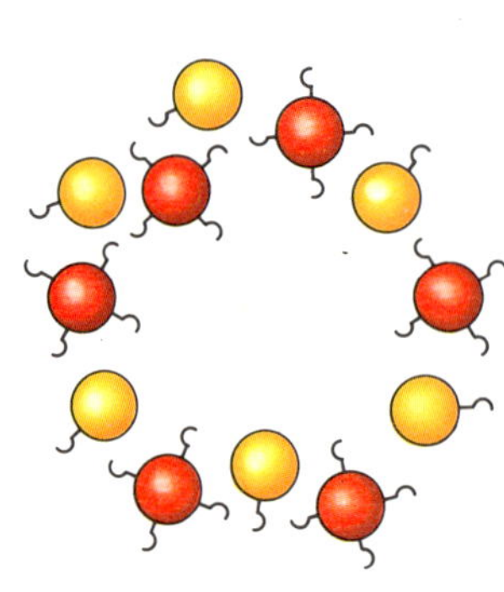

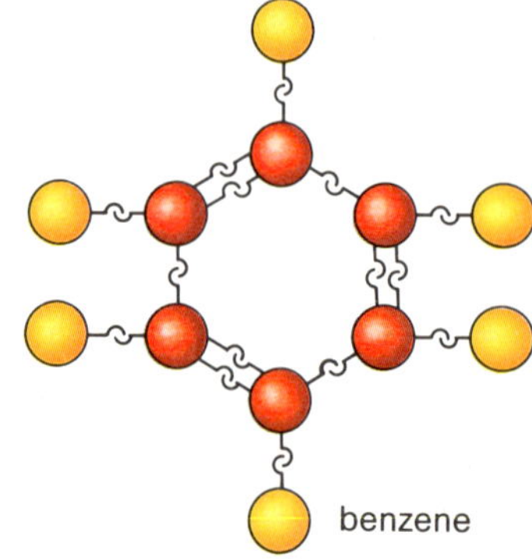

DREAMS CAN REVEAL not only the future but also, it seems, unsuspected truths about the world of the present. Many scientific innovations have made their appearance in dreams. One of the most celebrated had a revolutionary impact on chemistry.

In 1863 a gifted young German scientist, August Kekulé, was writing the second volume of a treatise on chemistry and had to deal with the problem of the chemical structure of the aromatic compounds. These were strong-smelling substances that contained hydrogen and carbon, and were derived from coal tar.

The smallest unit of any compound is called a molecule: it is a cluster of atoms, which can be pictured as linked by chemical 'hooks' called valence bonds. All the 'hooks' are linked to others, with none left free. Each type of atom has, in general, a fixed, small number of valence bonds. Carbon, for example, has four.

Kekulé had already shown how carbon atoms could form chains that were the 'backbones' of complex molecules. He had also cleared up some puzzles by showing that atoms could be joined by double or even triple links.

The structure of a molecule could often be explained by working out how the valence bonds of its constituent atoms could be linked. But no amount of ingenuity could form a chain of six carbon atoms with six hydrogen atoms, each of which had only one valence bond. Yet this was known to be the composition of benzene, the simplest of the aromatic compounds.

The solution came to Kekulé when he was dozing, half-way between sleeping and waking. He saw the benzene molecule as a snake that suddenly wriggled into a circle and swallowed its own tail. Kekulé woke and realised that the problem of benzene's structure could be solved if the six carbon atoms formed a ring, with the hydrogen atoms attached. An enormous field, the chemistry of the ring compounds, was opened up, and became the basis of the prosperous German dye industry.

A dream experiment

Another scientific breakthrough had its origin in a dream of the German-born physiologist Otto Loewi in 1921. He had been studying the transmission of signals along the nerves of animals. Nearly 20 years before, Loewi, like other scientists, had speculated that chemical processes were intimately involved in the mechanism of transmission of nerve signals, but little progress had been made with the idea. Inspiration came to Loewi in his sleep:

> The night before Easter Sunday of [1921] I awoke, turned on the light, and jotted down a few notes on a tiny slip of thin paper. Then I fell asleep again. It occurred to me at six o'clock in the morning that during the night I had

Right: Otto Loewi was a brilliant German-born scientist who devoted his life to studying the chemistry of the human body. A crucial experiment came to him in a dream. It showed how nerves control muscles, and answered a question that he had posed nearly 20 years before

A pact with the devil?

Giuseppe Tartini, a leading violinist of 18th-century Italy, was reputed to have made a compact with the Devil in a dream. The nocturnal visitor played a violin piece more ravishing than anything Tartini had ever heard. When he attempted to recapture it in the morning, he composed a sonata called *The Devil's Trill*, of truly fiendish difficulty. In Tartini's view it was a mere shadow of the music he had heard in his dream. However, his deal with the Devil led to worldly success. The story may have been prompted by the indiscretions of his early career, when he was arrested for marrying a protégée of the Archbishop of Padua. His prowess as a violinist may have contributed to the pardon that he received from the Archbishop.

written down something most important, but I was unable to decipher the scrawl. The next night, at three o'clock, the idea returned. It was the design of an experiment to determine whether or not the hypothesis of chemical transmission that I had uttered 17 years ago was correct. I got up immediately, went to the laboratory, and performed a simple experiment on a frog heart according to the nocturnal design. . . . Its results became the foundation of the theory of the chemical transmission of the nervous impulses.

Loewi's experiment threw light on the way in which electrical signals carried by nerves cause reactions in muscles – that is, how the brain controls the body. Loewi concluded from his experiment that in frogs the nerves do not stimulate the heart directly; specific chemical substances are liberated at the nerve terminals that modify the heart's functioning. For his work on chemical transmission of nerve impulses, Loewi shared a Nobel Prize with his old friend Sir Henry Dale in 1936.

These dream inspirations are not isolated incidents. Insights have frequently come to artists and scientists in their sleep. It is as if the sleep state enables the subconscious mind to take a leap that is not possible during its waking hours.

Above: Samuel Taylor Coleridge dreamed his poem *Kubla Khan*, including an ending that he later forgot

Below: Bernard Palissy was a gifted French potter, employed by King Charles IX and other members of the royal family. One of his elaborate rustic designs was inspired by a dream

Johann Wolfgang von Goethe, the great German poet, scientist and philosopher, reported that he solved many scientific problems and composed poems in his dreams. The Huguenot potter Bernard Palissy made one of his most beautiful ceramic pieces according to a design he had seen in a dream. The French composer Charles Nodier is said to have composed his piece *Lydia* in his sleep. Samuel Taylor Coleridge dreamed the whole of his poem *Kubla Khan* and simply copied it down the following morning. When he was interrupted by a visitor, however, the ending slipped his memory. The dream may have been brought on by the opium to which Coleridge was addicted.

Invention in sleep

Industrial inventions have been made in dreams. One is the technique of making lead shot by dropping molten lead into water from high towers. The drops of lead form perfect spheres during their fall. This process was conceived by James Watt, genius of the steam engine, and is said to have come to him in a dream about falling rain.

Such experiences are easily explained away as cases of the human mind employing its creative faculties more effectively than usual, and passing on the fruits of its activity in dreams. But they could be viewed as similar to those dreams in which the sleeper seems to acquire information that is not accessible to him by any normal means – such as dreams that reveal the identity of a murderer. The following examples of scientists' dream discoveries could be interpreted in this way.

The 19th-century Swiss palaeontologist Louis Agassiz was once trying to guess at the structure of a fossil fish from the faint and confused traces that were exposed on the surface of the stone slab in which it was preserved. He found it impossible to do so. In his dream, however, he saw the complete fish, with all the missing features perfectly restored. But when he awoke, the dream faded before he could record it. He examined the fossil again in the hope that it would bring the dream image back to him, but it failed to do so.

On the following night Agassiz had the same dream, but once again it faded from memory when he woke up. In the hope that he would dream of the complete fish on the third night, the scientist put pen and paper by his bedside. He was rewarded by another 'action replay' of the dream and was able to draw the fossil image immediately, while still half-asleep.

The following day the drawing did not impress Agassiz. He thought the form it showed to be most unlikely. But he went back to the fossil and began to chisel at the surface of the stone, using his sketch as a guide. To his astonishment he was able to reveal the missing parts of the fossil, which proved to be exactly what his dream of the previous night had depicted.

An interesting feature of this case is that Agassiz's conscious mind rejected the sketch because of the implausibility of what it showed. Did his subconscious perceive clues that escaped his observation? Or did he 'see' the shape of the fish by some unknown paranormal means?

Ancient secrets

Similar questions are posed by the experience of Professor Hilprecht, a scholar who was trying to decipher the words engraved on two small pieces of agate from ancient Babylonia. The *Proceedings* of the Society for Psychical Research for 1900 gave a detailed account of the remarkable way in which a solution to this intractable problem finally came to him.

Professor Hilprecht fell asleep one night after spending many hours in a vain attempt to understand the meaning of the inscription.

Right: on three consecutive nights Louis Agassiz had a dream that guided him in his study of a fossil fish

Below left: James Watt was a prolific inventor, best known for revolutionising the steam engine. A dream of rain gave him the idea for a method of making lead shot (below). Molten lead was poured through a grille at the top of a tower. The globules of lead formed into perfect spheres in their fall. They landed in a tub of water and cooled

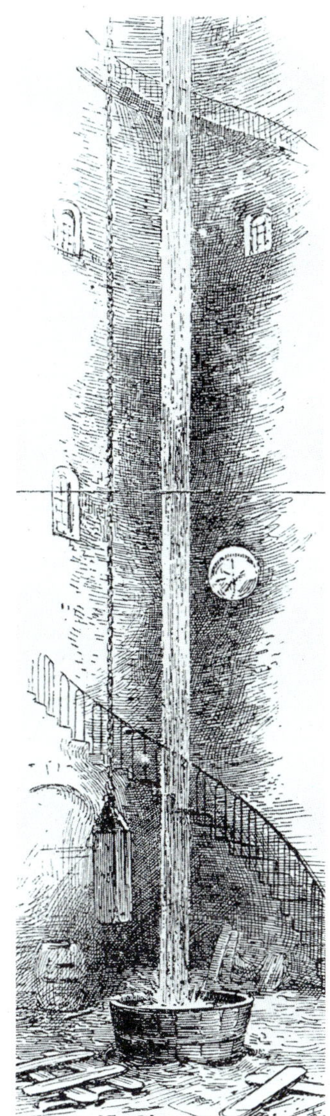

He dreamed that a tall, thin priest of pre-Christian Nippur (a sacred city near Babylon) led him to a treasure-chamber in a temple. They went into a small, low-ceilinged, windowless room in which there was a large wooden chest. Scraps of agate and lapis lazuli were scattered on the floor. The priest told the professor:

> King Kruigalzu [about 1300 BC] once sent to the temple of Bel, among other articles of agate and lapis lazuli, an inscribed votive cylinder of agate. Then we priests suddenly received the command to make for the statue of the god Ninib a pair of ear-rings of agate. We were in great dismay, since there was no agate as raw material at hand. In order for us to execute the command there was nothing for us to do but cut the votive cylinder into three parts, thus making three rings, each of which contained a portion of the original inscription. The first two served as ear-rings for the statue of the god; the two fragments which have given you so much trouble are portions of them. If you put the two together you will have a confirmation of my words.

The professor's wife testified to seeing her husband leap out of bed, rush into his study to examine the two pieces of agate, and cry out: 'It is so, it is so!'

Messages from the subconscious?

Many sceptics would favour a non-psychic explanation of this puzzle: that the professor's subconscious should take all the credit for fitting together the pieces of the jigsaw and communicating its findings in the form of a dream. The professor had simply slept on a problem and woken up with its answer, woven into a fantasy of a Babylonian priest.

But could it be that Professor Hilprecht was really in touch with the soul of the priest? Or is it possible that the scholar was unwittingly practising psychometry – 'object-reading'? Many psychics claim that just by holding something they can receive images and impressions concerning the object's past. Perhaps the same thing happened with Professor Hilprecht, and the dream was the means by which the images contained in the pieces of agate and gained in this way were transferred from his unconscious to his conscious mind, thus allowing him to decipher the mysterious markings.

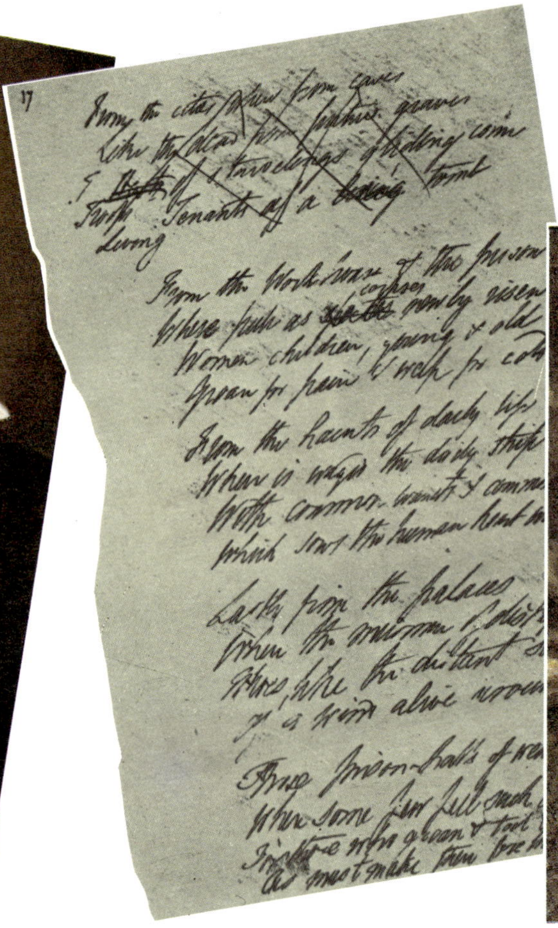

The genius within

How are works of genius produced? Their creators can rarely say; but time and again they insist that the credit is not theirs – and that they are merely the instruments of a power they cannot command

GENIUSES ARE OFTEN thought of as eccentric, abnormal, neighbours to the mad. The stock figure of the demented scientist still stalks horror movies, threatening the world with the latest product of an inspired but twisted thinking.

This popular picture may not be a true one, but genius is indeed strange and mysterious. Who can explain the masterpieces of art and literature, music, science and technology, philosophy and other creative spheres that have enriched human history – and sometimes changed it? What inspires the greatest creative minds?

While exceptional men and women have laboured, others have studied them and recorded their accounts of how they received their inspiration. Through such accounts runs a strange common thread: men and women of genius frequently ascribe their remarkable achievements to sources outside themselves. In case after case they claim that their discoveries, their poems, their music

Inspiration was impassioned and unpredictable for Percy Shelley (above left). The manuscript of his poem *The mask of anarchy* (above) shows the heavy revisions he made as ideas flooded forth

Robert Burns (right) was referring to the ancient idea that artistic creation occurred at the touch of a Muse when he wrote: 'The poetic Genius of my Country found me . . . at the plough, and threw her inspiring mantle over me.' Cartoonist Charles Addams of the *New Yorker* magazine made lighter use of the notion (far right)

Above: the popular image of the Muse, in a sentimental painting. She makes a last appearance to Chopin, as death embraces him

Left: William Wordsworth wrote of poetic inspiration as an 'awful Power . . . from the mind's abyss.' Is this an accurate picture of the creative faculty?

are *given* to them. One even gets the impression that their great works have been thrust upon them and that they themselves are mere instruments of some unknown creator. This notion is best considered by way of example.

The poet Percy Bysshe Shelley was found one day by his friend Edward John Trelawny among the pine forests near Pisa, Italy, sheets of manuscript lying beside him. Trelawny relates how scrawled the words were; many were scored out, corrected again and again in the heat of the poet's almost despairing effort to set down the images and words that came boiling up into his mind. 'Poetry,' Shelley said in explanation, 'is not like reasoning, a power to be exerted according to the determination of the will. A man cannot say: "I will write poetry." The greatest poet even cannot say it.'

Johann Wolfgang von Goethe claimed that the songs he wrote made him, not he the songs.

William Wordsworth, widely acknowledged as a poet of genius, was capable of examining his own mind in the throes of composition. On many occasions in his poetry he spoke of the 'sublime invasion' of material. In one place he writes:

> That awful Power rose from the mind's abyss,
> Like an unfathomed vapour that enwraps,
> At once, some lonely traveller. I was lost;
> Halted without an effort to break through;
> But to my conscious soul I now can say –
> 'I recognise thy glory'; in such strength
> Of usurpation, when the light of sense
> Goes out, but with a flash that has revealed
> The invisible world, doth greatness make abode.

The psychical researcher F.W.H. Myers put it like this: 'The influence rises from no discoverable source; for a moment it may startle or bewilder the conscious mind; then it is recognised as a source of knowledge, arriving through inner vision; while the action of the senses is suspended in a kind of momentary trance.'

George Eliot, the novelist, believed that when she was producing her most inspired work, some other personality seemed to take possession of her, dictating as if to a secretary. George Sand, the French writer, believed the same thing in regard to her own work. She has also left an account of the kind of creative struggle the composer Frédéric Chopin – her lover – went through to put down on paper the themes that had come to him. She wrote that his labour

> was a series of efforts, of irresolutions, and of frettings to seize again certain details of the theme he had heard. [He would] shut himself up in his room for whole days, weeping, walking, breaking his pens, repeating and altering a bar a hundred times!

Some famous authors have even talked about demons or brownies as the originators of their work. Rudyard Kipling said that he had learned to trust his personal 'demon' for advice, and William Thackeray wrote: 'I have been surprised at the observations made by some of my characters. It seems as if an occult Power was moving the pen.'

Robert Louis Stevenson obtained much of his most brilliant material from dreams, one of which was his well-known short story *Dr Jekyll and Mr Hyde*. In it he shows a realisation of the dark and sinister forces that can rule the subconscious. Talking about the role of his 'brownies' in his great literary output he said:

> The more I think of it, the more I am moved to press upon the world my

"We're looking for people who like to write."

Verse and worse

Geniuses usually have an unshakeable conviction of the value of their work; unfortunately, such conviction is no guarantee of its merits in the eyes of posterity. William McGonagall (1830–1902) was certain he composed his verses under 'divine inspiration'; and perhaps he did – if there is a god of bathos. One day he felt 'a strange kind of feeling' stealing over him – and then he penned his first verses, a tribute to his friend the Rev. George Gilfillan:

My blessing on his noble form,
And on his lofty head,
May all good angels guard him
while living,
And hereafter when he's dead.

Deaths among the clergy were a favourite theme of McGonagall's:

Friends of humanity, of high and
low degree,
I pray ye all come listen to me;
And truly I will relate to ye
The tragic fate of the Rev.
Alexander Heriot Mackonochie

Who was on a visit to the Bishop
of Argyle
For the good of his health, for a
short while;
Because for the last three years his
memory had been affected
Which prevented him from getting
his thoughts collected.

Stephen Pile puts it aptly when he says McGonagall 'was so giftedly bad that he backed unwittingly into genius'.

question: 'Who are the Little People?' They are near connections of the dreamer's, beyond doubt; they share in his financial worries and have an eye to the bank-book; they share also in his training; . . . only I think they have more talent; and one thing is beyond doubt, they can tell him a story piece by piece, like a serial, and keep him all the while in ignorance of where they aim.

That part of my work which is done while I am sleeping is the Brownies' part beyond contention; but that which is done while I am up and about is by no means necessarily mine, since all goes to show the Brownies have a hand in it even then.

Socrates, one of the greatest thinkers of all time, was often guided and advised in his affairs by a monitory voice, called variously the 'divine sign', 'divine voice', or the demon. He claimed that on many occasions it warned him against certain courses of action he proposed to take, and he believed that it was always right. It is an oddity of this mystical guide that it suggested only what not to do, never what the philosopher ought to do. Socrates seemed to feel that he was making the right decisions himself when the voice was silent. During the last days of his life, when his accusers sought his death, he drew strength and comfort from the fact that the voice intervened once only; this was to advise him against preparing a speech in his own defence.

Few would dispute that Wolfgang Amadeus Mozart – who wrote a complicated piano concerto at the age of four – was the greatest musical genius of all time. As far as we know, the creative power that activated artists such as Rembrandt and Mozart's younger contemporary Beethoven had to be developed, the latent spark fanned laboriously into flame. Mozart's genius was simply there, full blown. He himself had a simple explanation for his remarkable talents: he was in his own mind a 'receptor', an instrument through which some unknown power channelled glorious music.

As we have seen, great scientists have also acknowledged help from an indefinable source of inspiration. Kekulé, the father of structural organic chemistry, was one such. After fruitless struggles to determine the nature of the benzene molecule, he had a waking dream while travelling on a London bus. In the dream he saw the atoms grouping themselves in snake-like patterns in space. It was the breakthrough to the solution of his problem.

Bertrand Russell said of his mathematical creativity: 'Every evening [my mathematical] discussion ended with some difficulty and every morning I found that the difficulty of the previous evening had solved itself as I slept.'

Lord Kelvin had a marked intuitive gift. Solutions came to him in a flash of inspiration – and afterwards he had to labour consciously and exhaustively for proofs. Einstein too 'saw' solutions to his problems.

Player on the other side

There are in fact far too many cases of geniuses claiming that their works are in some way given to them, and that they simply polish them up, for us to ignore the possibility that in some strange way they are approaching the truth. However they put it, whether by referring to 'brownies' or 'demons' or 'subconscious mechanisms', for such people there seems to be a player or players on the other side of the boundary to consciousness – inspiring, teaching, guiding, desirous of helping them in their creative struggles. In these terms, the word 'genius' is most aptly applied to those human beings who, upon the penetration of their consciousnesses by inspiration when the barriers are down, have conscious abilities with

Below: Lord Kelvin made many brilliant discoveries concerning electricity and heat. Often they came to him in an instant: hours of laborious work were then needed to prove the results in a rigorous way

Left: Bertrand Russell was one of the many creative thinkers who find that, after lengthy and fruitless work on baffling problems, solutions are likely to come, fully formed, during the hours of sleep

Below right: the 'demon' of Socrates spoke to him for the last time while he was in prison, on trial for his life. It advised him not to write a speech in his own defence

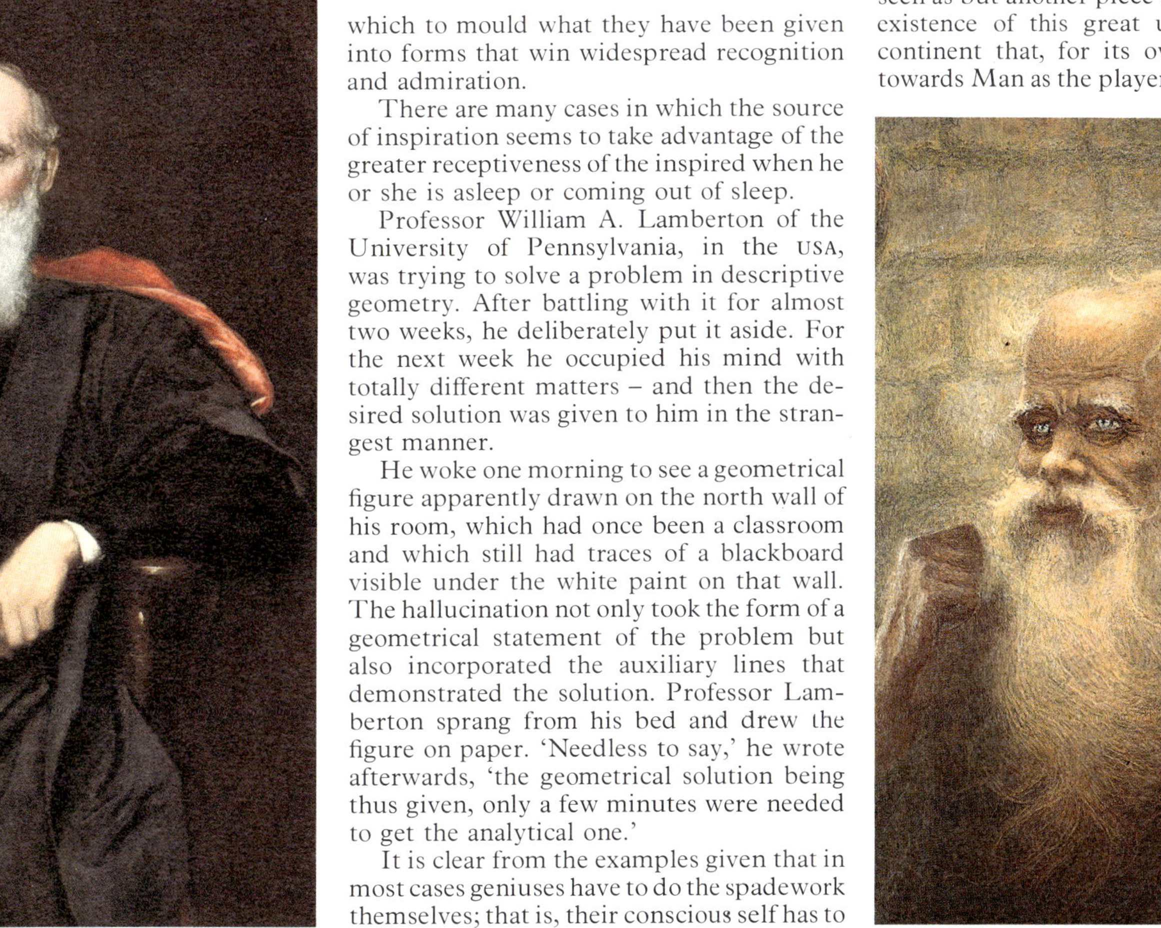

which to mould what they have been given into forms that win widespread recognition and admiration.

There are many cases in which the source of inspiration seems to take advantage of the greater receptiveness of the inspired when he or she is asleep or coming out of sleep.

Professor William A. Lamberton of the University of Pennsylvania, in the USA, was trying to solve a problem in descriptive geometry. After battling with it for almost two weeks, he deliberately put it aside. For the next week he occupied his mind with totally different matters – and then the desired solution was given to him in the strangest manner.

He woke one morning to see a geometrical figure apparently drawn on the north wall of his room, which had once been a classroom and which still had traces of a blackboard visible under the white paint on that wall. The hallucination not only took the form of a geometrical statement of the problem but also incorporated the auxiliary lines that demonstrated the solution. Professor Lamberton sprang from his bed and drew the figure on paper. 'Needless to say,' he wrote afterwards, 'the geometrical solution being thus given, only a few minutes were needed to get the analytical one.'

It is clear from the examples given that in most cases geniuses have to do the spadework themselves; that is, their conscious self has to sweat over the material both before and after the player on the other side intervenes. To that extent there is truth in the saying that genius is 10 per cent inspiration and 90 per cent perspiration.

But where, if that is the correct word, does the source of inspiration lie? No definite answer can be given, but there are many clues leading to a tentative 'model' of genius.

It must be accepted that our conscious personality is little more than a fraction of the human psyche or personality, and that most of that psyche is outside consciousness. F.W.H. Myers called those other reaches of personality the subliminal – that is to say, the parts below the threshold of consciousness. A limited definition of the subliminal or unconscious is that it contains everything, including our memories, that is not held within consciousness. But, as Myers, William James, Carl Gustav Jung, and indeed all those who have truly appreciated the complexity of human personality, have taught, the subliminal is much more than that. It merges with what Jung called a collective unconscious which is influenced to some degree by all men and women and which, by its structure and drives, in turn influences them. The evidence that a person's personality, both conscious and unconscious, is not a closed system is provided by telepathy, clairvoyance, and such ostensible cases of possession as those seen in the trance states of mediums. The inspiration of genius can be seen as but another piece of evidence for the existence of this great uncharted psychic continent that, for its own purposes, acts towards Man as the player on the other side.

The power behind the hunch

How can we explain overnight successes in the business world? Can the powerful 'hunches' on which many executives rely when making decisions be attributed to extra-sensory perception?

Above: the American Stock Exchange in New York's Wall Street district (right). Many of the men who successfully play the Stock Market admit that they are often guided by ESP

AFTER A TWO-YEAR development programme costing $2 million, the Electric Hydracon Company in Altoona, Pennsylvania, USA, discovered a serious flaw in its new extruded metal installation, which moulds metal by pushing it through dies. Only when the work was completed in 1961 did the company realise that if the machinery were run continuously the regular dies and tooling used would last only a week.

'Financial disaster would be our reward,' said Richard Haupt, who was then executive vice-president. He consulted five major companies to see what could be done and they all gave the same advice. If Electric Hydracon wanted its new plant to last longer it had to use *harder* materials for the containers, dies and tooling. But something told Haupt that it would be better to use softer materials.

'Our president directed me to abide by the

Dr Douglas Dean (above left), together with Dr John Mihalasky, carried out extensive research into the role of ESP in business life. Among the many top executives whose life and achievements he examined were: Conrad Hilton (top left), international hotel magnate; William C. Durant (top right), founder of General Motors; Charles Kemmons Wilson (above), chairman of Holiday Inns; and Chester Carlson (below), inventor of the Xerox photocopying technique

decision of the major steel mills,' Haupt recalled. 'Nevertheless, I followed my own intuition and spent two-and-a-half times more money for the softer material. The result was an outstanding success with the softer tooling. It lasts six times as long as harder steels. The entire industry has now followed this procedure.'

Richard Haupt, like many other top executives, recognises that there are times when an element of extra-sensory perception emerges in his decision-making, urging him to follow a course of action that often flies in the face of logic or expert advice. This talent, dubbed 'executive ESP', has been the subject of several studies.

Most businessmen would deny that they were psychic, and it is admittedly difficult to know where subconscious assessment from normal sensory clues ends, and extra-sensory perception begins. Executives who recognise that there is a difference between the two use many different words to describe it: sixth sense, business acumen, gut feeling, hunch or intuition.

Psychical researcher Dr Douglas Dean says that executive ESP is an essential ingredient in business life where decisions have to be made about future events, often without enough information to justify them. 'Businessmen use it every week, every month, every year, continually. And the best ones go on doing it very happily without worrying about it. They pile up tremendous profits year after year because they really are stupendous at this ability.'

Dean's statement is based on the research he carried out with the PSI Communications Project at Newark College of Engineering, New Jersey, from 1962. An English electrochemist with a keen interest in the paranormal, Dean worked on the project with a professor of industrial engineering who was originally sceptical – Dr John Mihalasky.

Among those who gave financial support to the project was the late Chester Carlson, inventor of the Xerox photocopying technique, who, through personal experience, had no doubts about the existence of ESP and other psychic phenomena.

During the course of the PSI Communications Project the researchers interviewed many top executives and looked at the lives of others. William C. Durant, the founder of General Motors, was typical. One of his colleagues, Alfred P. Sloan, a former president of the giant automobile company, said Durant, 'would proceed on a course of action guided solely, as far as I could tell, by some intuitive flash of brilliance. He never felt obliged to make an engineering hunt for the facts.'

Choosing the right sites for his hotels was the responsibility of Charles Kemmons Wilson, founder and chairman of Holiday Inns, Inc. He described the task as like 'going on an Easter egg hunt and sometimes you find the golden egg.' There were times when

Above: the London Hilton, one of an international chain of hotels established by Conrad HIlton. Considered by his associates to be an astute businessman, Hilton himself attributed at least part of his financial success to 'playing hunches'

he would insist on weeks of study by his company before he would make a decision on a site. But there were other times when he would give an emphatic 'no' for no other reason than 'I don't like the smell of it.'

Another hotel man who believed in following his hunches was Conrad Hilton. In the 1940s Hilton advised Duncan Harris, president of a large real estate firm, to buy Waldorf-Astoria bonds. Hilton himself had snapped up a considerable number at $4\frac{1}{2}$ cents, much to the surprise of other businessmen. The Depression had made the bonds tumble in price and wartime was adding to the difficulties of maintaining hotels.

Harris, too, was sceptical about his friend's advice and he invited Hilton to listen in on an extension when he telephoned his broker about the bonds. 'Some wild man from the West has forced them up to 8 cents,' said the broker with amusement. 'We're unloading by the bushel. This is the first time in years that anyone holding hotel paper has believed in Santa Claus.'

The man's cynicism did not dismay Hilton, who remarked later: 'Harris bought, and so, sweating and swearing, did a small faithful group who backed "Connie's hunches". Later hotel securities boomed and the wild man who bought at $4\frac{1}{2}$ cents was considered an astute fellow when he sold at 85 cents. Santa Claus had planted $22,500 and reaped almost $500,000. I've been accused more than once of playing hunches . . . I further believe most people have them, whether they follow them or not.'

Another of Hilton's hunches paid off when, during the war, he made a bid for the Stevens Corporation. He had wanted the Stevens Hotel, Chicago, but it had been taken over by the Air Force. He decided, when the Stevens Corporation came on the market, that its assets might prove profitable and, in time, if ever the government released the Chicago hotel, it would be his. But the Corporation's trustees called for sealed bids. The business empire would go to the highest bidder. In such a situation, interested parties run the risk of losing a bid by a narrow margin, or unnecessarily outbidding their rivals by many thousands.

'No businessman likes sealed bids,' Hilton remarked. 'My first bid, hastily made, was $165,000. Then somehow that didn't feel right to me. Another figure kept coming, $180,000. It satisfied me. It seemed fair. It felt right. I changed my bid to the larger figure on that hunch. When they were opened, the closest bid to mine was $179,800. I got the Stevens Corporation by a narrow margin of $200. Eventually the assets returned me $2 million.'

A similar situation arose in 1969 when the Alaskan oil lands were sold off. The international oil companies had to make sealed bids, and one particular area of 6 square miles (16 square kilometres) was of interest to many of them, including the Amarada-Hess-Getty Oil Combine. It had already made a bid but suddenly, on the weekend before the land was awarded, Leon Hess decided to increase the amount he was prepared to pay to $72.3 million. If he had not done so, he would have lost. When the bids were announced, his combine's offer was just $200,000 above its nearest competitor. Why did Leon Hess decide to boost his offer? 'I suddenly had a hunch,' he explained.

Playing the Stock Market successfully may also depend at times on a willingness to

Right: the San Francisco earthquake in 1906 destroyed miles of track belonging to the Union Pacific railway and the company's stock fell drastically. But one stockholder, Jesse Livermore, saved himself over a quarter of a million dollars – for only a few days before he had obeyed an impulse to 'sell short on Union Pacific'

Below: the oil pipeline that crosses Alaska. When the Alaskan oil lands were sold off in 1969, several companies showed interest in one small area. Sealed bids were invited and the Amarada-Hess-Getty Oil Combine made the highest offer – but only because, at the last moment and acting on a hunch, Leon Hess increased the amount he was prepared to pay

follow hunches. Jesse Livermore, a Wall Street multi-millionaire whose intuitive talents were well-known at the turn of the century, was so confident of his ESP powers that he even interrupted a holiday in order to obey a hunch to 'sell short on Union Pacific'. It was a strange decision to make because the railway's stock looked as solid as a rock, but he obeyed the impulse. A few days later the San Francisco earthquake wrecked miles of the railway company's track and its stock fell drastically. The hunch netted Livermore over a quarter of a million dollars.

So what is a hunch? The top executives who rely on it do not seem to know. Benjamin Fairless, former Chairman of the Board of US Steel, said: 'You don't know how you do it; you just do it.'

It would seem that executive ESP is often a deciding factor in an individual's business career, enabling those who possess the gift to rise to the top and help their companies to prosper. But would it be possible to spot such people in advance? Surprisingly, the answer that the PSI Communications Project came up with is a resounding Yes. Dean and Mihalasky, as well as interviewing top businessmen and testing them for ESP, also examined their outlook in a search for clues to differentiate between those who produced high scores in the tests and those who scored below average.

They were greatly influenced by the work of a leading American psychical researcher, Dr Gertrude Schmeidler, professor of psychology at the City College of New York. Dr Schmeidler had been investigating precognition for some considerable time and had compared the results of the participants in her experiments with their responses to a specially devised Time Metaphor Test. Individuals were asked if they thought of time as a dashing waterfall, a motionless sea, or in the form of an old man.

Those whose images of time were fast-moving were classed as 'dynamics' whereas those who regarded it as a motionless sea were said to be 'naturalistics'. For the few for whom time conjured up an image of an old man, the term 'humanistic' was used – they were the neutrals. When Dr Schmeidler analysed her results she discovered that the dynamics scored high in precognition tests where they knew they would subsequently be told the outcome.

Time and again in their tests, the two Newark researchers found dynamics outscoring naturalistics (whom they called oceanics) in ESP tests, which usually involved attempting to guess a number that a computer would generate randomly.

On one occasion, in November 1967, 40 top-flight executives were tested. Once again, the dynamics, as a group, outscored their oceanic colleagues. This time, Mihalasky also compared the results with the financial success of each individual's company. He comments:

'Some of the presidents were company owners. I asked if they were also the chief decision makers. If the answer was no, I discarded them. Others were chief decision makers but didn't have the title of president, and I threw them out too.' In this way he reduced the number to a dozen, all of whom were presidents who had held office for at least five years.

'Of these,' Mihalasky reports, 'every man who improved his company's profits by 100 per cent or more scored above the ten mark [average] on the precognition test.' He then combined the statistics with those attained at a similar survey of top executives, giving him 25 chief executives of small, medium and large companies. Twelve of these ran companies that had performed outstandingly, at least doubling profits in five years. When he checked their scores in the ESP test, he found that 11 of the 12 scored above average, and the twelfth man scored exactly at chance. Not one of them showed a negative ESP score.

An examination of the other 13 chief executives, who hadn't doubled their profits in five years, showed that five who had scored above chance had improved profits by between 51 and 100 per cent. One man scored at chance level, and of the seven who scored below chance only two had improved profits by more than 50 per cent.

Though not a large enough study to claim proof of the theory, these results do suggest very strongly that there is a correlation between profit-making and ESP abilities.

Obeying the inner voice

Abraham Lincoln, Winston Churchill, Franklin Roosevelt – all believed in psychic phenomena. How have these, and other, eminent and powerful statesmen been guided by ESP?

WINSTON CHURCHILL was entertaining three Government ministers to dinner at 10 Downing Street during the last war when he had a premonition. An air-raid had begun, as usual, and the dinner party continued without interruption. But the British Prime Minister suddenly rose and went into the kitchen where the cook and maid were working next to a high plate glass window.

'Put dinner on a hot-plate in the dining room,' Churchill instructed the butler, then he ordered everyone in the kitchen to go to the bomb shelter. The Prime Minister then returned to his guests and his dinner. Three minutes later a bomb fell at the back of the house, totally destroying the kitchen.

Churchill's intuitive powers were evident throughout his life and he learned to obey them. But it was during wartime that their influence was most dramatic. In 1941 Churchill made a habit of visiting anti-aircraft batteries during night raids.

Once, having watched a gun crew in action for some time, he went back to his staff car to depart. The near-side door was opened

Left: Winston Churchill on one of his many visits to anti-aircraft batteries in 1941. During the Second World War Churchill's 'inner voice' served him well; by heeding its advice he managed to escape serious injury and helped others to do the same

Above left: A. A. Lamb's allegorical painting of the Emancipation Proclamation, issued by Abraham Lincoln in 1863; and Negroes voting during the first state election in 1867 (above). Many Spiritualists believe that Lincoln decided to abolish slavery after talking to Nettie Colburn Maynard (above right) who, while in a trance, lectured the President at length on the subject

Top: Abraham Lincoln and the 'levitating' piano. It is said that the piano, played by a medium called Mrs Miller, rose in the air and began beating the time of the tune on the floor

for him because it was on that side that he always sat. But he ignored the open door, walked round the car, opened the far-side door himself, and climbed in. Minutes later, as the car was speeding through the darkened London streets, a bomb exploded close by. The force of the blast lifted the Prime Minister's vehicle onto two wheels, and it was on the verge of rolling over when it righted itself. 'It must have been my beef on that side that pulled it down,' Churchill is said to have remarked later.

When his wife questioned him about the incident, Churchill at first said he did not know why he had sat on that side of the car that night. But then he said: 'Of course I know. Something said "Stop!" before I reached the car door held open for me. It then appeared to me that I was told I was meant to open the door on the other side and get in and sit there – and that's what I did.'

What the British Prime Minister did was to listen to that 'inner voice' that we call intuition or a hunch, and heed its advice. He knew from experience that he could trust it, just as top executives have learned to be guided by ESP in making business decisions. Other statesmen have also been guided by intuition, or have allowed the psychic talents of others to guide them. The influence of the paranormal may well have shaped the destinies of some nations.

Many believe that American slaves owe their emancipation to the intervention of a teenager, Nettie Colburn Maynard, who gave spirit messages to Abraham Lincoln. While in trance, young Nettie is said to have lectured the President for an hour on the importance of freeing the slaves. Lincoln attended other seances, with different mediums, at one of which he and his bodyguard are reported to have climbed onto a piano which, despite its load, then lifted off the ground and began beating the time until the tune being played by a medium, Mrs Miller, was finished.

When a newspaper, the Cleveland *Plain-dealer*, published a story about some of Lincoln's alleged psychic experiences, he was asked if it was true. 'The only falsehood in the statement,' said the President, 'is that the half of it has not been told. This article does not begin to tell the wonderful things I have witnessed.'

No one knows how much the paranormal influenced the great Canadian statesman, William Lyon Mackenzie King, but his recently published diaries show that he had very bizarre beliefs and was certain that the spirits of dead politicians were in touch with him. When he visited England he always consulted top mediums, including Geraldine

Left: Canadian statesman W. L. Mackenzie King; he visited top mediums such as Geraldine Cummins (above)

Right: Richard Nixon in China in 1972. The pandas he took back to America created a huge demand for toy pandas – a demand that toy maker Herbert Raiffe had predicted the year before

Cummins who was particularly well-known for her automatic writings.

Franklin Roosevelt also consulted a psychic – Jeane Dixon, who is known as the Washington seer. And we should not be too surprised that modern politicians seek the help of those who claim to foresee the future: it is a tradition that goes back to the days of the Delphic Oracle.

There are times when ordinary citizens have premonitions about what presidents are going to do. In 1971, a Brooklyn, USA, toy manufacturer, Herbert Raiffe, had a hunch that toy pandas were going to be good sellers. There was no logic behind the decision but, nevertheless, he ordered that panda production should be increased at his factory.

In February of the following year President Richard Nixon visited China, toured the Forbidden City, and returned to America with a gift of two much-publicised pandas. No one was better placed to meet the sudden and unexpected demand for cuddly toy pandas than Raiffe whose intuition seems to have tuned into a rather trivial aspect of the President's China mission, long before the visit had even been arranged.

In America and Europe the police use psychics at times to help them solve serious crimes or find missing people. In Canada and elsewhere psychics have been able to guide archaeologists to the sites of long-buried ancient remains. And around the world, the ability of dowsers to locate subterranean water supplies and other resources is well known and documented. So why should we find it so odd that eminent men in the political arena are also prepared to open their minds to the influence of information that comes to them in a way that by-passes normal sensory channels?

Above: Franklin Roosevelt and Winston Churchill –

Not that it is always helpful to know the future. Abraham Lincoln, for example, awoke one day having had a vivid dream. In it he had heard the sound of sobbing and had followed it, through the White House, until he reached a room where he found a coffin draped with the flag. Lincoln, in his dream, asked a soldier who had died. 'It's the President,' came the reply. 'He has been assassinated.'

Days later Lincoln was dead . . . killed by an assassin's bullet.

Science and psi

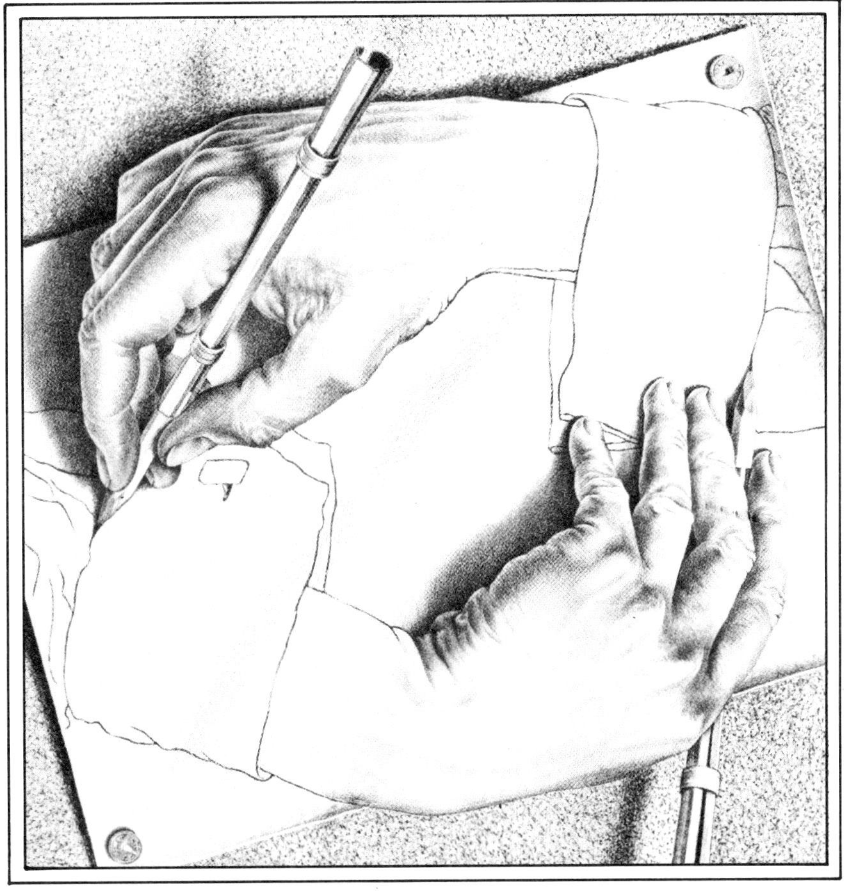

The traditional scientific point of view is that psychic phenomena are impossible, and belief in them is absurd, but modern theories about the nature of the Universe suggest that the paranormal may not be irreconcilable with science.

In the eye of the beholder

Can the scientist remain detached from the phenomena he studies? Or is he so bound up with them that he actually creates the effects that he observes? Scientific orthodoxy is challenged disturbingly by this novel concept

A DISTURBING IDEA has gained currency in certain scientific circles in recent years. It is an idea that conflicts completely with the basis on which most scientists conduct their experiments, the basis of 'naïve realism'. Most scientists, most of the time, assume that the physical world is 'out there', quite independent of themselves (though the scientist's own body, with its sense organs, is clearly a part of that world). Science is considered to be, firstly, a process of describing that physical world, and then of devising hypotheses as to how things work. If the hypotheses are good ones, they stand up under test, and assume the status of established theory. For example, the movements of the planets and other celestial bodies could be predicted with considerable accuracy by Newton's theory of gravitation which, after two centuries of successes, came to be regarded as unshakeable knowledge. When hypotheses do not stand up under test they are changed, or scrapped and replaced by better ones. Thus increasingly precise measurement showed Newton's gravitational theory to be inaccurate and it was replaced by Einstein's fundamentally different general theory of relativity of 1915, which now holds the field.

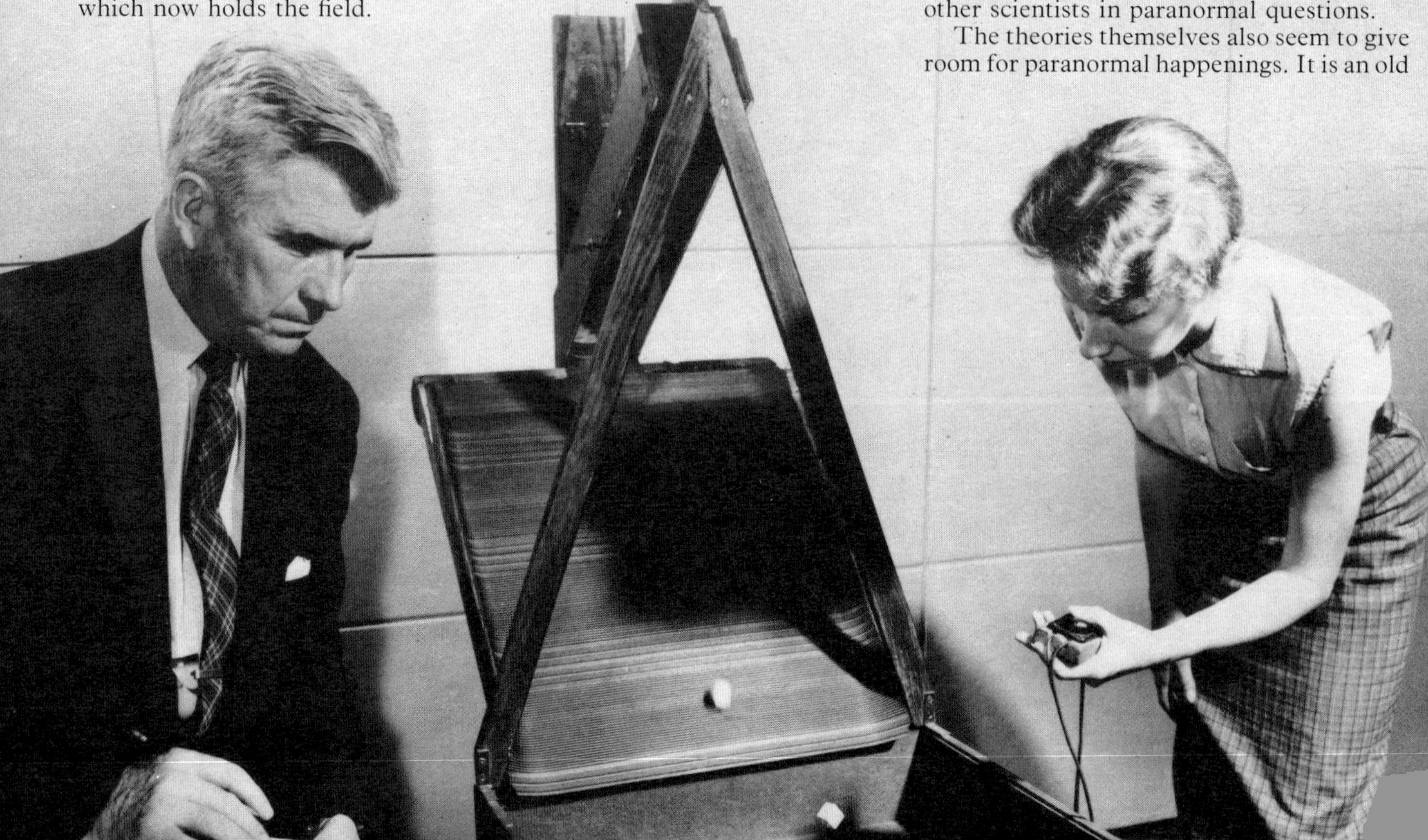

An experiment in psychokinesis (PK) under way in the parapsychological laboratory directed by J.B. Rhine, who is making notes. The results that he obtained in dice-rolling experiments convinced him that subjects could mentally control the numbers that turned up on the dice. If this can happen in a deliberately contrived PK experiment, could it also happen, unknown to the experimenters, in conventional research?

Most scientists would probably be willing to accept that, when constructing their theories, they were actually building mental 'models' representing experience. But they would probably react violently against the suggestion that the realist's view is not the whole truth about science. And if it were suggested that perhaps their mental activity could affect the results of an experiment they would probably be completely incredulous and point out that a most important step in the establishment of a scientific theory is that the relevant experiments should be repeatable by other experimenters in other laboratories, to provide the assurance that the result obtained was not the product of chance, error or self-deception.

The attitude of modern nuclear physicists is perhaps a little different. In the models they have devised to explain the behaviour of elementary particles some very strange things happen. Time runs backwards, and particles may disappear at one place and reappear in another without crossing the space between. Nuclear physicists on the whole do not worry too much about the physical interpretation of their equations, believing that, provided they lead to correct predictions of the outcome of experiments, their interpretation does not matter. Their mental models cannot be visualised – they are abstract and mathematical. The bizarre nature of their theories seems to predispose physicists to be more open-minded than other scientists in paranormal questions.

The theories themselves also seem to give room for paranormal happenings. It is an old

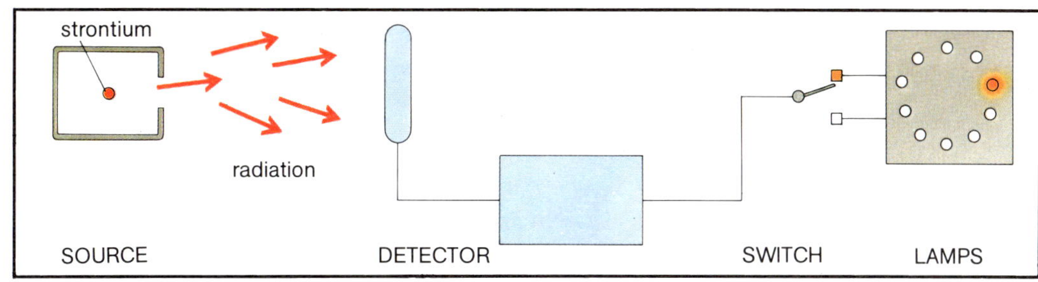

Left: the chain of events that takes place in Helmut Schmidt's PK experiments with a radioactive source. Radioactivity from strontium 90 triggers a detector, which controls a rapidly oscillating switch. The equipment is adjusted so that there is a 50 per cent chance of the switch being in either of its two positions. Lamps are lit up in a clockwise or an anticlockwise direction according to the position of the switch. Some subjects succeed in influencing the lamps to light in a particular direction. But in doing this, are they influencing the strontium, the detector, or some other part of the intricate circuitry?

Overleaf: Helmut Schmidt at work with a random number generating device

idea that, just as everything we can learn about or become aware of in the Universe influences us, directly or indirectly – otherwise we could not gain knowledge about it – so we influence everything else in the Universe, to some degree at least. In quantum mechanics this takes on a new twist. Some of the most eminent of physicists have claimed that, when a nuclear particle is observed by a scientist – or, perhaps, when a measurement is made on it by an automatic instrument – the observation directly affects the particle: if, for example, its position is measured, the particle acquires a definite position at that moment – having previously been in an indefinite, 'spread-out' state. On this view scientists intervene very directly in the phenomena they study – they create them as much as observe them.

Searching for PK

Such an interpretation of the process of measurement in quantum physics is not accepted by all scientists – the problems surrounding the question are profound and far-reaching. But many psychical researchers have been encouraged to look for the effects of influences of the mind on physical processes – psychokinesis, or PK – on the micro-level. One of these is Helmut Schmidt, who built a test machine using radioactive decay. The radioactive emissions from a sample of strontium 90 controlled a number of lamps arranged in a circle. When a Geiger counter recorded the arrival of radiation from the strontium, the equipment switched off the lamp that was illuminated at that moment, and switched on a neighbouring lamp. A rapidly oscillating switch determined whether the neighbouring lamp in the clockwise or in the counterclockwise direction was lit. Schmidt's subjects were asked to try to influence the lamps to light up in a specific direction – say, clockwise – and his results indicated very strongly that they could.

Psychical researchers have noticed apparent effects of mind on matter for many years, and many other experiments have been carried out to study the phenomenon. Dr Gertrude Schmeidler found, in experiments that have been repeated many times, that subjects who had a belief in the possibility of psychic phenomena were more likely to be successful. Equally remarkably, subjects who strongly disbelieved in the very possibility of such phenomena were more likely to get results that were worse than would be expected by chance. This too involves an interaction of an unknown type between the subject and the system that the subject is trying to observe or influence. Schmeidler called the believing subjects 'sheep' and the disbelieving ones 'goats'.

The psychical researchers have also put each other under scrutiny. Some researchers frequently get good results with their subjects: they are referred to as 'catalysts'. (The term comes from chemistry, and refers to a substance that promotes some reaction between other substances.) Other experimenters regularly fail to demonstrate PK effects, and have been described, unflatteringly, as 'inhibitors'. Usually such experimenters claim to be open-minded on the possibility of psychic phenomena occurring in their

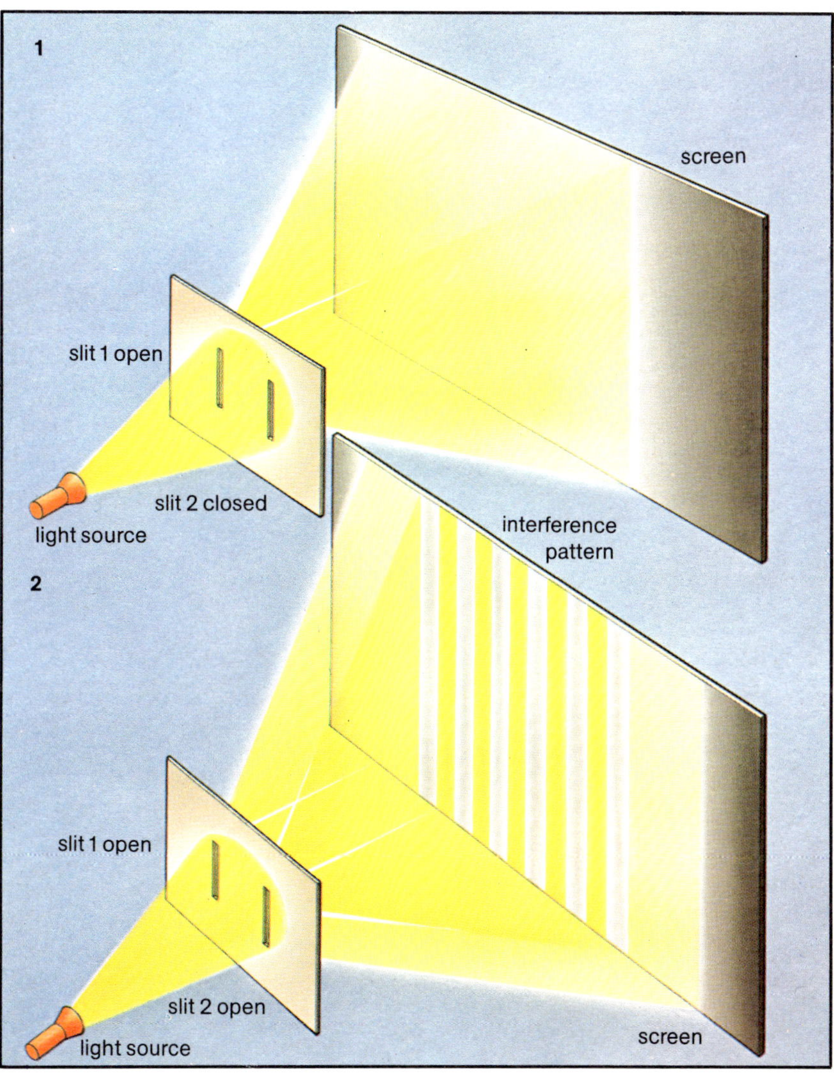

experiments: if, therefore, they are causing their own lack of success, one reason may lie in their unconscious minds.

Sceptics might suggest that the results of the 'catalysts' are actually due to fraud or incompetence. But many of these experimenters have unblemished reputations in other scientific fields: the doubters' speculations cannot be seriously entertained.

Many experiments have verified that the beliefs of subjects and experimenters are factors to be taken into account when conducting experiments in ESP and PK. The effects created by the 'Philip' group in Toronto, Canada, provide an example of this phenomenon. There the deliberate use of the imagination by a group of people, none of whom claimed to have exceptional psychic abilities, created a 'spirit' able to communicate with the group by means of paranormal rappings. The experiment has been repeated on a number of occasions, and there appears to be little doubt of its validity. It has been suggested that the experimenters, by their clear, detailed, and sustained thinking about the fictitious character Philip, created a 'thought form', a physical entity capable of producing sounds and other physical effects. The effects were weakened by the disbelief of

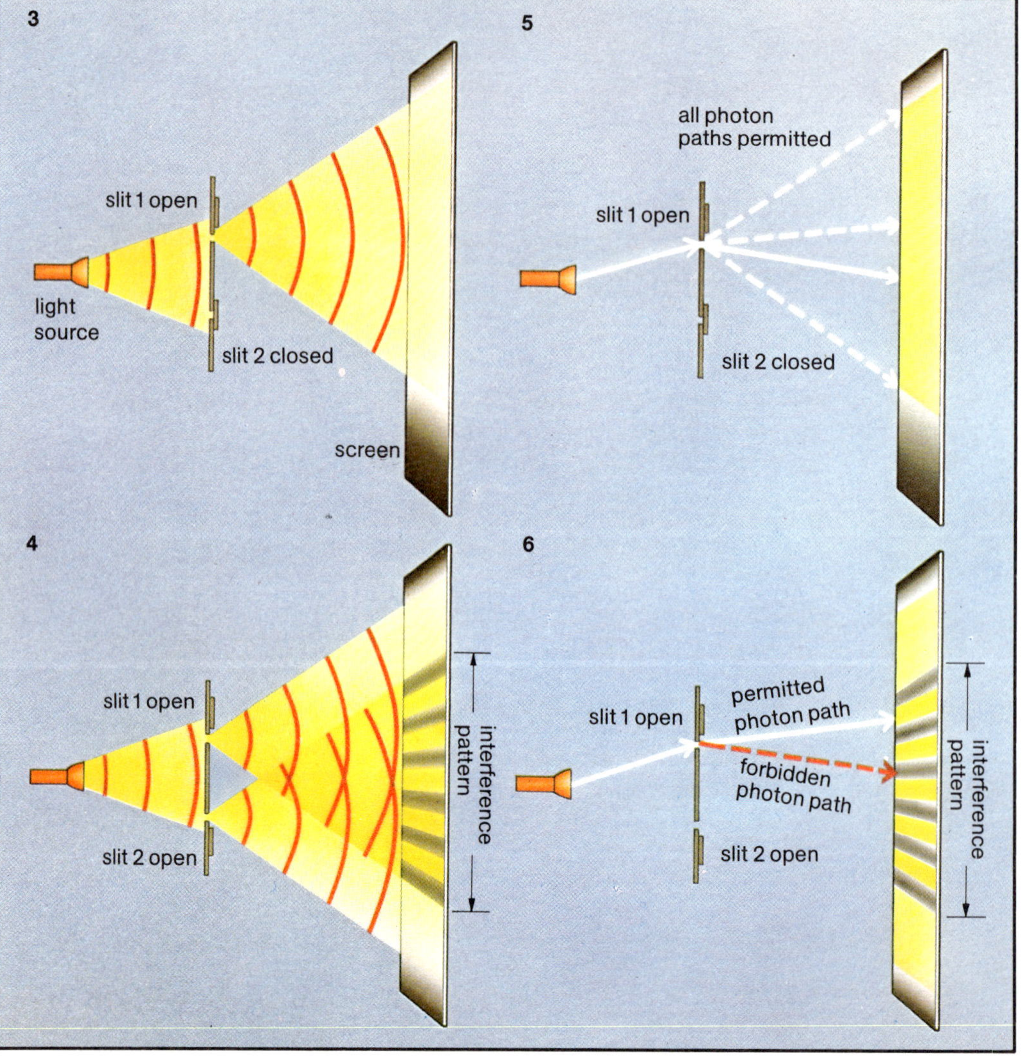

Nature abhors close observance. Light passing through a slit spreads to form a patch on a screen (1, previous page). When a second slit is opened, an interference pattern of light and dark bands is formed where the two beams overlap (2, previous page). Each beam can be seen as a train of waves (3, right). Where they overlap dark bands are formed at points where 'peaks' and 'troughs' cancel each other out (4). But other experiments show that light must also be viewed as made up of 'particles', called photons. In the one-slit experiment, each photon can follow a wide range of paths (5). But when the second slit is opened, certain paths are 'forbidden' – the photon cannot arrive in a dark band (6). But how can a photon travelling through one slit 'know' whether the other slit is open or closed? It seems that the photon 'goes through both slits at once' – it cannot be regarded as having a well-defined path in these circumstances

group members, and greatly strengthened by belief – even though this belief was of rather an unusual kind, for everyone in the group was well aware that they had 'made up' Philip.

What consequences for science in general follow from this? Suppose a scientist has a long-cherished belief in a particular physical theory, spends a great deal of time clarifying it in his mind and conducts experiments that are suggested by the theory; then it seems possible that physical effects confirming the theory can be *created* by this activity.

There are many cases of scientists who produced experimental results in accordance with some theory and were able to repeat them, while other workers were at first unable to do the same. This is usually attributed to the necessity for the other researchers to familiarise themselves with the experimental set-up and learn the skills necessary to conduct the experiment. But might it not also be that their own scepticism inhibited the effects that the original researcher achieved?

In some cases researchers have been unable to continue getting results, after an initial period of success. Could this be the result of discouragement by the unreceptive attitude of the scientific community?

Every year new, short-lived elementary particles are discovered. Frequently their existence is predicted before their discovery. It has been seriously suggested that these particles are being produced, rather than discovered, by the sustained mental efforts of physicists around the world. Although we have been conditioned to accept naïve realism by our scientifically based education, such an idea cannot be dismissed out of hand.

So naïve realism is an inadequate basis for an experiment in psychical matters. If the experiment involves the mind of a subject or subjects (and what experiment does not?) then it is essential to remember that the experimenter and any collaborators are parts

An indivisible whole

The amazing properties of the hologram are regarded by some scientists, such as David Bohm, as a vivid analogy for the indivisibility of the Universe. The hologram is a photograph of an object made by a special technique involving lasers. The light from a laser is of very pure colour – it has a single well-defined wavelength. The light waves are also very orderly – they are in phase, or 'in step' with each other. In making a hologram, no lens is used to form an image. Instead there is an apparently meaningless pattern of light and dark areas on the film. When the film is illuminated with laser light, however, a solid-looking image of the original object becomes visible (left, above). The film looks like a window through which the image is viewed; by shifting his viewpoint the observer can see details that are invisible from his original position. Ordinary stereoscopic photographs, by contrast, do not permit the viewer to 'look round the edge' of the image.

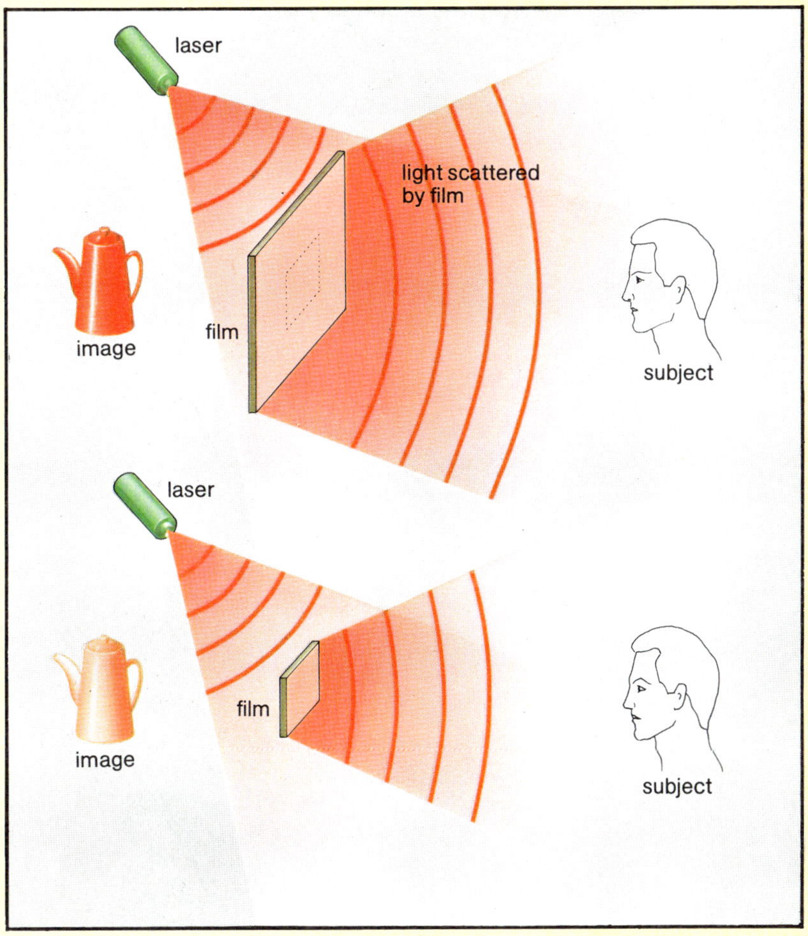

More strikingly still, cutting a small piece from the hologram and using that to form the image makes very little difference (left, below). The image loses some of its sharpness and must now be viewed through a smaller 'window' – but by shifting his position around, the observer can again view almost as much of the object as he could with the larger hologram.

Each small area of the hologram contains 'information', in 'coded' form, about the whole object, as seen from the position at which the hologram was made. That information is 'decoded' by the laser light to form a 'message' that is intelligible to us – the image. In a similar way, it may be that every object – or every mind – contains 'information' about the whole of the Universe – but in a coded form. Is this hidden unity of the Universe revealed when paranormal phenomena occur – and when the scientist discovers he is not separate from the Universe that he studies?

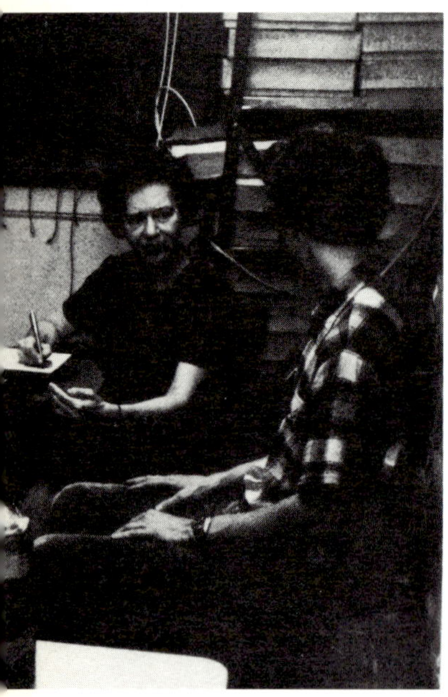

of the experiment too. In fact, the subject, the experimental team, their beliefs and their attitude towards the theory they are testing, the equipment, the laboratory and the world beyond, form a gestalt, an organised whole. It seems to be impossible to draw hard and fast divisions between any of these and say that they cannot influence each other, even though, in certain circumstances, that influence may be very weak.

The idea that all human beings are part of a greater whole, and are therefore inextricably linked, is a very old one. But it has only recently found its way into science, and most present-day scientists do not yet accept it. We are all – in the West at any rate – conditioned from an early age to accept the very inadequate view that human beings are no more than a mass of complex tissues surmounted by a living micro-computer, and that we are all quite separate from each other and from the physical Universe in which we find ourselves. It is very difficult for us to accept the clear evidence that it is not so. 'We are members one of another,' wrote Paul, and teachers from all the world's great religions have agreed with him. The scientific evidence that this is literally true grows. But the well-conditioned scientist meeting this evidence immediately responds with a well-developed defence reaction. It is interesting to see most of his scientific objectivity fly out of the window as he struggles to reduce the 'cognitive dissonance' (psychologists' jargon for a real or supposed mismatch between a subject's perceptions and his ideas of the way things should be). The greatest scientists do not fly from unfamiliar ideas in this way: genius seems able to resist the conditioning process, or to discount it.

Western exponents of the idea that human beings and the rest of the Universe are one whole, the evidence of which keeps breaking through in so many ways, are not uncommon. The eminent South African statesman Jan Christiaan Smuts put forward the idea in his writings on 'holism' – the doctrine that 'wholes are greater than the sum of their parts', having new properties that are not reducible to the properties of the parts. (The word 'holy' has the same root as 'holism' – denoting the idea of wholeness.)

The great psychologist C.G. Jung wrote about 'synchronicity' – the occurrence of meaningful patterns among things and events that are inexplicable by cause and effect. The writer Arthur Koestler in *The roots of coincidence* has championed these ideas and those of the biologist Paul Kammerer on 'the law of series'. This is the alleged occurrence of meaningful coincidences in series of events more frequently than we would expect by chance. Later, Koestler co-authored a work on various aspects of ESP and synchronicity, *The challenge of chance*. The evidence produced by psychical researchers by no means stands alone.

Above: paths of subatomic particles in a bubble chamber. The coiled tracks were produced by a stray cosmic ray; the roughly horizontal ones belong to artificially produced particles, which were the intended subjects of study. Is the intense thought devoted to these phenomena by the world's scientists actually helping to create them?

Top: Gertrude Schmeidler (left), who found that the attitudes of subjects and researchers affect the success of experiments in parapsychology. Others have confirmed her work

Guided evolution

The most recent – and extremely controversial – evidence in this area is that presented by the biologist Rupert Sheldrake. He postulates the existence of 'morphogenetic fields' – non-physical structure-forming fields that carry biological 'information'. The development of an individual organism, and the evolution of a species, are guided by these fields. The response issuing from that respected organ of the scientific establishment, *Nature*, was predictable in all but its intensity: the editor headed a leading article on Sheldrake's book with the phrase 'A book for burning?' The reaction of many physicists to David Bohm's controversial ideas has been similar.

The response of scientific orthodoxy to both these theories has been very like its response to Einstein's work. The evidence in the case of relativity finally became so strong that it was irresistible. The theories of Einstein are now 'establishment science'. Perhaps in due course Bohm's theories will receive the same recognition; in the meantime, it is unfortunate that they have had the same reception that greeted Einstein's.

The experimenter effect is, then, a phenomenon that does not accord with the basis of most modern scientific practice. However, there appears to be little doubt that it exists and cannot be ignored. Its occurrence could have been foreseen from the teachings of various traditions, especially those of Eastern religion and philosophy, and now seems to be confirmed by the findings in various areas of science. There can be little doubt of its profound importance. The recognition of the experimenter effect may presage radical changes in our ways of looking at the world and at mankind.

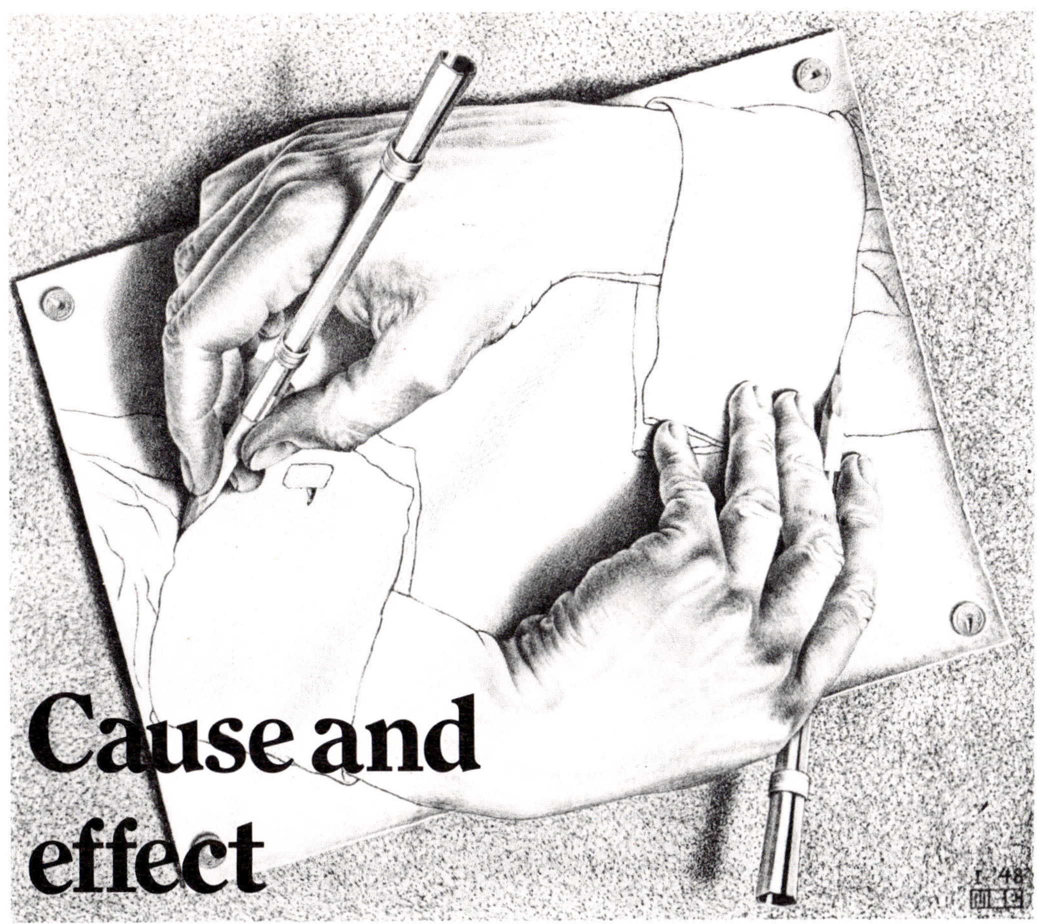

Cause and effect

Creator and creation are inextricably mixed in this arresting print by the Dutch artist M.C. Escher. A 'real' hand makes a drawing of a hand – which leaves the page, becomes 'real' and draws . . . the first hand. This is a striking metaphor for the emerging view of the Universe: the theories and beliefs of the scientist, apparently moulded by reality, become an important factor in shaping that reality

Scientists' confidence might be shaken if they were forced to acknowledge that they are unwitting actors in their own experiments. But some have already had to face up to this disturbing possibility

NEW SCIENTIFIC THEORIES that do not seem to agree with what is thought to be known are frequently rejected without a careful examination. Innovators who have been able to overcome their own educational conditioning to create original ideas are obliged to put up with this sort of response from the scientific 'establishment' until the day when their ideas become generally accepted – and, probably, become a new orthodoxy. The idea that scientific investigators and their collaborators are an integral part of their own experiments is such an idea.

Researcher A. J. Ellison experienced in his laboratory the inability of scientists to face this possibility. He was studying a famous British psychic who was apparently creating paranormal physical effects in a complex apparatus in which an infra-red beam was produced and its intensity measured electronically. He was evidently able to cause a sudden drop in the reading indicating the beam's intensity. (Whether it was the beam's actual intensity or the measuring instrument that was affected is uncertain.) The effect was repeated a number of times and seemed so clear and definite that Professor Ellison fetched three colleagues who were not part of the team, as independent witnesses. All fully understood the 'normal' electrical engineering and physics. They watched the effect being produced several times to order. Two of them were fascinated, declaring that they did not understand how it could possibly occur. They readily agreed to their names being quoted as witnesses. The third stated that 'there must be an explanation', even if he had not yet found it, and practically ran from the laboratory. He reduced the stress of this clash between what he was seeing with his own eyes and the received ideas of orthodoxy by refusing to admit the facts at all.

Brian Inglis, writer on the paranormal and consultant to this volume, has come across examples of biological experiments in which success or failure apparently depended on psychic influences from the researcher

Every researcher knows of experiments that did not give the expected results; the phenomenon is very common. Usually it is assumed that something went wrong and the experiment is repeated until it does give the 'correct' result. One wonders how many research students who do not clearly understand what the result of an experiment is supposed to be produce anomalous results – sometimes by their own unrecognised psychic ability – and are told to repeat the procedure until they get a more acceptable result. Perhaps the spoon-bending children who appeared following Uri Geller's television shows were able to produce paranormal results because they did not know that they were impossible – at least, according to their physics teachers.

The psychical researcher Rhea White has

made the point forcefully:

> the experimenter has been a neglected variable in parapsychological research. . . . There could hardly be a more significant area of investigation than the role of the experimenter, because not only may the achievement of extrachance results depend on the experimenter, but the experimenter may also affect the nature of the results obtained.

Perhaps the most important factor in successful experiments in psychical research is intense and sustained enthusiasm, and a desire on the part of the experimenter to get the best out of the subjects. This level of enthusiasm seemed to be present during the experiment with the British psychic mentioned above. It appears when the right people are present, and it must be carefully nurtured. Such an occasion is like a comet: its imminent arrival can be recognised, but it is not repeatable to order. The impressive paranormal events that can be brought about spring up and die down, and the skilful researcher must be ready for them – equipped to record them on audio- and videotape, and by other means, and to have witnesses present.

This phenomenon is by no means confined to psychical research. Brian Inglis describes the experience of the noted biologist Neil Miller. Miller wanted to find out whether rats could learn to control certain bodily functions – an ability that would upset conventional ideas about the workings of their nervous systems. With difficulty he found an assistant willing to collaborate on the experiments. They discovered that rats could indeed learn to alter blood pressure, heart rate, the temperature of one ear independently of the other, and other functions. Even though this sounded wildly improbable, other researchers were able to repeat the experiments and published their results during 1959.

Several years later Inglis visited Miller and discovered that he had been unable to repeat the results at this later date. The progressive decline of the results was inexplicable to Miller. He might have been completely discredited as a scientist if it had not been found in the 1960s that human beings could learn to control bodily functions, such as heart rate, previously thought to be completely automatic and independent of conscious control. Inglis suggests that psychic abilities of Miller or his assistant, or someone else involved in the experiment, might have played a role in his early success – and for some reason this ability declined subsequently.

A similar decline in experimental success occurred with Albert B. Sabin, the famous discoverer of a polio vaccine. He thought he had obtained reliable evidence that the virus

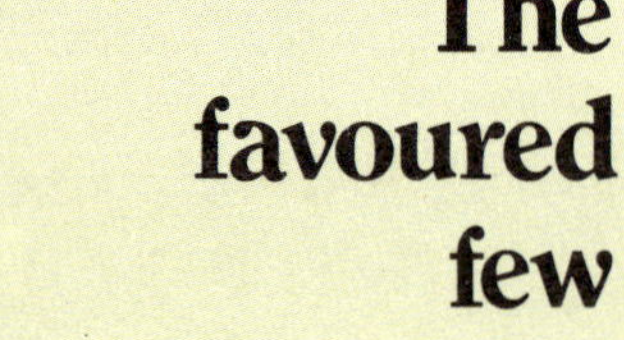

The favoured few

Psychologists are learning a great deal about the surprising ways in which human beings can influence the results obtained in supposedly objective tests. A classic demonstration was made by Robert Rosenthal and Lenore Jacobson in an American elementary school. They asked teachers to administer a non-verbal intelligence test to children in all six grades (ages 5 to 11). They then misled the teachers: they told them that the results indicated that certain children, who were named to the teachers, would show marked gains in their scores during the coming year. In reality these children had been selected randomly. They represented one fifth of all the pupils. Eight months later the teachers again administered the tests. The graph (left) shows the results. In all grades there was an average increase in test scores; but in grades 1 and 2 the children who had been marked out as promising made much greater gains than the rest. Some of the classes were tested by an educator from another school. She obtained the same results. In some unknown way the teachers' expectations about their pupils had called forth improved results.

Such effects can appear in very unexpected places. Before this work with schoolchildren, Rosenthal had studied behavioural scientists working with rats. Some researchers were told that their rats had been bred for intelligence; others were told that theirs had been bred for dullness. The results they obtained in such apparently straightforward tests as maze-running confirmed the supposed brightness or stupidity of the rats – which were, of course, a randomly selected sample.

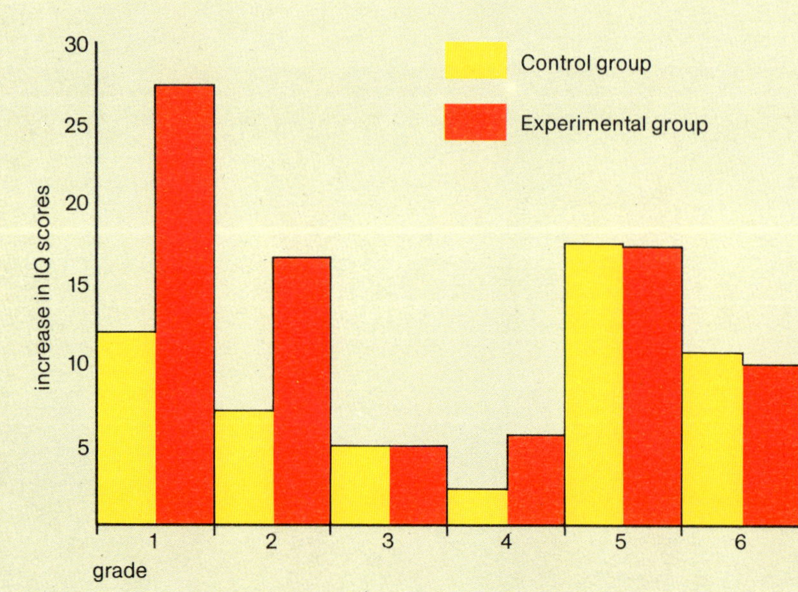

that causes herpes also caused many human cancers. Later he was quite unable to obtain the same results.

There are many examples of carefully controlled scientific trials that have produced such strongly conflicting results that the effects of the experimenters' beliefs and attitudes must be seriously considered. The best known data on the effects of the experimenters' expectations about the outcomes of the experiment were provided by Robert Rosenthal in 1966. They are widely quoted, but also widely criticised. However, he makes it clear that careful thought must go into the design of experiments in human behaviour, and experimental psychologists must be suspected of the same kinds of errors as parapsychologists.

An interesting study was carried out by the American parapsychologist J.C. Crumbaugh in 1958. He had been unsuccessful in his attempts to demonstrate paranormal effects and had decided that the personality of the experimenter must be an important factor. With the help of the staff at the Parapsychology Laboratory at Duke University, North Carolina, he designed a series of experiments. He worked with 16 subjects and 16 experimenters, working in long and short sessions. He studied the personalities and attitudes of both subjects and experimenters, and rated them according to their degree of self-confidence or insecurity, and their degree of belief or disbelief in ESP. He obtained results in the expected direction – that is, with the self-confident participants who believed in the possibility of success. He then refined the experimental design and repeated it, using only long sessions. No significant ESP results showed up.

Albert B. Sabin shows how his polio vaccine is administered. At one time Sabin thought he had demonstrated that certain human cancers are carried by viruses; but after a while he found himself unable to obtain the same experimental results. Was the change due to random disturbances – or to some change in his own attitude to his work?

Nevertheless, though he used 16 experimenters, Crumbaugh remained the principal experimenter: it is still possible that his own conviction that he could not succeed in ESP experiments inhibited his results. For there is no doubt that different experimenters obtain different results in similar psi tests.

Brian Inglis delivered the J.B. Rhine lecture to the Parapsychological Association in 1980. Its theme was of great importance in this area. His title was: 'Power corrupts; scepticism corrodes'. Many parapsychologists tend to be sceptical of the existence of the phenomena they study, though often

Getting the drift

When Einstein's theory of relativity became the orthodoxy of the scientific world, conflicting theories and experiments had difficulty in gaining a hearing – just as relativity itself had at first been rejected as inconceivable. The most distinguished physicist to bring contrary evidence was an American, Dayton C. Miller. He repeated the experiment of A.A. Michelson and E.W. Morley, first performed in 1887, which had come to be regarded as the cornerstone of the experimental evidence for relativity. It involved comparing the time of travel of two light beams along different paths. When Michelson and Morley performed the experiment, they expected that the 'wind' of ether (the hypothetical medium in which light waves travelled) would affect a beam travelling parallel to the Earth's motion more severely than a beam travelling at right angles to it. But they could find no difference, and it was gradually accepted that the ether does not exist.

From 1921 to 1926 Miller repeatedly carried out the Michelson-Morley experiment. His results varied – but he was convinced that they revealed an 'ether wind' with a speed of about 6 miles per second (10 kilometres per second) – one third of the Earth's speed around the Sun.

This work was sufficiently respected to win Miller a prize of $1000 from the American Academy of Sciences. No one had demonstrated any flaw in it by the time of Miller's death in 1941. But the implication that ether drift was detectable was rejected. Other experiments supported relativity, and in due course the Michelson-Morley experiment was repeated with other types of radiation, such as radio and radar, with no sign of ether drift.

In the 1950s Miller's results were closely analysed, and the investigators concluded that his results had been partly due to temperature fluctuations and partly due to random disturbances. But long before this reasoned criticism was made, the mass of scientists had assumed that something 'must' be wrong with such heretical results.

they are quite unconscious of this resistance. Consequently they refuse to accept almost any effect, no matter how unequivocal the evidence for it, for fear of being 'conned'.

The orthodox scientist will protest at this point. 'This is manifest nonsense!' he will say. 'You are suggesting that whatever nonsensical pseudo-scientific idea anyone comes up with is verifiable!'

Not at all: this does not necessarily follow. Take the morphogenetic field as an example. The presence of the field was postulated to explain the course of past evolution, and the development of living individuals throughout the course of their lives. These processes existed long before there was any Rupert Sheldrake to propose the existence of the field. But if its existence is confirmed at some future date, it will be by the demonstration of further effects and properties of the field manifesting themselves in new experimental arrangements. And it may be that, initially, some experimenters are more successful in demonstrating it than others. It is possible that these discoveries will not be made until scientific thinking is substantially in accord with them, when there will be a great weight of detailed thinking behind the notion of the morphogenetic field.

The opinions prevailing among the non-scientific public may also be highly important in determining what experimental results can be obtained. And these can be swayed by the opinions of noted scientists. However, it is probably the whole formed by the subjects and the experimenter that is of primary importance.

Patterns of guessing

There are, of course, ways in which the attitudes and beliefs of experimenters and subjects can influence the results without involving paranormal agencies. Subjects frequently tend to avoid calling the same card twice in a row during card-guessing experiments. This may be a quite unconscious habit, or it may be due to a belief that 'lightning doesn't strike twice in the same place'. In fact, if the drawing of the cards is truly random, all cards are equally likely to be drawn on any occasion, no matter what the previous card has been (provided each card is returned to the pack before the next draw). Someone else might have a preference for calling a particular type of card, and so on. If the card-drawing is not completely random, the biases of the subject may result in scores that are significantly above or below those that would be expected by pure chance – even if no paranormal factor is involved.

There is a tragic and highly controversial example of what may be an unusual case of the experimenter effect. The important experiments of S.G. Soal, a former president of the British Society for Psychical Research, have been widely regarded as outstanding in their class. They were card-guessing experiments that apparently demonstrated the existence of telepathy. A later computer analysis of his results indicated that the figure 1 had been altered to 4 or 5 in various places. Subsequently an independent observer at Soal's experiments claimed that she had seen him making alterations that agreed with these findings.

This was a shattering discovery to parapsychologists. Some of them have seriously suggested that an alternative to conscious fraud is possible. The changes may have been made quite unwittingly by Soal: his subconscious mind may have seized on this as a way of obtaining the results that he so passionately desired.

Cynics will scoff at this explanation, of course. They will classify Soal with those physical mediums who have been caught cheating when supposedly in trance during seances. But I am fairly sure that in at least some cases these mediums too were not cheating consciously and deliberately: they were in an 'altered state of consciousness', in which their normal mind was not in control.

Of course, it is deplorable that the experimental conditions during these seances and during Soal's experiments were so faulty that this 'cheating' could take place. We are learning rapidly, and the rate of learning is increasing. We can now record the activities of all participants in an experiment, and analyse the results completely automatically, thus circumventing most of these earlier difficulties. Thus the enthusiasm and optimism of experimenters and subjects are able to contribute to the success of the experiment, without distorting the results.

What the psychical researchers are bringing out – and this is perhaps the special importance of the topic – is the influence of human views and expectations in *all* experiments. This factor may well be the explanation of the anomalous results that do not find their way into the orthodox scientific literature. Gradually it is being appreciated by scientists – but not yet sufficiently.

Top: S.G. Soal conducted a classic series of experiments apparently demonstrating the existence of telepathy. But he had altered certain figures in his results, thus giving his subjects a spuriously high success rate

Above: J.B. Rhine and his wife Louisa. The most impressive demonstrations of ESP by the Rhines occurred early in their career, when, as J.B. Rhine believed, their enthusiasm was at its height

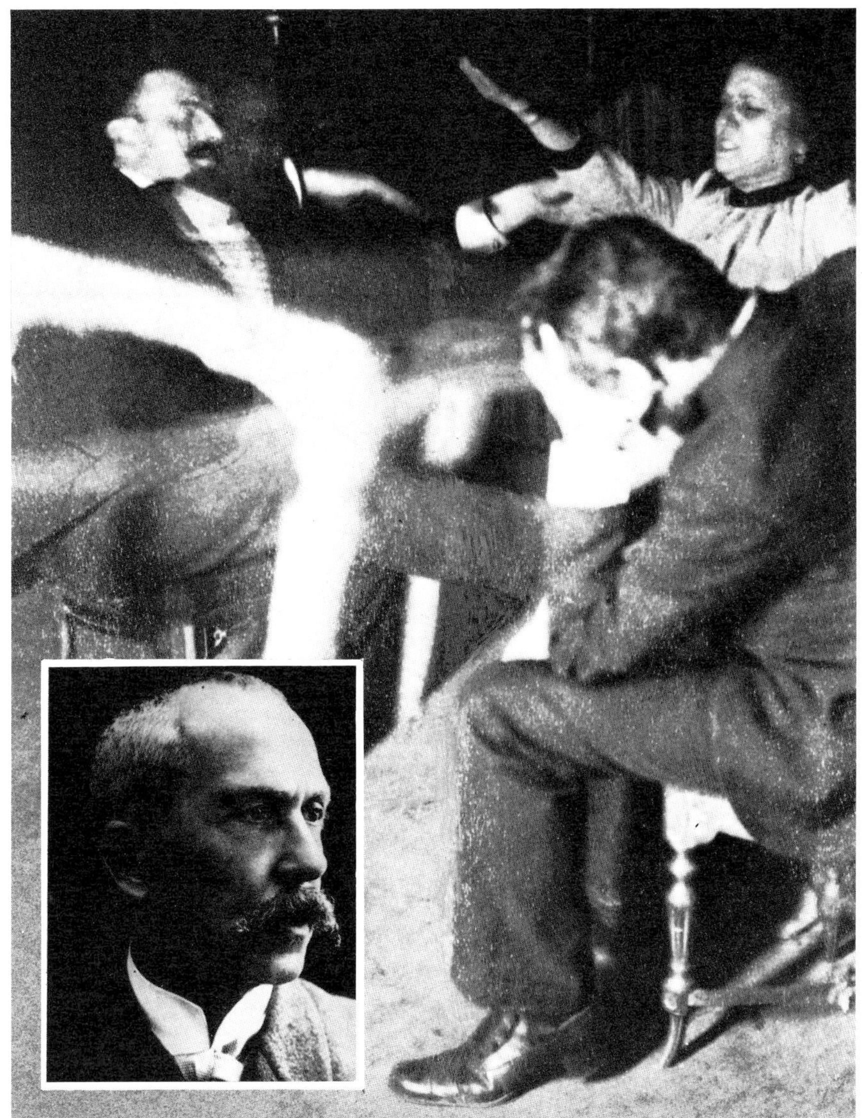

Outrageous and unthinkable

Psychical discoveries of the 19th century conflicted with the contemporary scientific picture of the Universe. But the complacency of the establishment was shaken as they were forced to adapt their ideas to their own 'irrational' findings

Above: a table levitates at a London sitting of Eusapia Palladino in 1903. Careful investigators ascribed some, at least, of her phenomena to 'some supernormal cause'

Inset: Charles Richet, a French physiologist, was convinced of Eusapia Palladino's genuineness

THE GREATEST OBSTACLE to acceptance of paranormal events is not the lack of evidence but the firmly entrenched belief that such events are impossible. Many eminent psychical researchers have drawn attention to this phenomenon – and, much to their dismay, have discovered it in themselves. Professor Charles Richet, a renowned physiologist and Nobel Laureate, a keen, sceptical and long-term researcher into alleged psychic phenomena, wrote the following after his carefully conducted series of tests of Eusapia Palladino, the famous – some would say notorious – physical medium:

> But at this point a remarkable psychological phenomenon made itself felt; a phenomenon deserving of all your attention. Observe that we are now dealing with observed facts which are nevertheless absurd; which are in contradiction with facts of daily observation; which are denied not by science only, but by the whole of humanity – facts which are rapid and fugitive, which take place in semi-darkness, and almost by surprise; with no proof except the testimony of our senses, which we know to be often fallible. After we have witnessed such facts, everything concurs to make us doubt them. Now, at the moment when these facts take place they seem to us certain, and we are willing to proclaim them openly; but when we return to ourself, when we feel the irresistible influence of our environment, when our friends all laugh at our credulity – then we are almost disarmed, and we begin to doubt. May it not all have been an illusion? May I not have been grossly deceived? . . . And then, as the moment of the experiment becomes more remote, that experiment which once seemed so conclusive gets to seem more and more uncertain, and we end by letting ourselves be persuaded that we have been the victims of a trick.

Everard Feilding, one of the most cautious investigators of the paranormal, also testified to the disorientating effect of prolonged contact with the incredible:

> The effect of all this on my mind was singular. I appeared to lose touch with actualities. Once admit the possibility of such things – and the mere fact of investigating them implied such an admission – where could one stop? I wrote at the time that I gradually began to feel that if a man seriously told me that the statue of the Albert Memorial had called in to tea I should have to admit that the question to be solved would not be the sanity of the narrator but the evidence for the fact.

Walter Franklin Prince, in his book *The enchanted boundary*, wrote of the strange spell psychic phenomena seemed to cast over many respectable men of science: they became so immediately antagonistic to the claims of psychical researchers that, without bothering to examine the evidence, they rushed into condemnatory print in terms so strongly emotive that, in any other field of scientific research, they would have lost any reputation they enjoyed.

One must not tumble, however, into the

Left: Katie King, allegedly a spirit materialised by the medium Florence Cook (visible at the left of the picture), photographed at a sitting in the home of Sir William Crookes. In the foreground is Dr Gully, another investigator. Katie was sufficiently substantial to be able to accept gifts of jewellery from an admirer. Crookes was one of the most eminent of those scientists who were open-minded enough to investigate mediumship and courageous enough to vouch for its authenticity

Below: dark ectoplasm is extruded from the navel of 'Margery' (Mrs Mina Crandon), an American medium active during the 1920s. Margery sat for a committee that was appointed by the magazine *Scientific American*. Her failure to convince them helped to strengthen the widespread conviction that science was in conflict with psychical claims. She was proved guilty of fraud on another occasion

common pitfall of believing that because a pioneer is at odds with the establishment regarding alleged new discoveries, he or she must be progressive, an unacknowledged genius unjustly persecuted by a hidebound and reactionary authority. As Marx put it – Groucho, not Karl –

> They said Galileo was mad, and he was proved right. They laughed at the Wright brothers, but they *did* fly. They thought my uncle Waldorf was cuckoo – and he was as mad as a hatter!

There is, of course, another strong motive for immediate antagonism towards psychical research and its findings from the intellectual establishments – a motive best expressed as a sort of equation of irrational identification:

> psychical research = spiritualism = the occult = black magic = witchcraft = the superstitious dark ages from which science has rescued mankind

In the second half of the 19th century especially, scientists and other learned men looked back in horror at the follies, the cruelties and the miseries imposed on the population of Europe by the superstitious persecution of 'witches'. It is estimated that during the witchcraft mania a quarter of a million people suffered torture and a hideous death at the hands of their tormentors. Nineteenth-century thinkers, having seen the light of science dispel the darkness of those earlier ages, were determined to withstand any movement that threatened to extinguish that light.

The belief in the impossibility of psychic phenomena was largely created because of the success of 19th-century science. It explained a host of celestial phenomena by applying Newton's law of gravitation and his laws of motion. One of the outstanding scientific successes of the century was the prediction of the existence of the planet Neptune, on the basis of its gravitational effects, before it was discovered with telescopes. Science came to understand a wide variety of natural phenomena, integrating in a seemingly universal theory of the physical world a large number of formerly separate fields, such as heat, light, electricity and magnetism. Clerk Maxwell's beautiful equations of electromagnetism gave an almost complete understanding of the electromagnetic field, leading ultimately to radio. In technology, too, Man's increasing use of his scientific knowledge in building bridges, ships, factories and trains, demonstrated how firmly based his mastery of nature was. It was not surprising that the only fear of scientists towards the end of the 19th century was that there seemed few, if any, jungles of ignorance left to be explored. One scientist expressed the belief that most scientific effort would henceforth be devoted to measuring physical constants to more decimal places.

The billiard-ball Universe

In this climate of opinion, most informed people believed that space, time, mass, the atom, energy, and so on were clearly understood. A body was made up ultimately of hard, billiard-ball-like atoms. Each atom always had a well-defined position and velocity. One could describe its space coordinates – its position – to any desired degree of accuracy, and by bringing in Newtonian time, which flowed uniformly, the rate of change of its space co-ordinates – its speed – could be expressed uniquely. Matter was indestructible: it could change its form from solid to liquid to gas, but it could never disappear – or appear. Energy likewise was indestructible, though it, too, could change its form. The potential for useful work stored

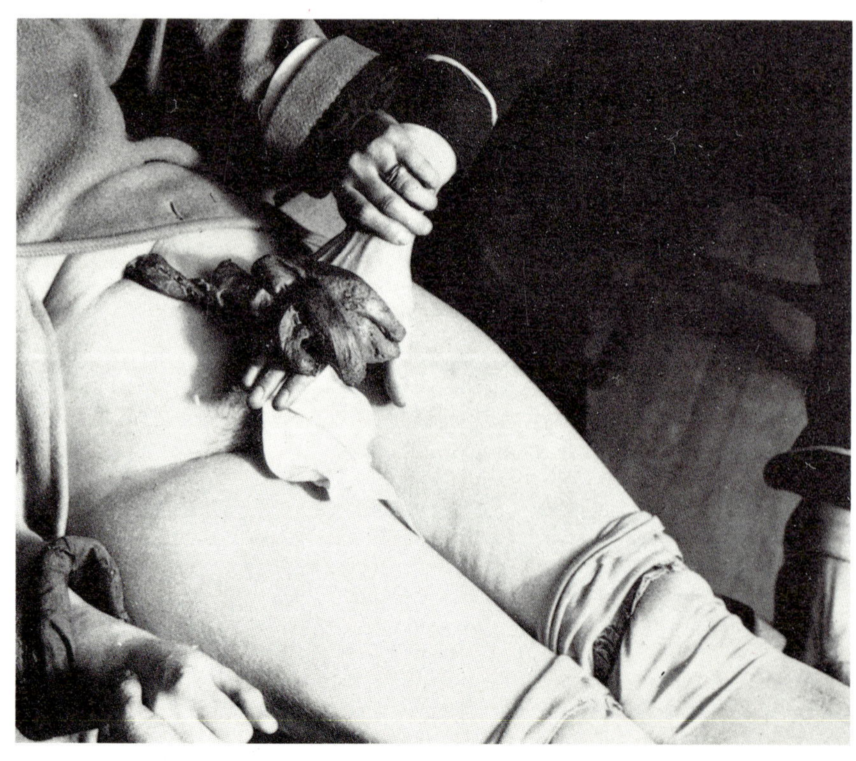

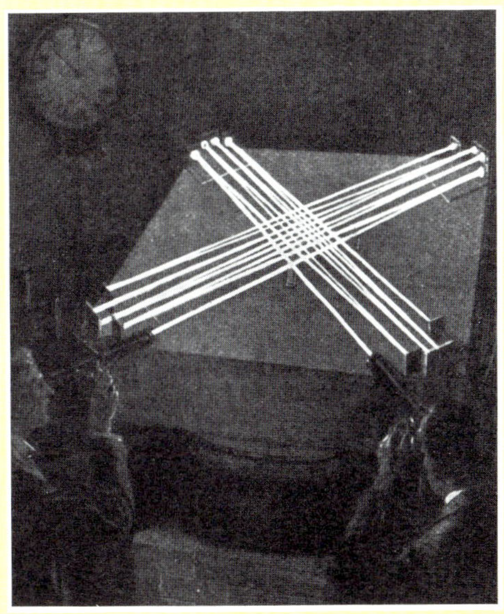

In search of the ether

Left: a massive table floating on mercury provided a stable support for the optical instruments used by Michelson and Morley

Below: a light ray is split into two components. One travels parallel to the supposed ether wind, one at right angles to it

The crisis of Victorian science was marked by many baffling experimental results. One of the most important was obtained by the American physicists A. A. Michelson and E. W. Morley in 1887. Light was a form of wave motion and so, it seemed, must be carried in some extraordinarily tenuous and all-pervasive fluid, as sound waves are carried in air. Since the Earth moves in its orbit around the Sun at 18 miles (30 kilometres) per second, a strong ether 'wind' must be blowing over the planet. Michelson and Morley devised a sensitive experiment to detect it. A light ray was sent to a 'beam splitter', a mirror that partly reflected and partly transmitted the light. The whole apparatus could be rotated. In the orientation shown, one beam (A) would first be slowed down as it travelled against the ether wind, and then speeded up as it travelled with it. The net result would be that it took longer to make the round trip than beam B, which travelled across the ether wind. Michelson and Morley compared beams A and B and could find no difference in their travel times. Yet it was unthinkable that the Earth did not move. The only tenable solution was Einstein's theory of relativity, which abandoned the concept of the ether and drastically revised our ideas of space and time. Light is now regarded as sometimes behaving like a wave motion – though not requiring any physical medium for its transmission – and sometimes behaving like a stream of particles.

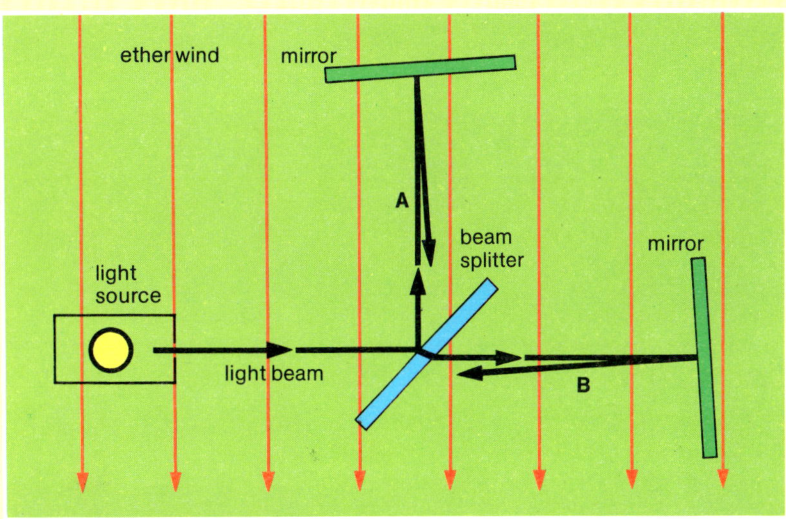

in a coiled spring, in an electric storage battery or in a hot gas was energy in its different manifestations.

It looked, too, as if the functions of plants and animals could ultimately be resolved into physical and chemical processes. Man, too, was beginning to be understood. The great physiologists and neurologists such as Hughlings Jackson seemed to be demonstrating by their pioneer studies of neural processes that a sound mind presupposed a sound brain. The impairment of personality and mental functions caused by brain lesions of various kinds led many to the belief that the concept of 'mind' was superfluous. More and more researchers were adhering to 'epiphenomenalism', which asserted that mental events were purely a side effect of brain activity – reflecting it but not influencing it, so that an understanding of brain activity would be sufficient for an understanding of all mental processes.

There were two other major theories, though they were losing their adherents. Parallelism regarded mental and neural events as running in parallel, without either being the cause of the other. This also made understanding of the brain sufficient for scientific purposes. Interactionism maintained that mind was as real as brain, existed separately from it, yet interacted with it. This would make an understanding of mental processes dependent on, but not entirely reducible to, processes in the brain. Very few thinkers at the end of the 19th century still believed this.

As far as the soul was concerned, it is fair to say that a good proportion of intelligent people refused to entertain such an outmoded and elusive concept. Lip service was still paid to the Church but, more and more, death was looked upon as the final annihilator of all human hopes. Most people, in fact, refused to think seriously about it at all until faced by the grim reality. Frederic Myers, the great pioneer of psychical research, was once in the company of a Victorian businessman whom he attempted to engage in conversation about Man's possible survival after death. The businessman was obviously uneasy and embarrassed. He refused to discuss the matter. Finally Myers

The brilliant physicist James Clerk Maxwell, who conjectured that light waves were undulations in a subtle medium, the ether. The overthrow of the concept of the ether marked the fall of Victorian physics

asked point blank: 'What do you think will happen to you when you die?' His companion's answer was: 'Why, I suppose I will enter into the joy of my Lord, but why talk about such an unpleasant subject?'

It is no wonder then that the alleged phenomena studied by psychical researchers found no lodging in the house of late-19th-century science. Telepathy, clairvoyance, psychokinesis, precognition and retro-cognition – all these branches of the paranormal were inexplicable according to the 19th-century world model. They were, in fact, downright impossible. Only a deluded and gullible fool would believe them.

And as if these weren't enough, what about the bizarre phenomena of the seance room, where mediums went into trances, were controlled by spirit guides and claimed to bring together the spirits of the dead and those still incarnate in this world? There were also many fully investigated cases of hauntings, both of places and of people.

Again, these things were impossible according to science and most scientists still ignored them or dismissed them with generalities about faulty reporting, fraud and human gullibility.

Yet among psychical researchers over the next century there were to be numbered some of the keenest and best-trained minds in Europe and the United States. For example, of the 52 presidents of the British Society for Psychical Research, 26 have held chairs in science or philosophy in universities, 10 have been Fellows of the Royal Society, four have held the Order of Merit and three have been Nobel Laureates. They have included the physicists Lord Rayleigh, J. J. Thomson, and Sir Oliver Lodge, the philosophers Henri Bergson and Henry Sidgwick, the classical scholar Gilbert Murray, the psychologist and philosopher William James, and many others equally renowned for their intellect and research achievements.

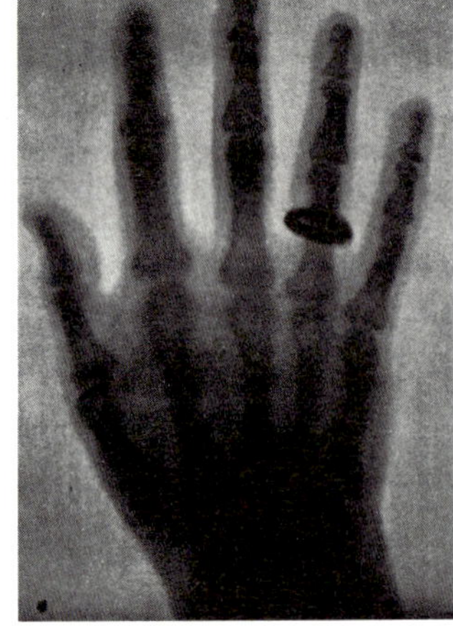

Top: the Great Exhibition of 1851, held in London, showed off the machinery and manufactures of the Age of Progress. Superstition was in headlong retreat before science, which, it seemed, would make mankind the master of the planet

Above: matter proved to be transparent to x-rays – a 'paranormal' discovery of science, made by W. K. Röntgen in 1895

A change of climate

The critical and condemnatory atmosphere of former times has to some extent changed since the 1950s. Controlled experiment in psychical research has confirmed the occurrence of many types of psychic phenomena, such as telepathy, clairvoyance, psychometry, precognition and psychokinesis. For almost half a century, ever since the pioneering researches of J. B. Rhine in the newly created Parapsychological Laboratory at Duke University in North Carolina, workers in various parts of the world have conducted carefully controlled laboratory experiments on the paranormal. They have amassed results that could not be due to mere chance. If these had been produced in some other, 'respectable', research field they would have been universally accepted as valid.

An increasingly large number of departments engaged in parapsychological research in the United States, Europe and Russia have enlisted the aid of modern science and technology. Among the more interesting have been the psychic dream experiments carried out at the Maimonides Medical Center in New York City, where dreams were analysed to see if they had been influenced by the pictures studied by experimenters in other rooms while the subjects lay sleeping. At Cambridge University's Department of Psychology, Dr Carl Sargent and his collaborators found that scenes watched by others influenced the images in the minds of conscious volunteers who had been relaxed and subjected to sensory deprivation.

The new climate of opinion among professional scientists is mainly due to a growing realisation that the 19th-century model of the Universe is no longer valid. The physicists of the 20th century have demolished the old structure and in its place have installed a model possessing such wild properties that it makes the world of paranormal phenomena appear staid. With the construction of a new scientific world view, it no longer seems impossible that paranormal phenomena could be reconciled with science.

This new model could not have been foreseen by the Victorian physicist. It resulted from totally unexpected discoveries made towards the end of the 19th century. In 1881 two American physicists, Michelson and Morley, tried to measure the Earth's velocity through the luminiferous ether, a medium supposed to carry light waves and to pervade the whole of space. They found themselves totally unable to detect its presence. It required the advent of relativity theory to provide an explanation for this baffling state of affairs.

In 1895 W. K. Röntgen discovered x-rays: a year later A. H. Becquerel noticed the blackening of an unexposed photographic plate in the presence of uranium and potassium compounds, thereby stumbling on radioactivity. By 1897 J. J. Thomson had reached a stage in his epoch-making researches where he was able to show that electrons – electrically charged particles – were over 1000 times lighter than the lightest atoms. The first steps into the strange world of the atom had been taken. Soon Einstein published his first papers. At the same time late-Victorian certainty was being further shaken by a parallel revolution, stemming from the discovery of the subconscious mind. Freud and Jung were embarking on their researches, which were to demonstrate that Man was not even master of his inner sanctum, the mind. In the world of the psyche, laws operated that were as alien to common sense as the new laws of quantum mechanics.

The bestiality and irrationality still present in that psyche became all too plain during the 20th century. Science was the handmaiden of many of the century's worst excesses, and forfeited its claim to be the guardian of progress. Science was no longer regarded as possessing a veto over claims formerly considered superstitious – at the very time that its own internal development was permitting it to become more open to paranormal phenomena.

Warfare in the modern age – Vietnamese children flee a napalm strike on their village. In the 20th century human beings have inflicted suffering on each other on a larger scale than ever before. The human race – sadder and, perhaps, wiser than the crowds who thronged the Great Exhibition in 1851 – looks towards the future not with confidence but with a grim foreboding

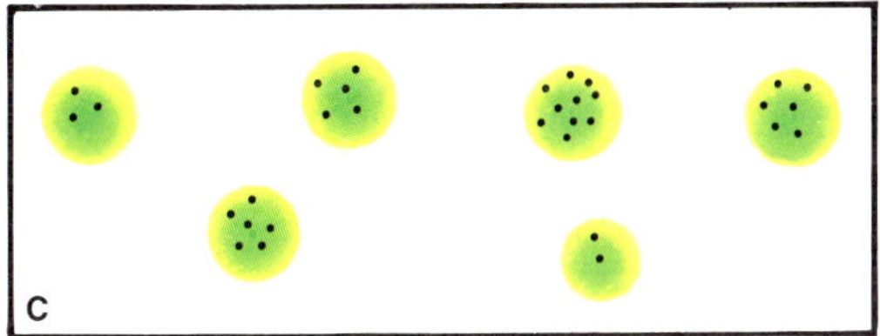

Left: the evolving concept of the atom. Democritus, a Greek thinker of 400 BC, regarded atoms as indivisible and made of one basic kind of 'stuff' (A). Differences in their shapes determined how they joined together and accounted for the properties of compounds. In 1803 John Dalton proposed that there were scores of qualitatively different types of atom (B). He was able to work out the relative weights of some of them. Only with the discovery of the electron was it realised that the atom was made up of smaller parts. J. J. Thomson suggested that atoms consist of electrons (negatively charged), surrounded by a cloud of positive charge (C). But Rutherford showed that electrons orbit around a central nucleus (D). Thus matter, apparently so solid, is largely empty space

The phantom universe

There seems to be no place for 'common sense' in the bizarre new scientific theories of the 20th century. In the complex world of modern physics, time flows at varying rates or even goes backwards, and matter and antimatter are in a state of constant flux

THE LATE-VICTORIAN MODEL of the Universe seemed a steady, reliable and enduring construction. Yet within half a century it was shattered by quantum mechanics and the theory of relativity.

The first suspicions that nature was not as it had seemed came when the Michelson-Morley experiment failed in its attempt to detect the Earth's movement through the luminiferous ether, as we have seen. The physicists Hendrik Lorentz and G. F. Fitzgerald suggested an explanation: physical objects had sizes that depended on their speeds – a moving object shrank in the direction of its motion. They also postulated that the measurement of the passage of time by a clock depended likewise on the clock's velocity. The expression 'time flies' took on quite a different meaning! They suggested that the Michelson-Morley null result could be explained by such changes in the measuring apparatus.

Lorentz gave a special mathematical expression that related the space and time measurements made by a moving observer to those made by an observer at rest. Speeds in Man's everyday life are very small with respect to the velocity of light – which is 186,000 miles per second (300,000 kilometres per second) – and so these effects would be unnoticeable. But if light travelled at the speed of, say, a racing car, then even in past centuries people might have taken it as quite normal for arrows and cannonballs to shorten perceptibly in the direction of travel, regaining their former length when they stopped, and for a clock's hands to turn more slowly while it was moving.

Some of Lorentz's ideas appeared, in a different form, in Einstein's theory of relativity, published in 1905. But Einstein went further by denying any distinction between moving and stationary objects. An observer in a high-speed rocket would see an apparent shortening of 'stationary' objects and a slowing down of 'stationary' clocks, just as observers on Earth would see these changes in him and in the rocket.

Einstein showed that this curious velocity effect also altered the mass of an object. As its velocity increased, its mass increased, making the object harder to accelerate. As its speed approached the velocity of light, the mass became enormous. Einstein obtained the result that the velocity of light was a limit that no physical object could reach. Nowadays, physicists are able to accelerate charged particles to within a few per cent of this velocity, at which speeds their masses are observed to be many times their rest mass.

A photograph of individual atoms. Each spot of light in this picture represents a single atom in the tip of a tungsten needle. The symmetrical patterning of the atoms reflects the crystalline structure of the metal. To make the picture, an intense electric field was applied at the highly sharpened tip of the needle. Electrons were torn from each atom and formed images where they struck the film

In addition, Einstein assumed that the velocity of light as measured by any observer was a fixed quantity, no matter at what speed the observer moved. This again was contrary to common sense. If two cars, each travelling at 50 miles per hour (80 km/h) as measured by a stationary observer, are approaching each other, we would expect that an observer in one of the cars would see the other as approaching at 100 miles per hour (160 km/h). In fact, as Einstein showed, the relative speed is actually less than this by an infinitesimal amount.

Furthermore, if the cars were beams of light, and the speed of light were only 50 miles per hour (80 km/h), then a measurement of its speed would always give that result – no matter what the speed of the observer. In essence, he would be carrying out Michelson and Morley's experiment, and finding what they found – that no variation in the speed of light is detectable.

Treating space and time as separate and independent quantities was now shown to be mistaken. In 1908 Hermann Minkowski suggested that the concept of 'spacetime' could be used to remove the barriers to our acceptance of such strange effects as these changes in time and size. He claimed:

> Henceforth space by itself, and time by itself, are doomed to fade away into mere shadows, and only a kind of union of the two will preserve an independent reality.

In Minkowski's conception the Universe is represented as having four dimensions: the three dimensions of space – length, breadth and width – and the dimension of time. The history of a body (a human being, a picture, anything) is represented by a 'world line', mapping its course through space and time from its creation to its dissolution. There is no movement or change in this representation of the Universe. Past, present and future are introduced by human consciousness. The slice of space-time consciously perceived defines the present moment for the observer. Some theorists have supposed that consciousness travels like a tiny point of light along the observer's world line. Although the four-dimensional block Universe is static and unchanging, he is under the illusion that 'things happen' – rather like the illusion experienced by a driver at night when trees that are actually static seem to appear in the headlamp's beam, rush past and disappear.

On closer examination this model of space, time and consciousness reveals difficulties, but it remains useful when paranormal phenomena relating to time and consciousness are studied, if only to help the theorist break free from common-sense conceptions or prejudices about such matters.

Above: Hermann Minkowski, who conceived 'spacetime'

Below: a snooker game, shown in 'snapshots' (left), from the bottom upwards, and in space-time (right), in which the vertical dimension represents time. Each object's history is shown by its 'world line'

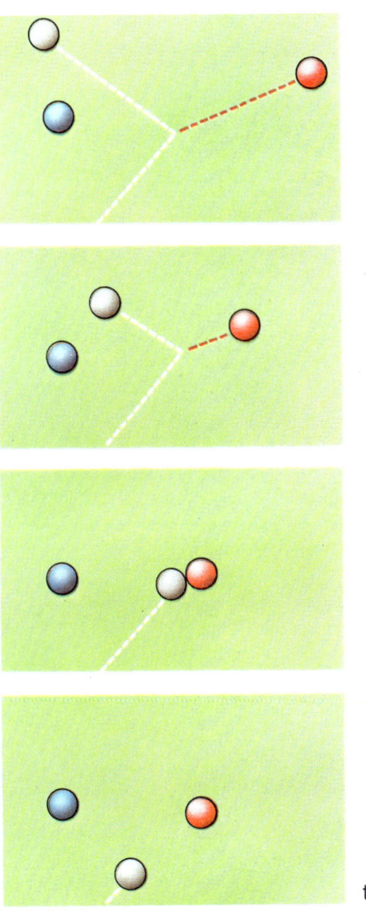

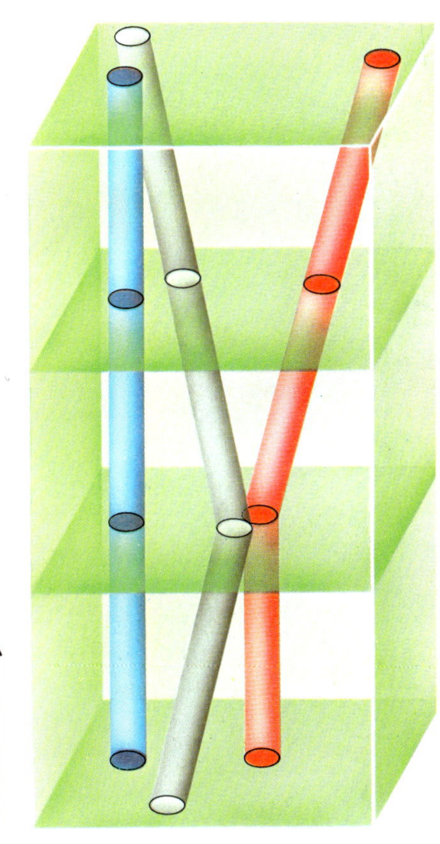

Into the atom

After the theories of Einstein and Minkowski, still worse assaults on common sense were to follow. J. J. Thomson showed that the electron was an entity with less than a thousandth of the mass of the hydrogen atom. Other experimenters discovered the proton and the neutron. Both had essentially the same mass as a hydrogen atom but, whereas the proton carried a charge equal to that of the electron but of opposite sign, the neutron was electrically neutral. Ernest Rutherford postulated that every atom consisted of a nucleus of protons and neutrons surrounded by a screen of electrons, held in orbit by the attractive force between their negative electrical charges and the protons' positive charges. The electrons circled the nucleus like miniature planets moving round a miniature Sun. Like our solar system, the atom now became largely composed of nothing. If it had been a sphere the size of the Earth, then the nucleus would be a cathedral at its centre, circled by electrons the size of bungalows.

But the Danish theorist Niels Bohr went further. To any orbital radius there corresponded an energy level. Using the long-established idea that in atomic processes energy comes in multiples of a basic energy unit, the 'quantum', he showed that only certain orbits were possible for the electrons in atoms. But the theory gave little insight as to why such limitations should exist in nature. Furthermore, electrons apparently jumped from one orbit to another instantaneously. But even though the theory's assumptions seemed against all common sense, it became accepted because it worked.

Other researchers were now demonstrating additional strange features of these subatomic particles. When an electron collided with another atomic particle, it behaved like a tiny cannonball, but in other experiments electrons behaved as if they were made up of waves, as light is. The electron could equally well be regarded as a wave or as a particle. Sir William Bragg quipped: 'Electrons seem to be waves on Mondays, Wednesdays and Fridays, and particles on Tuesdays, Thursdays and Saturdays.' Perhaps on Sundays they took the day off to recover from their Jekyll and Hyde transformations.

This dual quality of the particles of nature is recognised in Bohr's principle of complementarity:

> The concept of complementarity is

Left: the atom, once thought to be indivisible, has a complex structure. Swarms of electrons, carrying negative electric charge, circle a heavy nucleus consisting of positively charged protons and uncharged neutrons. The electrons follow orbits grouped in 'shells', and are responsible for the atom's chemical properties

meant to describe a situation in which we can look at one and the same event through two different frames of reference. These two frames mutually exclude each other, and only the juxtaposition of these contradictory frames provides an exhaustive view of the appearances of the phenomena.

Bohr cited many examples of complementary relationships among ideas from outside physics: for example, moral *judgement* and psychological *explanation* of human actions may be mutually incompatible, yet equally necessary to give a full picture of them. Later we shall discover that the principle of complementarity can be usefully applied to the world of paranormal phenomena.

Below: Niels Bohr proposed in 1913 that in the atom only certain orbits are 'allowed' for electrons – a restriction that could not then be explained

Werner Heisenberg, who had made crucial contributions to the task of replacing the 19th century's conception of a hard, material Universe by the insubstantial world-web of 20th-century theoretical physics, stated his principle of indeterminacy: that for subatomic entities it is impossible to know their position and velocity simultaneously and exactly. Since subatomic particles are wave-like it is not possible to talk about position in any precise fashion. In fact the equations of theoretical physics refer merely to possibilities or probabilities, not to facts. Henry Margenau said of them:

> The equations say nothing about masses moving; they regulate the behaviour of very abstract fields, certainly in many cases non-material fields. . . .

This field theory implies that matter is composed of wave-like processes, that the seemingly solid material Universe perceived by our physical senses is an illusion. In addition, the seeming separateness of objects within that Universe is also an illusion. On the subatomic scale, there are no 'objects' of invariant 'mass' and given 'volume' separated by 'distances' and acting on each other with 'forces' of the simple push-pull type of mechanics. The entity we conveniently call an electron has no definite position at a given time, no definite velocity and no isolation from the rest of the Universe. Quantum theory states that, whatever location is specified, there is a small but finite probability of

A crisis of identity

One of the triumphs of 19th-century science was the demonstration that light consists of waves. These were explained as consisting of fluctuations in electric and magnetic fields, and their wavelengths were accurately measured. But although the evidence for this view was overwhelming, it could not explain the fact that light waves can knock electrons out of atoms (below right). This 'photoelectric' effect is used in photographers' light meters – the electrons ejected by the light form an electric current, the strength of which indicates the intensity of the light. Even an extremely faint light can eject electrons – a fact baffling to physicists. Albert Einstein, in the same year that he proposed the theory of relativity, suggested that light behaves in this experiment as if consisting of a stream of particle-like 'photons'. This picture accounts for the behaviour of light in some experiments, while in others the wave picture must be used.

The same ambiguity was discovered in what had been regarded simply as particles. The fact that electrons can sometimes behave like waves was demonstrated in 1926. Like the photoelectric effect, this phenomenon has practical uses. One type of electron microscope (above) uses a beam of electrons like a beam of light, focusing it and forming images of an object, such as that of the water flea (above left). The wavelength of the electrons is so short that they can reveal details hundreds of times smaller than those that can be seen with a light microscope.

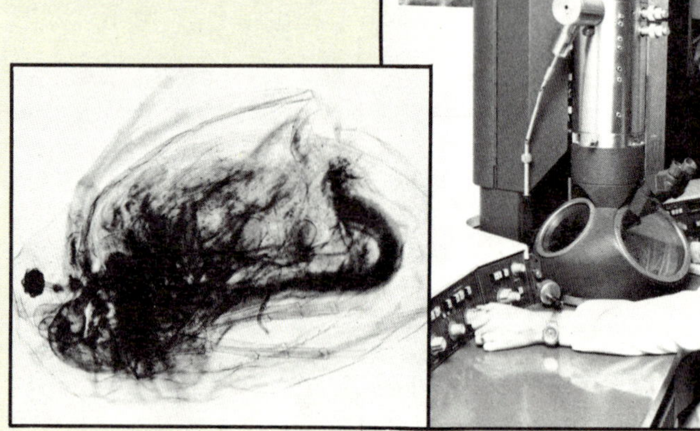

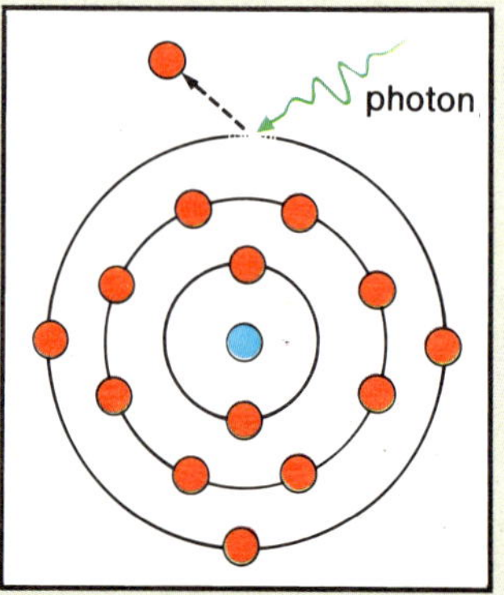

the electron being there. It, and every other subatomic particle, is in some way related to every part of the Universe.

Instinctively we react to these ideas by assuming that the uncertainty in our knowledge of position, velocity, and so on is simply due to the imprecision of our measurements. But this is not so. The uncertainty is built into the microworld because of the nature of subatomic particles.

In countless experiments every day, mass is transformed into energy and vice versa; streams of neutrinos (particles that have no mass, no electric charge, no magnetic field), travelling from remote regions of space, pass through the 'solid' Earth, as if the planet were a ghost; experimenters work with 'antimatter' particles, the mirror opposites of the particles of the everyday Universe.

The existence of one such antimatter particle, the positron, was predicted by the British theorist P. A. M. Dirac in 1931 and confirmed experimentally in 1932 by Carl Anderson. It has the same mass as an electron but is of opposite electric charge. When it meets an electron, both are annihilated, resulting in the creation of high-energy gamma rays. The physicist Richard Feynman proposed that the positron *was* an electron – but an electron moving backwards in time. Certainly the mathematical theory suggested that if an electron could do this it would behave in experiments exactly like a positron. Feynman went further, suggesting that all antimatter particles were ordinary particles travelling backwards in time.

A collision on the subatomic scale. The picture shows events in a bubble chamber, a tank filled with liquid hydrogen. A pion, a short-lived particle, enters at left. The hydrogen boils along its path, leaving a track of tiny bubbles. The pion strikes a hydrogen atom's nucleus, consisting of a single proton, which disintegrates to produce a cascade of particles. Their properties are revealed by the length, thickness and curvature of their paths

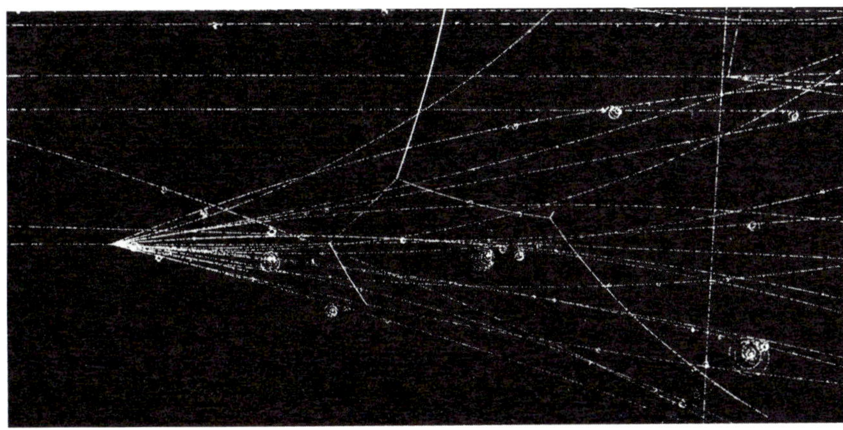

Dirac had been led to his prediction from his study of the solutions of the quantum-mechanical equations that he himself had proposed. For every solution he found describing an electron of given energy, there was another one predicting an electron with negative energy of equal amount – no matter how large. But if these negative energy states existed, why did electrons not fall into these bottomless pits of negative energy, causing atoms to collapse and the Universe to be annihilated in one blaze of radiation? Dirac suggested that all the negative energy states were already occupied by an infinite 'sea' of electrons. Now Pauli's 'exclusion principle' states that two electrons cannot occupy the same energy niche; so, with all possible negative energy states filled, ordinary electrons are kept in existence.

Normally this infinite electron 'sea' is no more perceptible in atomic processes than the air around us is perceptible to our senses. On occasion, however, a negative-energy electron can acquire enough energy to climb out of its 'hole' in Dirac's sea. To the observer it then simply materialises as an ordinary electron. But the hole in the sea also becomes manifest, as an electron of positive electric charge – the anti-particle that Dirac had predicted, the positron.

Such paradoxical concepts have given Man the insight to manipulate the microworld, split the atom and, ultimately, create nuclear power stations. Emulating the legendary Prometheus, who stole fire from heaven, he now attempts in his fusion experiments to bring down to Earth the energy-releasing processes of the stars themselves. Some parapsychologists hope that our modern quantum-mechanical understanding of the Universe will inspire similarly fruitful theories in the equally strange field of the paranormal.

Below: P. A. M. Dirac suggested the existence of a 'sea' of unperceived electrons of negative energy (left). Ordinary electrons have positive energy. A photon of very high energy can knock an electron from the 'sea' (right). The electron appears to be created, together with a 'hole' in the sea – an anti-electron, or positron

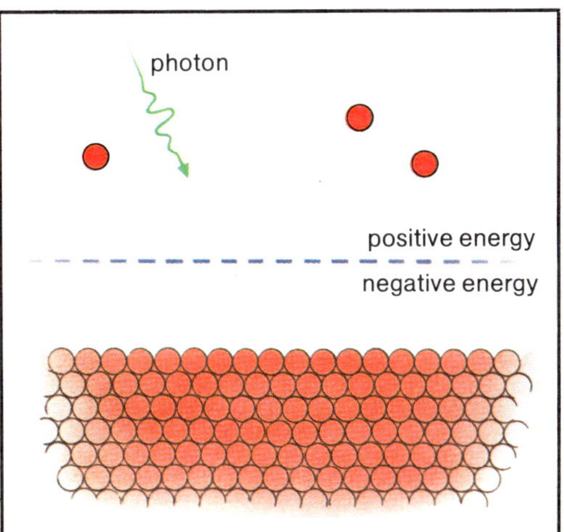

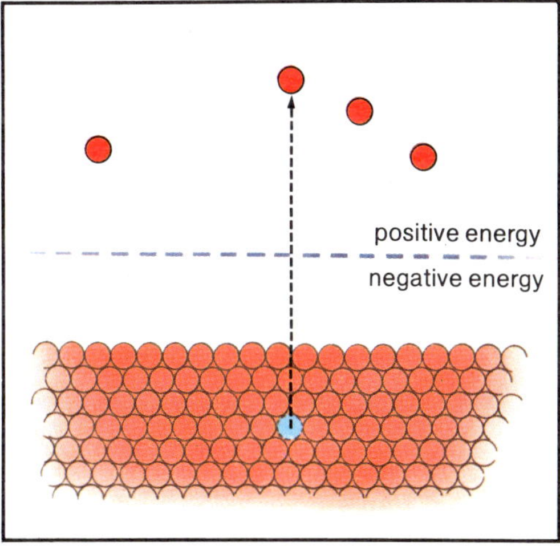

The new view of reality

The mind seems able to leap over barriers of space, time and even death itself. Modern science has made daring and repeated attempts to account for these strange human powers

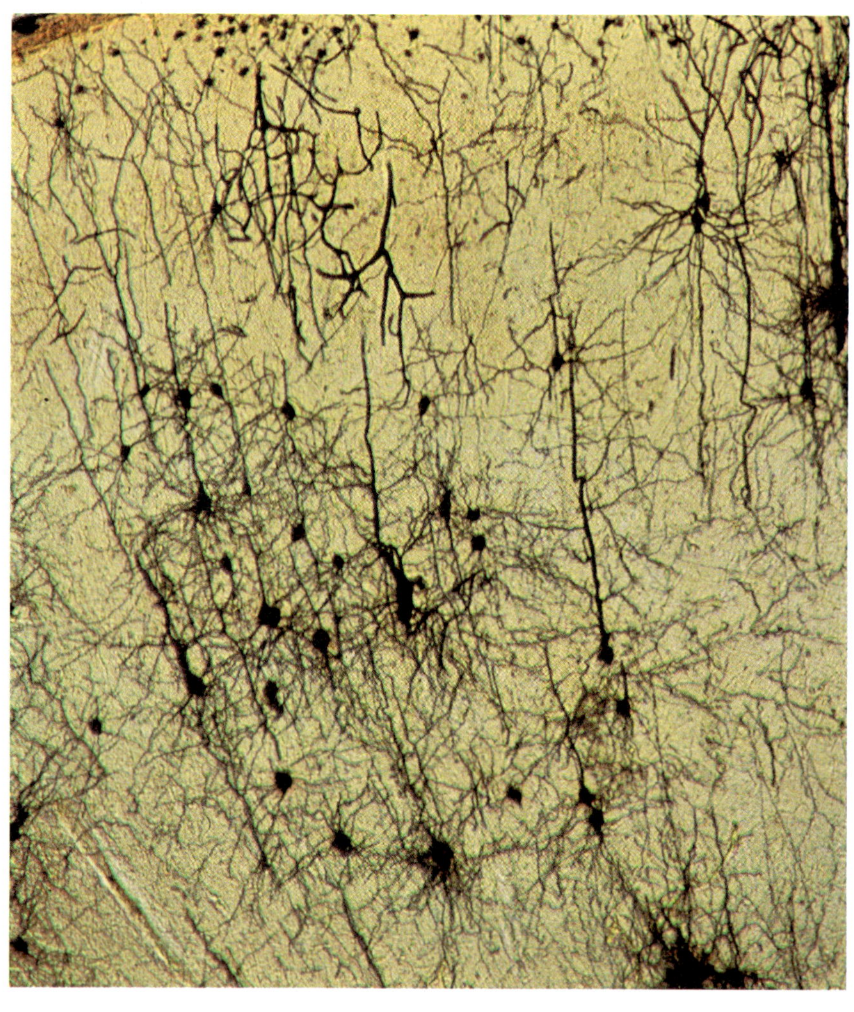

THE STRANGE and beautiful Universe discovered by the brilliant researches of 20th-century physicists is forever hidden from our senses, adapted as they are to the macroworld. The entities of the subatomic Universe elude everyday concepts: they are related to each other in a web of mathematical probabilities in a shadow game whose rules are the laws of relativity and quantum physics. The statements of physicists about the nature of reality and about the immediate sensory world resemble more and more the statements of mystics, both eastern and western, and those of mediums regarding the operations of their psychic faculties.

The medium, the mystic and the physicist find themselves in unexpected accord. The odd man out is the one who still believes that the 19th-century picture of the Universe is adequate to the whole of reality. A few quotations are sufficient to illustrate this.

The physicist Sir Arthur Eddington: 'The stuff of the world is mind stuff.'

The mystic Evelyn Underhill: 'The game of give and take that goes on between the human consciousness and the external world. . . .'

The physicist Louis de Broglie: 'In space-time everything which for each of us constitutes the past, the present, and the future is given *en bloc*. . . .'

The medium Eileen Garrett: 'In the ultimate nature of the Universe there are no divisions in time and space.'

The Zen Master Dogen: 'It is believed by most that time passes; in actual fact, it stays where it is. This idea of passing may be called time, but it is an incorrect idea, for since one sees it only as passing, one cannot understand that it stays just where it is.'

From a Buddhist text: 'It was taught by the Buddha . . . that . . . the past, the future, physical space . . . and individuals are nothing but names, forms of thought, words of common usage, merely superficial realities.'

The physicist Henry Margenau: 'The central recognition of the theory of relativity is that geometry is a construct of the intellect. Only when this discovery is accepted can the mind feel free to tamper with the time-honoured notions of space and time.'

The principle of complementarity was forced on theoretical physicists because of the dual nature of subatomic particles: they behave sometimes like traditional notions of particles, sometimes like waves. The principle is relevant in the paranormal field. The point of view provided by our senses in everyday life is evidently only one aspect of reality, a model geared towards a human being's immediate physical survival. The modern physicist's picture, totally different from the sensory one, represents nature in a different way, revealing quite different aspects of reality. Instead of conferring importance on objects, masses, positions, distances and a linear time of past, present and future, it emphasises patterns, fields and relationships in divisionless time. Individual identity is illusory, position a matter of probability. The physicist, from this second point of view, is able to set up experiments that reveal new aspects of nature and confirm his theories, or force him to modify them. The points of view of science and of common sense are complementary. Both work in their own fields.

Lawrence LeShan, medical man, psychologist and psychical researcher, has tabulated the characteristics of such viewpoints. His

Below: Arthur Eddington, an innovative theorist, believed that the results of scientific research are largely determined by our methods of investigation – in studying nature we 'discover ourselves'

'sensory reality' (SR) corresponds roughly to the sensory viewpoint: his 'clairvoyant reality' (CR) is the clairvoyant's or medium's view of the world. He finds that the CR view is not at all different in major respects from that of the modern theoretical physicist, or indeed from what the mystics of all ages have told us about the world.

One may then hope that psychic phenomena such as telepathy, clairvoyance, psychometry, precognition and retrocognition can take their place in a body of CR theory analogous to the theories of quantum mechanics and relativity. Like these theories, it may have to begin by agreeing that in the world of the paranormal ordinary concepts of space and time are inadmissible. There are indeed good grounds for believing this, since the ability of a sensitive to acquire information seems totally independent of distance or time intervals.

Left: some of the billions of cells in the outer layer of the brain. The extreme sensitivity of brain cells could explain how some people pick up 'psychic' impressions

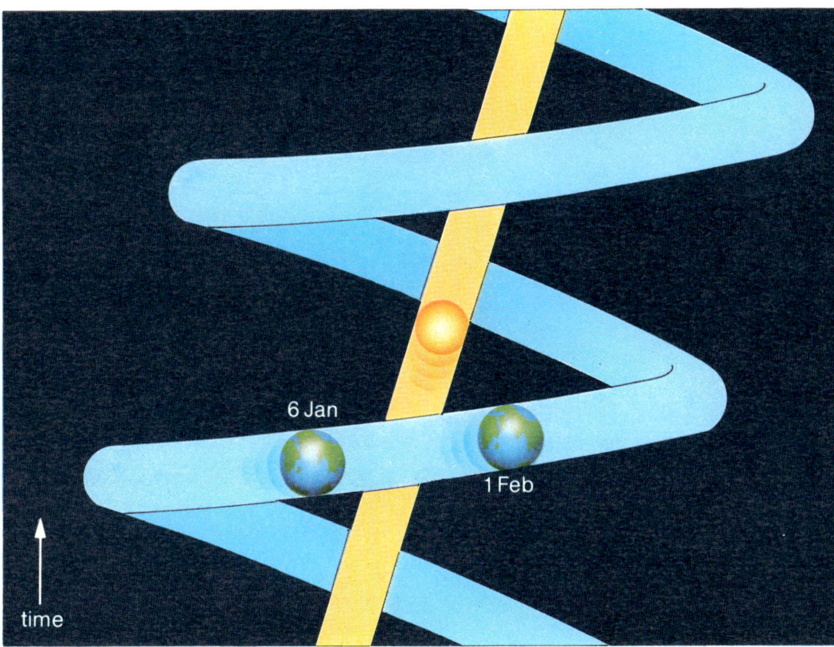

Below: the physical distances involved in predictions are immense. An event on 1 February is not only 4 weeks later than one on 6 January – because of the movement of the Earth, it is also 42 million miles (67 million kilometres) away in space

The Dutch sensitive Gerard Croiset could predict certain detailed events to be experienced during the following month by a person he had never met. In one case he made predictions on 6 January concerning the experiences of a woman, Mrs M, on 1 February. The idea of a brain-to-brain 'mental radio' breaks down here. What is not usually appreciated is that a further spatial difficulty arises if one supposes that Croiset's brain was somehow reading the physical memory traces that were to be laid down in Mrs M's brain a month later. On 1 February Mrs M was 42 million miles (67 million kilometres) away from Croiset's position on 6 January, because of the Earth's motion around the Sun. Thus it seems that mind cannot be localised in time and space.

What could correspond in the 'psychic mechanics' of clairvoyant reality to the non-material fields of quantum mechanics? Strangely enough, the first steps along the road to such a concept may have been taken by certain researchers in the very period when the demolition of 19th-century science was under way. At that time brilliant psychologists such as the American William James, the Austrian Sigmund Freud and the Swiss Carl Gustav Jung were exploring another world invisible to the senses: the world of the unconscious mind, the strange, often paradoxical operations of which covertly influenced human thoughts and actions. All three were interested in the paranormal – James and Jung intensely so – for the light it might shed on the dark continent of the psyche. James, the founding father of American psychology, used the idea of the four-dimensional 'block universe' in attempts to understand the psychic phenomena. He postulated the concept of the 'specious present', a tiny interval of time containing everything being experienced by the individual at that moment. Jung, who later collaborated with the physicist Wolfgang Pauli in an attempt to come to grips with synchronicities (meaningful coincidences) was well aware of the revolution in physics going on throughout his long life. He introduced the concept of the collective unconscious, in some ways related to James's own idea of a psychic repository or record of all human experience. A major feature of the Jungian collective unconscious, however, was that it was not merely a passive record but a dynamic, creative one, giving rise to dream, myth, religion and artistic creation.

Below: Lawrence LeShan, a medically trained parapsychologist in the United States, has made rigorous tests of the powers of psychics and mediums, notably the 'object-reading' abilities of Mrs Eileen Garrett

The memory of the race

The existence of the collective unconscious – the racial memory of mankind – is supported by dream analysis, by the universality of myths and by paranormal phenomena. It looks, too, as if this great, submerged continent of the psyche exists outside space and time. Like an island in the ocean, each human mind lies separated from all others above the threshold of consciousness. But just as all islands join below the ocean surface, so Jungian teaching suggests that below the conscious level, at greater and greater depths of the psyche, there is a merging of each personal subconscious. As Jung himself put it:

> The deepest we can reach in our exploration of the unconscious mind is the layer where man is no longer a distinct individual, but where his mind widens out and merges into the mind of mankind – not the conscious mind, but the unconscious mind of mankind, where we are all the same.

The pioneers of quantum mechanics replaced gross matter with non-material fields, accepting that their nature was indefinable and only the laws of their behaviour could be sought. Similarly, the depth psychologists for the most part ignore questions regarding the nature or 'whereabouts' of the collective unconscious, seeking merely to discover and understand its laws by studying its transactions with human beings. Just as the theoretical physicists have recognised various kinds of subatomic particles within the fields they study and have deduced their laws of interaction, it may be expected that the explorers of the psyche – psychologists, psychoanalysts, psychical researchers – will discover more about the structures of the collective unconscious.

People and programs

For example, if the collective unconscious is a record or psychic store of all human experience, does it contain, like an electronic computer, the 'program' of everyone who has ever lived? Is it possible that sensitives who enter a psychic state gain the ability to activate and 'run' certain programs – the programs of people now dead?

Running such a program may not be at all analogous to running a cassette on a tape recorder. The tape is passive, non-reactive and fixed in content. By contrast, there are pocket computers that are 'intelligent' enough to give you a very good game of chess. And it is possible to program computers with medical programs that can 'converse' with a patient via a screen and a typewriter keyboard so fluently that the patient finds it difficult to believe that he is not dealing with a sympathetic doctor.

When Rosemary Brown receives music from the composers Liszt, Chopin and Beethoven, or Luiz Gasparetto's hands are guided by the painters Picasso or Toulouse-Lautrec, are these two sensitives merely interacting with programs stored in the collective unconscious – programs that contain information not only on the lives of these great men, but also their musical and artistic techniques, their memories, their personality traits and even their drives?

Above: Sir John Eccles shared the 1963 Nobel prize for medicine for his researches on nerve cells. His work led him to speculate on the interaction between mind and brain

It seems reasonable to suppose, if we accept the hypothesis of a collective unconscious stocked with records of the lives and personalities of every human being, that the 'communicators' contacted by mediums will behave according to the beliefs and knowledge possessed by their originals. The ghostly figure may still act as if it believed itself damned for its sins. It may still try to invoke the aid of the living to solve the problems it left behind at the end of its earthly life.

It is also reasonable to suppose that the words, pictures, music and other produc-

Above: the prolific artist Pablo Picasso who died in 1973. His genius seems to have survived – appearing in the 'automatic' paintings of some psychics, notably those of Luiz Gasparetto

Left: before numerous witnesses Luiz Gasparetto demonstrates the remarkable rapidity with which he can produce drawings and paintings in the style of artists no longer living. His facility strongly suggests that during these sessions his normal personality 'program' has been supplanted by that of the deceased artist

tions of such a communicator will be strongly influenced by the mind through which they are channelled – as the performance of a computer program is modified by the capabilities of the machine on which it is run.

This picture of human minds influencing and being influenced by the collective unconscious raises the mind-brain problem with increased force. The relationship between the mind and brain has long been a thorny problem for interactionists. The perplexing mystery of how the will operates the brain and hence the neurones that control the muscles has been tackled by, among others, Sir John Eccles, the world-famous physiologist. Grossly over-simplifying his ingenious arguments, it may be said that the brain is a structure of an enormous number of neurones, many of which are critically

poised between firing and not firing. Eccles suggests that tiny amounts of mental energy, well-directed by the mind, will operate such 'hair-trigger' neurones by psychokinesis (PK). Each in its turn fires others, initiating in a fraction of a second a chain reaction involving hundreds of thousands of neurones. In this mind-brain influence, which would operate also in the other direction, we see the possibility of a theory incorporating some paranormal phenomena. If the minds of A and B connect at their deepest levels with the timeless collective unconscious (CU), sensory data entering A's brain could surface as imagery in B's brain.

Various researchers have attempted to generalise quantum mechanics to include paranormal phenomena. Martin Ruderfer suggested that neutrinos are responsible. Neutrinos are particles without electric charge and, to the best of our present knowledge, no mass. They react with matter extremely infrequently. In fact they are ghost-like in their behaviour: billions of neutrinos pass unimpeded through the Earth every second. Interstellar space is filled with neutrinos, created in nuclear reactions within the stars and travelling in all directions. This 'neutrino sea' might be capable of initiating psychic phenomena.

Top: a computer in combat with a chess master, David Levy (at keyboard). The computer could be given new skills by equipping it with a new program. In a similar way the mysterious abilities and knowledge that psychics can acquire may also be some kind of 'change of program'

Above: illustration of the interconnection of human minds, as conceived by Carl Jung. The conscious minds of individuals seem separated, as islands are separated by the ocean. Below the 'surface' each individual has a personal unconscious mind that is similarly isolated. But at the deepest level each mind merges with the collective unconscious, a shared racial memory that unites individuals as the ocean floor links the world's islands

Adrian Dobbs, a mathematical physicist, put forward a two-dimensional model of time and postulated the existence of 'psitrons', particles that travel faster than light and can never be slowed below the speed of light. (This concept is in accordance with orthodox relativity theory.) In his closely argued theory (no more bizarre than much of quantum mechanics) he tries to account for telepathy and precognition.

Precognition or PK

The physicist and parapsychologist Helmut Schmidt persuaded volunteers to try to predict single quantum processes: emissions of electrons from a radioactive strontium 90 source. The time of occurrence of such an event is completely unpredictable and yet Schmidt's volunteers obtained scores that would have been expected to happen by chance only once in every thousand million experiments. It is, to understate it, difficult to explain Schmidt's experiments without invoking precognition or psychokinesis. If the former is involved, the mind is acquiring information about future events. If the latter, then the mind is causing events on the subatomic level, in a manner recalling Eddington's assertion, quoted at the beginning of this article, that the world is made of 'mind stuff'.

We are still at the beginning of our understanding of such matters. Some new Einstein or Newton may already be waiting in the wings to show how a more generalised quantum-mechanical model will embrace paranormal phenomena. On the other hand, it may be that quantum mechanics will be of value to the study of the paranormal only by the shining example of its creators' courage in postulating totally new and seemingly irrational concepts. On one famous occasion the sign of approval bestowed on a new scientific idea was the reaction: 'It's just mad enough to be right!' Perhaps a scientific theory of the paranormal will have to be very mad to stand a chance of being right.

Now you see it...

Some of the most sophisticated attempts to explain psychic phenomena are derived from quantum physics. Among these are the 'observation theories' – which would appear to suggest that we are constantly performing psychokinesis

HOW DOES ESP WORK? Many theories – more and less fantastic – have been put forward to explain it; but perhaps the most exciting to have emerged since the mid 1970s are the so-called 'observation theories'. These attempt to explain the physics of ESP from the basic assumption that psychic events are essentially quantum events writ large. The two principal founders of this approach are both physicists – Helmut Schmidt and Evan Harris Walker. Schmidt's theory was originally formulated as an elegant mathematical model of ESP, one that made very few physical assumptions and was not concerned with the physiology or psychology of the psychic. By contrast, the observation theory formulated by Walker *does* concern itself with the physiology and psychology of the psychic; it proposes a new role for the 'hidden variables' that may underlie quantum reactions, and attempts to formulate a comprehensive theory of ESP and PK that embraces a novel view of consciousness and the bizarre world of quantum physics.

Walker's theory is a quantum theoretic model. To understand it even in outline, it is necessary to have just a smattering of quantum physics.

In our everyday lives most of the events we observe involve objects of what is, to us, 'normal' size. These objects are composed of billions upon billions of atoms, and the behaviour of such huge assemblies of atoms irons out the essentially irregular behaviour of tiny entities such as neutrons or electrons.

The behaviour of 'normal' sized objects follows, essentially, the laws of Newtonian physics – unless they are accelerated to near light speeds, when strange relativistic effects begin to appear. We live in a world of 'billiard ball causality'. If a billiard ball cannons into a billiard table cushion at a certain angle and speed, it will follow exactly

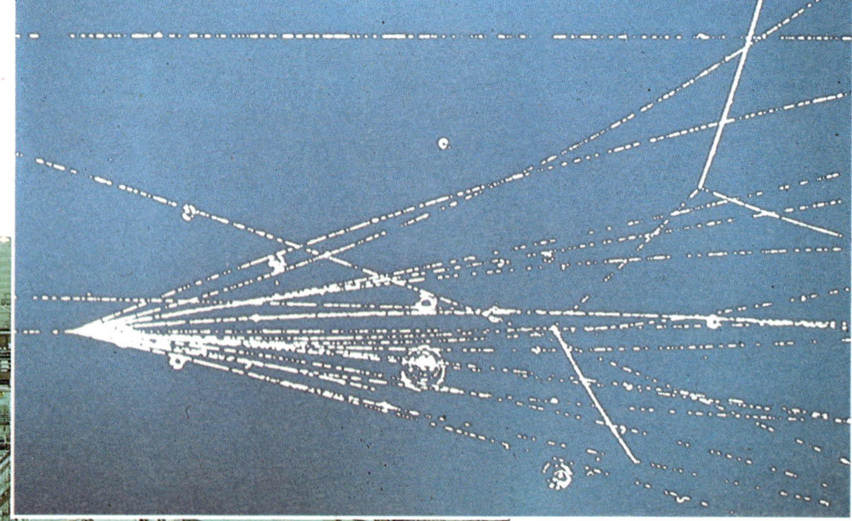

Left: the antiproton accumulator at the European Organisation for Nuclear Research (CERN) at Geneva, Switzerland, and (above) tracks made in a hydrogen bubble chamber by subatomic particles. According to one interpretation of quantum mechanics, events at the quantum level – for instance, subatomic reactions such as those that go on within the antiproton accumulator – remain indeterminate until perceived by a human being – for instance, as particle tracks in cloud chambers

Above: Alex 'Hurricane' Higgins, the British snooker player, lines up a shot. His skill depends on the assumption that a billiard ball, hit at a certain angle at a certain speed, will always rebound in the same way (right, above). This, however, is untrue at the quantum level: imagine that the billiard ball represents an electron and the billiard cushion an atom. Then the electron will bounce off the atom in a number of possible rebound trajectories (right, below) – and it is completely impossible to predict which one it will follow in any given experiment

the same rebound trajectory every time. It is this predictability that enables Hurricane Higgins, the famous British snooker player, to play so well. This would be impossible in the quantum world of atomic particles: if, for instance, the ball were an electron and the cushion were an atom, each shot would have completely unpredictable consequences. The electron would bounce off the atom in a myriad of possible directions.

This outcome is not completely lawless, however, since there is a certain statistical likelihood that the electron will follow any given one of the possible rebound trajectories. If a large number of electrons are fired, one after another, at the atom, the number following each possible trajectory will be in accordance with the probabilities for the interaction – and these do not vary from instance to instance of the interaction. Thus quantum events show statistical predictability – the overall behaviour of large groups is predictable, even if no one can say in advance what any particular quantum particle will do.

This state of affairs holds for all quantum

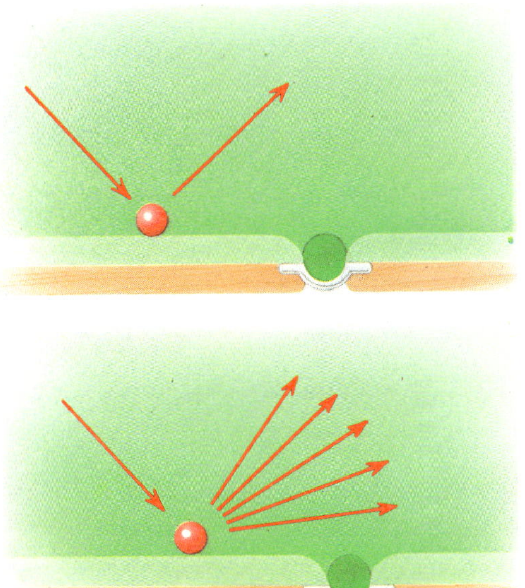

reactions. The implication for the observation theory of psi is that predictions about psi events can also be only probabilistic, and that the nature of psi is probabilistic. This is very much in accord with the practical results of psi research – an experiment works, then it doesn't, then it does, and so on. The theory may, indeed, help to explain why psi is so elusive and such a slippery fish to catch. So psi may be probabilistic – but it is also well known to transcend the boundaries of time and space. Precognition and telepathy over great distances clearly establish these properties – and any theory of psi must explain them. Walker's does so elegantly, by putting some very strange hypothetical properties of quantum reactions to work in the service of psi.

Albert Einstein – and others – put forward the idea that there may exist a special set of factors that governs the behaviour of quantum systems, apart from the generally accepted, known ones. He called these extra determining factors 'hidden variables', because they are not apparently measurable like the normal factors that affect quantum reactions – energy, mass, charge, and so on. He suggested that, if only we knew the values of these hidden variables governing a given quantum reaction, we could predict exactly what would happen each time, instead of having only statistical predictions available. Some brilliant theoretical work by the mathematical physicist John S. Bell proved that if such hidden variables really do exist, they must be 'non-local'. In physics, 'local' variables are those that can be tied down in time and space as being at a given place at a certain time. 'Non-local' variables can interact across space without limit and – astonishingly – also through time. Systems having non-local properties could, theoretically, interact with each other across space and time in ways that are not possible for systems having only local properties. One bold hypothesis, discussed by David Bohm, one of the leading proponents of hidden variable theory, in his book *Wholeness and the implicate order* (1980), states that all quantum reactions are, in principle, accessible to each other across space and time by interaction through their hidden variables. This provides Walker with exactly the theoretical mechanism he needs to explain the space- and time-transcending features of ESP.

Parapsychology has echoed this view by proposing the existence of a special time-crossing type of PK, which is known as 'retro PK'. The extraordinary properties of retro PK become easier to understand in the context of the 'measurement problem' of quantum physics, which leads us to the heart of the quantum view of reality.

Quantum problem

During the development of quantum theory in the 1920s and 1930s a problem arose that remains the subject of active controversy within the scientific community. This is the 'measurement problem' of quantum physics. In essence it is as follows.

An examination of the mathematics describing quantum reactions shows, as with the billiard ball example, that the outcomes are probabilistic. But – and here the quantum world takes a lurch away from everyday common sense – the way in which the mathematics of the quantum billiard ball collision is set up means that, until you actually measure the position of the ball, that position is indeterminate, and more: until you measure it, you could regard the ball as simultaneously bouncing back along *all* its possible trajectories!

To provide instant reassurance that physicists are not completely mad, it should be stated immediately that they concede that whenever one makes a measurement or observation of a quantum system it is always in just one of its possible states, never in the confused state of the hypothetical quantum billiard ball rolling along every one of its possible rebound trajectories.

Another analogy may help to clarify this situation. Imagine an egg sitting in a refrigerator egg rack. The egg represents the quantum system. Its states are represented by the places it can occupy in its egg rack. While the refrigerator door is closed, the mathematics says that the position of the egg is indeterminate – that the egg cannot be regarded as occupying any particular compartment of the egg rack – or, indeed, that it simultaneously occupies all the spaces in the rack. But whenever we open the door to make an observation – or measurement – there is the egg sitting as good as gold in only one place! Just as the refrigerator has to be opened deliberately to peek inside, the states of quantum systems remain indeterminate between specific measurements of their state.

Consciousness and science

What is it that collapses the indeterminate quantum system into only one of its possible states? Various schools of thought have been developed to provide interpretations of the mathematical language describing quantum reactions. One of these, the 'Copenhagen' interpretation developed by the Danish physicist Niels Bohr, suggests that the factor that causes the collapse is observation by a conscious observer. If the measurement were performed by a non-conscious machine, the Copenhagen interpretation states that every possible state would still be present – until a conscious being made an observation of the system. In this way, the Copenhagen interpretation binds human consciousness into the heart of physics, seeing the observer as bringing definite form out of the chaos of the indeterminate quantum state.

It is only a short step from regarding the observer as able to force the quantum system into definite form to asking whether the observer could not, in principle, decide which particular state the system should be in when observed. Such an action would, of course, be PK. To test this notion, it would be necessary to construct a PK target system in which the target actually consisted of quantum events. But in fact the random event generators (REGs) often used in PK experiments depend on random quantum events – the breakdown of radioactive atoms – that are amplified so as to make them accessible to our senses.

A test of retro PK has been devised by Helmut Schmidt. His PK machine used an REG that derived its random events from the quantal breakdown of radioactive strontium 90 atoms. The radioactive emissions caused by this breakdown were registered on a Geiger counter connected to electronic circuits that, when the counter detected something, produced one of two possible output states. The REG was thus essentially – and in a very sophisticated manner – producing a random alternation between two states that was very similar to those produced by tossing a coin. Over long runs of experiments, left to itself, Schmidt's REG produced, as expected, almost exactly 50 per cent 'heads' and 50 per cent 'tails'. PK agents were asked to will one state to be produced more than the other. Although about 3 per cent bias was generally the greatest to be produced, over runs of tens of thousands of experiments this becomes extremely significant – the probability of such results occurring by chance amounts to around one million million to one. The most crucial aspect of the interpretation of these results is that the PK does not apparently represent an input of energy – it is, instead, an ordering, a slight de-randomising of normally random events.

Left: a thought experiment that may help to clarify the measurement problem of quantum mechanics. Imagine an egg in a refrigerator egg rack. With the refrigerator door open, you note the egg's position (top), then shut the door. Common sense says that the egg must remain in the same position while the door is shut – but quantum mechanics says that the position of the egg is indeterminate. In fact, it could be occupying *any* of the spaces in the rack – or, indeed, *all* of them (middle). But whenever the door is opened and an observation of the egg is made, it is in its original compartment (bottom)

Above: a game of dice. Because, at the subatomic level, all matter is in motion, at that level the exact shape of the die is dependent on random quantum fluctuations. Evan Harris Walker has attempted to prove mathematically that the behaviour of a bouncing die depends not so much upon how it is thrown as upon the quantum fluctuation in its shape. The observation theories suggest that psychokinesis (PK) operates on quantum events – and Walker's alleged proof suggests how

This is equivalent to the addition of *information* to the system, not energy.

The Copenhagen explanation of the 'collapse' of a quantum state by an observer carries with it the implication that a necessary condition of the observer's being able to collapse it is that he does indeed 'measure' the outcome of the collapse of the quantum event in some fashion. And the observation theories agree with this view. The exact way in which this is done does not matter, and may vary – the observer may read a dial, see a light, hear a tone or even read a computer printout. The crucial event, according to the Copenhagen interpretation, is the very first observation made by a human being. On this view, subsequent observations are completely irrelevant because the first observation 'fixes' the quantum outcome. From here on, however, the observation theories differ from the Copenhagen interpretation.

Evan Harris Walker considers the role of the consciousness of the human observer in much more detail than does Schmidt. He believes that three important data processing systems can be ascribed to the human brain. One of these is the data processing system of the non-conscious brain, which is parapsychologically uninteresting. The second data system is that associated with brain processes that give information to the conscious mind. Walker believes that the part of his theory dealing with consciousness is a central and important part of his overall theory. The third system is more complex. Walker argues that the nerves associated with consciousness are interconnected on a quantum level – not just by the normal processes of chemical transmission. This produces a vastly complex quantally connected entity that can be regarded as having one complex quantum state. The consciousness of the person is, according to Walker, equivalent to the 'hidden variables' of the quantum state of the conscious brain cells, thus 'steering' the state of his own brain. Some of this data processing capacity is available to accomplish the 'collapse' of indeterminate quantum states outside the brain. This is what Walker terms the 'will', something that is free to exert PK on the world and is the source of all psi phenomena, including ESP. He maintains that 'consciousness' is thus real, but not an ordinary physical entity, and that it can have real physical effects on the world by means of its power to manipulate the 'hidden variables' of quantum systems.

However – and here Walker departs from the conventional Copenhagen interpretation – because the will can manipulate the non-local 'hidden variables' of quantum systems, its activity is not limited by time or space. This creates the astonishing and counter-intuitive prediction – that it is possible for us to influence *past* events!

Above: Helmut Schmidt with one of his PK-testing machines. This is a two-stage random event generator in which the events are generated by radioactive decay, a quantum process that is therefore, Schmidt believes, susceptible to PK influence

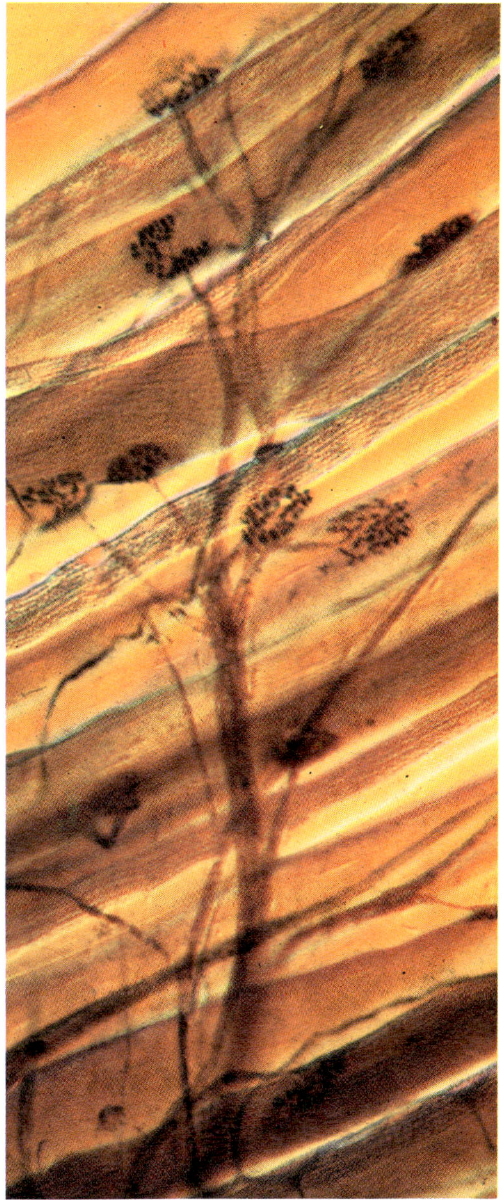

Right: human nerve end-plates. Physicist Evan Harris Walker argues that the nerves in the brain are connected on the quantum level – and that consciousness is equivalent to the 'hidden variables' of the quantum state of the brain

Power over the past

The observation theories of psi raise the extraordinary possibility that psychokinesis can change events that have already happened. Is there any validity in this claim, and can the theory and its implications be tested?

IF NO LIMITS in time or space can be placed on the possible influence of observers of a given quantum event, then *every* observer of a quantum event is potentially free to contribute his pennyworth of influence. The event itself will reflect the balance of all future influences contributed by various observers; it is as if the quantum event is an election result that shows the outcome of all the 'votes' – psychokinetic (PK) influences – to be cast in each direction by all future 'voters' (observers). The quantum event does not alter once it has happened, but happens in such a form as to reflect the overall effect of all later observers. This concept may seem extraordinary, but there is some evidence to show that this 'retro PK' effect really does exist. The implications for the science of parapsychology are staggering. First let us look at a now classic experiment to demonstrate the retro PK effect, which was performed by the German physicist Helmut Schmidt in the late 1970s.

Schmidt arranged for a laboratory assistant, who knew nothing of the details or purpose of the experiment, to run a computer-linked random event generator (REG) and to generate 12 sets of data consisting of the output states of the REG, which were not examined by anyone until the end of the experiment. Each of the 12 sets of data was stored in two forms – as audible clicks on audio tape cassettes and as holes in punched paper tape. The paper tape records were made because Schmidt thought that, while PK might alter the audio cassette records, it seemed impossible that it could punch holes or fill them in on paper tape. Comparison of the paper tape records with the audio tape records would reveal any discrepancies.

Several months after the 12 sets of data were generated, they were sorted into two sets of six by a random method. One set was simply kept securely until all the data were analysed. The other set was replayed, section by section, to a PK agent. The PK agent had succeeded in influencing the REG's output of clicks in previous experiments in which he had listened to its output 'live'. This time he listened to its several-month-old output, but was not told that he was listening to recorded, rather than live, clicks from the REG. The PK agent thought it was a normal PK experiment just like the previous ones.

Schmidt then used a computer to analyse the data on all 12 cassettes and paper tapes. The paper tape records and the cassettes all agreed exactly. Those that had not been selected for playing to the PK agent contained REG output states in a random distribution. But those he had listened to showed a divergence from chance that was statistically significant – retro PK was apparently real. In subsequent experiments, Schmidt tried playing another set of REG target clicks four times to the PK agent – and found that the divergence from chance of those clicks was approximately four times that of the first set.

Other experimenters have also succeeded in demonstrating retro PK effects and, however counterintuitive, or absurd according to the ordinary rules of common sense, retro PK may seem to be, it seems likely that it may exist. It also explains many of the results in parapsychology that have so far proved utterly baffling. If so, retro PK is of the first importance and must be taken into account: its implications for the evolution of parapsychology as a science are extremely far-reaching. First, however, the role of retro PK

In 1981, the author experienced what appeared to be a successful case of the use of retro PK. Watching the runners being paraded in the collecting ring before the Grand National (below), he had a sudden hunch that Aldaniti was going to win. He placed a bet, deciding to act consistently with the observation theories and provide himself with vivid and repeated feedback of the result. Aldaniti won (bottom) – and, by pure chance, the author happened to watch no less than six replays of the finish of the race on television. He thus boosted his retro PK – which may account for his hunch

as the mechanism behind all ESP must be clarified.

Suppose you are acting as a subject in an ESP test using playing cards. You pick up a card, face down, and try to guess its identity. Since there are no clues given, in guessing you could legitimately be seen as acting as an REG of a rather complicated and imperfect sort. After you have called out your guess, you are allowed to turn the card over. Now, as soon as you know the real identity of the card, you can, if you wish, immediately try to influence yourself in your own past – of a few seconds ago – by exerting retro PK to make yourself call out the correct card. If quantal reactions in your brain are responsible for your card calling, you could regard yourself as a quantum-driven REG accessible to retro PK!

But, the sceptic will object, if the call is wrong, no amount of retro PK will make it right, and so in that case retro PK is completely pointless. If it is correct, retro PK is unnecessary because nothing will change a right call into a wrong one, so in neither case is it worth attempting to use retro PK. However, this is just where 'common sense'

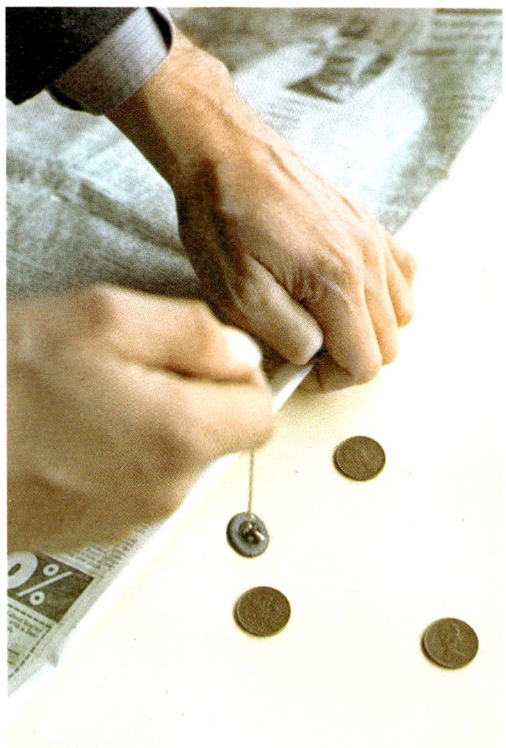

A dowsing experiment that can be carried out at home to test retro PK. You need a button on a piece of string to act as a pendulum, and some coins to act as targets. Place the coins on a table, and swing the pendulum over them, noting how it reacts when it is above a coin (left). Go out of the room, and ask someone to rearrange the coins and cover them with a newspaper (below left). Swing the pendulum above the newspaper and, when you feel sure of the locations of the coins, lift the newspaper to reveal their true positions. According to the observation theories, this is the important moment of the experiment – you now send a telepathic message concerning the true positions of the coins across time to yourself of just a few moments before, as you swung the pendulum

can lead the sceptic into logical falsehood. Yes, if one found, on turning over the card, that the call was incorrect, one would not bother to exert retro PK. But the accuracy of the call always reflects the amount of retro PK you are going to exert in the future – so one way of increasing the percentage of calls you get right is to attempt to produce lots of retro PK for all of them. If you don't bother, Schmidt's theory clearly predicts failure.

Now of course participants in ESP experiments have never – yet – deliberately tried to exert retro PK on themselves, and yet many ESP experiments have had high success rates. Thus, if ESP is indeed mediated by retro PK, it must be possible for this to happen without the conscious knowledge of the person concerned – and here very far-reaching consequences of the observation theories begin

The numbers racket

Many parapsychological experiments rely heavily on the use of statistical analysis. In particular, many of them use the mysterious notion of statistical significance. This is actually no more than a measure of the unlikelihood of the event in question occurring by chance. If, for example, the results of an experiment are said to be significant at the 5 per cent level, this means that there is a probability of no more than 5 per cent of them happening by chance.

In Helmut Schmidt's experiment, the cassettes and tapes cannot be checked at the beginning of the experiment, as their form then becomes immutable and retro PK can have no effect. The only alternative is to assume that they originally carried a record of a truly random REG output – and measure how much the records altered by retro PK differ from a random distribution. In Schmidt's experiment, the cassettes and tapes showed a divergence from chance that was statistically significant. But it is just possible that the original records may not have contained random distributions – and a solid proof of the existence of retro PK would require a far greater number of experiments.

to become apparent. There is no reason in principle why *everyone* involved in the experiment – experimenters, score checkers, analysers, even the people who, at some future date, read reports of the results of the experiment, should not influence the ESP subject at the point at which he makes his call. And this is, indeed, what the data of parapsychology experiments imply.

The problems for parapsychology may go even further. As soon as the results of experiments are published they are made accessible to a large number of people, all of whom can then produce effects.

However, the observation theories have produced a number of practical guidelines for increasing the effectiveness of your own ESP. First, do not tell sceptical people about your ESP experiences and experiments – they are thereby given access to influencing your results. Second, be careful in selecting the people who are to be involved in your psychic ventures – they too will affect your results. Third, try to view your role as an ESP percipient as passive. You are not as it were reaching out to the world to wrench off information, but acting merely as a passive object to be acted upon by your own retro PK and the retro PK of later observers of your efforts. Fourth, try to arrange things in such a way that you become acquainted with the results of your ESP attempts at a time when you are feeling happy and optimistic, not ill, tired or depressed. Fifth, ensure that a number of people 'observe' your results – this should increase the chances of your ESP guesses being correct. This is not a fruitless exercise, as your guesses will reflect the total amount of retro PK that you are able to bring to them. If you can recruit a group of highly psychic friends to examine your results, so much the better. Lastly, you can use real-life situations as a training ground. Here are some examples.

In 1981 the author experienced a spontaneous ESP experience that illustrates the observation theories in action. It was on the occasion of the Grand National. The author happened to be sitting watching the television, which was showing the horses parading in the collecting ring prior to the race. At the sight of Aldaniti the author felt a striking feeling of certainty that *this* horse would win. The author is not a betting man and has never had a similar experience, and a battle ensued between his habitual disinclination to visit a betting shop and his intuitive certainty that Aldaniti would win. Eventually he placed a bet, deciding to try as far as possible to act consistently with the observation theory and provide himself with as vivid and repeated feedback of the race as possible, in order to increase his chances of winning the bet. He then watched the race, and Aldaniti duly won. However, and this is the point of the story, by pure chance (the author watches little television) he happened to watch a number of other replays of the finish of the 1981 Grand National on television; in all, he saw six. This is the only race of which the author has ever seen more than one replay, and it seems an interesting and suggestive coincidence that this is the only race about which the author has had an ESP 'hunch'. The repeated and emotionally exciting feedback provided by the six replays of the race should, according to the observation theories, boost his retro PK massively. This incident seems a textbook demonstration of the use of retro PK to provide accurate ESP impressions.

In what was possibly an example of retro PK engineered by the cosmic joker, a Mrs Jones was out driving one day (below) when she was struck by a sudden fear that her house might be burning down. She hurried home – to find her house perfectly safe, and some fire insurance literature tucked into the front door (bottom). Was this retro PK – or was it merely a case of precognition in which the 'noise' obscured the 'signal'?

The observation theories form part of an exciting frontier area of parapsychology and may one day solve the riddle of how psi works. Many of the ideas involved may at first sight seem bizarre and counterintuitive – but then it is perhaps hardly surprising that something as strange as psi should demand an equally exotic explanation. It is interesting to make informal tests of some of the predictions of the observation theories, which can easily be done in real life. But understanding the observation theories is trickier than it may seem – before you claim to know what they are about, try explaining them to a friend!

Psychology and parapsychology

Many mental conditions – hypnotic trances and epilepsy for example – were once the object of superstitious dread, yet they are now regarded as perfectly natural, if not wholly explicable. Will 'paranormal' phenomena such as psychokinesis and telepathy ever lose their aura of mystery?

Squatters in the mind

Some individuals seem to possess a host of different selves who come and go continually. Sometimes a new self is a temporary visitor – sometimes it claims to be the sole true personality. Investigators have long been puzzled by these cases of fluid and uncertain identity

THE HISTORY OF MAN'S ADVANCE since the medieval period has been the story of his gradual realisation of how little he seems to matter in the scheme of things. From the pre-Copernican view that he lived at the centre of the Universe, a Universe that was not very much larger than the Earth, he has been forced by modern astronomical discoveries to accept that the Earth is an insignificant dot in the Galaxy, and the Galaxy, in relation to the visible Universe, is the size of a speck of dust in a cathedral. His fond conceit that he was Lord of Creation over the beasts of the field has been swept away by Darwin and his successors; to many he seems to be simply an animal species that grew a large brain and is now in serious danger of following the dinosaur and the dodo to extinction. And in the 19th century his assumption that he was at least in charge of his mind, overseeing its workings and guiding it according to rational purposes, was undermined and demolished by Freud's theories of the subconscious mind. He discovered that large tracts of Man's thinking processes lay behind a barrier; often decisions were taken there and then surfaced, so that he was fooled into accepting them as his own. In implementing them he was cast more in the role of public relations officer than that of managing director.

Nevertheless, notwithstanding these withdrawals to more modest estimates of his position, the average man could still console himself with the belief that at any rate his mental processes, conscious and unconscious, originated within his skull, woven on the marvellous electrochemical loom of his brain. The raw materials feeding the brain came through his five senses and the nerves monitoring his body.

The spiritual factor

This view is held by a large proportion even of those who still pay lip service to the religious teachings that there is a non-material factor – the spiritual – capable of influencing and being contacted by human beings. They believe that their thoughts are their own, that their dreams, by night or by day, are the products of their mind and brain. Their fantasies, their wishful thinking, belong solely to them. If they are surprised or terrified by the events in their dreams, they attribute this to the fact that the dream

Above: *The sleep of reason brings forth monsters*, by Goya. But are the monsters the products of our own unconscious minds – or are they sometimes intruders from outside? The evidence suggests that our 'ordinary' minds may not enjoy undisputed possession of our bodies

Right: in *The three faces of Eve* (1957), Joanne Woodward played Eve, a famous multiple personality victim. One of her selves was an uninhibited girl, seen here with her psychiatrist (Lee J. Cobb)

producer, the 'master of ceremonies', is their unconscious, or that they have had too much to eat for supper or that they are worried about something. In their dreams they are like a person at the cinema who views a film he has had no hand in producing. 'What an imagination I have!' they say admiringly.

Unfortunately not all people can believe this to be the case. It appears indisputable that certain human beings have to come to terms with the fact that their control of their bodily mechanism can be challenged. Among such people are the multiple personality cases, in which a number of distinct personalities dispute the possession of one body. In some of these carefully studied cases it is possible to believe that the original personality has been shattered by one or more traumatic experiences and has given rise to 'secondary' personalities. But others, equally carefully studied by psychiatrists, demonstrate such bizarre features that the possibility of invasion by independent personalities, or parts of personalities, has to be seriously considered. If such a theory seems to the man in the street to be a woeful return to the superstitious twaddle of the Dark Ages then, its proponents would reply, he is simply ignorant of the facts.

During the last 100 years, some scores of multiple personality cases have been treated and carefully studied by authorities such as Freud, Jung, William James, Morton Prince, Walter F. Prince and others. Many have common features but it is rash to assume that the same explanation covers all of them.

Let us suppose that the everyday personality is a girl. Often she is quiet, reserved, joyless, hyperconscientious. Often she has had a very unhappy upbringing, the product of a home broken by violence. She may find herself puzzling over lost stretches of time, the events of which she cannot remember. Strange clothes appear in her wardrobe and she gradually comes to fear for her sanity. If she consults a psychiatrist she may be fortunate enough to find one who recognises her condition. He will encounter one or more secondary personalities that from time to time surface to take control of the body and obliterate the dowdy everyday personality.

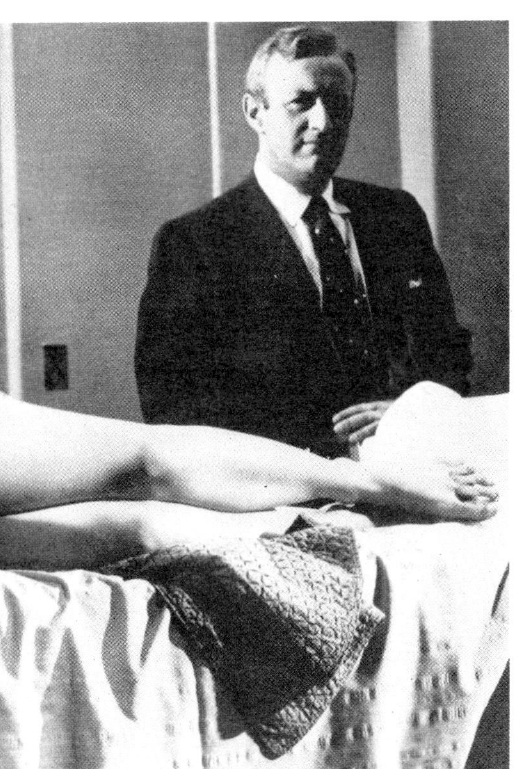

Dr Walter Franklin Prince, a minister of religion and a psychologist, who investigated many cases of multiple personality and of apparent possession by spirits. One of his most celebrated cases was Doris Fischer, who had five personalities – one of whom claimed to be a guardian spirit

In a number of cases, the major secondary personality turns out to be bright and fun-loving, openly contemptuous of the quiet girl she shares the body with. The dislike and contempt of the secondary personality may find an outlet in playing tricks upon the bewildered rival, who has no knowledge of the fun-lover's existence, nor has any memories of the experiences of the other. On the other hand, the fun-lover is often fully aware of everything the dowdy one experiences when the latter is in control. So different are the two characters that the psychiatrist treating the case knows which personality is in control immediately the girl enters the room, a knowledge due not only to different tastes in fashion but also to an almost physical transformation of the patient's face. Truly, Robert Louis Stevenson displayed remarkable insight into the complexities of the human mind when he wrote *Dr Jekyll and Mr Hyde* in the late 19th century.

One body, five occupants

Five or six separate personalities in one body, quite distinct in their beliefs, ethics and mental ages, have been displayed in a number of cases. In the case of an American woman, Doris Fischer – studied by Dr Walter F. Prince of Pittsburgh – there were five personalities: Doris, Margaret, Ariel, Sick Doris and Sleeping Real Doris. Doris was the 'normal' quiet, bewildered personality, Margaret the mischievous one who got Doris into trouble. Ariel appeared when Doris was asleep and always claimed to be a spirit who had come to protect her. Sick Doris gave the impression of being a dull, nervous, timid, almost simple-minded person. Sleeping Real Doris seems to have had predominantly the role of guardian of memories: she had no marked separate personality, but could reel off memories of past events, like a living tape recorder. Dr Prince described her as 'sleeping' because this ability lay dormant most of the time.

Dr Prince and his wife took the sorely troubled girl to stay with them, almost as a daughter, and thanks to the Princes' care and psychiatric treatment, the girl's mental and physical health improved over the next few years. During that time the complex relationship among the five personalities inhabiting the body of Doris Fischer altered. At first Margaret had access to the contents of Doris's and Sick Doris's minds, while Ariel was acquainted with the minds of all

three. Sometimes quarrels would occur for control of the body. As time went on, Doris extended her control as Sick Doris and then Sleeping Real Doris gradually deteriorated and finally disappeared. It was then the turn of Margaret, the sharp, fun-loving one. Slowly she receded until she too vanished.

There is a touching and thought-provoking account of the last days of Sick Doris. As she began to disintegrate she seemed to realise that she was going to 'die'. She accompanied Dr Prince on a last walk and she left a letter for Margaret. One of the ways by which each entity communicated with the others was by writing letters when she was in control, to be read when the appropriate personality took over the body. In her letter Sick Doris instructed Margaret as to what to do with her possessions and tried to leave her sister personality some helpful advice.

To the end Ariel maintained her claim that she was a spirit sent to look after Doris. In his account Dr Prince admits that to him she was the most mature and the wisest of all the personalities and that he had to consider seriously the hypothesis that her claim was in some way the truth.

The Christine Beauchamp case displayed many similarities to the Doris Fischer case and is quite often confused with the latter, especially since it was treated by another Dr Prince – this time Dr Morton Prince, a professor at the Tufts Medical School in Boston, USA. Christine Beauchamp was a student; she was approaching a nervous breakdown when she consulted him. He tried hypnosis, finding that she was a good subject. To his surprise a distinct, separate personality emerged – a relaxed, very much calmer version whom Prince called B-2 to distinguish her from the first Christine (B-1). But more was to follow. B-2, under hypnosis, was always rubbing her closed eyes. Prince discovered that it was a third personality, at first called B-3, who did the rubbing in an effort to get them open. B-3 insisted that she had a right to see and on a subsequent occasion she at last managed to open Christine's eyes. From then on she insisted on being known as Sally. She was a bright, mischievous person, not nearly so well-educated as Christine but exhibiting perfect health in contrast to Christine's debilitated and nervous state. She seemed to hate Christine and claimed that she never slept – that she stayed awake while the other personality was asleep. She continually tormented Christine with practical jokes. According to Dr Prince, Sally went out into the country where she collected in a box some snakes and spiders. She packed them up and addressed the package to Christine, who opened the box in due time and went into screaming hysterics – not surprisingly, since she had a horror of snakes and spiders.

Sally would also force the straitlaced Christine into embarrassing situations in which she would have to tell lies. In spite of Dr Prince's efforts, this feud continued until, quite suddenly, a fourth personality, B-4, surfaced. B-4 was a mature, responsible, firm personality who defended the luckless Christine from Sally's torments by giving Sally as good – or as bad – as she gave Christine.

Left: the transformation of the decent Dr Jekyll into the bestial Mr Hyde. This film version of the classic tale by Robert Louis Stevenson (inset) was made in 1931 and starred Frederic March. Hyde is really a fragment of a personality – the repressed evil side of Jekyll's nature. Stevenson, writing in 1886, anticipated Freud in his view of a potentially destructive dark side of the mind that threatens the world of reason and light. By contrast, the 'extra' selves in multiple personality cases may be complete, rounded individuals – and sometimes even an improvement on the ordinary self

Dr Prince decided that if he could merge B-1 and B-4 and suppress Sally he could obtain the true Christine. Using every hypnotic skill he possessed, he attempted to achieve this goal. It is not surprising to learn that Sally resisted to the end, claiming that she had every right to live and enjoy life. But Dr Prince succeeded in producing a more complete personality for Christine, though not quite eliminating Sally. As the years went by, Sally appeared from time to time, as if revisiting old haunts, to indulge herself by playing tricks on Christine.

If a personality under shock can shatter into fragments, so that each fragment is made up of a fraction of all those moods, emotions, beliefs, prejudices, desires that contribute to the normal person, then, even though in the Doris Fischer case Ariel claimed to be a spirit, we can still cling to the belief that no outside and alien influences are at work. But, as we shall see, there are cases that to a number of investigators stretch this hypothesis to breaking point.

The in crowd breaks out

Perhaps the official population figures for the United States should be increased – so many of its citizens seem to be afflicted, or favoured, by extra personalities. William Milligan (below) was found guilty of raping four young women in Columbus, Ohio, in 1976. He was diagnosed as having 10 personalities – of whom the guilty one was an 18-year-old lesbian. One of the psychiatrists who hastened to interview Milligan was Dr Cornelia Wilbur; she had previously treated 'Sybil', the subject of a book and a film, who had 16 personalities.

But these cases are excelled by that of 'Charles' – the pseudonym given by a psychiatrist to what he hoped was the core personality of someone who was called Eric when he was found wandering in a daze in Daytona Beach, Florida, in February 1982. Eric immediately 'split' into two selves – 'young Eric' and 'older Eric'. Young Eric told a (fictitious) tale of being brought up by drug dealers, being raped and witnessing murders committed by his stepfather. Further personalities emerged over a period of weeks – violent Mark, arrogant Michael, blind and mute Jeffrey – until there were no fewer than 27. The youngest was a foetus. Many of the selves were in conflict and created problems for each other: Michael, for example, was athletic and went on a long jog that left Eric – and all the other occupants of his body – aching for days. 'Charles', supposedly the true personality, said afterwards: 'I've lived through hell. I'm surprised I didn't go crazy. . . .'

The mind at large

Just as a person can apparently be invaded by other selves, so it seems that the 'normal' self can wander to far-off times and places. Writer Archie Roy is able to offer a personal account of his own involvement in such a classic case of 'distant seeing'

OVER THE PAST CENTURY there has been collected an impressive body of evidence that certain human beings have the clairvoyant faculty – an ability to acquire data about people and places without using the normal five senses. Some of these clairvoyants – or 'sensitives' or 'paragnosts' – have been studied by the most careful and skilful psychical researchers, who have had to come to the conclusion that their gift is genuine. But while one can be intellectually convinced of the reality of clairvoyance by their evidence, one is unlikely to be totally convinced unless one experiences it in person. I had just such an experience with a Glasgow sensitive, Albert Best. A friend took me to visit him at his home, without telling him my name or address. Mr Best, who believes that spirits of the dead work through him, told me that a number of people who had died wished to give me greetings and best wishes. He then proceeded to name them and gave me some characteristic details about each, including the addresses they used to live at, complete with street name and number. All were in the vicinity of the address at which I now live, and yet I had never heard of most of them.

Below: Albert Best, a psychic who practises in Glasgow. He interprets his own skills as the result of the spirits of the dead working through him. Other explanations are possible, however: for example, that he gains information about the dead telepathically from friends or relations present at the sittings

On making enquiries subsequently, I found that these people had indeed existed and had lived at the addresses Mr Best had given me. In some cases, however, they had lived there 10 years or more before I had moved to that district. It is interesting that these messages should be so concerned with

Right: the French psychical researcher and doctor Eugène Osty. He made many noteworthy experimental investigations of mediums and psychics of all descriptions. In his studies of psychometrists, or 'object readers', he found that they preferred to work with such items as hair or fingernails from the absent person with whom they were trying to establish rapport

Left: Alison Goodall was apparently put in touch with her dead father (inset) at a sitting with Albert Best. Mr Best correctly stated that Miss Goodall's work involved writing – she was in fact a journalist. Among the many accurate personal details he gave about her father, he said that he had been connected with the law: Mr Goodall had been a police Chief Superintendent. At another sitting Mr Best was equally impressive when he passed on 'messages from the dead' to the author (above)

the deceased persons' addresses: Mr Best had formerly worked for many years as a postman. This is typical of the way in which the personal characteristics of a psychic seem to influence the nature of the messages that come through him.

This test was, of course, in no way conclusive but was certainly worth following up. I asked Mr Best if I might bring a friend to visit him in a fortnight's time. I was particularly careful in making this arrangement not only to avoid giving the name of the friend – indeed at that time I had not even decided whom to invite – but also to avoid using the words 'he' or 'she'. When I took my friend to Mr Best's flat it was the first time he had met her. I was careful, of course, not to introduce her by name to him.

Mr Best, like a number of sensitives, goes into an almost imperceptibly altered state of consciousness to operate. In that state he claimed that my friend's deceased father was present and that he was providing information. Mr Best made the following statements:

> Your father is dead, your mother is still alive. You have one brother but no sisters. Your father was connected with the law. He died very suddenly. When reading and in his slippers he would place the heel of one on the toe of the other and had a habit of pushing the heel off his upper foot with the toe of the other slipper. His strongest drink was milk, and it was a bit of a joke in the family. When you and your mother would try to persuade him to travel abroad he would say such things as 'No, my heart's in the Highlands' and refuse to go. He had two watches. One is still in the family house; the other, a wristlet watch, has had a new strap put on it during the past week. I see you with a lot of other people. You are all writing, scribbling away. But you're not a novelist.

Afterwards my friend, who is a journalist and whose father was a police superintendent, confirmed that every single statement was correct – even to the watch, which she happened to be wearing. It had belonged to her father and she had put a new strap on it a week previously.

During the same meeting a number of other facts were given with the claim that they referred to my life and family, some of them going back 30 to 40 years. All were correct – if the two sets of statements, referring to me and to my friend, had been switched round, they would have failed lamentably to fit us. The whole experiment markedly strengthened my conviction that, whatever interpretation one puts on it, such a gift exists.

Among the psychical investigators who have studied sensitives with such gifts have been Dr Osty, a French physician who

Right: Dr J. Hettinger, who studied psychometry and obtained enough evidence to write two books on what he called the 'ultra-perceptive faculty'

became director of the Institut Métapsychique International in Paris, Dr J. Hettinger, who wrote two books describing his experiments and conclusions, and Professor W.H.C. Tenhaeff of the University of Utrecht's Parapsychological Institute. All three made a particular study of so-called psychometrists, sensitives who seem to obtain their best results when they are allowed to hold some object, letter or document belonging to the 'target' person, who may be alive or dead.

A permanent link

None of the researchers believed that the object in some mysterious way stored up information that was somehow 'read' by the sensitive. All that it did was to allow the sensitive to achieve a psychic connection with the person or persons to whom it had belonged. Once that had been achieved, even should the object be destroyed or taken away the sensitive could still obtain data psychically from the owner of the object. Neither did it matter how long ago the person had last handled it. Once the psychic contact had been made, even events in the life of the person following the time he or she had last touched the object could be perceived by the sensitive. And even more startling was the fact that sensitives, or at least some of them, could predict future events in the life of the 'target' person. This ability of a psychic to look ahead in time is repugnant to many people's cherished beliefs concerning the nature of time and free will; nevertheless the evidence, looked at without prejudice, is strong.

One of the most famous cases of psychometry is that of Señora Maria Reyes de Z., studied by the psychical researcher Dr G. Pagenstecher in the 1920s. The case of the Spanish traveller is completely characteristic of the ability of a psychometrist seemingly to merge with the mind of another human being and obtain information from it.

Dr Pagenstecher gave Señora de Z. a sealed envelope, the contents of which were unknown even to him. The woman said that she seemed to be aboard a great liner. There was an atmosphere of panic although the sea was calm. Many people wore lifejackets. She saw a large man of pale complexion with dark eyes and black hair, with a beard and moustache. Over one eye he had a scar. He seemed Spanish in appearance. She saw him tear a page from his notebook and write a few lines on it. While he did so, she heard a number of explosions. The man finished his note and put into a bottle, which he sealed and threw overboard. The ship was obviously sinking and Señora de Z. heard the man cry out in Spanish: 'My God, my children!'

After the lady came out of her trance Dr Pagenstecher allowed several witnesses to examine another envelope and confirm that it was securely sealed. Then he opened it. In it was a statement that the first envelope contained a torn piece of paper, carrying the message, in Spanish:

> The ship sinks. Good-bye, my Luisa. Take care of my children and see that they don't forget me. Havana. May God protect you and me. Good-bye.

The two sealed envelopes had been sent to Dr Pagenstecher by an attorney. They came from a man who knew a woman whose husband had almost certainly been drowned in the sinking of the *Lusitania* some years previously. The liner was a victim of a U-boat on 7 May 1915. The torn scrap of paper had been taken from a bottle washed ashore after the sinking and had finally been sent to Havana. It is probable that the message came from Señor Penoles, the husband of the woman. It is recorded that a description of the appearance of Señor Penoles fitted

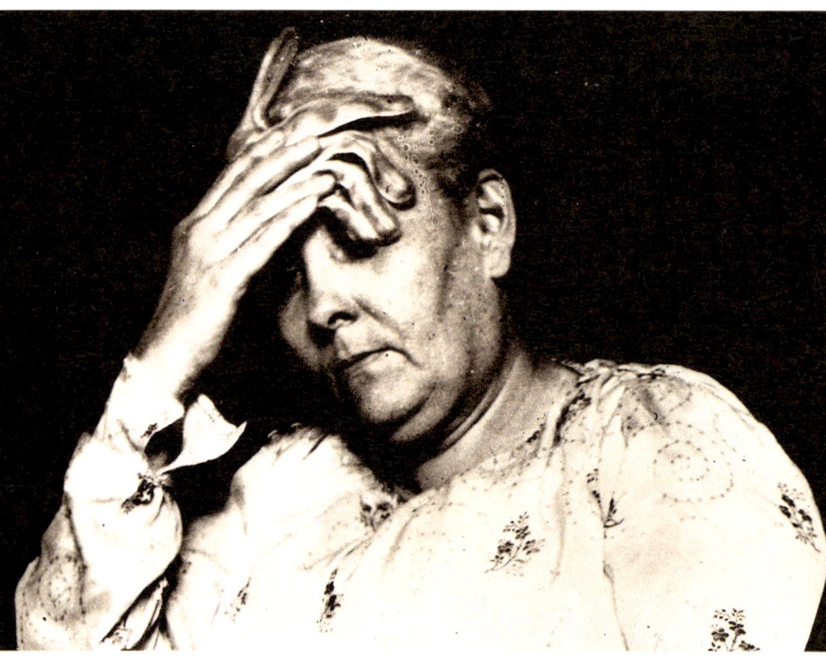

An object reader working with the glove of a person with whom she is attempting to establish rapport. Researchers generally do not believe that the objects used in such sessions are stores of information about the absent person: rather they are the means by which a link with the person (whether alive or dead) can be established. If the object is subsequently destroyed the link between the person and the medium may persist

Left: Dr Gustav Pagenstecher, a German doctor living in Mexico, who was a tireless investigator of the mind's apparent ability to perceive remote places and past events. He concluded that a sensitive was most likely to perceive events in an object's history if they were of a type that had occurred frequently, were associated with extreme emotion, or were very recent

perfectly with the description given by the psychic of the man she had 'seen'.

Osty, Hettinger and Tenhaeff have collected scores of cases that are just as impressive. Over many years Professor Tenhaeff studied a number of 'paragnosts' (the name he gave to such psychics). He found that with some of them the rapport with the 'target' people, whether alive or dead, became so strong that they seemed to enter into the paragnosts. The psychics tended to 'become' those other persons, to feel sensations and emotions characteristic of them, as well as sharing their memories.

Mr C.H. known in Tenhaeff's files as Delta, was an extreme case of this: he identified with the target person to such an extent that he was virtually possessed by the other. He set up as a psychic detective and was often employed to find missing persons. In one such case an elderly man, E. G., went missing and Delta was called in. In a report to Professor Tenhaeff he subsequently described how he went to the old man's bedroom to obtain psychic 'impressions'. He had already experienced strong feelings that had led him to the conclusion – later proved correct – that the old man had drowned.

> G. manifested himself once again . . . I felt myself becoming very unwell. It was as if there was something in the way on my chest. It was the same feeling I had with a bad cold. I further noticed that G. was sobbing through me. Tears came into my eyes . . . I went through the house once more and walked up the stairs. I did this in the same way in which G. had done so during his lifetime. I also had very strong eructations (which I never have). I was told that G. had been much troubled by this. All the feelings of G. had become mine.

Several of Professor Tenhaeff's paragnosts expressed the fear that sooner or later they would be unable to 'throw off' the personality with which they had entered into rapport and so become truly possessed. Delta told Tenhaeff that if he feared that he was no longer in complete control of the situation and in danger of being entirely overwhelmed by the other personality, he could nevertheless restrain the other and become himself again. There are, however, cases on record where possession seems to have been total and 'the other' has taken up residence like a squatter of the mind, displacing the rightful owner of the body to limbo. Whether that 'other' is essentially an alien personality or a secondary personality created around the memories and experiences with which the sensitive makes contact is a matter for debate.

The sinking of the British liner *Lusitania* by a German submarine in May 1915 resulted in the deaths of 1000 people. Years later, in Mexico, a sensitive seemed to get in touch with this scene. Holding an envelope whose contents were unknown to her, she 'saw' a scene of panic on a ship, amidst which one passenger put a note in a bottle and threw it overboard. The envelope she was holding contained just such a message, allegedly washed ashore after the *Lusitania*'s sinking. And there had indeed been panic on board the *Lusitania* as the great ship had listed to one side and lifeboats capsized as they were launched

Not like her at all

Claiming to be possessed by the spirit of a young woman long dead, a 13-year-old girl played the role to the full – by moving in with the dead woman's parents and living as their daughter. A small American town was the scene of this strange reincarnation

Above: Watseka, Illinois, as it looked in the late 19th century. People were very willing to hear tales of returned 'spirits' at this time, for Spiritualism was the rage in America

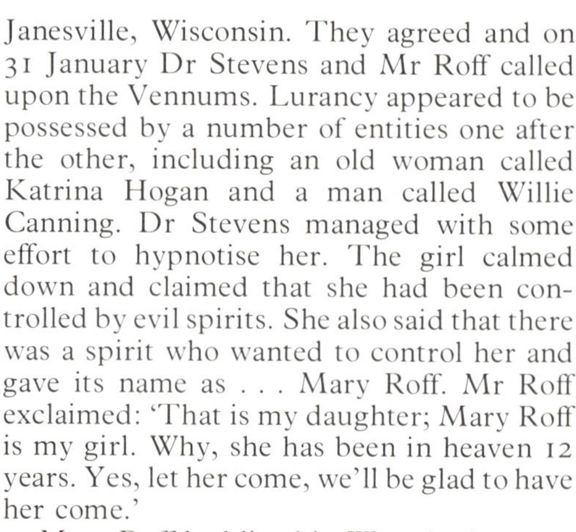

Right: Lurancy Vennum, who was besieged by numerous 'spirits' before one of them took up exclusive residence for a few months. It claimed to be the spirit of Mary Roff (far right), who had died 13 years before, aged 18. Mary had been subject to curious seizures, during which she allegedly produced psychic phenomena. Did she enjoy a brief reincarnation in Lurancy's body?

ONE OF THE MOST EXTRAORDINARY and best-authenticated cases of ostensible possession is that of the 'Watseka wonder'. The person at the centre of events, Mary Lurancy Vennum, was born in April 1864 in the American township of Milford, about 7 miles (11 kilometres) from Watseka, Illinois. Until the age of 13 Lurancy enjoyed good health. Then, one day in July 1877, she told her family: 'There were persons in my room last night, and they called "Rancy! Rancy!" and I felt their breath on my face.' The next night she left her bed, protesting that she could not sleep because every time she tried to sleep she heard voices calling 'Rancy! Rancy!'

This episode was followed a few days later by some kind of seizure. The next day, 12 July, she had another, which led to her announcing to her family that she could see heaven and angels and people, now dead, whom she had known. These incidents, in which she seemed almost entranced, continued and, together with her wild statements, persuaded onlookers that she was insane.

Early in 1878 two acquaintances of the Vennums, Mr and Mrs Roff, suggested that they should call in Dr E. W. Stevens of Janesville, Wisconsin. They agreed and on 31 January Dr Stevens and Mr Roff called upon the Vennums. Lurancy appeared to be possessed by a number of entities one after the other, including an old woman called Katrina Hogan and a man called Willie Canning. Dr Stevens managed with some effort to hypnotise her. The girl calmed down and claimed that she had been controlled by evil spirits. She also said that there was a spirit who wanted to control her and gave its name as . . . Mary Roff. Mr Roff exclaimed: 'That is my daughter; Mary Roff is my girl. Why, she has been in heaven 12 years. Yes, let her come, we'll be glad to have her come.'

Mary Roff had lived in Watseka for most of her life, until her death when she was still less than 19 years old, in July 1865. (Lurancy at this time was just over a year old.) From the age of six months Mary had suffered from violent seizures, which became worse during her life. Allegedly her illnesses made her notorious in the neighbourhood during her lifetime: and she was regarded as having clairvoyant powers, which were investigated by a number of the town's citizens.

After Lurancy's announcement that Mary's spirit had returned, the excited Mr Roff assured her that Mary, because of her own sufferings in life, would be able to help her. Lurancy seems to have taken the advice of some of the other spirits as well. She announced that Mary would displace the other spirits. Mr Roff made the further suggestion that Lurancy's mother should bring her to the Roffs' house '. . . and Mary will be likely to come along, and a mutual benefit may be derived from our former experience with Mary.' One can imagine very easily the welter of emotions – fear, hope, wishful thinking, terror, bewilderment, despair – tearing at the two families. The following day Mr Vennum called upon Mr Roff to tell him that his daughter now gave every sign of *being* Mary Roff. During the next week, the girl was 'mild, docile, polite and timid, knowing none of the family, but constantly pleading to go home'.

The 'Mary Roff' personality maintained its control. About a week later, Mary Roff's mother and sister paid a visit to the Vennum household. 'Mary', seeing them coming along the street, exclaimed: 'There comes my ma and sister Nervie.' The name 'Nervie' was one that the late Mary Roff had used for her sister – by this late date now married – when she was a girl. When they entered the house, 'Mary' was overcome with emotion and pleaded to be allowed to 'go home' with them. The Vennums agreed, and on 11 February 'Mary Roff' went home.

It is on record that 'Mary' remained there for three months, behaving exactly as if she were indeed the Roffs' dead daughter, recognising everyone she had known when she had been alive, remembering scores of incidents from her past. Some of these events had happened 13 to 25 years before. When she met friends or relatives of the Roffs whom she had not seen for many years – if it is accepted that she *was* 'Mary Roff' – she would still recognise them but comment on changes in their appearance. Some days after she arrived at the Roffs' house, a Mrs Parker and her daughter-in-law, Nellie Parker, came to visit the Roffs. Mrs Parker had been a neighbour of the Roffs in Middleport in 1852 and in Watseka in 1860. 'Mary' immediately recognised them as if she had last seen them the day before, although it was 17 years since the Roffs' daughter Mary had last seen them. Particular clothes, a box of letters and a collar the dead daughter had sewn were seized on by 'Mary', in a number of cases with comments that showed she knew the exact circumstances concerning their relationship with the dead girl.

Naturally the unhappy Vennum family visited the Roffs on occasion to see how their daughter – if indeed she was still their daughter! – was progressing. The girl did not seem to recognise any member of the Vennum family or the Vennums' friends and neighbours. As the visits continued, however, she became more friendly towards them, but gave every indication that to her they were strangers that she was just coming to know.

This extraordinary situation continued until 7 May. On that day 'Mary' told Mrs Roff that Lurancy was returning. The girl sat down, closed her eyes and almost immediately opened them. She looked around and exclaimed: 'Where am I? I was never here before.'

Mrs Roff reassured her but the girl had

Below right: Richard Hodgson, a sceptic who exposed several fraudulent mediums, but was convinced of the genuineness of some. He studied the Lurancy Vennum case and believed that it had to be explained in terms of a spirit taking over Lurancy's person

now taken on the personality of Lurancy. She pleaded to be allowed to go home. She was still pleading five minutes later when a reversal took place and the 'Mary' personality took over once more. From then until 19 May the girl's body continued to be occupied by the 'Mary' personality, though more and more frequently she would be transformed into 'Lurancy'. On 19 May, for example, while Lurancy's brother Henry was present, 'Lurancy' came through and recognised Henry; then the reversion to 'Mary' again took place.

In the record kept by Mr Roff we find him writing on the morning of 21 May:

> Mary is to leave the body of Rancy today, about eleven o'clock, so she says. She is bidding neighbours and friends good-bye. Rancy to return home all right today. Mary came from her room upstairs, where she was sleeping with Lottie, at ten o'clock last night, lay down by us, hugged and kissed us, and cried because she must bid us good-bye, telling us to give all her pictures, marbles, and cards, and twenty-five cents Mrs Vennum had given her, to Rancy, and had us promise to visit Rancy often.

One of 'Mary's' last acts was to arrange that after she and Mrs Alter – her supposed sister – had said their goodbyes, Mrs Alter should take Lurancy to Mr Roff's office. By the time Mrs Alter had arrived at the office, Lurancy was firmly back in control. She obviously accepted the Vennums as her own family when she got to their house and settled in contentedly.

Lurancy Vennum's subsequent life was essentially a normal one. She married a farmer, George Binning, in January 1882 and had a family. In 1884 they moved farther west. It is on record that occasionally 'Mary' would return, in a manner reminiscent of a 'spirit control' taking over an entranced medium, but the days of full possession were over.

When Lurancy Vennum 'became' Mary Roff, she moved into the Roffs' home (above). The new 'Mary' recognised many of the family possessions. After a few months' stay 'Mary' said goodbye; Lurancy took her place and was welcomed back into the Vennum home (below). The disturbances that had once alarmed her family now virtually ceased

This extraordinary story raises a number of questions. The first, naturally, is: what authenticity can we ascribe to it?

The first account of the case was written by Dr E. W. Stevens, the man who had been called in by the Vennums on the advice of Mr Roff. Dr Stevens kept a close watch on the progress of the case, interviewed the chief witnesses and had his written account confirmed by both sets of parents. A paper by him was published in the *Religio-Philosophical Journal* in 1879, followed after a short time by a pamphlet entitled *The Watseka Wonder*.

Visit from a sceptic

The celebrated and notoriously sceptical psychical researcher Dr Richard Hodgson visited Watseka in April 1890 and questioned the major witnesses in the case still living in the neighbourhood. His account of what they told him was subsequently published in the *Religio-Philosophical Journal* for 20 December 1890.

> I have no doubt that the incidents occurred substantially as described in the narrative by Dr Stevens, and in my view the only other interpretation of the case – besides the spiritistic – that seems at all plausible is that which has been put forward as the alternative to the spiritistic theory to account for the trance-communications of Mrs Piper and similar cases, viz., secondary personality with supernormal powers. It would be difficult to disprove this hypothesis in the case of the 'Watseka

Will the real Mrs Piper...

Mrs Leonora Piper first discovered her exceptional abilities as a medium during her twenties, when she fell into a trance while she was being treated by a psychic healer

One of the most closely studied of American mediums was Mrs Leonora Piper of Boston, Massachusetts. While in her trance state she was ostensibly taken over by one or more psychic 'masters of ceremonies', or 'controls'. Some showed humour, wit and knowledge; others talked arrant nonsense; others seemed to be psychic confidence tricksters.

The psychical researcher Richard Hodgson was at first sceptical of the 'spiritistic hypothesis' to explain these happenings. He was inclined to the opinion of his colleague Mrs Sidgwick that the controls were 'phases or elements' of Mrs Piper's personality. But then a control appeared claiming to be George Pelham.

Pelham had been a friend of Hodgson and had promised that, if he were to die first and find himself still existing, he would devote himself to proving the fact. Two years later he *did* die, in an accident. After several years' study of the 'Pelham' control, Hodgson was finally forced to report: 'Out of a large number of sitters who went as strangers to Mrs Piper, the communicating G.P. has picked out the friends of G.P. living, precisely as the G.P. living might be expected to do . . . I cannot profess to have any doubt but that the chief communicators to whom I have referred . . . are veritably the personalities that they claim to be, that they have survived the change we call death.'

> Wonder', owing to the comparative meagreness of the record and the probable abundance of 'suggestion' in the environment, and any conclusion that we may reach would probably be determined largely by our convictions concerning other cases. My personal opinion is that the 'Watseka Wonder' case belongs in the main manifestations to the spiritistic category.

Hodgson is saying, then, and the present writer must agree with him, that there is no way that the strange case of Lurancy Vennum can be explained away by normal means. It has to be explained in one of two ways – in terms of spirits or of multiple personalities. These two types of explanation can be applied to a large body of psychic phenomena.

The spiritistic hypothesis, namely that in this case the spirit of Mary Roff took over the body of Lurancy Vennum, receives support from a similar case studied by Professor Ian Stevenson of the Department of Neurology and Psychiatry at the University of Virginia, USA. A little Indian boy, Jasbir Lal Jat, $3\frac{1}{2}$ years old, was pronounced dead of smallpox. Some hours later, however, he revived and exhibited a brand new personality. He now claimed to be a man from a different village who had been poisoned. His detailed knowledge of the man's past life convinced the little boy's parents that he was not fantasising. It was found that the man had died at about the same time that the child ostensibly died, suggesting a bizarre spirit analogue of musical chairs.

Professor Ian Stevenson, a leading American authority on cases of apparent reincarnation

This interpretation has to be studied as an alternative to the straightforward reincarnation theory in conjunction with the remarkable collection of ostensible reincarnation cases collected by Dr Stevenson and others. The 'Watseka wonder' and the case of Jasbir Lal Jat demonstrate the necessity of keeping in mind the 'possession' hypothesis.

Hodgson's other theory was that a secondary personality of Lurancy Vennum's utilised extra-sensory perception or paragnostic powers to acquire details of Mary Roff's past life from those still living and then dramatised them into a pseudo Mary Roff personality. This is also capable of fitting the facts of the case. For what reason Lurancy Vennum's subconscious should do this we can only guess. It is clear, however, that the girl was surrounded by people who were sympathetic towards the spiritistic hypothesis: if she was suffering attacks of hysteria, she might well, on the subconscious level, wish to give them what they wanted. To do this, however, she would have had to have psychic powers to gather a multitude of details from the memories of Mary Roff.

Whatever the truth of the matter, it seems certain that Lurancy Vennum, as 'Mary Roff', demonstrated that a human being can suffer psychic 'invasion' for a period measured in months, to the extent that the 'legal tenant' of the body is displaced as if he or she had never been.

All in the mind?

Occasionally, entire groups of people are struck down by a strange epidemic with all the symptoms of serious illness – and yet a few hours later they are completely recovered. What is the weird mental contagion that causes such outbreaks? Why do they happen?

IN THE SUMMER OF 1980 the inhabitants of Kirkby-in-Ashfield in Nottinghamshire, England, put on a big village show; and among the treats laid on for the occasion was a marching jazz band that was to appear – weather permitting – in the open. The weather relented; the contest was proceeding according to plan – and then, suddenly, all was chaos. Children began to collapse, as if losing the use of their limbs. Many vomited. Questioned by anxious parents, they said they had headaches, twitches, miscellaneous pains, constricted throats. Nearly 300 of them were taken to hospitals, along with a few adults who had also succumbed. But the great majority recovered in a few hours, seemingly none the worse for their ordeal.

This was a classical example of mass hysteria in the symptoms displayed, the age of the victims, the rapidity with which the epidemic spread, and the quick recovery rate. Yet mass hysteria was at first hardly even considered as a diagnosis. The first thought was that it was food poisoning, and an unfortunate ice cream vendor was in fear, for a time, that he was about to be lynched. Then a neighbouring farmer was denounced for having allowed indiscriminate spraying of weed-killer; a horse, it was alleged, had died in the field shortly before – one of many rumours that turned out to be unfounded. And, needless to say, 'a virus' was blamed, and laboratory workers were kept busy trying fruitlessly to identify the culprit. It was even surmised that the epidemic was caused by an emanation of noxious gases, and the field was dug up in search of their source.

Dangerous diagnosis

Why the reluctance to diagnose mass hysteria, when the outbreak had so many of the stock indications of that disorder? There were two main reasons, the immediate one being that any doctor in the vicinity who had offered that diagnosis would have risked the fury of the children's parents. For most of them, it would have implied that their offspring had only pretended to be ill, or were crazy, or perhaps a mixture of both.

The other reason was that the medical profession has been conditioned to think of illness, and particularly epidemics of illness, as organic: the consequence of physical or chemical processes – the depredations of germs or viruses, or the absorption into the lungs or the digestive system of toxic matter. From the beginning of the 20th century until

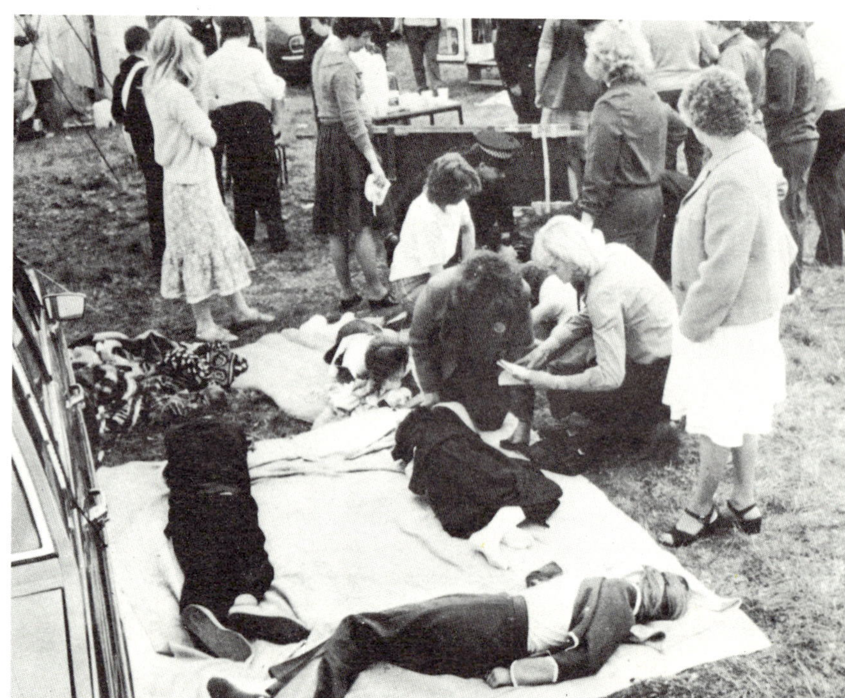

Children at a village fair in Nottinghamshire, England, were victims of a sudden and mysterious epidemic of an unknown disease in the summer of 1980. Over 300 were taken to hospital (top); most of those affected were young children (above). What was the nature of the strange disease? Only after thorough investigation proved fruitless did doctors reluctantly make the obvious diagnosis – mass hysteria

the late 1970s most medical students were actually taught that *real* disease symptoms are always necessarily organic – in a different category from the neuroses and hysteria. And although research into the effect of the mind and the emotions on physical and chemical processes in the body, in particular with hormones and enzymes, has shown this to be fallacious, many doctors continue to think in organic terms – much as many physicists continue to think in Newtonian terms, in spite of the fact that Einstein and, still more, the quantum physicists have upset their cherished assumptions.

There is a further complication: 'hysteria' has three distinct meanings. And until they are sorted out, any attempt to explain outbreaks such as the one at Kirkby-in-Ashfield can only promote confusion.

Colloquially, the meaning of hysteria is clear enough. In effect, it describes a state in which we lose conscious control over ourselves, our movements, and our behaviour. Its most familiar form is a child's tantrum: kicking, screaming, crying. Hysteria is not, however, necessarily anti-social. When somebody sobs hysterically with grief over a bereavement or the behaviour of a faithless lover it may be an embarrassment to those who have to put up with it, but they may subsequently feel that the emotional release has been 'good for' the sufferer.

Above: 'a child more easily conceived than described' – a childish tantrum, from a Victorian illustration

Below: hysterical behaviour at a pop concert – a new phenomenon in the 1950s

With laughter, most of us regard those occasions when we have found something or somebody hysterically funny, so that we have 'fallen about', and tears have coursed down our cheeks, as memorable, to be cherished. Hysteria induced by tickling is for most children a joy – as long as it is not carried too far by over-enthusiastic adults.

Yet even if the term 'hysterical' – as in the often heard pub-anecdote phrase, 'it was hysterical' – has amiable connotations, 'hysteria' has none. It implies the existence of a disorder, of a disreputable kind. The loss of control, the implication is, comes from weak-mindedness or bloody-mindedness – or, as in a child's tantrum, an unwelcome and disquieting mixture of both.

The power of the mind

Clinically, hysteria has another meaning altogether. Loss of control is still indicated, but of a different kind. What it amounts to is that the mind has the power, on certain occasions, to produce symptoms that exactly mimic those of organic disease – and not just of disease. The most notorious form of hysteria in this category is pseudocyesis, or false pregnancy. It is rare today, because more sophisticated methods of testing can reveal whether or not a woman is pregnant. But until the mid 20th century false pregnancies were commonly reported, some completing the full term, with morning sickness, cessation of menstrual periods, swelling breasts, swelling stomach, and ultimately labour pains.

More sophisticated tests have also helped to eliminate hysteria from the reckoning in terms of diagnosis of disease. A glance at the medical textbooks of the 19th century shows that it was considered one of the most widespread of diseases, as well as being extremely difficult to detect. 'You hear of hysteric coughs,' Sir James Paget, surgeon to Queen Victoria, told his students, 'of hysteric dyspepsias and paralysis, of hysteric joints and spines.' He went on to say that hysterical illnesses were extremely common, needed careful handling, and must be watched for because there was hardly any common illness that was not imitated, the mimicry being 'so close as to make the diagnosis very difficult'.

Paget wanted to make a distinction between hysteria in its colloquial sense, which he considered to be disordered behaviour – a mental, or emotional, breakdown – and in its clinical sense, a real illness, he insisted, that he christened 'neuromimesis'. For a time the term was used by doctors and it is still to be found in medical dictionaries; but unluckily it failed to catch on, so that confusion between the two has remained ever since. Yet in one respect that confusion is justified. The two are linked – as the Kirkby-in-Ashfield 'epidemic' illustrated.

What infuriated parents when reporters from the newspapers (and a psychiatrist on BBC radio) told them that mass hysteria was being suggested as a possible explanation, the other suspects having one by one been cleared of guilt, was that their children had not behaved hysterically. They had suffered from *real* symptoms – the fainting, the aches and pains, the vomiting, the constricted throat – how could this be 'hysteria'? But this is, in fact, precisely the form mass hysteria most commonly takes. The first person to contract the symptoms sets the pattern: the rest follow it, as if imitating it.

The idea that epidemics of hysteria are triggered off by an 'index case' has been confirmed by recent research into outbreaks in factories and workshops in the United States. Two psychologists, Michael Colligan and Michael Smith of the US Department of Health, Education and Welfare, have unearthed a great many reports of hysterical outbreaks and shown how consistent the pattern is. Less work has been done in this area in Britain, but there have been a few revealing investigations.

Two were carried out by Anne Maguire, and recorded in the *Lancet* in 1978, after she had been called in to advise the management about what action to take in epidemics of what were assumed to be infectious or contagious skin diseases. In both cases, she found the initial victim – the index case – had indeed contracted dermatitis, but it was not connected with the employee's job. The other workers had the same symptoms, but not, it turned out, the same disorder; anyway, the symptoms disappeared once it was established that there was nothing in the work they were doing or the materials they were handling that could be blamed for their skin condition.

If such outbreaks are common, why are they so often not reported? One clue is given by the fact that Anne Maguire was called in as a dermatologist. In the great majority of cases psychiatrists or clinical psychologists are not consulted. 'The investigative team,' Colligan and Smith found, 'is likely to consist of an industrial hygienist, a nurse or medical assistant, a physician, and possibly a toxicologist.' Only when they can come up with no explanation is hysteria considered as a possibility. By that time, with the epidemic as a rule a thing of the past, the management will be tempted to terminate the enquiry, and 'the final report is unceremoniously buried in the agency files.'

The psychic link

The third meaning of hysteria is 'psychic contagion': in other words, we are thinking of the mechanism, as yet unexplained, by which the symptoms (whatever form they may take) are transmitted. And here, not merely is ignorance almost total, but very little research is being done. Many outbreaks in schools are never investigated at all – not, that is, unless the symptoms are of a kind that might encourage parents to sue. And then almost invariably there are two prime suspects, the meals and the central heating or ventilating system. If pathogenic bacteria or gas leaks are not found, headmasters naturally prefer to have the whole episode hushed up, in case hysteria should be diagnosed.

Schools are easily the most fertile breeding ground of epidemic hysteria, however; and a few outbreaks have been carefully investigated and surveyed in reports in medical journals. The symptoms vary, but they generally include some, if not all, of the standard indicators: dizziness, fainting, headache, shivering, loss of feeling, a sensation of cold (or heat), pins-and-needles, miscellaneous pains, muscle spasm, panting, constricted throat, nausea and vomiting. Sometimes there are symptoms of the kind that the term hysteria suggests, such as

Above: Sir James Paget, who believed hysteria to be a clinical illness

Since the 1950s, mass hysteria among pop audiences has become commonplace. The behaviour of Beatles fans is notorious; at the London opening of the Beatles film *Help* in July 1965 (above) nearly 40 were treated for hysteria. Ten years later fans of the Bay City Rollers were exhibiting the same kind of behaviour (left)

convulsions and dissociation – talking in a strange voice, sometimes in a strange language. But these usually affect only a tiny minority of the victims.

In the majority of cases there is a strong element of what appears to be imitation. Witnesses often refer to children 'falling like ninepins'. But the imitation cannot be entirely conscious. Many of the symptoms reported could hardly be imitated deliberately – the constricted throat, the loss of feeling, the pins-and-needles, the muscle pain. And sometimes children who collapse are not within sight of each other: they may be in different parts of a school – even in different schools, as in an outbreak in Wales in 1956, where thousands of children collapsed at around the same time.

The historical evidence is abundant – and not all of it relates to disease. The disciples at Pentecost, after all, were clearly caught up in an outbreak that they so far lost control over their limbs that they reeled about as if drunk (St Peter had to explain to onlookers that they would hardly be drunk at that hour of the morning). The disciples also dissociated, 'speaking in tongues'. However they certainly did not think of themselves as having been ill: on the contrary, their possession by the Holy Spirit, as they thought of it, was to be the second decisive event in their lives, their encounter with Jesus having been the first; and, indeed, it led to the founding of the Christian Church.

Other outbreaks, however, have been horrendous; notably the epidemic in the Loudun convent in the 1630s, agonisingly described in Aldous Huxley's book *The devils of Loudun* (and travestied in the film). It is possible, too – indeed likely – that Hitler owed his ascendancy over the German people to his exploitation of mass hysteria at the Nuremberg rallies and elsewhere. Yet there are other features of hysteria that could conceivably be exploited for our benefit – for example, it can provide a remarkable degree of immunity not just to pain, but also to actual injury – if they were better understood; and this should now be one of our major objectives.

But even so we are left with a number of unsolved questions. What is the cause of such outbreaks? Why do they take their eccentric pattern? By what process are the victims selected (for not everybody succumbs)? Why should school children be particularly susceptible? And what is the agency that transmits the disorder?

Adolf Hitler (below left) had an instinctive understanding of the hysterical behaviour of people in crowds – and how to exploit it. In the Nuremberg rallies (below) he was able to make hundreds of thousands of Germans forget any doubts they might have had about his politics and swear their undying devotion to him as their leader

A shameful affliction

In primitive societies hysterics were often regarded as favourites of the gods, and mass hysteria was frequently used therapeutically. Yet many doctors today refuse to recognise the phenomenon

MASS HYSTERIA has three components: loss of control, mimicry and contagion. The loss of control may be of a mental or physical kind, or both, and it tends to take much the same form in all victims of the same outbreak, as if some kind of mimicry were involved. The way in which the symptoms spread from person to person is as yet unexplained: epidemics break out suddenly and usually unexpectedly, and spread too quickly to be accounted for in terms of virus transmission. The reason for the epidemics remains a mystery; but a look back over the historical background of the phenomenon offers some clues to its solution.

It is important to realise that many societies show little of the fear hysteria provokes in the West; indeed, in tribal communities it is still commonly held in respect, even reverence. The tribal shaman, witch doctor or medicine man, as anthropologists soon discovered when they began to investigate tribal life, was usually chosen precisely *because* he was an hysteric – that is, because he periodically went into trances in which he became clairvoyant or clairaudient. Often it was assumed that his inspiration came from the spirit world, that he transmitted messages from dead ancestors telling where the tribe could find game, how to escape enemies or treat a sick warrior, or where to find a sorcerer.

Voodoo dancing in Ouidah, Benin, in west Africa. In this form of mass hysteria, the participants believe that divine beings select certain people and put them into trances; the gods are then briefly incarnated during the stylised ritual voodoo dances

Induced hysteria was also commonly used in tribal life for therapeutic purposes. With the help, if necessary, of drumming, dancing and drugs, sick individuals would be put into trances in which they would have convulsions, talk in voices not their own, and collapse into comas. Sometimes the entire tribe would join in, hysterically imitating the symptoms of the sick member; at other times the whole tribe would become hysterical in order to shake off some collectively felt physical or mental ill. This was done in the belief that the convulsions and dissociation (speaking in strange languages) that hysteria induces are a way of throwing or shrugging off physical and emotional shackles and allowing health to return.

The belief that hysteria was linked with spirit forces continued in highly advanced societies, as the Old Testament reveals. The prophets acquired their role by their ability to go into trances in order to hear what the Lord had to tell the tribe. Homer, too, tells that the 'seer' was a respected figure – although he was often hard put to it to keep up with what the gods were doing, what with their continual in-fighting and capricious changes of mind. But in the *Hippocratic collection*, an anthology of medical writings from the third century BC, hysteria is for the first time diagnosed, not as a gift from the gods, but as an illness. People who traded on the fact that they had fits, claiming that they were divine in origin, were denounced by Hippocrates and his followers as no better than 'witch-doctors, quacks and charlatans'.

How this change came about cannot now be ascertained with any certainty, but there is a plausible theory to account for it. The more civilised the community – and ancient Greece, the cradle of Western thought, was highly civilised – the less attention people paid to the gods and their utterances. Sacrifices were offered and observances kept up, but interest in what the gods had to say – and in their mediums, the hysterics – waned. Where divinely inspired hysterics still existed, their activities had become highly formalised, as with the oracles whose prophetic utterances were induced by fasting and hallucinogenic drugs, and were strictly controlled by their priests and priestesses. Spontaneous hysterical dissociation in public had ceased to be respectable.

One of the major incidents of hysteria as a divine or spirit force occurred at the first Pentecost, when the disciples' convulsions and dissociation convinced them that the Holy Spirit, promised them by Jesus before his death, had indeed possessed them. Henceforth they could follow in Jesus's footsteps and actually receive his word directly through clairaudience – or have it passed on by angels. Within a couple of centuries, however, as the Christian Church began to establish itself, against considerable odds, hysteria and its consequences came to be viewed as a threat to the security of the Church – the lack of control might, it was feared, breed heresy, and without a firm ideological base the Church would be vulnerable.

Above: in the strange Good Friday procession of flagellants in the Philippines, hundreds of masked men whip themselves until the blood flows. This self-scourging, or flagellantism, was also common in Europe during the late medieval period

Below: religious ecstasy at Thaipusam, a Hindu ceremony, in Kuala Lumpur, Thailand

God could hardly be working through so erratic a medium of transmission as hysterical fits. The Devil could work miracles, just as he could cite scripture, for his own purposes. The fact that her visions and voices were of angels did nothing to protect Joan of Arc: she suffered the fate of a witch.

'Possessed by the Devil'

For centuries, mass hysteria was taken to be a symptom of diabolical possession. The most notorious epidemic in Europe was a dancing mania, 'St Vitus's dance', a convulsive neurological disease that periodically broke out in areas ravaged by war or famine towards the close of the Middle Ages. Later epidemics of mass hysteria were reported chiefly from institutions such as the Loudun convent where, as we have seen, investigators sent by Louis XIV watched the Prioress and her nuns writhing in convulsions and screaming foul obscenities.

Occasionally, however, it had to be admitted that the forces at work were potentially beneficial. By the time of the protracted epidemic at St Medard, near Paris, a century after the Loudun case, the naïve belief in the Devil had been considerably eroded; and it was noticed that the *convulsionnaires*, as they were called, developed extraordinary immunity not only to pain, but also to injury. They could be beaten with heavy mallets, jabbed with pointed sticks, suspended above fires, without any sign of injury. Even the Scottish philosopher – and arch-sceptic – David Hume had to admit that the evidence for these miraculous powers, even though he himself could not accept it, had been proved by judges of unquestioned integrity and, as he phrased it, 'attested by witnesses of credit and distinction in a learned age'.

Some churchmen began to argue that the convulsions and dissociation observed in hysterical subjects were not necessarily diabolic in origin. On the contrary, they could represent a struggle to throw off the Devil or his demons. A Swiss priest, Johan Gassner, attracted great crowds to what were, in effect, services in which healing was induced by hysteria, hundreds of people joining in mass exorcism. The early Quakers, and Shakers, adopted much the same technique; its Christian origins were in Pentecost, but its beginnings went much further back in tribal medicine.

Franz Mesmer tried to put a scientific interpretation on the force that swept through participants on such occasions. He called it 'animal magnetism' – a form of magnetism capable of conversion into biological energy. Contrary to common belief, Mesmer did not use what we now call hypnotism in his healing sessions. He set out to induce hysteria in his patients so that they had fits, dissociated, and sank into comas – and, although the hostile investigators appointed by Louis XVI at Marie Antoinette's request rejected his theory of animal magnetism, they had to admit that many patients seemed much better for their treatment.

'Spinal irritation'

By this time, however, doctors were beginning to search for a rational explanation of the phenomenon. They could not accept that people who were induced to have fits and talk like lunatics might actually be benefiting from the experience. Mass hysteria came to be regarded as a nervous disease (described as 'spinal irritation' or as a manifestation of religious mania, as indeed it could be: descriptions of revivalist meetings reveal that congregations frequently became hysterical – as they still do.

Even the fact that, in the hysteric condition induced by Mesmer's techniques, people lost all feeling of pain was rejected by the medical profession. Periodically, painless surgery was demonstrated upon 'magnetised' patients – an inestimable boon, had doctors been prepared to use it, in an age that knew no anaesthetic drugs – but orthodox surgeons claimed that the patients were only pretending to feel no pain.

By the beginning of the 20th century, the fact that hysteria had some valuable properties had been forgotten. In individuals it was taken to be disordered behaviour; in groups, an indication of self-indulgence, whether by silly schoolgirls copying each other, or by members of revivalist sects becoming over-excited. Psychiatrists even began to express doubts as to whether the clinical condition of hysteria actually existed: might not all cases of apparently hysterical behaviour be accounted for by physical disorders such as epilepsy, psychoses such as schizophrenia, or simple play-acting?

Gradually, however, epidemics of hysteria in schools began to push their way back into the news, until in 1964 the medical correspondent of *The Times* suggested that a diagnosis of mass hysteria, 'even if in these days of scientific materialism it is verging on

An extraordinary outbreak of mass hysteria occurred at St Medard, near Paris, in the 1730s. The victims, or *convulsionnaires,* developed what seemed to be a total immunity to both pain and injury; this contemporary engraving (bottom) shows them being kicked and beaten by interested observers without showing any sign of pain. Even the arch-sceptic philosopher David Hume (below) was impressed by the evidence for their remarkable powers

lèse majesté,' was sometimes the only one that fitted the facts.

What he probably had in mind were certain outbreaks in hospitals, for some of these epidemics had an embarrassing feature. The victims were not the patients in the hospital beds. They were nurses, ancillary staff, medical students, junior doctors and even – perish the thought! – consultants.

A case in point was the epidemic that occurred at the Royal Free Hospital in London in 1955, when nearly 300 members of the staff succumbed to a mysterious illness whose symptoms followed the classic pattern of mass hysteria: loss of feeling, muscle spasms or tremors, diffused aches, giddiness, constricted throat, and so on. But relief that, in most cases, recovery was rapid, was soon overshadowed by embarrassment: as no physical cause for the outbreak could be found, it might have to be put down to hysteria.

Whatever name such outbreaks are given – the Americans, who have had the same experience in hospitals and other institutions, prefer 'epidemic neuromyasthenia' – they clearly belong to the same family as those reported from schools, convents and factories. The signs and symptoms vary in different outbreaks, but the resemblances are more striking than the differences. To try to pretend that the symptoms are organic, *real*, in hospitals, but hysterical in schools, is childish.

Misleading diagnosis

Because epidemic hysteria is not a notifiable disease, because it is often put down to some cause such as a virus, even when none can be traced, because it is so often in the interests of those in charge of the schools, hospitals or factories in which it occurs to hush it up – for all these reasons, there is no clear evidence of how prevalent it is. Even the medical journals now concede that it is much more common than it used to be.

Yet mass hysteria remains a mysterious disease, and the outbreaks are investigated less with a view to finding out more about it than simply to eliminate all other possibilities. Only when the bacteriological and other tests have proved negative is mass hysteria considered as a possibility – and then, as a rule with, as it were, a shrug of the shoulders, as if to imply that it really isn't worth investigating any further.

But of course it *is* worth investigating further, because the historical clues suggest that it has two extremely important, and potentially useful, features. One is the way in which hysterics feel no pain and suffer no injury in circumstances where they would ordinarily be in agony from burns or bruises. It requires little imagination to realise how valuable it would be if this latent faculty could be developed.

The other feature is the process by which hysteria is transmitted within a group of people. All that can be said within the limits of present knowledge is that, for want of a better description, it appears to operate through some kind of psychic contagion. Materialist science rejects the concept of psychic contagion; but the very foundations of materialist science are shifting. Medical researchers are prepared to consider factors that they would once have ignored. Whatever form the transmission takes, in any case, it should certainly be explored – for a better understanding of it could have a profound importance for the study, not only of hysteria, but of epidemics, physical and emotional, in general.

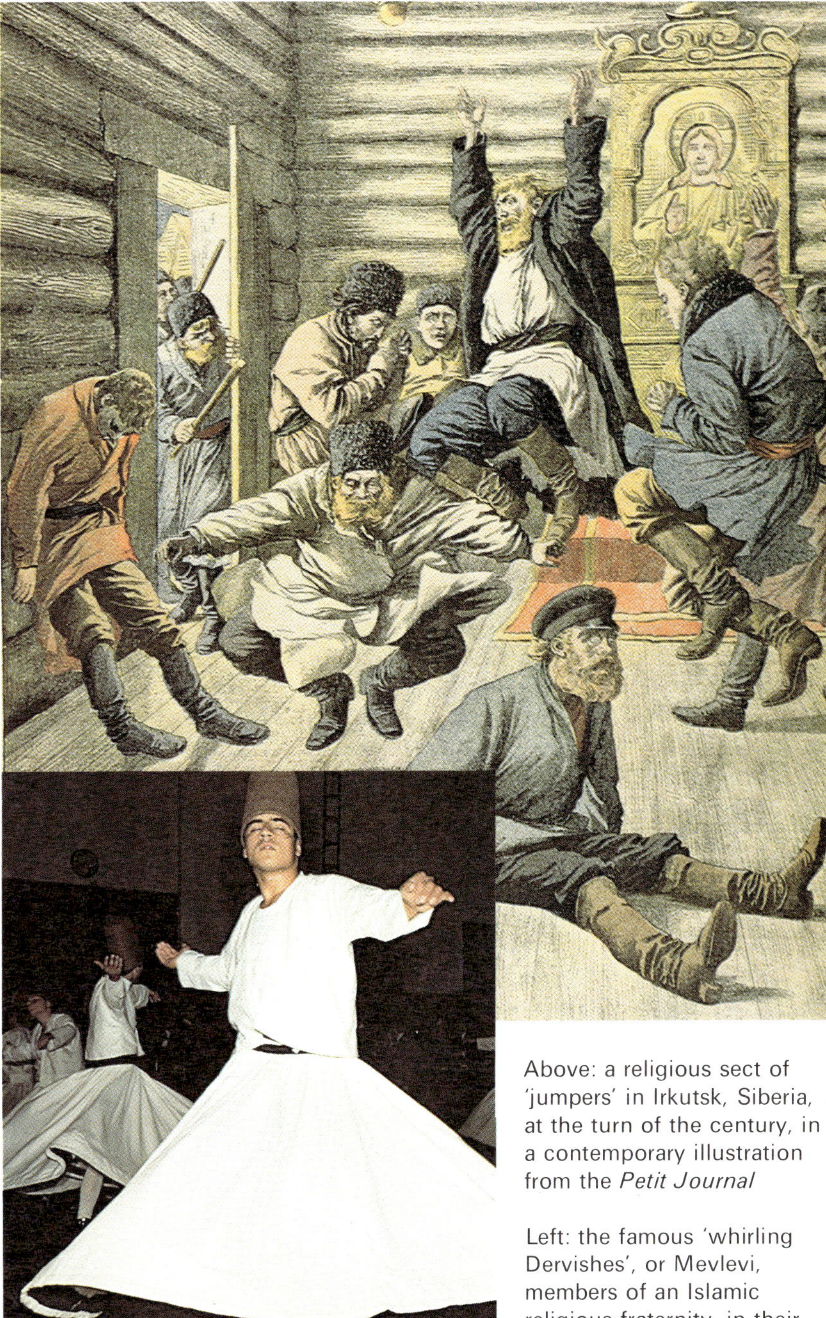

Above: a religious sect of 'jumpers' in Irkutsk, Siberia, at the turn of the century, in a contemporary illustration from the *Petit Journal*

Left: the famous 'whirling Dervishes', or Mevlevi, members of an Islamic religious fraternity, in their ecstatic dance – a central part of their faith

A psychic contagion

The symptoms of mass hysteria are often similar to those of serious illness – but hysteria spreads faster than any known disease. How can this be possible? Could there be a link with ESP?

REPORTS OF OUTBREAKS of mass hysteria in places throughout the world, together with what little research has been done on the subject, strongly suggest that certain long-accepted assumptions about the phenomenon should be revised. Three aspects, in particular, need reconsidering.

First, it is unwise to think of hysteria as a disease – let alone as simple self-indulgent shamming. A better description would be 'breakdown': a breakdown, whether nervous or physical, may provide a form of protection from an intolerable situation by removing the victim from it. In this role, it can perform the same valuable function as a fuse-wire in an electrical circuit.

Second, the symptoms of hysteria are not necessarily those we associate with the term. They tend to manifest themselves in the symptoms associated, in the society in which they occur, with breakdown of normal behaviour. Thus lack of control among the nuns of Loudun, at a time when hysteria was taken to be the work of the Devil, resulted in their lecherous and obscene behaviour. Nowadays, when such outbreaks are generally assumed to be the work of a virus, people tend to behave as if they were suffering from a neuropathic disorder – unless they are taken up in some high religious frenzy, when they may imitate the disciples at Pentecost.

Third, the diagnosis 'hysteria' should not be regarded as the equivalent of saying that there was nothing really wrong with the victim. The prevalence of such outbreaks suggests that they should be carefully investigated to find out how they occur and for what reasons.

What *is* the force that takes over a group of people and, in effect, breaks them down, inducing a range of symptoms that may vary enormously in different circumstances, but that are generally quite consistent within a single outbreak? What, in other words, is the nature of 'psychic' contagion – the term *psychic* indicates some unexplained mode of

A flock of starlings in flight. It has been suggested that the weird human behaviour that we call mass hysteria is a vestige of the instinct that keeps flocks of birds together – a kind of collective mind

The Jonestown madness

transmission – that results in scores or even hundreds of people breaking down at, or around, the same time, in much the same way – even when they are not all within sight of one another, so that simple imitation can be ruled out?

When dealing with such problems, it is always worth looking back over Man's evolutionary past, to see if there are any parallels. In this case, there are. Many species appear to have some method of communication that biologists have yet to explain.

At its most basic level, this communication seems to take place between *cells*. In his book *Supernature*, Lyall Watson describes the remarkable capacity of the common or bathroom sponge – a colony of cells – in its natural ocean habitat, to reconstitute itself in similar form if destroyed. 'Some sponges grow to several feet in diameter,' Watson observes, 'and yet, if you cut them up and squeeze the pieces through silk cloth to separate every cell from its neighbour, the gruel soon gets together and organizes itself – and the complete sponge reappears like a phoenix to go back into business again.'

In his delightful book *The soul of the white ant* (1937), the South African scientist Eugène Marais describes his experiments with colonies of ants. These revealed that, although groups of ants and even individual ants were engaged in separate pursuits at any given time – feeding the queen, collecting the food for her, storing it, building larders for it, or fighting off intruders – the activities of all of them were dictated by what, for want of a better word, he felt bound to call a soul, although as a good Darwinian naturalist he would have preferred a more scientific term.

Late in November 1978, a horrified world learned of the appalling mass suicide at Jonestown in the jungles of Guyana, on the northern coast of South America. The victims – over 900 of them – were members of a California-based religious sect known as the People's Temple, led by the psychopathic Reverend Jim Jones. They killed themselves by drinking potassium cyanide mixed with a sweet, fizzy drink.

Many theories have been advanced as to how so many people could be induced to disregard their own instinct for self-preservation to the extent of killing themselves on the order of a madman. But the answer is obvious: it is a clear case of mass hysteria – that strange vestige of the instinct that, in animals, enables the will of the group to triumph over that of the individual.

The thousands of termites that live inside each nest organise their highly specialised activities in such a way that everything contributes to the welfare of the entire community. They have developed a special instinct to do this; mass hysteria may be produced in human beings in a similar way

Birds of a feather

The behaviour of starlings is a good example of such collective behaviour on a larger scale. Thousands of starlings roost in London, but they spend their days in the countryside, where food is more plentiful. At a certain time in the evening starlings all round London – as far away as Essex and the Home Counties – will begin to make the same inward journey, so that day after day the flocks can be tracked on radar, looking like the ripples on a pond after a pebble has been dropped in – spreading outwards in the morning, moving inwards in the evening.

Even more remarkable is the behaviour of starlings in the flocks as they fly out and back. They do not follow a leader; it is as if, in their whirlings, they are directed by . . . well, there is still no scientific alternative to the word 'soul'.

The most plausible explanation of this kind of behaviour is that it depends on a form of communication that developed early in the evolutionary process. In the case of ants, it was a form of diversification, enabling the community as a whole to survive while various groups within it performed their various different tasks. In birds it developed into a mechanism for the protection of the group, providing large flocks of birds with collective guidance for their movements.

Could it be that mass hysteria is a relic of a similar collective human instinct – an evolutionary device that has largely outlived its usefulness?

This seems a likely hypothesis – but we are still no nearer an explanation of the way in which the symptoms are transmitted in an outbreak of mass hysteria.

How does it operate? The most promising line of research in this connection has been into *pheromones*, the free-floating scent molecules whose discovery has helped to account for the way in which, for example, males of a species will come clustering round a female on heat.

In her novel *The group*, Mary McCarthy claimed that women living in close contact with each other tend to menstruate at the same time; and research at Harvard and elsewhere has since shown that this is correct. Room-mates' periods tend to move into synchronisation; so do those of close friends who spend a great deal of time together. Pheromones are currently front runners in the search for an explanation. But if pheromones are the channel of communication in this case, may they not serve the same purpose in other epidemics that have hitherto been thought to be spread by infection?

Hysteria and the common cold

In a fascinating research project, the astronomers Fred Hoyle and Chandra Wickramasinghe have demonstrated that, contrary to common assumption, influenza does not spread by person-to-person contact – a fact that had already been established globally, as large-scale epidemics do not follow the course that would be expected if person-to-person infection were the agent of the spread of the disease. The same phenomenon has been confirmed at the Common Cold Research Unit at Salisbury in England. Coughs and sneezes seem to be the obvious suspects – but they are not guilty.

If this is the case, how *do* epidemics spread? An alternative theory is that viruses are constantly here, there and everywhere, but we can resist them unless, and until, an epidemic is signalled – by pheromones. They may also be the messengers in other circumstances – for instance, in the romantic encounters familiar to all of us (seeing a 'stranger across a crowded room'), or in the witch-doctor recipes for 'smelling out' witches.

Pheromones, however, take us only part of the way on this voyage of discovery. Eugène Marais, who knew nothing of pheromones but had convinced himself that the secret of ant communication must lie in scent, was imaginative enough to recognise that the kind of scent involved was not quite the kind we generally think of. It was misleading, he argued, to assume the existence of a gas, or microscopic particles. 'Perfume is not entirely a physical substance. You may scent a large room for ten years with a small piece of musk, and yet there will not be any loss of weight.' Scent, he felt, should be thought of in terms of 'waves in the ether'.

Much of Marais's work has been superseded by subsequent research, but it remains stimulating. In *Tuning in to nature* Philip S. Callaghan, professor of entomology at the University of Florida, has followed up Marais's idea, and come to the same conclusion: the sensory mechanism involved in ant communication is not 'straight' smell. Insects, he claims, 'smell' odours electronically, by 'tuning into the narrowband infrared radiation emitted by sex and host-plant scents'. If this turns out to be correct, and Callahan presents impressive evidence for his theory, traditional assumptions about

Above: the common or 'bathroom' sponge. The cells of this colony seem, in some mysterious way, to be able to communicate – if they are dispersed, they will regroup in a similar form

Below: Iranians in Tehran mourn the death of Ayatollah Taleghani in 1979. Outbreaks of mass hysteria often occur at moments of heightened emotion

The link with ESP

In 1944 an epidemic of strange incidents took place in the small town of Muldoon in the United States. It began when a woman reported to police that a man had sprayed her legs with gas, leaving them paralysed. The incident was reported in the local press – and a spate of similar events began. Police were unable to catch the 'phantom anaesthetist of Muldoon' – who was remarkable for being able to spray several different women simultaneously in different parts of the town.

When it was suggested that the epidemic was not one of paralysis but of mass hysteria, the flood of reports ceased. This was followed by a period during which reports of all kinds of unusual phenomena fell below average.

The story bears a remarkable resemblance to the histories of many paranormal phenomena – notably the 'men in black' of UFO sightings. In general, the people who report the incidents have no knowledge of other similar cases. Nevertheless, the knowledge spreads, as in other outbreaks of mass hysteria, by a mysterious 'psychic contagion' that may have something to do with the method of communication involved in telepathy. Further study of mass hysteria may give us an insight into these other phenomena.

Left: celebrations of the anniversary of the October revolution in Red Square, Moscow. Thousands of people attend this event, and the Soviet authorities use the occasion in effect to mesmerise their audiences – at home and abroad – by showing off some of the Soviet Union's advanced weaponry

the way in which epidemics of all kinds are spread will need to be re-examined.

The origin of a number of serious diseases is still uncertain; these include epilepsy, Parkinsonism, multiple sclerosis and myasthenia gravis. Some are of the epidemic type – most recently, Legionnaire's disease. The whole weight of research into their causes and spread has been on the quest for some common biological factor – germ, virus, biochemical mix-up, toxic substance. So far, this research has achieved little.

Looters on the rampage

Sometimes, researchers find what they *believe* to be the cause – and it is triumphantly paraded, much as captured kings were paraded through the streets of Rome. But soon, other contributory factors are found – or the suspected virus is found in the bodies of perfectly healthy people. The whole idea that illnesses are caused by viruses is, in fact, beginning to fall into discredit. It is now thought likely that their role is more like that of looters, who come out on the rampage only when law and order – in this case, the orderly and healthy functioning of the body – have broken down.

But what causes this breakdown? This brings us back to the question, why do epidemics occur? The answer, of course, is that we do not know. But a study of mass hysteria might bring us closer to an explanation.

To sum up: mass hysteria has three components. The first is loss of control, or breakdown in normal behaviour; the second is mimicry, or the similarity in the abnormal behaviour of the victims of any single outbreak. The third is the missing link: the actual process by which the disorder spreads. Do pheromones elicit the responses that result in the epidemic? Or can it be that pathogens from outer space, falling to Earth, are responsible, as Hoyle and Wickramasinghe suggest? Or infra-red radiation? Or is there some as yet undiscovered psychokinetic force – as reported so often in accounts of hauntings or poltergeist activity – that can affect groups?

Above: lemmings making their suicide leaps into the sea. Here again, the instinct that in humans has become mass hysteria is at work: lemmings kill themselves when the population has grown to such numbers that their habitat can no longer support them

More serious and systematic investigation of mass hysteria could provide the answers not merely to these questions, but to much that is imperfectly understood, or misunderstood, about disease in general; and also, in all probability, help solve many of the problems that have baffled biologists in their study of animal, bird and insect behaviour, and psychologists in their study of the ways in which men and women communicate when no communication through the ordinary senses seems possible.

Freud's guilty secret

Sigmund Freud, the great pioneering psychoanalyst, was known to revile what he called 'the black tide of occultism'. Yet at the same time, Freud was actually a believer in some aspects of the paranormal

THOUGH MANY PEOPLE are aware of the work of Sigmund Freud and its importance for our understanding of mental illness, few know of his life-long interest in the paranormal. This is not surprising, however, as Freud himself felt very ambivalent about the subject, and especially about making his interest public. Indeed, most of his writing on the subject was published late in his life, and one of the most important papers only after his death.

Freud's interest in the paranormal centred mainly on telepathy; he never seriously considered the possibility of precognition, asserting:

> The notion that there is any mental power, apart from acute calculation, which can foresee future events in detail is on the one hand too much in contradiction to all the expectations and presumptions of science, and on the other hand corresponds too closely to certain ancient and familiar human desires which criticism must reject as unjustifiable pretensions.

When he further took into account the 'untrustworthiness, credulity, and unconvincingness' of reports of precognition, Freud felt there was nothing in them of interest to science.

However, Freud took a very different line about what he called 'thought transference' or telepathy. Throughout his career his opinion as to whether telepathy existed swung wildly from the most pronounced scepticism to total belief. Frequently his letters declared that he was now 'convinced' of the existence of this phenomenon, but within a short time he would express a desire to forget the whole unsavoury area.

Far left: Sigmund Freud (1856–1939), the founder of psychoanalysis, who – as a refugee from the Nazis – spent his last year in England (below, far left: his London consulting rooms). To Freud, sexuality was the most important single factor in determining the mental health of every adult; a view that was at first received with outrage by the Victorian society in which he grew up, but that became increasingly respectable and influential. Indeed, after reading the bulk of Freud's work, Laurence Olivier built his film *Hamlet* (1943) around Freudian concepts – particularly that of the Oedipus complex, or unnaturally deep, sexually tinged relationship between mother and son. Olivier, who directed the film and also played the title role, deliberately chose a younger actress, Eileen Herlie, to play the part of Queen Gertrude, Hamlet's mother (left), thus conveying as explicitly as possible the attraction between mother and son. Significantly, although Freud was extremely wary of becoming involved in the paranormal, his favourite quotation from *Hamlet* was 'There are more things in heaven and earth, Horatio,/ Than are dreamt of in your philosophy'

Throughout his life, Freud declared his belief that these phenomena were worthy of scientific investigation – he was a member of both the English and the American societies for psychical research – and indeed he frequently attempted to investigate those incidents in his own life that he felt might have been psychic in origin. For example, a month after he had become engaged, he accidentally broke the engagement ring his fiancée had given him. He wrote to ask her if she had been less fond of him at the time the ring broke. On another occasion, while a student in Paris, he heard what he took to be his fiancée calling his name. He carefully took note of the times of these incidents and wrote to her to find out what was happening at these precise moments. However, Freud found no correlation between what was happening to him and his fiancée's thoughts or actions.

And, in spite of this personal interest in the subject, Freud never had what he regarded as a telepathic dream. Neither did he find any evidence of such dreams among his patients. This failure did not prevent Freud engaging in one of his favourite pastimes, telling stories of strange or uncanny happenings, especially after midnight. Freud was intrigued by the more mysterious aspects of these stories, and when challenged about their validity would reply with his favourite quotation from *Hamlet*: 'There are more things in heaven and earth, Horatio,/Than are dreamt of in your philosophy.'

Freud did, however, have some success in thought transference experiments he held with his close friends. He found the results were 'remarkably good, particularly those in which I played the medium'. Perhaps the most important reason why Freud did not publish the results of these experiments, or declare more forthrightly his belief in telepathy, was his fear that the opponents of psychoanalysis would make use of such 'dubious' testimony against the infant science. Freud had devoted most of his life to establishing the validity of psychoanalysis – its theories and its practice. During much of this time, the science was under attack from many quarters, largely because of its concern with infant sexuality.

Escaping 'the black tide'

Freud was loath to bring psychoanalysis under further attack and was frequently urged by his more conservative followers not to publish anything concerning the paranormal. For example, Ernest Jones, Freud's leading disciple in England, thought Freud was wrong to pursue his enquiries in this area and criticised him heavily for publishing an article favourable to the existence of telepathy. Freud replied that he was sorry to have offended 'English sensibilities', but that he had to tell the truth as he saw it. On the other hand, Freud warned Carl Gustav Jung, who was at the time sympathetic to Freud's beliefs, not to get involved in the 'black tide of mud of occultism' and he was distinctly chary of Jung's interest in astrology and mysticism.

In spite of his ambivalent attitude, Freud's work and the new science of psychoanalysis produced several major advances in our understanding of psychic phenomena. Indeed, the methodology of the most successful modern experiments was also foreshadowed in the practice Freud invented.

In 1900 Freud published *The interpretation of dreams*, a work in which some of his most important discoveries in psychology were made public. In it, he described a 'psychological technique which makes it possible to interpret dreams' and further enables us to 'elucidate' the processes to which the strangeness and obscurity of dreams are due'.

Freud called this technique 'free association'. His patients were asked to say everything that came into their minds, to communicate every idea or thought that occurred to them without exception. Free association required two preliminary steps. First, the

patient had to concentrate on his own innermost perceptions. To help make this easier, Freud arranged his office so that the patient lay on a couch, and the analyst sat on a chair behind him, so the patient could not easily be distracted by the analyst's movements or facial expressions. It was also important that the room be quiet, so the patient could enter a free-floating mental state.

The second aspect of the preparation involved, as far as possible, the patient becoming an impartial observer and reporter of his own thoughts as they arose, without rationalising or 'editing' them in any way.

When the patient followed these instructions and spontaneously said everything that came into his mind, Freud found that matters that had been previously hidden from consciousness came to the fore. What he was especially interested in, of course, was the meaning and origin of the patient's symptoms, and the way in which they found expression in dreams.

Free association is remarkably similar to the modern parapsychological practice of free response experiments, for example the Ganzfeld (sensory deprivation) procedure. In these tests, the subject is asked to say everything that comes into his or her mind for a set period of time. Distracting external stimuli are screened out, so that the subject can have access to his innermost thoughts. And indeed, subjects are often warned not to censor their thoughts with reason but to wait until after the experiment to make a rational evaluation of what they have said. The main difference between the two procedures is simply that Freud looked to free association to supply information about the patient's deep-seated emotional problems, and the parapsychologist is seeking to bring to awareness unconscious psi.

The second major contribution to parapsychology of *The interpretation of dreams* involves Freud's theories about *how* unconscious thoughts become conscious. He described how, in each of us, an unconscious 'censor' seems to operate, which examines our thoughts and perceptions and decides which ones are 'suitable' to be allowed into our consciousness. If the censor feels a particular thought is unsuitable, it is distorted, as in dreams, which makes it difficult for our conscious minds to understand the 'unacceptable' message. The different ways in which this distortion can happen are outlined in *The interpretation of dreams*.

The censor steps in

It is rare that precognitive dreams, for example, accurately and literally reveal a future event. Often important details are shifted around, or altered slightly – which may be attributable to the censor. In order for the dream to be understood correctly, these details have to be translated into their original form – and Freud discovered a means of doing this to some extent.

Through the application of this theory, Freud discovered a new class of psychic phenomena, which he felt was not subject to the usual sceptical objections. It was by analysing the *unsuccessful* prophecies of professional fortune tellers that Freud felt he had found a hidden psychic component.

For example, Freud had a patient who was a childless woman, 43 years of age. Her emotional problem was the result of an unusually intense attachment to her father, for whom she hoped to substitute her husband. But frustratingly for her, her husband turned out to be infertile. When she was 27 she took a trip to Paris and visited a palmist who told her that she would have two children before she was 32. This prophecy had, of course, been proved incorrect by time, and yet Freud wondered what was the source of the two numbers in the fortune teller's prediction. He found out that the woman's mother had married her father at the age of 30 – and when she was 32 she had given birth to two children in the course of one year.

Freud felt that the fortune teller had picked up by thought transference his patient's intense desire to be just like her mother, and had satisfied it by telling her that she, too, would have two children at 32.

Another similar incident was discovered in the life of an intelligent young medical student who visited Freud because he felt himself incapable of taking his final examination. Analysis helped the patient to face the task and also revealed a curious story. The young man told Freud how he had consulted an astrologer who was known for being able to make specific predictions about someone on the basis of his birthday alone. He gave the astrologer the birthdate of a man

Left: Freud with his English disciple Ernest Jones in 1919. Freud had been intrigued by the successful results of 'thought transference' (or telepathy) experiments in which he and close friends had participated and published a paper on the subject, but Jones – and others – urged him to leave such subjects well alone if psychoanalysis were to be taken seriously. It seems, however, that parapsychology lost a champion in Freud, for he was also fascinated by the nature of some *unsuccessful* predictions of fortune tellers (below), believing them to mask a special kind of significance

Above: psychical researcher Hereward Carrington, to whom Freud wrote in 1921: 'If I had to live . . . again, I should devote myself to psychical research . . .'

Below right: mother and baby. Freud thought that a child, feeling hungry, believes he has actually created his mother who brings him food. It is, Freud said, at this stage that we begin to develop our lifelong superstitions

who was his rival for the attentions of someone he loved dearly. The astrologer had predicted that the rival would die in July or August of that year, from eating crabs or oysters. Freud asked the young man what was so remarkable about this prophecy, since his rival was still very much alive. The young man replied that the summer before the prediction, his rival had been poisoned by eating oysters and nearly died of it: the astrologer had become aware through telepathy of the young man's intense secret wish – that his rival should die – and also of the incident of the previous summer. Her 'prophecy' was thus indicative of thought transference and not precognition.

However much Freud came to believe in the possibility of telepathy he felt that most omens, presentiments, prophetic dreams and superstitious practices had no foundation in external reality. Rather, he tended to understand these phenomena in the light of the internal reality that psychoanalysis had uncovered. He felt most of these phenomena could be accounted for either by assuming a regression to an earlier stage of thinking, or by the activation of deeply repressed infantile experiences.

The child as God

The earlier stage of thinking that Freud felt was present in much belief of supernatural occurrences was called the stage of 'infantile omnipotence'. Perhaps, this stage can most easily be understood in the relationship of a baby to its mother and her breast (or bottle). The baby feels hungry and wishes his mother were there to feed him – and suddenly and miraculously she is. The child comes to feel that it was his mere thought that brought his mother – bearing food – into being. Later, when the baby comes to understand that it was not his thought that created his mother, and that she and others do not necessarily do what he wishes, he grows out of this stage of development and becomes more realistic. Freud felt that though most of us grow out of this childlike thinking, there are occasions in our later life when we go back to it, and it is especially at these times that we are prone to be superstitious.

The second factor that Freud evoked to explain the belief in superstition was concerned with the activation of forgotten infantile experiences. Superstition was, in Freud's opinion, derived from suppressed hostile and cruel impulses. For example, if a child wishes ill on a parent or sibling, but knows that this is wrong, he may come to repress these thoughts and feelings. Later, he may project them onto the outside world and come to imagine there are evil or destructive spirits, ghosts or demons around. Through this kind of explanation, Freud hoped to 'tame' the supernatural, relegating it to a category of unconscious psychology.

Whenever he attempted this kind of explanation, Freud was careful to add that he did not believe that all paranormal phenomena could be explained in this way; some – a small core of objectively verifiable incidents – he felt should be taken seriously and carefully analysed. Freud did not feel that the existence of telepathy would upset the findings of psychoanalysis, especially those concerning the structure and symbolism of dreams. In fact, he believed it would be possible to incorporate a belief in telepathy into dream analysis, assuming that telepathic material is often used by the unconscious mind as a basis for some dreams. Freud proposed that the psychoanalyst should treat the telepathic contribution in the same way as the other dream material – thus providing further proof of the efficacy of psychoanalysis.

In fact, in a letter written in 1921 to psychical researcher Hereward Carrington, Freud said: 'If I had to live all over again, I should devote myself to psychical research rather than to psychoanalysis.' He also stated that 'it would be a great satisfaction to me if I could convince myself and others on unimpeachable evidence of the existence of telepathic processes.' It was such doubts that probably prevented Sigmund Freud making a more outstanding contribution to our understanding of the paranormal and the subtler workings of the human mind.

Jung: no shame in psi

When Freud and Jung had a fierce argument about psi, a bookcase exploded with sound – an example of the PK that scientists did not believe possible. Later, Jung became an outspoken champion of the paranormal

FOR CARL GUSTAV JUNG, the great pioneering psychologist, parapsychology was much more than a subject for scientific research, academic debate, and theory, because his own life was enriched by almost every kind of spontaneous psi. While his now famous writings on synchronicity may help us to understand its dynamics, without his own psychic experiences he might never have become a psychologist at all.

Carl Gustav Jung (1875–1961), the Swiss psychologist whose open belief in the significance of the mystical and the paranormal caused a final rift with his teacher and friend Sigmund Freud. Fascinated by the efficacy of the two great fortune telling techniques, the Tarot cards and the *I Ching*, Jung was also one of the first to propose a psychic origin for 'flying saucers'

At the age of 23, Jung was a student living in a well-to-do Swiss home, pondering a possible future in surgery. As he sat with his textbooks, a sound like a pistol-shot rang out from the dining-room next door where his mother was knitting. The astonished pair looked at the walnut table – the wood had split right through, and not along any joint. Jung wrote: 'I was thunderstruck. . . . A table of solid walnut that had dried out for 70 years – how could it split on a summer day in the relatively high degree of humidity characteristic of our climate?' And just two weeks later, Jung came home to find that his mother and sister had been terrified by a similarly loud report, this time from a sideboard. Jung checked it; inside lay a shattered breadknife. This knife was to play a leading role in Jung's striking demonstration of psychokinesis (PK) to Sigmund Freud, which significantly altered Freud's attitude to the paranormal.

It was not surprising, perhaps, that such dramatic paranormal effects occurred in the Jung home; his mother kept a diary of precognitions and odd 'coincidences', and his grandmother was noted for 'second sight' and seeing spirits of the dead. And, by one of those odd coincidences, very shortly after the twin PK events Jung heard that certain relatives of his had been taken with the table-turning craze and that a school-girl cousin was showing signs of becoming a medium. Jung undertook a long study of her circle, and eventually submitted his doctoral dissertation on the psychology of the medium.

Dominant 'part souls'

At that stage he was not convinced of any evidence of paranormality, and certainly detected fraud in his cousin's later career. His primary interest concerned the way in which 'part souls', the strange and almost autonomous fragments that appeared to have split off from the unconscious mind, dominated the medium in her trance state. Jung stressed that these 'part souls' complemented the conscious mind – this being the origin of his famous theory that the conscious and unconscious minds can balance and complement each other. The young medium was simple and childish; but the dominating 'part soul' was aristocratic, distinguished and poised. Jung's first views on the 'spirits of the dead' were that they are fragments projected from the unconscious. Later, however, he was to revise this opinion.

His interest in mediumship brought Jung to psychology, to the study of schizophrenia,

and to his work at the prestigious Burgholzli mental hospital in Zurich; between 1900 and 1907 he studied the nature of psychosis intensively, conducting what was to become famous research with word-association tests. Jung identified what he termed *complexes* (one of many household words deriving from Jung) from the results of such tests – these were manifested when the patient made unusual associations between groups of linked words, accompanied by strong emotion. These complexes were the result of emotional conflict in the individual – conflict usually created by friction between the unconscious and the conscious mind.

When he came to write up the results of his word-association experiments, Jung could not justify ignoring the work of another champion of associations, Sigmund Freud. Even threats by the medical establishment – 'If you support Freud you'll regret it, it will damage your reputation, etc.' – did not alter Jung's views about the importance of Freud's ideas, and after some correspondence the two met in Vienna in February 1907. They talked virtually non-stop for 13 hours. As far as Freud was concerned, Jung rapidly became 'favourite son' in the psychoanalytic movement; but Jung was uneasy in the role.

The main area of contention between the two was the importance of religion and spirituality. Freud had no time for either, while Jung claimed that Freud had made sexuality his substitute religion. Gradually, Jung grew to think that the rejection of the spiritual by Freud reflected the older man's flight from that element in himself. Disagreements between the two grew. Against this background of divergence, in 1909 Jung visited Freud in Vienna and, among other things, asked him for his views on parapsychology – in particular, on the incident of the broken knife in the Jung home. 'Bosh,' replied Freud. 'I had some difficulty in checking the sharp retort on the tip of my tongue,' Jung recalled. And then, as he said, 'I had a curious sensation. It was as if my diaphragm were made of iron and were becoming red-hot . . .', and a loud report issued from a bookcase, just as it had from the table in Jung's home. Speaking in the kind of jargon of which many 20th-century parapsychologists might be proud, Jung told Freud this was a 'catalytic exteriorisation phenomenon', but for Freud it was just more 'bosh'; until Jung told him it would happen again – which it promptly did. Freud was shaken, and Jung never again discussed this feat of PK – which almost certainly was due to him – with Freud.

Top: a group of distinguished psychologists in 1909, including Sigmund Freud (sitting, left) and C. G. Jung (sitting, right). Later that year Freud and Jung argued about the paranormal – 'bosh' Freud called it – and the famous 'explosion' of the bookcase happened, twice, apparently directed by Jung's own PK powers. In his youth, his mother (right) had been alarmed by a similarly loud report from a table, which split. Two weeks later an explosive sound came from a sideboard; inside they found a shattered knife (above)

A balancing act

As it was, Jung's increasingly heretical views on the unconscious had made him unacceptable to other hard-core psychoanalysts. Jung saw the understanding of the unconscious as a potentially positive force for health in the personality. He believed that most young people tended to develop their conscious minds in an unbalanced way, fostering the general trait of what he called *extroversion*, their attention being primarily directed to the outside world. And so the unconscious mind would often develop a compensating *introversion* – an inwards-looking attitude. We need a balance, Jung argued; both outer and inner worlds are essential to us. And, above all, he stressed that sexuality is only one of a number of primary psychological drives. This was heresy and, as far as his colleagues were concerned, Jung had to go – like Alfred Adler before him and countless others after. The psychoanalytic movement lost its deepest thinker.

During the next decade Jung developed his ideas on the unconscious, while spontaneous psi continued to occur in his life. He had a telepathic awareness of a patient's suicide, and experienced crisis cases of

spontaneous ESP with his own family. In 1920, while staying in England, Jung encountered a ghost; and in the 1920s he worked with the psychologist Baron von Schrenck-Nötzing and the psychiatrist Eugen Bleuler at the Burgholzli Hospital, studying the PK of Austrian medium Rudi Schneider. Jung does not seem to have kept detailed records of these investigations, but materialisations apparently occurred, and he confided to his long-standing friend and helper Aniela Jaffe that he considered them genuine. Jung was certainly not a gullible witness; on several occasions he did *not* see phenomena that other sitters reported.

After this he did little research work, but began to develop a framework for understanding psychic happenings. This is perhaps his most distinctive contribution to both psychology and parapsychology. Jung was surely right in arguing that the major problem with psi is not the data, but the fact that there was no sound theory to explain it. Yet natural 'laws', Jung argued, are true only in statistical terms – they are not inflexible dogma; in the realms of the infinitesimally small and the infinitely great they break down. And the collective unconscious is infinitely great.

Jung rapidly realised, as he pondered the symptoms of neurotics and schizophrenics – and, increasingly, other areas of human thinking and belief such as dreams, fairy-tales and folklore and myths – that certain themes and motifs tended to recur. Certain symbols are found in many different cultures and at different times; such as that of a snake swallowing his own tail, or the Earth Mother. For Jung, it was significant that these symbols and images were what he called *numinous* – they had emotional significance for people other than the individual dreamer, or the patient who drew them

Above: the Burgholzli mental hospital in Zurich, where, between 1900 and 1907, Jung studied the nature of psychosis. He had become interested in psychology as a direct result of investigating the nature of mediumship

in art therapy (another Jungian innovation). The emotive power, and universality, of these symbols and themes led Jung to suggest that certain elements in the unconscious are collective; they are not acquired, but are at best slightly modified by individual experience. And key elements at the unconscious level are the archetypes, primordial organising factors in our psyches.

We cannot ever perceive the archetypes directly; but we infer their existence. Place some paper over a magnet and sprinkle iron filings on it; the filings fall into place along the magnetic lines of force – but you cannot see a magnetic field, even though you know there must be one there. Similarly, archetypes cannot be seen directly; but certain patterns of experiences, daydreams and images fall into place just like the iron filings, and one knows *something* lying deep in the mind is creating the patterns that form. Jung believed that the 'deep' form of archetypes can never be known; for, in his most radical writings, he expressed his belief that they

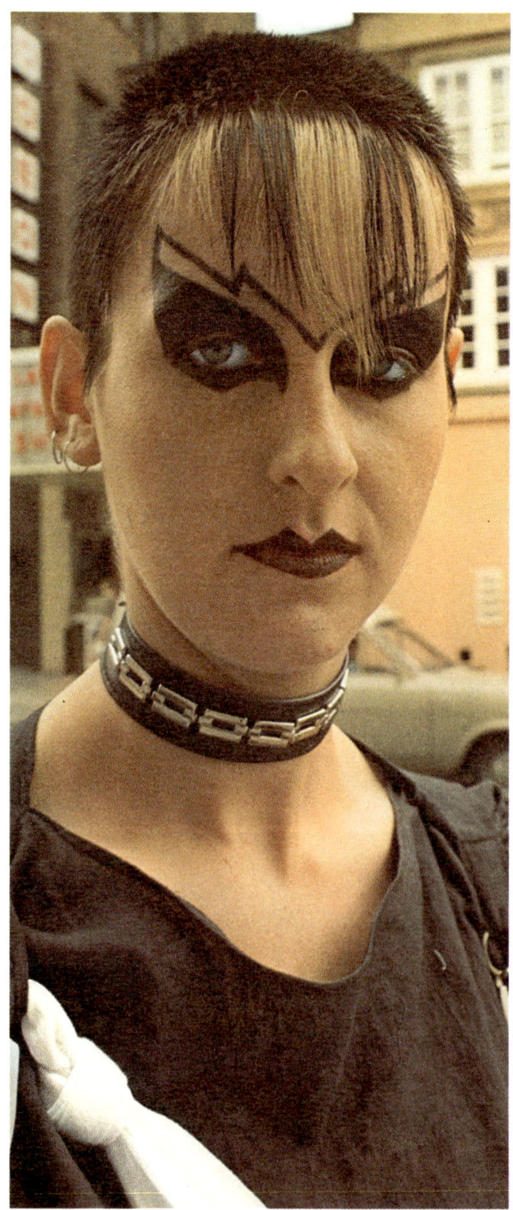

Right: a young punk of the 1980s, seemingly proof of Jung's assertion that young people tend to develop their conscious minds in an unbalanced way, generally producing noticeably extrovert ways of dressing and behaving. At the same time the unconscious is striving towards a healthy balance – even this girl may be a natural introvert behind the elaborate façade

exist not just in individuals, not just in mankind as a whole, but somehow in some continuum outside space and time. For how else, he argued, could the coincidences – which he termed *synchronistic* – be explained?

Jung reported a case of a woman who told him how, at the death of her mother and grandmother, a flock of birds had gathered outside the window. Her husband was a patient of Jung's whose neurosis had responded well to treatment – but soon Jung suspected his patient had heart disease and sent him to a specialist. After this visit the man collapsed and died in the street, even though the specialist had given him a clean bill of health – and despite the fact that Jung himself had thought the man's symptoms very slight. When his body was taken home his wife was already very anxious – a flock of birds had alighted on the roof just after her husband had left. For Jung, an archetypal force moving synchronistically within and without generates a coincidence, and in this case the woman's story to him was the external event.

In the psychologists most famous case, a young woman patient was telling him of a dream in which she was given a golden scarab, and at that very moment, an insect flew in at the window – a rose scarab, the European relative of the golden scarab. Jung handed it to her, saying, 'Here is your scarab.' He reports that this upset the patient's sceptical rationalism and greatly facilitated her treatment.

How can one interpret these events? Did the wife cause the flock of birds to appear through PK? Did Jung similarly cause the rose scarab to appear? Jung's coincidences are often reinterpreted by ardent devotees of the psi-mediated instrumental response theory put forward by parapsychologist Rex Stanford, which argues for unconscious need-related PK, but this type of causal analysis perhaps misses the point. Jung's argument was that this kind of reductionist 'explanation' is not going to lead anywhere; we will understand the psychodynamics of coincidences only by accepting that something *outside* the individual must be involved; some kind of organising principle that also exists outside the confines of space and time. These coincidences contain characteristic themes, which make them meaningful to us, being universal and numinous; archetypes are involved.

Jung also ferreted out instances of synchronicity in other aspects of the paranormal such as astrology and cases of déjà-vu – areas where rational explanations failed. His belief in synchronicity compelled Jung to rethink his earlier ideas on survival after death; for, if archetypes exist outside normal space and time – and ESP and PK seemed to prove it – then perhaps the human psyche itself could exist outside space and time after the death of the body. But Jung was prepared only to speculate on the matter.

What are we to make of Jung's argument for synchronicity? Is it worthy of serious consideration or, as the American philosopher Stephen Braude has suggested, is it just 'deep nonsense'? If Jung is right about archetypal themes being common in most cultures throughout history, then it seems that we are approaching the discovery of an organising principle outside of space and time. The idea is, of course, happily accepted by most cultures, notably oriental ones – hence the rationale for (and Jung's interest in) the ancient Chinese *I Ching* and other oracular systems. Perhaps the very acceptance of synchronicity is in itself archetypal.

Below: a rose scarab, one of which made a timely appearance in Jung's most famous case of 'synchronicity' – when a patient was telling him of a dream about a scarab. Jung did not believe that either he or his patient had caused the scarab to appear – as would some modern parapsychologists. Rather he thought that something outside of us, and probably also outside of space and time, causes such things to happen, reverberating with archetypes – timeless key factors in our psyches. Such a factor is the Earth Mother, common to many cultures throughout history (bottom: an ancient Turkish 'primitive Venus')

ESP on test

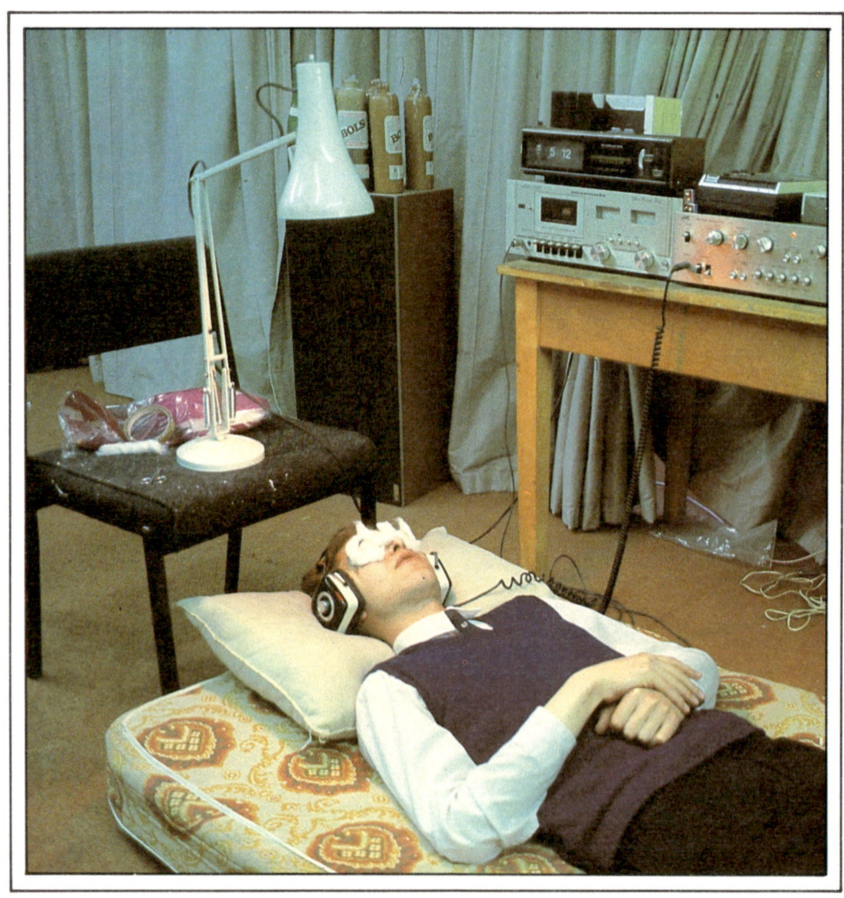

The idea that phenomena as intangible as telepathy and precognition can be subjected to experimentation seems incongruous, but orthodox science demands proof and there have been many determined attempts to provide it – with startling results.

Paranormal phenomena tend not to happen in laboratories; therefore, said the scientific establishment, they never happen at all. Why then are more and more scientists enthusiastically investigating the world of parapsychology?

The Cinderella science

OF ALL THE SCIENCES, that of parapsychology has the most far-reaching implications for Man. Yet, since its beginnings in the 1930s, it has met with bitter opposition, intolerance and hostility from other scientists – so much so that parapsychology is barely recognised as a legitimate academic discipline, and those few brave scientists who seek to study it have either to approach it through an accepted field of study – such as psychology – or pursue it as a sideline, through such organisations as the Society for Psychical Research (SPR).

Why is this? For parapsychology (which means 'beyond psychology') is the study of psychic phenomena – such as psychokinesis (PK), poltergeist phenomena, ESP and dream telepathy – among other unexplained abilities of the human mind. And such happenings, history assures us, have been observed for thousands of years.

All too often, however, strange phenomena have been associated with demons, angels or fairies, and have accumulated a combination of religious, superstitious and occult connotations. Even today parapsychology is frequently shunned because of an 'occult' tag and is bracketed with the activities of the deluded and the deranged.

Before J. B. Rhine began his pioneering laboratory work into the search for 'psi' – or the unknown force behind psychic phenomena – in the 1930s, parapsychology was known as 'psychical research'. It was the province of enthusiastic members of the leisured classes, such as Sir William Crookes and Sir Arthur Conan Doyle, and revolved mainly around the investigation of mediums and the quest for proof of the afterlife.

Rhine, however, was more interested in phenomena that are demonstrably products of the human brain (such as ESP) and concentrated on examining these effects in the laboratory experiments for which he became famous. Since those early days, telepathy, out-of-the-body experiences (OOBEs), PK, dreams and metal bending have been studied in laboratories all over the world. And still the scientific establishment tends to sneer and withhold its financial support.

Before laying the blame squarely at the door of sceptical scientists, it is worthwhile considering a point raised by Dr Charles Tart of the University of California during the fifth international conference of the SPR in Bristol in 1981. He proposed the theory that scepticism about the existence of psi was

Trial and error

'I felt as if the whole framework with which I viewed the world had suddenly been destroyed. I seemed very naked and vulnerable, surrounded by a hostile, incomprehensible universe.' So said John Taylor, well-respected professor of mathematics at London's King's College, in 1973 after witnessing Uri Geller bending metal through mind power alone.

With the characteristic fervour of a convert, Taylor threw himself into a scientific investigation into the paranormal, especially metal bending. But instead of congratulating him on his open-mindedness his colleagues ridiculed and openly ostracised him. So, ironically, it was the scientific establishment, not paranormal phenomena, that ultimately made Taylor's world 'hostile'. He began an attempt to explain metal bending as a function of electromagnetics. When this failed he denounced the entire paranormal spectrum as nonsense or the product of fraud.

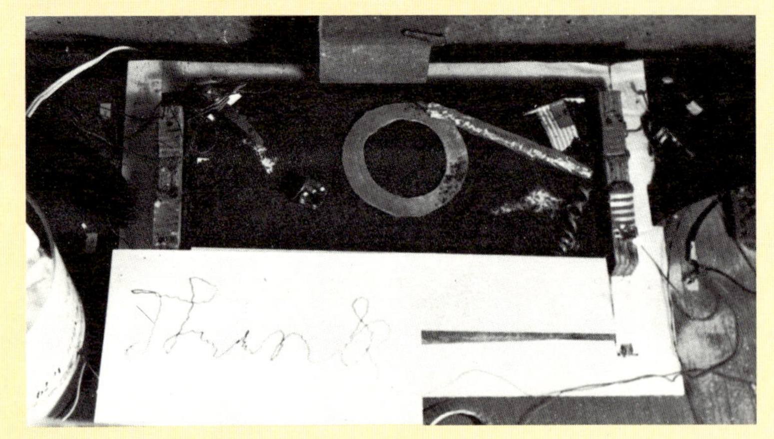

Cox's think tank

An upturned fishtank containing, among other things, separate leather rings, a pen and blank paper – this is the world's most exciting new parapsychological tool, the 'Cox's mini-lab'.

Pioneered in the 1960s by William E. Cox of the Society for Research on Rapport and Telekenesis (SORRAT) at Rolla, Missouri, USA, this simple kit has produced astonishing evidence of PK. 'Encouraged' by the presence of one or more sensitives the leather rings have linked and unlinked, while teleporting from inside to outside the mini-lab, and the pen has written by itself on the paper provided (above). The activities in the lab triggered a movie camera to provide a permanent record.

By 1981 parapsychologists in other parts of the world were building their own mini-labs amid growing anticipation from researchers in the field.

Previous page: it has been suggested that it would further the cause of parapsychology as an academic subject if a permanent paranormal object' – such as rings linked by PK – could be found and put on display in a museum. Is this such an object? The shapes, cut out of plywood, are firmly linked, but the question is how this came about. Were they ingeniously made that way or were they linked paranormally?

not only entrenched in our rationalist world but is, to a certain extent, necessary for society to function at all. If we 'gave in' to what he believes to be a natural ability – telepathy – and we could all read each other's minds, politics, commerce and personal relationships would fall apart. Scepticism about, and indeed actual resistance to, psi has kept civilisation together.

There is also evidence to show that believers in psi (known in parapsychological jargon as 'sheep') perform random ESP tests more successfully than unbelievers ('goats'). This has been proved time and again in laboratory tests; the 'hits' are significantly higher for sheep than for goats. So we come to a momentous conclusion: an openness to psi tends to encourage phenomena, whereas scepticism quells them. A sceptic will, in fact, appear to prove his prejudice, but then so will a believer. Dr Tart further pointed out to an august assembly of professional and amateur parapsychologists that workers in their own field were not immune to scepticism. Researchers into psi were just as likely as anyone else in our civilisation to exhibit the social fear of strange phenomena. This is frequently shown, he claimed, by their results; such as scoring 'marginally above chance' in ESP card guessing, enough to justify further study perhaps but not enough to shake the world – or themselves. But those researchers who have successfully faced their ingrained fear of psi and 'trained it out' of themselves have had the most remarkable results. However, one has to be a very thick-skinned and single-minded researcher to be open-minded enough to encourage spectacular psi results.

It is safer and, many would say, more scientific to try to investigate the paranormal purely in terms of the known laws of physics. This may be a rather arrogant approach, assuming as it does that our knowledge of such laws is complete.

But science is based on cautious evaluation, and caution in a field notorious for past frauds and hoaxes is no bad thing. Besides, scientific 'goats' demand watertight evidence for the alleged phenomena, and it is true that there is no theoretical explanation for psychic phenomena that can be tested and developed. Researchers have had notions and ideas about the underlying force responsible for these phenomena, but nothing as substantial as a set of laws has been established. Rhine speculated that there is probably an unknown force or energy – psi – at work. What its characteristics are, how it behaves, and how it affects the material world, he could not say. It still remains to be discovered.

A source of embarrassment

In addition the scientific establishment demands replication. In any other science if a successful experiment cannot be repeated by other scientists using the same methodology in other laboratories then the results are almost certainly invalid. Apart from anything else, replication rules out the possibility that the results were produced by fraud, collusion between experimenter and subject or any other experimental shortcoming. And here parapsychology faces its greatest obstacle and richest source of embarrassment.

For, as reports of telepathy, precognition, clairvoyance and other psychic phenomena show, paranormal events are mainly spontaneous. There is a wayward elusiveness about them. You may, as it were, take your psychic horse to water, but you cannot necessarily make him drink. Metal benders may produce astonishing effects in their own homes, but put them in a laboratory and you may wait until doomsday for a spoon as much as to twitch.

But parapsychology and controllable experiments are not incompatible. John Hasted, professor of physics at Birkbeck College, London, has run a continuing series of experiments on metal bending over several years. Since his investigation of Uri Geller's abilities in the early 1970s he has studied the strange powers of several other gifted youngsters. Despite the scorn of his colleagues he persevered and has devised experiments that he believes have provided important data. Nevertheless, he is fully aware that the phenomena cannot always be produced – or, more significantly, *reproduced* – to order, and his work has involved many hours of patient waiting. His experience as a psychical researcher has taught him to take a more flexible approach; he will often go to the subject's home and encourage the phenomena there rather than plunge the youngster into a clinical atmosphere at the laboratory.

A further problem is the resistance to positive results. When American parapsychologists Harold Puthoff and Russell Targ published the results of their successful 'remote viewing' experiment – to see whether subjects could 'see' and describe by means of ESP a site visited by a target team – they met with a storm of protest from both within and without the parapsychological fraternity. They were accused of bad methodology and poor analysis of data. They refuted the criticisms in a detailed reply. Subsequently similar experiments have been run elsewhere – with positive results.

Above: Helmut Schmidt of the University of Freiburg, West Germany, demonstrates the random number generator he developed for use in ESP tests. Subjects attempt to guess or even influence a sequence of flashing lights; over several years a number of remarkable 'hits' have been scored

Guessing which light

Another experiment that has yielded promising results is based on the use of a random number generator. This machine, first developed for the purpose by Helmut Schmidt of the University of Freiburg in West Germany, turns coloured lights on and off in a random sequence while the subject attempts to predict – or even influence – which light will come next. Schmidt has claimed significant results over 10 years of experiments with the machine and one or two other laboratories have also succeeded in producing positive results.

But predicting the colour of the next light or the shape on the next Zener card inevitably means long and often intensely boring hours, days and even weeks in a laboratory. And whereas the technicians involved may be used to such an uninspiring environment, the subjects frequently find their surroundings bleak, intimidating and negative. All this tends to inhibit the very phenomena they seek to bring forth.

One of the few experimental processes that actively encourages the subject to perform in a pleasurable atmosphere uses the 'Ganzfeld' technique. This involves three participants: an agent, who attempts to transmit an image by telepathic means; a subject (or receiver) in the Ganzfeld state – totally relaxed under a soft, diffused light, sensory deprivation and muted white noise; and an experimenter, who records the subject's spoken impressions (or 'mentation') during the transmission period.

One of the leading exponents of experiments based on the Ganzfeld technique is Dr Carl Sargent of Cambridge University, England, who is concerned that the subjects enjoy the experience, that it should be *fun*. He is an exuberant advocate of the positive approach to parapsychology and so far his results have been outstanding. For example, one target image was William Blake's painting *The ancient of days* (showing God kneeling and holding a huge pair of compasses). The sender transmitted the thought 'dividers hurtling through space' and wrote it down on a piece of paper, which was then sealed in an envelope. The subject said he got the impression of 'dividers hurtling through space'. This type of success appears to be most common among experimenters who *encourage* positive results.

Naturally a run of such startlingly successful experiments lays itself open to accusations of bad methodology and even downright collusion between subject and experimenter. While insisting that he takes the most stringent precautions against fraud, Dr Sargent declares that the most important aspect of the experiment is the phenomena, not 'what the neighbours think'.

There will always be critics, including those who doubt the evidence of their own eyes, and the new mood among researchers is to aim first to get the phenomena. Doubts about replication of results, fraud-proof test conditions and assessment of significance over chance must all come afterwards.

The phenomena must come first; without them there is nothing to investigate and the subject becomes unreal. If studying real phenomena attracts academic scorn, then working on secondhand data – hearsay – would make parapsychology a mockery.

And judging by the evidence, the future of psychical research, or more properly, parapsychology, may hang more on the attitude of the researchers themselves than on that of their academic standing.

Below: Stephen North, the young English boy who has proved to be one of Professor John Hasted's 'star' metal benders

View from afar

Can the mind somehow travel many miles, tour a target location and report back with an accurate description? Many controversial claims have been made for the phenomenon of remote viewing

WHEN RUSSELL TARG and Harold Puthoff published *Mind-reach* in 1977 they were not modest about its claims: they had, they asserted, made the final breakthrough and established scientifically that the phenomenon known as remote viewing was fact, and they considered it to be 'probably a latent and widely distributed perceptual ability.'

Remote viewing – a kind of ESP – was not a new subject for discussion and experiment. Papers covering aspects of the phenomenon had appeared in the early 1970s in the British science journal *Nature* and in other highly respected publications. Although controversial, it was believed to be a subject to be taken seriously, and Targ and Puthoff's work in this field especially so, for they were both established physicists on the academic staff of California's Stanford Research Institute (SRI).

Their standing as reputable scientists and the confident way they presented their case made it impossible to ignore their claims. Their research was subjected to intense scrutiny – and the reaction they received was little short of savage.

Targ and Puthoff were accused of everything from deliberately misreading the results and prompting the subjects to unscientific methodology. Even so, they invited other scientists to try to reproduce their results; indeed, since 1977 many others have tried, and with very little success. To many psychical researchers it seemed that remote viewing, like so many other similar 'breakthroughs', was a kind of mirage. Was it possible that the researchers trying to reproduce the results of Targ and Puthoff's work had missed some element in the experiments? Or was it that the two physicists had, in their enthusiasm, pushed their conclusions too far?

Targ and Puthoff began their experiments with a series of remarkable successes, using as subjects New York artist and psychic Ingo Swann and retired police commissioner Pat Price. Both showed remarkable aptitude for remote viewing; in some cases they even named the target location instead of merely describing it. Sometimes they were given only map co-ordinates and asked to describe in detail what they 'saw'.

These and other successes inspired Targ and Puthoff to mount more tightly controlled experiments to validate beyond doubt the

Russell Targ (left) and Harold Puthoff (right), respected physicists of California's Stanford Research Institute. But their pioneering work into remote viewing was savagely attacked by scientists and psychical researchers alike

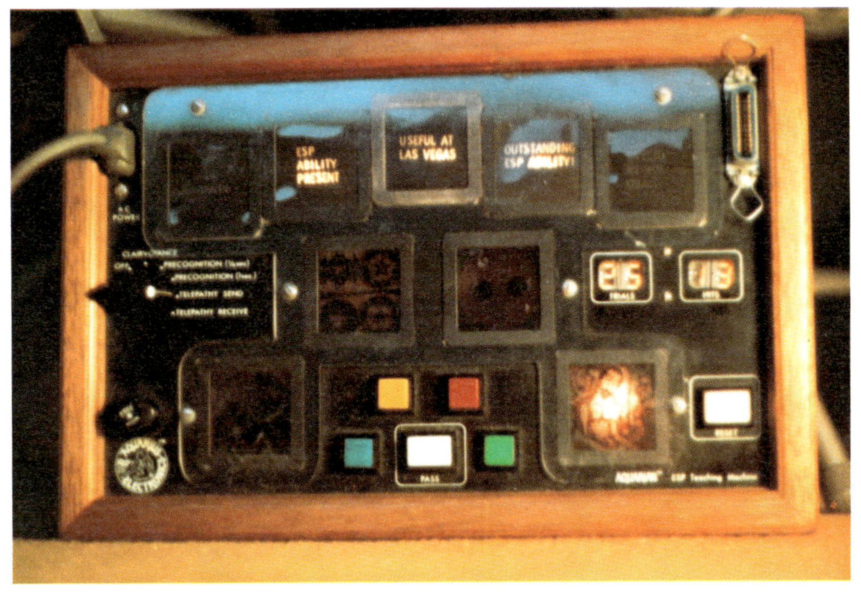

phenomenon of remote viewing.

Altogether there were nine experiments using Pat Price, which were duly written up and published in *Nature* in October 1974. In these a high proportion of the transcript description is very specific; some might have thought suspiciously so. Perhaps it was for this very reason that this series provoked the most hostile reaction.

Price had been set nine target locations in the Stanford area; these were noted down, and each was sealed in an envelope before being locked away in a safe. Pat Price and an experimenter – usually Russell Targ – stationed themselves in a room about 30 minutes before remote viewing was due to begin. Meanwhile Harold Puthoff, together with at least one other member of the target team, selected an envelope at random from the safe, opened it, and set off for the specified location. Neither Price nor Targ had any communication with the rest of the team from the very beginning of the test.

A perfect description

The first site was a well-known landmark on the Stanford campus, the Hoover Tower. Not only did Price immediately describe a tower-like structure, but actually specified it as the 'Hoover Tower'.

This seemed almost too good to be true. The protocol of the experiments was then tightened to prevent any security leaks. The divisional director, whose function it was to open the target envelope, now drove the team to the site *before* revealing its identity to them. The first time they did this the target was Redwood City Marina. Price's first taped words were: 'What I'm looking at is a little boat jetty or . . . dock along the bay.'

Another bull's eye description was given for the seventh target on the list: an arts and crafts plaza with shops, flowers, ceramic ornaments, fountains, paths and vine-hung arbors. In the report Price's unedited transcript is quoted verbatim. Targ and Puthoff claimed his 'description is accurate in almost every detail'.

Indeed, Price's 'viewing' contained much that was specifically relevant to the arts and crafts plaza. He said, for example, 'I'm looking at something that looks like an arbor. . . . Seems to be cool, shaded. Doesn't seem to me that they're [i.e. the target team] out in the direct sunlight. . . . there's lots of trees, in an arbor area.'

Startlingly accurate though much of this was, many of Price's transcripts also included much that was incorrect. The researchers began to see a pattern in his remote viewing, noting 'the occurrence of essentially correct descriptions of basic elements and patterns coupled with incomplete or erroneous analysis of function was to be a continuing thread throughout the remote viewing work.' In other words, he was often muddled or wrong.

Left: a sketch of a target as 'seen' by one of the SRI subjects, and a photograph of the actual location – San Andres airport in Colombia, South America. It is a remarkable 'hit'

Top: a student tests his ESP ability using a machine devised by Targ and Puthoff. The subject has to indicate which image is going to flash on a screen seconds before it appears. This apparatus is also used in psi testing by Professor Hans Bender and Elmar Gruber of the Freiburg Institute in West Germany

He also, they noted, drew target locations or objects as mirror images, which proved – to them – that the right hemisphere of the brain was somehow involved in the process, for the right side of the brain is believed to control holistic, pattern-making and intuitive thinking.

Impressive as Price's results were to those who worked with him closely, the real test came when the transcripts and drawings were compared with the target areas by an independent judge who visited the nine sites and then rated the descriptions on a scale of one to nine, best to worst match. He had been presented with Price's unlabelled narratives in a random order, so he had no hint as to which site Price had been referring – except from the scripts themselves. Having carried out this evaluation, the judge awarded him

Right: the late Dr Kit Pedler with biologist Dr Beverley Rubik at the target selected for a remote viewing test, Indian Rock, Berkeley, California, in 1980. Although the subject – many miles away – noted a few correspondences with the target, most of her report described Codornices Park, which she later verified by visiting it. Dr Pedler did not consider this a complete 'miss' but was convinced that she had, in some way, 'seen' the park through the displacement effect that is so often noted by researchers. This in itself raises further perplexing questions

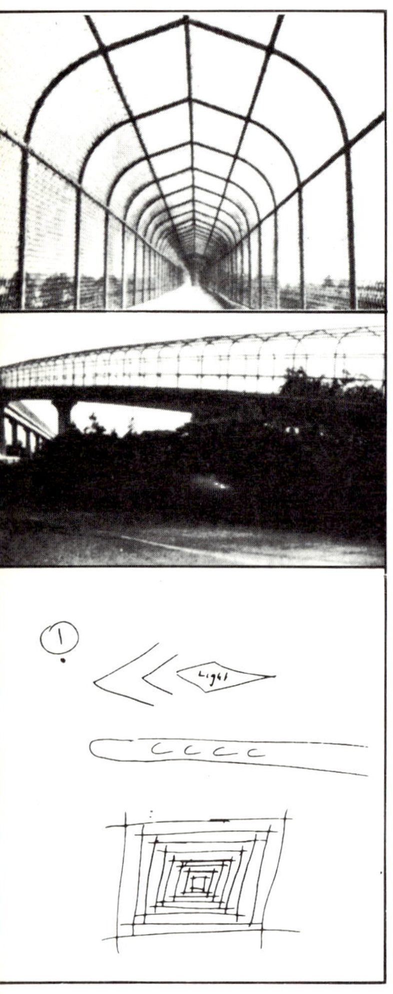

Above: Hella Hammid's drawing of the target that she described as 'some kind of diagonal trough up in the air'. Compare it with the target, a pedestrian overpass; the perspective is particularly accurate

seven direct hits out of nine, a strikingly significant result, the odds against this happening by chance being at least 35,000:1.

A further back-up was provided when a separate group of SRI scientists, so far unassociated with the Targ/Puthoff programme, were asked to match the scripts against the targets. The same procedure followed as before: unlabelled, randomly ordered transcripts were distributed to the team of five, who then visited the sites independently.

Chance alone would have provided five correct matches overall, but in this test, the correct correlation was much higher: individually the investigation team scored them seven, six, five, three and three.

The fascinating aspect about Price's involvement was that he, although obviously a successful 'viewer', did not claim to possess any special gift for it, merely saying that he was willing to give the experiments a try. If it were true that he had no special 'talent' and yet was so strikingly successful, the researchers wondered if anyone could do it.

They found a suitable guinea-pig for the next stage in the series in Hella Hammid, a professional photographer. Another nine-experiment series was mounted, along similar lines to that using Price. The only difference was that Hammid's remote viewing time was cut from 30 to 15 minutes.

Drawing conclusions

Hammid preferred to make drawings of her mental impressions, rather than describe them verbally as Price had done. Some of these 'doodles' were remarkably accurate.

Again an independent judge was brought in to repeat the matching process and the results were just as impressive: five direct hits and four second ranks. The odds against this were given as 500,000:1.

Following up this success, Targ and Puthoff ran a further four series of tests involving seven other subjects. All but one test proved to be statistically significant.

These results should indeed, as *Mind-reach* claimed, have proved beyond a shadow of a doubt that remote viewing is *fact*. However, the experiments and their results were not always straightforward nor easy to evaluate. For example, when the late Dr Kit Pedler was making his series *Mind over matter* for British television he visited Stanford and took part in an experiment himself, and certain problems emerged.

Hella Hammid acted as subject while Dr Pedler and Dr Beverley Rubik, a biologist who had joined up with the team for the experiment, drove off to one of the six randomly selected sites in the vicinity. Television viewers saw Pedler and Rubik wandering round a rocky incline, while Hammid – locked in a hotel room – was being filmed speaking and drawing her mental impressions of what they were seeing.

After a specified period Pedler and Rubik

returned to the hotel and compared notes with Hammid. Then Hammid was driven to each of the six sites with the task of identifying the target with only her previously recorded impressions as guides. As it happened, she was convinced she had not 'seen' the target – but instead identified one of the other sites on the list, Codornices Park, as the place she had 'seen'.

Dr Pedler found the very nature of this 'miss' intriguing. Though some may think his reasoning merely desperate rationalisation in an embarrassing situation, he pointed out that there is a well-known, if little understood, factor called the 'displacement effect'. This is an extremely mysterious process, found also in other telepathic experiments, which operates when the subject homes in, not on the target itself, but on one of the others in the target pool. The phenomenon frequently goes unremarked because researchers are concerned solely with totalling up direct hits. To many, including Dr Pedler, this aspect of telepathic experiment was potentially just as exciting as getting direct hits all the time.

But in the case of the Puthoff/Targ experiments more mundane objections were also raised. On only very few occasions was the received image unambiguously clear. There may indeed be a number of correct correspondences, but in most cases there is an abundance of over-generalised description: trees, roads, flowers, hills and so on – easily guessed components of many likely target sites. Sifting out the relevant from the 'padding', agreeing on the significance of each phrase in the transcript is clearly not quite as easy as the experimenters stated.

Yet, despite these quibbles, Targ and Puthoff did seem to present a strikingly positive case for remote viewing. So why did the critics attack them so fiercely?

Close-up on remote viewing

Not only sceptical scientists but also fellow psychical researchers took issue with Targ and Puthoff over their remote viewing experiments at SRI. But why? What is the background to the controversy over this elusive phenomenon?

THE RESEARCH BY Russell Targ and Harold Puthoff into remote viewing certainly made an impact. For many people on the fringe of parapsychology, including students and interested laymen, their work had the full weight of authority behind it, for both men were physicists of some standing. If they were prepared to put their reputations at risk by stating so positively that remote viewing *exists*, then who could doubt the validity of their work? However, their fellow scientists, many of them prejudiced against parapsychology in the first place, and some who were merely cautious, were not so ready to hail the results as a breakthrough.

Two of the sceptics were David Marks and Richard Kamman, both psychologists at New Zealand's Otago University. Their students, reading of Puthoff and Targ's conclusions, had begun to bombard them with questions about remote viewing and parapsychology in general. The Stanford Research Institute (SRI) had suddenly become the centre of attention.

Neither Marks nor Kamman had, until that point in the late 1970s, any special interest in ESP and they admitted their relative ignorance about parapsychology. But the pressure from their students was so intense that they realised they would have to learn. They were interested in the SRI experiments particularly because Targ and Puthoff had claimed that almost anyone, psychically gifted or not, could be successful in remote viewing. It was also claimed that the results of the experiments were easy to reproduce.

So, between 1976 and 1978, Marks and Kamman ran 35 trials similar to the SRI

In an article written in 1927 Sir Oliver Lodge cited as evidence for 'telepathy at a distance' the case of the Misses Miles and Ramsden. They undertook a series of experiments in telepathy, which were similar to those carried out in the 1970s at SRI. Miss Miles photographed Henbury Church in Cheshire (above), while Miss Ramsden, in Scotland, drew her mental impressions of the image being transmitted (left). Miss Ramsden, however, felt dissatisfied, saying 'something is wanting, as it seemed bigger and more imposing'. The lack of ivy and the slit windows suggest she had 'picked up' an early version of the church

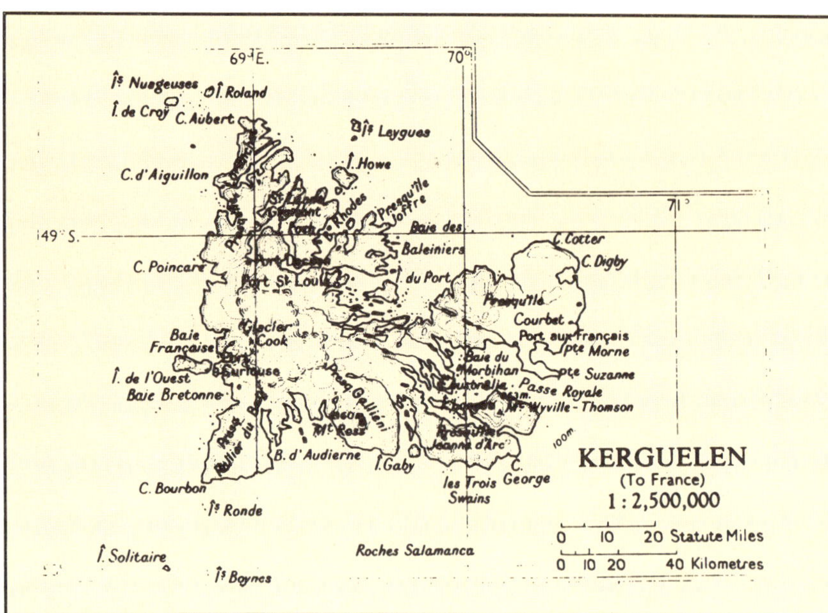

sessions. They used five subjects: a graduate psychologist, a hypnotist, a housewife, an arts student and a medical undergraduate. All of them expressed the belief that they had some psychic ability.

Marks and Kamman followed the SRI routines as faithfully as possible. The target team was given 20 minutes to reach its specified destination, then the subject – back at the laboratory – noted down any feelings or impressions about the unknown target for 15 minutes. The team returned, collected the subject and all then went to the target site to check the subject's transcript against the location. Marks and Kamman were pleased to find encouraging correspondences at the early stages of their project. One of their subjects was so confident that he said, 'If the judges can't match my descriptions accurately, there will be something wrong with them.'

Unfortunately this confidence was misplaced – the independent judges, brought in to try to match transcripts with actual target locations, failed to do so in every case they were asked to consider.

Up to this stage everyone at Otago had felt very positive about the outcome of the experiments; so what had gone wrong? Marks and Kamman decided to accompany one subject and the target group on one of their joint trips to the target location after the actual remote viewing had taken place. This was to reveal serious flaws in the nature of the experiment – and by implication the experiments of Puthoff and Targ, whose methodology they had followed so carefully. The New Zealanders labelled the problem *subjective validation*; put simply, this means that if you want an experiment to work it will,

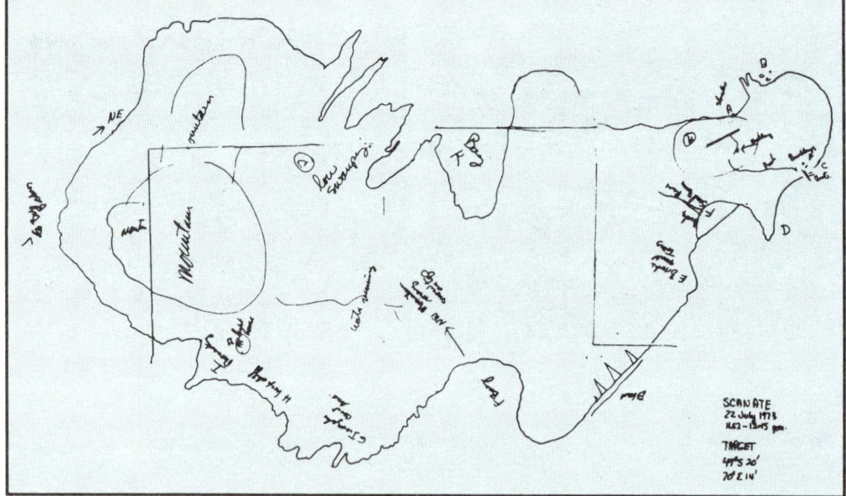

Project Scanate (scanning by co-ordinate) was one of the most controversial areas of SRI's remote viewing experiments. A map co-ordinate would be given to the team by telephone and the subject asked to describe the location, which would later be checked. According to Puthoff and Targ, psychic Ingo Swann (left) showed remarkable talent for this. The map co-ordinates for Kerguelen Island in the Indian Ocean (top) were given to Swann who responded with an extremely accurate verbal description of the location. His version of the map (above) is, however, much less convincing, especially considering that Swann is also an artist and is used to thinking in visual terms

because you will tend to select the results you were seeking and reject the rest. Since all the subjects had been strongly motivated to succeed, they had tended to grasp at correspondences – between their impressions and the target – that, according to the judges, simply did not exist. 'The fact is,' concluded Marks and Kamman, 'any target can be matched by any description to some degree.'

For their part, the judges had tried hard to match transcripts against targets and they felt they had come up with the best matches possible. Unfortunately they were not the same details seized upon as 'proof' by the experimental team.

The Otago team then asked the obvious question: if we have had this difficulty, then how did Targ and Puthoff manage to achieve so many direct hits? They began to investigate the SRI findings in closer detail and came up with some provocative discoveries about the way the transcripts had been judged.

For example, they noticed that the SRI transcripts were unedited, including all manner of material in addition to the subject's actual narrative. Only some scripts were dated, and others – significantly – carried references to previous experiments. One of remote viewer Pat Price's transcripts – the Redwood City Marina test – expressly mentions the previous day's target: 'I've been trying to picture it in my mind and where you went yesterday on your nature walk. . . .'

Marks and Kamman saw this as a potential cue to the judge, who was ostensibly trying to evaluate the material on its descriptive content alone. In effect this apparently throwaway remark could be telling the judge that whatever the target was, it was *not* a nature walk, because that was yesterday's target. With such cues the judge could have worked out the series of targets, consciously or subconsciously, and given higher scores as a result.

What the SRI trials had not included, and what they badly needed according to the Otago team, was an attempt at remote *judging*. Was it possible, they wondered, that the judges could come up with good matches armed only with the transcripts – not visiting the target site at all?

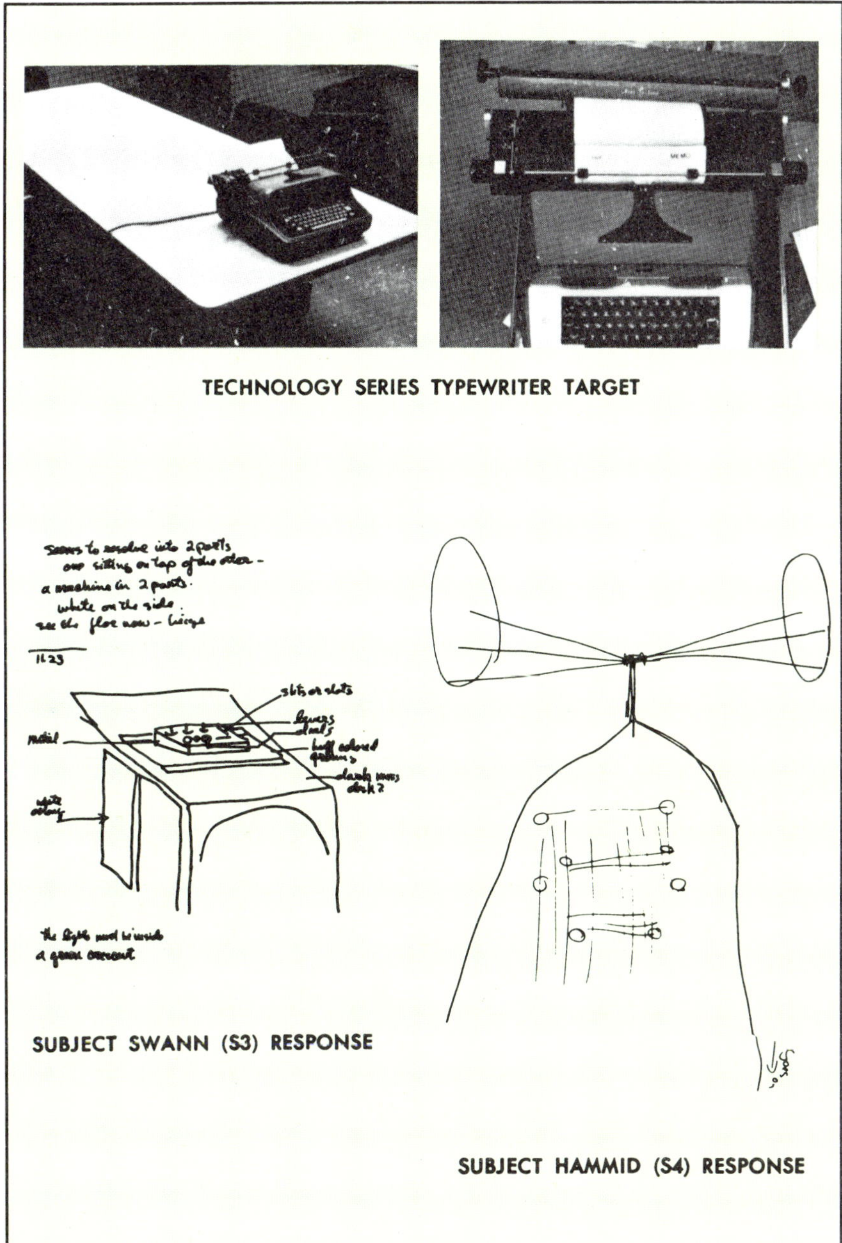

Two SRI 'stars' draw their impressions of the target, a typewriter. Ingo Swann's sketch (on the left) seems strikingly accurate, though he did not actually name the object, noting instead that it 'seems to be in two parts, one sitting on top of the other'. Hella Hammid's sketch (on the right) is not impressive although the grid effect could be seen as a keyboard

The two psychologists acquired five of the Price scripts that had not been published from a consultant to the SRI project. These appeared to be covered in cues such as references to 'yesterday's two targets', more specifically 'the second of the day', and Targ's encouraging comment on one transcript, 'nothing like having three successes behind you'. Other subtle cues included mention of the time of day of the experiment, useful when more than one experiment is staged in one day. In a rigidly controlled scientific experiment there should have been nothing but the subject's impressions on the transcript, and only references to that particular remote viewing session. Any extraneous matter was not only bad methodology, but suspicious.

Right on cue

With a little intelligent guesswork, and a little reading between the – added – lines, Marks correctly matched all five transcripts to the targets, 'solely on the basis of the cues contained in the transcripts, and no visits to target locations . . . prior to the successful matchings.'

Marks and Kamman argued that the SRI judging could hardly be said to have been blind. Their conclusion, as it was published in *Nature*, says:

> Our investigation of the SRI remote viewing experiment with Pat Price forces the conclusion that the successful identification of target sites by judges is impossible unless multiple extraneous cues which were available in the original unedited transcripts are utilized. Investigators of remote viewing should take more care to ensure that such cues are not available. Furthermore, the listing of targets given to judges should be randomized and not presented in the same sequence as that which occurred in the experiments.

And what about the astonishingly successful SRI remote viewing tests using Ingo Swann and Hella Hammid? On balance, Marks and Kamman seriously doubted whether tighter controls had been involved in those. Their final, damning verdict, published in their book *The psychology of the psychic* (1980), is that 'It appears to us that the remote viewing effect is, at present, nothing more than a massive artifact of poor methodology and wishful thinking.'

They did admit that they had been working with incomplete data and, of course, they had not been present during the SRI tests.

However, Robert Morris, who reviewed *The psychology of the psychic* in the *Journal* of the American Society for Psychical Research (ASPR), investigated the New Zealanders'

One such case took place during one of Dr Carl Sargent's Ganzfeld tests at Cambridge, England, in June 1981. Peter Brookesmith (Editor of the magazine *The Unexplained*) acted as 'sender' and Lynn Picknett (Deputy Editor) as subject. A target picture (left) was chosen from four randomly selected, sealed envelopes, yet the subject received vivid and detailed impressions of one of the other pictures – *which was still in its sealed envelope* (below). No one was 'sending it, so how did it happen?

Absent-minded

Dr Kit Pedler noted the curious phenomenon called the 'displacement effect' that occurred during remote viewing experiments at SRI. But bypassing the actual target and homing in on one of the rejected targets instead is intriguingly common in other ESP experiments. And such 'misses' are often more interesting than direct 'hits', although researchers frequently overlook them.

criticisms and, in turn, found much to criticise. They had, he asserted, jumped to as many conclusions as, in their opinion, had Puthoff and Targ. Marks and Kamman, said Morris, had overstepped the mark by juggling with incomplete or improperly understood data and had reached the wrong conclusions. Morris conceded that the SRI experiments had required tighter controls and that there had been some serious weaknesses in the methodology employed. But the debunkers seem, like so many debunkers of psychic matters, to have missed the point. Sloppy methodology is one thing, but does it totally invalidate the basic premise that different people, in different places, can somehow 'see' with each other's eyes, telepathically?

Nothing but the scripts

Still with the SRI judging routine – and its inherent weaknesses – in mind, Marks and Kamman countered, they say, by trying another version. In this they removed the cues from the SRI scripts, gave the judges the targets and analysed the matches, assessed on the basis of the transcript alone. But they came up with only chance results.

However, Dr Charles Tart, of the University of California, also took up the challenge. He combines the qualities of being a refreshingly positive parapsychologist with a reputation for employing strict controls in all his experiments. Having edited out all extraneous information and cues, he resubmitted the scripts to a judge who had previously been successful at matching free-response material, though not at SRI. This judge matched the scripts to the targets at *above* chance odds.

So, imperfect as they were, perhaps the SRI remote viewing trials did prove that there is a strange, telepathic ability that so far we have only glimpsed. Puthoff and Targ's enthusiastic claims that everyone can score a direct hit with remote viewing seems, at present, a little fanciful. Yet there is an increasing body of evidence that suggests very strongly that other psychic abilities – metal bending for example – *can be learned.* There is also mounting evidence in other areas of psychical research that a positive attitude to psi can actively encourage phenomena to occur.

So perhaps the Puthoff/Targ experiments should not be despised. True, no one else has been able to come up with the same high number of direct hits, but perhaps no one else has been enthusiastic enough to encourage such positive findings. And even if they were muddled and ended up, in themselves, proving nothing, they have inspired others to take up the challenge to discover the hidden powers of the human mind.

Telepathy without tears

Sensory deprivation can be an instrument of torture, but in parapsychology it has provided the means for some remarkably successful experiments in telepathy, some of which were carried out at Cambridge University

THE SUBJECT LIES DOWN on a mattress on the floor of a quiet room in the psychology department of the University of Cambridge in England. Halved ping-pong balls are taped over his eyes, a red light is switched on a few feet above his head, and through the headphones he wears, an amplifier beams a steady stream of hissing, crackling 'white noise'. He is not about to be hypnotised – or tortured. He is in what psychologists call the *Ganzfeld* (German for 'whole field'), a state in which, though fully conscious and alert, he has been deprived of normal visual and auditory impressions. He is about to take

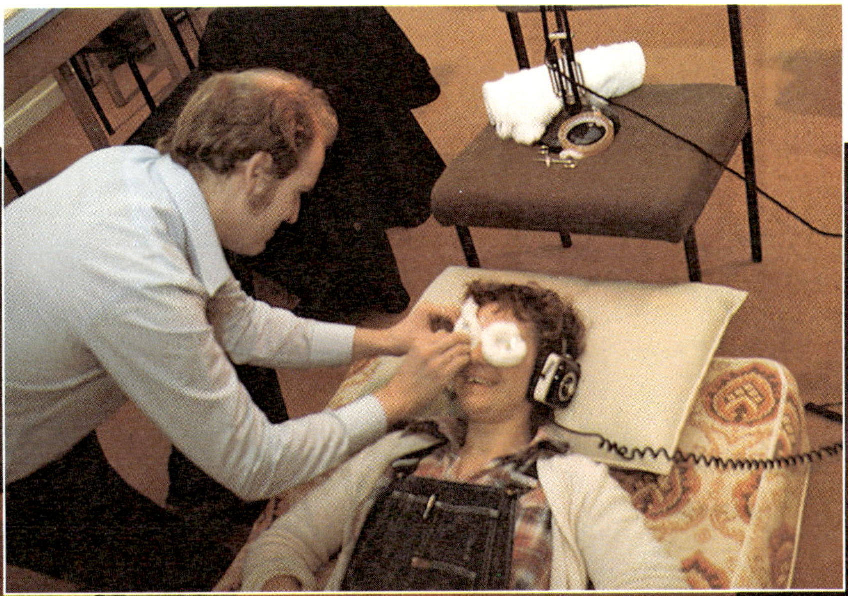

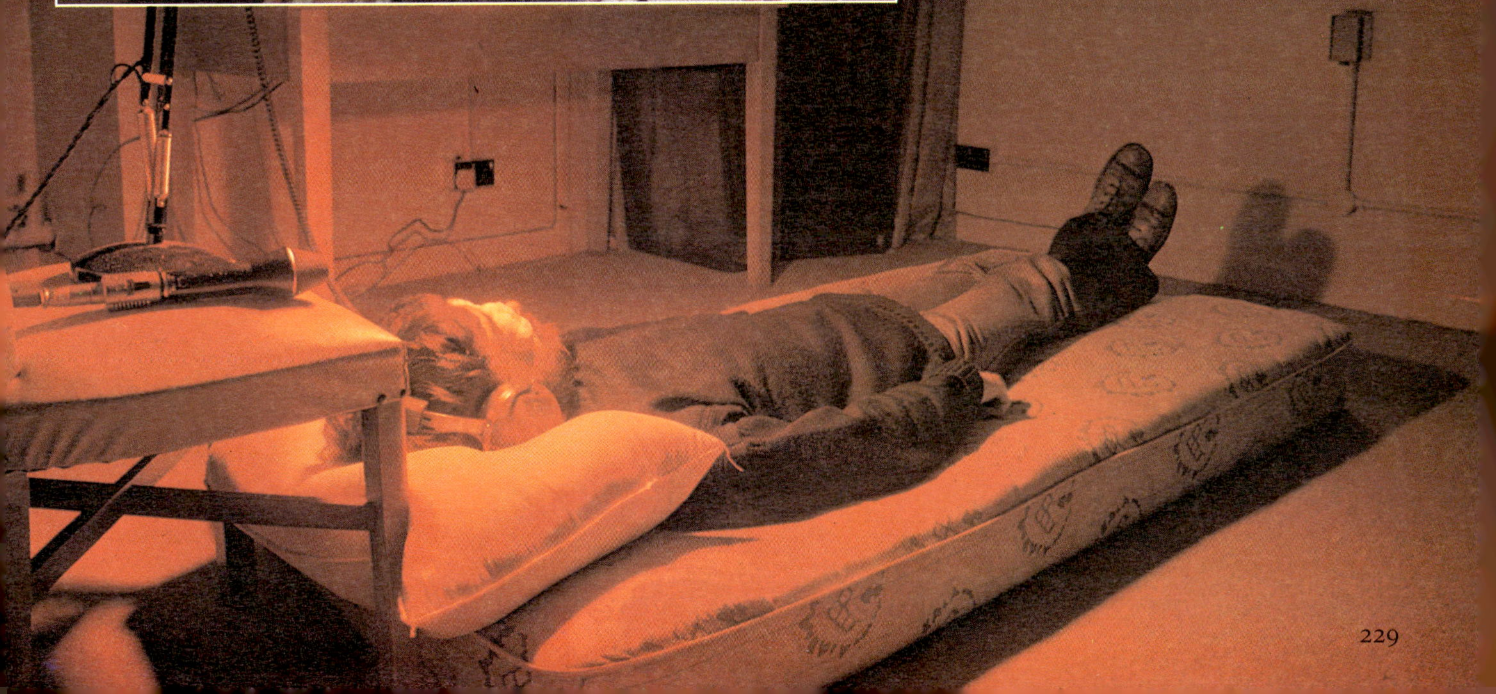

Bottom: throughout a Ganzfeld session the subject is bathed in a red light

Inset: subject Heidi Bartlet relaxes while Dr Sargent adjusts halved ping-pong balls over her eyes. These – and the red light – effectively block out all visual 'noise' (normal sensory stimulation), while Heidi listens to muted white noise through the headphones

Previous page, top: Dr Sargent adjusts the level of white noise so that it blocks out all sound – while remaining comfortable for the subject

Right: while the subject speaks her mental impressions into a microphone, Dr Sargent writes them down in the next door control room. Although her 'mentation' is taped, the written record is the basis for the later marking session

part in an experiment in planned telepathic transmission.

'Our brains are programmed to respond to changing events,' explains Dr Carl Sargent, who is in charge of the Ganzfeld experiments at Cambridge. 'And if there is no change in our visual or auditory input, then maybe the brain will respond to the ESP channel.'

He clicks his stopwatch. 'Right,' he says, 'the experiment has begun.' In the adjoining control room, his assistant switches on a tape recorder and watches the subject through a one-way mirror. Then Sargent goes down the corridor to another room, sits down, and begins to stare at a picture, one of a set of four that has been selected for the occasion from 60 sets by a complex random process, so that neither he nor anyone else has any idea in advance what it will be.

Today's target picture is a landscape painting by the 19th-century Italian artist Giuseppi Palizzi. It shows a peaceful rural scene. In the foreground, an animal is being led towards the rustic house on the left, passing a large rock behind which there is a flat and barren landscape dominated by a large triangular-topped mountain, like a flattened pyramid, with a circular lake below it.

Sargent's task is to try to 'send' the contents of the picture into the mind of the subject in the other room. He focuses all his attention on the painting – its shape, colours and content – and he writes down some of the associations it has for him. 'Rather like the surface of the Moon,' he notes.

Meanwhile, the subject has settled down in his Ganzfeld environment. He finds it pleasant and relaxing, and soon, as instructed, he begins to speak into the microphone beside him, saying whatever occurs to him. After seven minutes, he says:

'Ah yes, there we go! Very clear. Dark animal standing on a rock, and a blue background. Mountain, blue – very clear, that.' A few minutes later, he adds: 'Looks more like the detail of a rock now. Very clear.' And:

'Like a pyramid seen from the air – rocks – same as before. Like the top of Mount Everest or something. It's a very bleak landscape. . . . Big blob in the middle – perhaps it's the hole in the Earth?'

Finally, after 21 minutes in the Ganzfeld, the subject appears to score a direct hit:

'I'm still getting this desolate *Moon landscape*.'

Dipping into the pool

When the experiment ends, after about half an hour, the assistant comes in, helps the subject remove the ping-pong balls, and shows him a duplicate set of the four pictures from which the target was selected. At this stage, the assistant has no idea which one it was. She then goes through her notes, and asks the subject to match each statement he made to one or more of the pictures, scoring from 0 for no resemblance at all, to 99 for very strong resemblance.

The first picture is a news photograph of a naked undergraduate riding a bicycle along King's Parade in Cambridge. The second is a painting of some china ornaments and animals, the third is the Palizzi landscape, and the fourth is a cartoon by Heath Robinson showing an elderly couple rowing a boat.

The subject is confused. He immediately sees that the general shape and appearance of the cartoon are similar to those of the image he saw: the artist has drawn the white waves in such a way as to suggest a jagged lunar landscape, and the boat is roughly the shape of the rock he described. But there are several elements in the Palizzi that correspond to his impressions, and the second picture shows a china animal standing on a rock against a blue background. He seems to have picked up certain features of three of the four pictures, but when his scores are added up, the cartoon comes first and the Palizzi second, the china ornaments third and the naked student last.

Sargent now comes into the room and

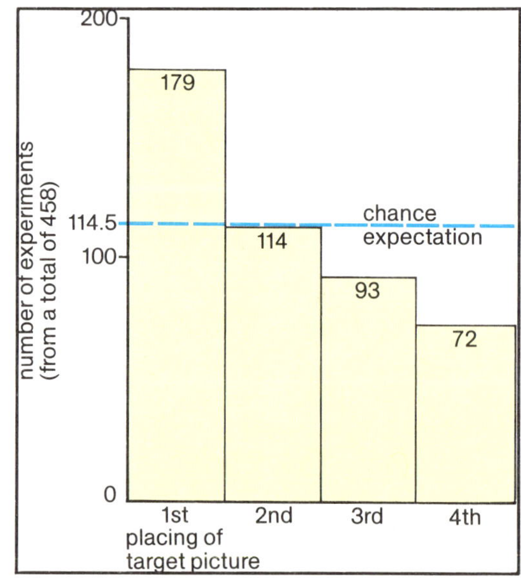

Right: a graph showing where Dr Sargent's subjects placed the target out of a pool of four pictures. By November 1981 there had been 458 experiments; out of these no less than 179 placed the target picture first, 114 placed it second, 93 third and 72 fourth. The 179 who were successful represent 39.08 per cent of the total number of experiments – the probability of getting such a high score is one in 100 million

evening, with Sargent 'sending' a picture from his Cambridge home to the subject in London. It was agreed that the session would begin at 11.45 p.m., and for half an hour the subject, lying in his darkened bedroom with his eyes closed, received no impression at all. Then, 35 minutes after Sargent had actually stopped trying to transmit, the subject had a clear vision of a figure standing on a pedestal with a bright light behind it. After trying for a further 10 minutes, he saw the same image again, and then went to sleep, after jotting down his impression. Later, he learned that the picture Sargent had been concentrating on was Blake's *Glad day* – which shows a figure standing on a rock with a bright light behind it. Another coincidence?

Some successful subjects have described their target picture in uncannily precise

shows the subject his notes and the correct target picture. With hindsight, the subject wonders why he did not choose the Palizzi, and is impressed by the fact that both he and Sargent should refer specifically to a Moon landscape.

This single experiment proves nothing. Chance alone would predict that the subject should, at the end of the experiment, pick the correct target out of the target pool once every four times, giving a success rate of 25 per cent. But by the end of April 1981, after running a total of 412 sessions involving 146 different subjects, Sargent had come up with results that are very difficult to ascribe to chance alone. In these sessions, 37.9 per cent of first choices have been correct, and the percentages of rating the target picture respectively second, third and fourth have been 25.2, 20.4 and 16.5. In other words, there have been over 50 per cent more correct first choices than chance should predict. That this is due to consistently successful guesswork is statistically highly improbable. It is also of interest that almost twice as many first- or second-choice guesses as third or fourth have been correct.

In one series of experiments, Sargent set out to see if previously successful subjects would do better than previously unsuccessful ones. They certainly did. While the latter group scored 27.3 per cent correct first choices, almost exactly what they could be expected to score by chance or guesswork, the former achieved a hit rate of 83 per cent, a figure that could be attributed to guesswork only six times in 100,000. Successful Ganzfeld subjects, it seems, are likely to become more successful. In other words, *telepathic receptivity can be learned.*

The subject who had failed to score a correct first choice in the experiment described above decided to see if he, too, could improve – straight away. At his suggestion, he and Sargent held a test session later that

Top: Heidi Bartlet chooses the correct target picture out of the pool of four. Dr Sargent has discovered that Ganzfeld subjects can *learn* to get direct 'hits' consistently

Above: the scene by the 19th-century Italian artist Giuseppi Palizzi, which was the target picture in one notable experiment. Dr Sargent, who was the 'sender', noted down the phrase 'rather like the surface of the Moon'. The subject remarked during his mentation period, 'I'm still getting this desolate Moon landscape.' Coincidence?

detail. Hugh Ashton, one of Carl Sargent's regular collaborators, remarked during a test with himself as subject: 'I keep thinking of firemen and a fire station.' The target picture was of firemen in training at a fire station, and Ashton even mentioned that one fireman had his face towards the camera, a detail Sargent had not consciously noticed while transmitting. Such incidents raise the question of whether the sender is in fact sending by telepathy or the subject is receiving his impressions by clairvoyance.

There is even evidence for some unexpected precognitive side-effects in Ganzfeld studies. A Dutch journalist dreamed the night before his test that the target would be a surrealistic painting by Magritte. It turned out to be a Dali – the only surrealist work in Sargent's entire pool of pictures. Writer Roy Stemman made a correct first choice on his first attempt, but also reported images of Spanish dancers and a Mayan temple, which had nothing to do with the target. He then went home, switched on his television and found himself looking at Spanish-style dancing in a film about Mexico.

The original idea for Ganzfeld research

came from US parapsychologist Charles Honorton, while he was at the Maimonides Medical Center in New York carrying out experiments in dream telepathy. He kept noticing that most reports of spontaneous telepathy over the previous century had come from people who were in a highly relaxed state at the time, whether asleep, convalescing, or just doing nothing in particular. Therefore, he reasoned, instead of making people sit and guess ESP Zener cards *ad nauseam*, why not try to recreate the conditions under which telepathy seemed to happen in real life?

Alert – but dreaming

Attempts to transmit images to dreamers were highly successful, he found, but they took far too long. All night, in fact. He considered that the Ganzfeld environment was an analogue of the dream state, and that by placing somebody in it he would be creating an environment in which psychic experience could be expected to flourish, as indeed it did. By 1977, Honorton was able to report that not only had his own eight experiments, involving a total of 267 sessions, given significant positive results, but that 10 other researchers had been able to repeat them just as successfully or more so, to a degree he described as 'highly significant by the most conservative estimate'.

Carl Sargent makes no secret of his enthusiasm for his Ganzfeld work, which he first tried, with himself as subject, on a visit to Honorton's laboratory in 1978. 'It had a very powerful effect on me psychologically,' he says. 'I found it really did produce an altered state of consciousness, and I even had an incipient out-of-the-body experience.' Subsequently, he achieved considerable success both as subject and as sender, and has found, by studying the psychological questionnaires he gives all his subjects, that extroverted types are far more likely to be successful than introverts.

He himself is the most exuberant of extroverts. 'Ganzfeld work is, above all, tremendous fun,' he says. 'People really enjoy it, and they keep coming back for more.' Yet however much he enjoys his work, he takes it very seriously. As the first person to be awarded a Ph.D. for a thesis on a parapsychological topic, and as a full-time parapsychologist (of whom in 1981 there were only about half a dozen in the whole of Britain, and probably not more than 30 in the West), he is well aware of the need to achieve scientific respectability if his subject is to attract the attention of other scientists and to encourage funding. Thanks to him, parapsychology became part of the syllabus for Cambridge undergraduates, and by 1981 eight had volunteered to train in it.

Ganzfeld research is one of the most promising fields of parapsychology to have emerged since the metal bending of the mid 1970s, and it offers considerable promise for at least two reasons:

First, it has produced a very consistent and high repeatability rate, and second, it is largely fraud-proof, as there is no opportunity for the subject to cheat – deliberately or subliminally. It is also a clear example of a parapsychological hypothesis being put to the test and successfully repeated elsewhere, a standard requirement of science.

Moreover, unlike metal bending, it is of practical value in itself. Not only is it enjoyable and relaxing for most subjects, but regular practitioners have found it gives them an overall increase in sensitivity and awareness. For the first time in more than a century of psychical research, it seems that 'paranormal' abilities can, given suitable conditions, be learned and produced to order in the laboratory.

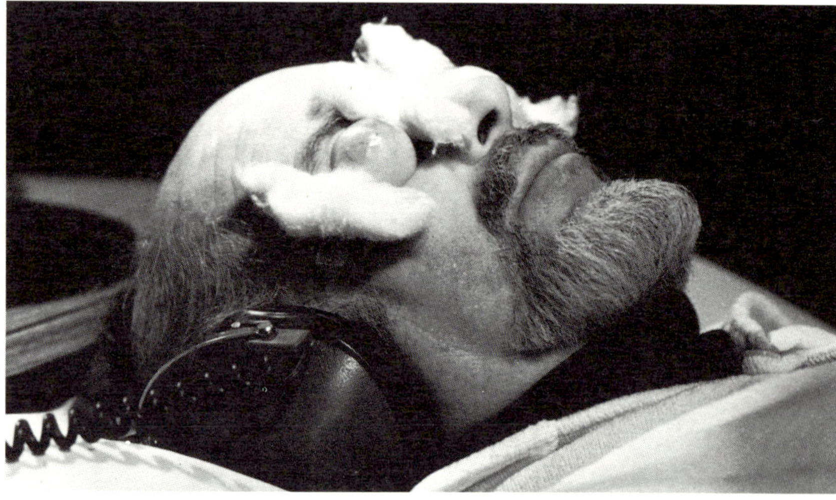

Top: the late Dr Kit Pedler taking part in a Cambridge Ganzfeld experiment

Above: Charles Honorton, the US parapsychologist who discovered the efficacy of the Ganzfeld

Left: *Glad day* by William Blake. This was a target that the subject failed to place first – but successfully picked up during a long-distance telepathy experiment that night

ESP unlimited

The Ganzfeld experiments, designed to encourage telepathy in special laboratory conditions, have had the unexpected result of producing spontaneous ESP. How does this curious 'spin-off' happen?

Left: Dr Carl Sargent, head of the Ganzfeld experiments at Cambridge. He himself participates in the tests, acting both as sender and receiver at various times

Below: a subject in the Ganzfeld state, ready to try to receive telepathic messages from a sender in another location. In the Ganzfeld environment, the subject is deprived of normal sight and sound

SPONTANEOUS ESP in the laboratory? It seems a contradiction in terms, but it occurs. Indeed, ESP experiments at the University of Cambridge have shown that the laboratory can even *stimulate* spontaneous ESP – a powerful rejoinder to those who object to scientific 'testing' of psi.

As described earlier, a particular kind of ESP experiment has dominated parapsychological work at Cambridge since 1978 – telepathy of subjects in the Ganzfeld state. Using pictures as targets, the 'receiver' in the experiment is kept in an environment of unchanging uniform light and sound for 30 minutes or so. For much of this time, a 'sender' at a distant location looks at one – and only one – randomly chosen target picture. This picture could be almost anything: a newspaper cutting, greeting card, art print or cartoon, for example. The receiver is asked to talk about his or her visual or auditory images, physical feelings, stray thoughts, everything, while the experimenter writes down everything said. At the end of the experiment the receiver is shown a set of four different pictures, one of which is a copy of the target picture viewed by the sender. Even the experimenter does not know which one it is. The receiver tries to pick it out on the basis of the impressions he or she had while in the Ganzfeld environment. The experiment is more sophisticated than this in detail, but this is the essence of it.

What the experimenters are looking for is a scoring rate that is well above the chance level. If chance alone operated, the correct picture would be chosen one time out of four, or 25 per cent of the time. In fact, the 'direct hit' rate from nearly 500 Ganzfeld test sessions at Cambridge is just over 39 per cent, notably higher than chance.

These simple and unobjectionable statistical tests give clear evidence of ESP in operation. But it is also clear that the statistics are not measuring all the ESP that occurs – after all, spontaneous ESP by definition cannot be detected with pre-designed statistical tests.

The receivers in the Ganzfeld tests often exhibit ESP unconnected to the target picture. For example, one receiver was plagued with a pain in his lower back during his session, although he typically did not suffer this. Later we learned that medical students had been listening to a lecture on rheumatism in a nearby lecture theatre. In another session filmed for television, an experimenter squashed a beetle that was crawling across the page on which he was writing down a receiver's comments. The receiver reported hearing The Beatles singing *Please please me* – an ironic verbal pun. Sometimes receivers pick up extraneous aspects of the feelings of other participants in experiments. Once, when I sat in my office fretting over a personal difficulty, a receiver experienced severe anxiety during her session. Such cases

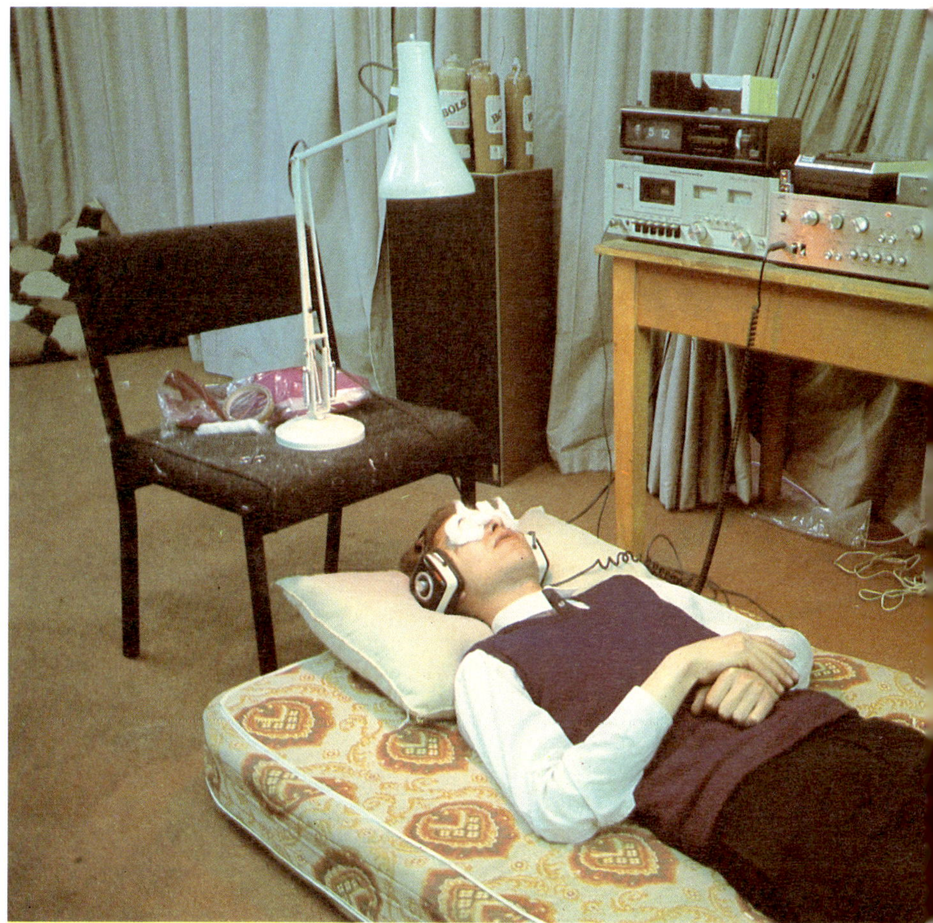

Two minds as one

The similarities – or correspondences – between two consecutive Ganzfeld experiments at Cambridge University on 25 August 1980 illustrate what is meant by 'crosstalk'. With no contact between them, Trevor Harley picked up on and described elements of Carl Sargent's responses in the earlier of the two tests. The remarks below are the exact words of the subjects.

Sargent's session

Cross shapes, crucifixes, floating.

A stag's head . . . very clear, or maybe a horse. Even a giraffe; the horse's head grew as I looked at it.

A huge variety of animals. It's like a bloody Noah's ark.

Harley's session

Someone being crucified.

Crucifix shapes and crosses.

A giraffe with its neck outstretched reaching up to a tree. Now its head turns into a horse's head.

The white dove hovering, branch in beak, looking at the ark. Noah is looking at it.

Below: the lady of the lake, the legendary figure who was supposed to have given King Arthur the great sword Excalibur. In independent tests held on the same day, two Ganzfeld subjects received impressions of her – an example of 'crosstalk'

of ESP have been reported from other laboratories. Stanley Krippner of the Maimonides Medical Center in New York reported a dream telepathy session in which he, as sender, was preoccupied with a stomach pain that he feared might require an operation. The dreamer picked up the theme of the stomach operation in detail, but not the target picture Krippner was looking at. Indeed, in all these cases cited, the receivers were not successful in picking up the target. Perhaps only so much ESP can operate at any one time.

Receivers may even 'crosstalk' – that is, detect and report elements from another receiver's session. In the Cambridge files are two transcripts in which the theme of 'the lady of the lake' – and more specifically, of her hand holding Arthur's sword aloft – is described. They were collected on the same day from two subjects who had no contact with each other.

This kind of crosstalk may be put down to common features in the environment – maybe the newspaper both receivers read that day contained something on Arthurian legends. But another example shows this cannot be the whole explanation. On 25 August 1980 I myself acted as a subject in a precognition experiment starting at 12.16 p.m. I scored a direct hit on a W. Heath Robinson picture of Noah's ark, called *Spring cleaning on the ark*. At 2.15 p.m. another subject, Trevor Harley, started his session in the same experiment. I had been careful to say absolutely nothing about my session to him, but the correspondences between his experiences and mine are really remarkable (see box). Incidentally, Harley had scored badly on the target picture. His ESP had been distracted by going through my memories rather than concentrated on receiving the target picture.

Receivers may also demonstrate precognition as well as ESP in their sessions. One student subject confided before a session that

Bottom right: a cartoon of Noah's ark by W. Heath Robinson. This painting has assumed a special place in the Ganzfeld tests, having more than once been the focus of crosstalk

he had a very strong impression that the target was going to show a Highland stag, because he had dreamed about such an animal being in the laboratory the night before. An antlered buck deer was a prominent feature of the target picture, and only two of the 220 potential targets then available contained such an animal.

Hugh Ashton, one of the regular receivers in the Cambridge Ganzfeld tests, has the strange facility of turning into a sender during his sessions. Ashton is a 25-year-old statistician who doubles as bass and keyboards player in a Cambridge band. He has made several outstanding ESP hits on targets. In the first session undertaken with this receiver, I acted as sender. When I opened the sealed envelope containing the randomly selected target picture for that session, it was a piece of feminist art. I knew at once, with complete certainty, – and correctly as it turned out – that Ashton had already identified the target and I knew exactly which part of the picture he had detected first. It was as if he had sent that information to me to be recognised when I saw the target.

A more dramatic example of a receiver-turned-sender occurred in a session on 27 March 1979 when the target picture was Renoir's *Le moulin de la galette*. This picture shows a group of people at a French outdoor café, with a bottle and glasses on a table. In Ashton's mind these objects became a ouija board and he became a physical medium. (Anyone doubting that the Ganzfeld procedure can induce a genuinely altered state of consciousness should have heard his respiration rate treble.) As sender in that session, I had the most bizarre mental sensations I have ever experienced. I found it impossible to concentrate and 'send' the picture. It was like the mental equivalent of trying to walk through water, and in my session notes I specifically wrote, 'It feels as if I'm being hypnotised at a distance.' It is intriguing that I should have had this sensation at the time that Ashton imagined he was a medium.

Senders have also frequently and correctly noted impressions about what the receiver is experiencing and feeling – for example, being very anxious, feeling physically disorientated, experiencing floating sensations. But the senders could logically, if unconsciously, infer that anyone in the artificial Ganzfeld state might have such feelings.

Sometimes crosstalk occurs between experiments. In the course of one dream precognition experiment, the subject dreamed that the next two targets would be a B and a D picture. These were wrong for this experiment – but correct for another test going on at the same time.

The most striking cases of spontaneous ESP are the extended correspondences, of which two instances can be given. Hugh Ashton again figures in one. In a session run

on 27 November 1981 he acted as the receiver. I was the sender and a student, Julie Milton, was the experimenter. His first comment was that I had an envelope on which the number 39 was marked. Then he said that the picture was W. Heath Robinson's cartoon of Noah's ark. Now, this target (is there something significant about this particular picture?) had been used for a session on 20 November 1981 with me as receiver, Julie as sender, and another student, Sheila Bennett, as experimenter. Hugh knew nothing of the previous test and had no idea that this cartoon was in our pool of possible targets, by now expanded to over 340 pictures. He had exactly specified the target of the earlier test. The number 39 was the number of the set of pictures used in the next session involving myself, Julie and Sheila, but not Hugh. He seems to have picked up information from the past and future, with a startling exactness.

The second example is also intriguing. On 14 June 1981 a student subject tested by two other students gave as a first impression of the target a picture by the French artist Seurat. It must be said that such specific impressions are rather rare. Four days later, on the morning of 18 June 1981, a student experimenter, who knew nothing of the earlier session, woke and gazed at Seurat's picture of *The bathers*, which hung on her wall. That would make a nice target for the day's session, she said to herself. And it did so happen that it was the target picture that day. As was the practice, it was selected at random. The fourth student experimenter who picked picture set number 17 by chance had no idea that picture 17A was Seurat's *The bathers*. This ESP concentrated on Seurat continued: on 20 June yet another subject reported an impression of – indeed, the same painting. Apart from the two mentions on the 14th and 20th, sandwiching the test session in which *The bathers* was the actual target, I have only one other specific citing of Seurat from nearly 500 transcripts.

In my final illustration of spontaneous ESP in the laboratory, I cannot give full details because the sender wishes to remain anonymous. On the occasion in question, I was acting as experimenter. The sender reported seeing quite clearly an apparitional figure of me walk through the locked door of the room in which she was sitting, and look around.

What are we to make of all this – the receiver crosstalk, the receivers acting as senders, timeslips and even apparitions in the laboratory? As with anything spontaneous, it is impossible to prove paranormality. But to demand such proof is to miss the point. What is important is that spontaneous events do occur in the laboratory and that they are common to many experimenters. The laboratory is not after all hostile to spontaneous ESP. Indeed, the atmosphere of the experimental laboratory may even spark it. And perhaps we should not lament the fact that scientists cannot trap all the possible ESP in experiments with pre-planned statistical measurements. Although recent successful lines of experiments, such as the tests for altered states of consciousness, have a better repeatability record than anything previously reported in parapsychology, it is oddly satisfying to know that ESP still remains somewhat erratic and unpredictable. It may be of interest to know that my experience in the session with Hugh Ashton on that March night in 1979, when I felt my mental processes paralysed, did more to convince me of the reality of psi than any number of statistics. As far as I am concerned, ESP certainly exists – I literally felt it.

Below: Georges Seurat's *The bathers*, another of the target pictures for the Ganzfeld tests. During a four-day period in 1981, this particular picture sparked off a series of telepathic impressions from such unrelated sources that the events could only be described as spontaneous extra-sensory perception

Previous page, top: Hugh Ashton, a regular participant in the Ganzfeld experiments. Ashton has made several outstanding hits on ESP targets and has been known to turn into a sender during sessions when he is receiving

Previous page, bottom: *Le moulin de la galette*, a painting by the French Impressionist Renoir. This picture was a target on one of the occasions that Ashton reversed roles from subject to sender

Index